3 5209 00419 7014

wmaln
HD2791 .A77
Asch, Peter/Economic theory and the anti

Lewis and Clark College - Watzek Library

DUE

D1020403

Antitrust Dilemma

PETER ASCH

New York · London · Sydney · Toronto

HD
2791
.A77

Copyright © 1970, by John Wiley & Sons, Inc.

All right reserved. No part of this book may be reproduced by any means, nor transmitted, nor translated into a machine language without the written permission of the publisher.

Library of Congress Catalogue Card Numbr: 78-127658

ISBN 0-471-03443-6

Printed in the United States of America

10 9 8 7 6 5 4 3 2 1

For My Mother and Father

34255

Preface

Economists are sometimes a critical, even cantankerous, lot. We are especially prone to complain about public policies formulated in ignorance of the lessons of economic analysis or, worse yet, based in "bad" economics. Antitrust policy has thus been forced to compete with other areas for its share of criticism but, all things considered, it has more than held its own.

The main purpose of this book, of course, is not to complain. Instead, it is to survey and analyze the important issues in American antitrust from an economic viewpoint. Antitrust decisions invariably affect the structure and behavior of firms and industries, and rational decision processes must take account of these influences. It is here that economic analysis can prove most useful.

The precise role of economics in antitrust is often misunderstood. Consider the case of huge corporations in the United States. These firms, by their very existence, enrage some and enchant others. There is no objective way to determine who is right or wrong—if, indeed, these words have meaning here. Yet there is a good deal of pertinent information to be had. The enraged should know, for example, that big companies may contribute significantly to our national output and living standards; and the enchanted should know, for example, that there is a sense in which large and powerful concerns may adversely affect society's welfare. Both costs and benefits are associated with large firms (or with the absence of such firms). Economics, as such, *cannot* define the socially appropriate level of firm size because it cannot tell us what we *ought* to desire. It *can*, however, help to define the costs and benefits associated with policy decisions that affect size. What we, collectively, do with this information depends on the results we want. But the information itself is vitally important. Without it, neither the enraged nor the enchanted can hope to reach judgments that are rational from their own point of view.

The purpose of this book, then, is not merely to "cover" antitrust materials, but to indicate something about the potential and actual contribution of economic analysis to policy formulation. The organization of the book reflects my own biases. I do not believe that any sensible discussion of antitrust can proceed without some knowledge of relevant economic theory and measurement. These topics thus receive substantial attention, although in retrospect it appears that they might have been pursued even further. I hope that this book will be useful not only to students in courses dealing with antitrust but also to those individuals (policymakers included) who have a general interest in the area. The theoretical and empirical sections assume relatively little background on the part of the reader. Although some previous exposure to microeconomic theory is helpful, it is not absolutely necessary.

Like most authors, I owe a very large debt to others. I have benefited immeasurably from a critique of an earlier draft by Franklin M. Fisher, and from many acute criticisms by Burton G. Malkiel, Matityahu Marcus, Jesse W. Markham, David McFarland, R. W. Pfouts, Richard E. Quandt, and Joseph J. Seneca. And also I have been greatly helped on a number of specific points by the comments of Gary W. Bowman, John F. Graybeal, and Stanley H. Masters. Any weakness in the book remain despite the best efforts of these individuals. Sometimes an author just cannot be saved from himself.

I am most grateful to Mrs. Geraldine Dructor, who typed successive drafts of the manuscript with care and skill, and to the Rutgers University Research Council for generous financial support.

Finally, I owe a real debt to my family. My wife Rita not only provided the necessary moral support but helped with the thankless tasks of reading and editing the final manuscript. My children, Eric and David, are also to be thanked and congratulated for tolerating the past months cheerfully, if not silently.

Rutgers College
1970

Peter Asch

Contents

ECONOMIC THEORY AND THE ANTITRUST DILEMMA

Introduction

The antitrust laws of the United States encompass a large, and sometimes bewildering, group of provisions designed to encourage competition. The rationale for the laws is complex, involving social and political as well as economic motives. Yet it is clear from the written record that the presumption in favor of competition—both within economics and without—is deeply ingrained in American life. A free society tends to distrust concentrations of power, whether private or public; and competition, although subject to varying definitions, often is associated with the absence of dominance by one or a few interests.

Anyone taking even a superficial glance at the present economy is likely to be struck by an apparent gap between the competitiveness that we advocate and the centralization of power that we tolerate. Most corporate wealth and income is accounted for by the 200 largest firms. Many of our major markets are dominated by a few large companies,[1] and the recent growth of giant conglomerate enterprises whose activities span many industries has been dramatic. Such observations raise fundamental questions about our economic system and the priorities of society. Have the antitrust laws failed to meet their stated purpose, and if so, why? Do we really desire competition, or is this merely a word to which we devote empty lip service? Alternatively, is competition something that we desire but cannot define simply in terms of the size and power of business units? These are some of the general questions to which this book is addressed.

---

[1] This is especially true in the manufacturing sector. In such important markets as automobiles, cigarettes, detergents, and most primary and fabricated metal products, the four largest firms account for more than 50 percent of total production and sales.

Competition: The Economic Rationale

If we accept the writings of Congress and the courts at face value, an important motivation for antitrust legislation and enforcement has been economic. Here the antitrust rationale rests on a number of familiar propositions: that producers and sellers put forth their best efforts when threatened by effective rivals; that the economic desires of society are fulfilled when no individuals or groups within the marketplace possess the power to exploit; in short, that competition as a market force compels the best possible economic results.

The intuitive sense of these propositions can be illustrated simply. Consider, for example, an individual stranded in an automobile, out of gas on a country road. If a second motorist should come along and offer to supply enough gas to reach the next town, we may expect that some transaction will occur. But what will be the terms of this transaction? If the second motorist happens to be a good Samaritan, the gas may be offered free of charge or at cost, but suppose instead that he seeks to extract the maximum possible profit. The price that he can obtain for his gasoline cannot be specified without more information; for example, how anxious is the stranded driver to get going? How repugnant to him is the idea of walking to the next town? It is likely, however, that the price paid for the gas will be, in some sense, abnormally high. Why? In simplest terms, because the stranded driver has no alternative except to forego the gasoline. The seller has no competitors and is thus under no compulsion to offer a particularly attractive bargain; indeed, the price he can obtain is limited only by the buyer's desires and ability to pay.

It may be objected that there is a missing element here, that the abnormal price paid for gasoline may result not simply from the presence of a monopolistic seller but also from the unusual circumstances in which a gallon of gasoline may be valued more highly by the buyer than it ordinarily would. This is a valid observation, yet the fact remains that the transaction might be very different if, for example, four motorists appear simultaneously, each offering to sell the required gasoline and each willing to compete for the sale; or if the motorist runs out of gas near an intersection containing several service stations. The seller's power, deriving from the absence of competitors, does influence the terms of the exchange.

Examples of monopolistic exploitation are commonplace. Prices charged at a 24-hour general store located some distance from shopping centers are likely to be relatively high because the store enjoys a partial monopoly in both location and time. The price of a soft drink at a theater intermission or a sandwich on a train may similarly reflect a degree of monopoly power. This is not to imply, incidentally, that the entire differential between such prices and more "ordinary" prices is attributable to monopolistic control. The general store, for example, may well incur higher unit costs than a supermarket, and its best (profit-maximizing) price may thus tend to be higher for reasons of cost as well as by reason of its monopoly position. Freedom from competition, however, does make a difference. The ability of the store or the train or the theater to charge more depends on the difficulty customers encounter in going elsewhere.

It should be made clear at this point that the economic argument in favor of competition does not rest simply on intuition or homey examples of exploitation. As we shall see, economic analysis demonstrates, in a formal and rigorous fashion, the inevitable superiority of competitive market results. It concludes, in other words, that there is some sense in which competition always benefits society more than partial or complete monopoly.

Despite the clarity of this conclusion,[2] our competition-promoting antitrust policies today are in a state of some disarray. What is confused is in part the legal status of complex and somewhat ambiguous provisions. But the more basic confusion—and a major source of policy dilemmas— concerns the relationships between what the law does on the one hand and what economic analysis might suggest on the other.

This is not to imply that antitrust policies generally run contrary to the lessons of economics. Much, and perhaps most, public competition policy possesses a cogent economic rationale, and antitrust very likely has had a positive effect on the competitiveness of the American economy. The problem is rather that some apparently straightforward theoretical conclusions have not provided a clear basis for policy action. We have a highly developed economic theory of competition, but an ambiguous policy for its maintenance and encouragement. A primary task of this book is to explore the reasons why it has proved difficult to move from a theory of competition to a policy about competition. Once these reasons are seen explicitly, it may be possible both to define limitations to the relevance of theory for policy and to suggest ways in which policy may be brought into closer accord with economic analysis and its implications.

[2] The conclusion of competitive superiority is at this point nothing more than an assertion. Its validity will be discussed in Chapter 1.

Competition: Economic Desirability and Noneconomic Objectives

Economists have long recognized the benefits of competitive markets, yet public policies toward competition are not motivated solely—perhaps not even primarily—by economic objectives. Social and political factors also are important, and, although these are not our direct concern here, it would be myopic to pretend that they do not exist. Interestingly, the presumption in favor of competition that is made on noneconomic grounds is closely related in some ways to economic arguments.

As we shall see in Chapter 1, the economic "case" for competition is in effect an argument that competitive markets are the most efficient form of industrial organization. Efficiency, however, is defined in a rather specific way: the competitive market is said to be efficient because it most accurately reflects and executes the desires of individuals in society—that is, the desires of the community as a whole. In a free society a premium is placed on democratic decision making. If competitive markets make economic decisions efficiently as it is defined here, then such decisions are made in an essentially democratic fashion. That is, the decisions reflect the desires of the community without the distortions that powerful interest groups could impose.

There are, however, important reasons for not carrying the economic optimality argument too far into the noneconomic realm. It is true that competitive markets do an efficient job of allocating resources, and that they may be democratic in the sense that the dollar votes of consumers are directly translated into the desired output decisions. It may well be, however, that the dollar votes are themselves distributed in an undesirable or undemocratic fashion. Consider, for example, a society in which the majority of income and wealth is held by a very small group. If such a situation is itself considered undemocratic, resources may still be allocated efficiently by a competitive market system; but this kind of efficiency will not necessarily be desirable in light of the initially undemocratic distribution.

Competition: The Gap between Theory and Policy

Whether or not we consider economic objectives to be paramount, there can be no question that they comprise a relevant motivation for antitrust. It therefore follows that the general formulation of antitrust policies must take account of economic implications, even though these implications may not always be the controlling factor in policy decisions. Much of the economic literature of recent years has attributed policy failures and confusion to a gap between theory and action. Some observers have argued that policy makers frequently ignore or fail to understand the economic implications of what they are doing. It has been argued specifically that there is a legal-economic dichotomy in approaches to antitrust problems, and that policy makers sometimes pursue these matters in an economically illiterate fashion.

This dichotomy is certainly a real one, yet the legal-economic distinction at best provides only a limited explanation of the current status of antitrust. Indeed, if we ask why there is a gap between economic theory and public policy, there is a rather large variety of possible answers, each with some claim to truth. Many of the arguments familiar to students of industrial organization rest on a common point: for one reason or another, it appears that we cannot decide whether theoretical conclusions about competition are fully *relevant* to policy formulation.

This ambivalence is not too surprising. Often there is a question in economics as to whether theoretical conclusions apply directly to policy problems of the real world. In the area of competition this question is acute because the conclusion of competitive superiority is derived under a number of rather restrictive assumptions. If the abandonment of some restrictive assumptions could alter the conclusion, then there is no firm a priori basis for determining an appropriate public competition policy.

A second source of ambivalence lies in the impure nature of real markets. The conclusion of competitive optimality rests on a comparison between the economist's strict definition of a purely or perfectly competitive market and other market forms. Policy decisions, however, do not involve choices between perfection and imperfection, but rather between various kinds of imperfection. Theoretical implications for such choices are relatively weak, and even if we could decide as a rule to opt for "more competitive" markets, there is serious difficulty in defining and measuring what this means.

Although theoretical conclusions may be quite meaningful, then, there are some real difficulties in moving from theory to policy. To the extent that objective analysis falls short of providing full prescriptions for policy, it becomes necessary to look at empirical evidence—that is, to examine what actually happens in different kinds of markets. As we shall see, a good deal of information on market behavior has been gathered. The data yield a number of useful clues about the ways in which performance patterns vary with the structure or type of industry. It is not clear, however, that this evidence brings us much closer to categorical statements about the kinds of policy that will yield particular ends.

If both theory and evidence are inconclusive, we cannot predict accurately the effect of policy moves. It is not appropriate to be too pessimistic at this point, however. We may be able to say a good deal about the likely effects of alternative policies, even if such statements cannot be made with complete precision or confidence. Moreover, improved predictions in the future—based especially on new empirical clues—are always a real possibility.

It must be pointed out that, whatever the current status of economic theory and measurement, even perfect predictions of policy effects might not be conclusive. The question of what public competition policies ought to be adopted obviously depends on the effects of the alternatives, but it depends as well on *society's evaluation* of these effects. This statement appears self-evident, but it is not trivial. Society has numerous economic objectives. We would be pleased to have, for example: an equitable distribution of income, efficient resource allocation, rapid innovation, wise resource conservation, and so on. But even assuming that we could agree on the meanings of these noble aims, the appropriate policy for their implementation might be unclear.

The objectives conflict in that a policy that emphasizes one (or more) must also de-emphasize one (or more). The question then becomes: how does society assign priorities, that is, decide which goals are more important? This kind of question cannot be answered on the basis of economic analysis or empirical evidence. Such information is helpful in delineating society's alternatives, but it cannot itself tell us what sorts of policies are desirable or undesirable.

The Theoretical Foundations
of Antitrust

This section sets forth the area of economic theory that contains the pure economic justification for American antitrust policy. The economic rationale of antitrust rests in the traditional body of price theory, and specifically in the theory of market behavior. Although it is rather easy to show intuitively that competition may benefit consumers more than monopoly, the casual demonstration leaves a number of questions unanswered. It does not tell us, for example, whether a competitive market *inevitably* yields superior results, or whether under certain conditions economic problems may be better resolved by monopoly; nor does the casual, common-sense approach tell us whether *all* economic problems are best solved by competition.

It therefore is useful to examine in a more precise fashion the analytical basis of statements about competition, monopoly, and intermediate market forms. This will clarify the meaning of our presumption in favor of competition, and will make it easier to evaluate actual policies in light of their economic implications. The first task in this examination of market theories is to define the exact nature of competitive market results. It will be shown that competition yields an *optimal* solution of the fundamental economic problem; that is, a solution that is not only preferable to a monopoly result, but is in some sense the *best possible* outcome. This much having been shown, it will be necessary to append a number of significant qualifications. It will be shown that the conclusion rests on certain assumptions that, while perfectly legitimate from a theoretical standpoint, may cast doubt on a policy that single-mindedly pursues "more competitive" markets.

It will also be useful to analyze in some detail the workings of imperfectly competitive and oligopolistic markets, which contain elements of both competition and monopoly. Policy decisions deal most frequently with these intermediate markets, and they are therefore of considerable practical interest. It is also in this area, however, that theories of market behavior have proved least satisfactory, and some of the reasons behind fundamental policy difficulties should become quickly evident.

Finally, in this section a number of recent interpretations of the firm and of market behavior will be examined. It is widely recognized that orthodox economic theory fails to explain a good deal about a modern and complex economy. Some new explanations, made in light of this failure, indicate how observed behavior may better be reconciled with theoretical expectations.

Competition and Monopoly

It is a basic and familiar conclusion of microeconomic theory that differently structured markets behave in fundamentally different ways. A convenient starting point in the analysis of market behavior is the comparison between the extremes of pure or perfect competition and pure monopoly. These market forms, although they are infrequently (if ever) encountered in the modern American economy, yield much insight into the processes by which prices and output levels are determined.

A. Competition

The economist's benchmark in discussions of market behavior is pure or perfect competition. A perfectly competitive market is one that is characterized by:[1]

1. *Many firms.* The number of firms is sufficiently large, and each firm individually is sufficiently small, that none can influence the terms on which it supplies goods and services to the market.
2. *Homogeneous products.* The products offered by firms are identical not only in physical characteristics but in the minds of consumers. That is, consumers

[1] The terms pure and perfect competition are sometimes used as if they were synonymous. When a distinction is made, pure competition is often taken to refer only to the first two characteristics: many firms and homogeneous products.

have no preference whatever for the product of one seller over that of any other.

3. *Free entry and exit.* There are no unusual or artificial barriers that might deter firms from entering or leaving the market.

4. *Perfect knowledge.* No participants in the market can be exploited because of ignorance.

5. *Independence.* Firms make decisions individually, that is, without collusion.

A number of consequences relevant to market behavior can be inferred immediately from these characteristics. For example, the firm in pure competition faces a perfectly elastic demand curve such as DD' in Figure 1.1. This follows from the fact that the firm is insignificantly

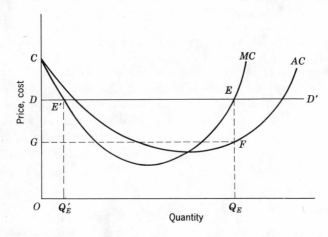

Figure 1.1

small in the market and cannot affect the market price. The horizontal demand curve indicates that the firm can sell any amount it produces at the prevailing market price, OD; there is no meaningful pricing decision for the firm in a purely competitive market. Were it to charge more than the market price, it would sell nothing. Yet, if the firm desires maximum profits, there is no incentive to charge less than the market price; all that can be produced will be sold at the prevailing rate.

If we now specify that the firm confronts conventional marginal cost and average cost curves, CMC and CAC respectively in Figure 1.1, the short-run equilibrium position of the firm is defined at point E.

Q_E is the firm's profit-maximizing output because it is at this output
level that marginal cost (CMC) equals marginal revenue (given by
DD').[2] At any output less than Q_E, the firm is forgoing profits on additional units for which marginal revenue exceeds marginal cost; at any
greater output, the firm is producing some units whose marginal cost
exceeds marginal revenue, and are therefore unprofitable.[3]

In the example of Figure 1.1, the price obtained for each unit (OD)
exceeds the average cost of production (OG). In other words, the firm
is earning profit DG on each unit it sells, and its total profit is represented
by rectangle $DGFE$. Referring back to the characteristics of the competitive market, however, it can be seen that such a situation will not
persist. If entry and exit are free, the existence of net profits should
induce other profit-seeking firms to enter the market. The new entrants
increase the supply of goods to the market and tend to drive down the
market price. From the firm's point of view, demand curve DD' will
fall.[4] Entry will continue until profits are entirely competed away and
the inducement for new firms to enter disappears. This brings us to the
long-run equilibrium position of the competitive firm, depicted in Figure
1.2.

Equilibrium again occurs at a point, E, involving an output level,
Q_E, at which marginal cost and marginal revenue are equated. In the
long run, however, the equilibrium occurs also at a point for which price
and average cost are the same. At equilibrium, then, the firm's average
revenue from sales just covers its average cost. Total revenue just
covers total cost, and the firm is said to be in a *zero profit* position.[5]
This is an important element of the long-run competitive equilibrium,

---

[2] A horizontal demand curve is also a marginal revenue curve (and, for that matter,
an average revenue curve as well). This is so because as successive units are sold, the
price of the last unit—and of previous units—remains unchanged. The net addition to
revenue, or the *marginal revenue* of the last unit, is thus simply its price.

[3] Note, however, that point E' in Figure 1.1 (output Q'_E) is *not* a profit-maximizing
point, even though marginal cost and marginal revenue are equated. (It is actually a
profit-minimizing position, since marginal cost exceeds marginal revenue for every
unit sold.) Although profit-maximization requires the marginal cost–marginal revenue
equality, not all such equalities imply maximization. It is necessary to add a second
maximization condition, namely, that the marginal cost curve cut the marginal revenue
curve *from below*.

[4] Entry of new firms may or may not shift firms' cost curves as well; the possibility
that costs will be altered is ignored here.

[5] Zero profit might be more accurately termed zero *excess* profit. The firm must
earn some profit with which it retains its management. This "normal" profit can be
treated as an economic cost—the cost of hiring the entrepreneurial factor of production.
Thus zero profit means that the firm earns no profit *beyond* what can be defined as an
economic cost.

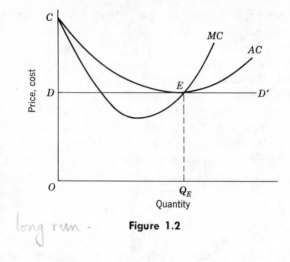

long run.

Figure 1.2

and its inevitability is easily shown. If the average cost curve, CAC, intersects demand curve DD' as it did in the short-run example of Figure 1.1, the process is as described above: there are profitable output positions, new entry is induced, and the market price falls. If, on the other hand, CAC were to lie entirely above DD', every output level would imply a net loss; firms would thus be forced to exit from the market, and market price would tend to rise. So long as profitable positions exist, entry continues; similarly, so long as all positions are unprofitable, exit continues. Equilibrium is attained only when there is no net entry or exit that would tend to push the market price up or down—that is, when the average cost curve, CAC, is tangent to the demand curve, DD'. The firm's profit-maximizing position occurs at this point of tangency, because this is precisely where the marginal cost curve, CMC, must intersect the demand curve, which is here the marginal revenue curve as well.[6]

Industry equilibrium is portrayed in terms of conventional supply and demand curves, as in Figure 1.3. The industry demand curve, DD', shows the usual relationship between price and quantity demanded. The precise derivation of the industry supply curve, SS', varies slightly between the short and long run, although its broad meaning is the same in both. The supply curve shows what quantities will be forthcoming at various prices. Obviously the amount that the industry will supply at

[6] The marginal cost curve must intersect the average cost curve at the latter's minimum point. But the minimum point of the AC curve must also be the point of its tangency to a *horizontal* demand curve.

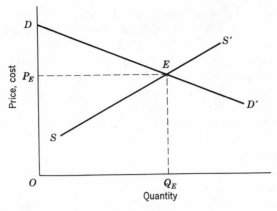

Figure 1.3

any given price is the sum total of what all firms will supply at that price. In the short run the amount that any firm will supply at some price can be read off directly from the firm's marginal cost curve. Thus the short-run industry supply curve is simply the (horizontal) summation of the marginal cost curves for all firms in the industry (and the supply curve for the firm in the short run is its marginal cost curve.)

The definition of the long-run industry supply curve is somewhat more complicated since it must take account of adjustments such as the affect of entry and exit on cost functions. That is, we cannot discuss the supply terms of various quantities without knowing something about the way in which cost curves may shift as the industry undergoes expansion and contraction. It is possible to short-circuit such difficulties for our purposes by observing that in the long run all competitive firms, and thus the competitive industry, tend toward equilibrium at zero profit. This implies that supply prices in the long run (i.e., the prices at which supply is offered) tend to equal average costs, and the long-run industry supply curve may thus be said to approximate the long-run average cost curve for the industry.

B. Pure Monopoly

Pure monopoly, the other market extreme, is a case in which a single firm is the sole supplier of a commodity for which no close substitutes exist; the firm and the industry are the same. The monopolist thus faces a conventional downward-sloping demand curve, such as DD' in Figure 1.4, and maximizes profits at that output level for which marginal cost equals marginal revenue. In Figure 1.4 the monopolist will produce output Q_M and will charge price P_M, the price which the market will pay for that quantity. The portrayal of equilibrium for monopoly is essentially the same in both the short and long run.

A number of interesting observations may be made with respect to monopoly equilibrium. First, it is obvious that the monopolist succeeds in doing something competitive firms cannot do: charging a price in excess of marginal cost, and perhaps in excess of long-run average cost. The reason again is that competitive firms have no power over price and are assumed to act independently. Were the competitive firms to conspire, they too could take advantage of the downward-sloping industry demand curve, and presumably could arrive at a price-quantity solution similar to that of the monopolist. It is worth noting that the monopolist's ability to exploit the market (in the sense that he charges a price in excess of marginal cost) does not imply any undesirable motivation such as extreme greed (nor is the competitive firm more altruistic). Under the assumptions of traditional price theory, all firms seek maximum profits. If the monopolist succeeds better than most, it is only because the market is less effective in restraining his actions.

A further observation of interest is that there are some constraints on the monopolist. He cannot pursue maximum profits "without regard to supply and demand forces," as some naive statements would make it appear. Quite the contrary; his maximizing calculations must take account of the demand and cost curves precisely as the competitive firm takes account of these factors. It is even possible that monopoly will be unprofitable. Note, for example, that there is no average cost curve drawn in Figure 1.4. If the firm's average cost curve were to lie entirely above demand curve DD', there would be no price-output combination that would enable a monopolist to stay in business in the long run. This indicates simply that even a monopolist cannot earn profits on a product that no one is willing to buy at a price equal to or higher than the average cost of producing it.

Finally, it may be observed that there is really no such thing as a monopoly supply curve. The monopolist establishes prices according to the position of the demand, marginal revenue, and marginal cost curves. But we cannot read off the output that will be forthcoming at various prices by referring to any single curve. It is, in fact, easy to see that, for a given MC curve, the equilibrium price-quantity combination may occur at various points on the diagram, depending on the position of DD' and DMR. Given appropriate shifts in demand, a particular output

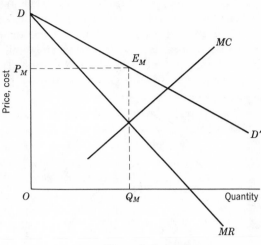

Figure 1.4

level may be priced differently, and a given price may be associated with different outputs.

C. Monopoly and Competition: The Initial Comparison

The usual comparison of market results under pure competition and pure monopoly may be examined in Figure 1.5. In the short run competitive equilibrium occurs at point E_C, the intersection of the industry supply and demand curves. Monopoly equilibrium occurs at E_M, reflecting output Q_M (the level at which marginal cost and marginal revenue are equal) and price P_M (the highest price at which industry demand will accept quantity Q_M).

This extremely simple comparison constitutes the standard demonstration of competitive superiority to monopoly. The competitive industry produces more and charges a lower price for its output, a result that most would agree is preferred.[7] There are several problems and

[7] This is something of an oversimplification. It may be agreed that more goods generally are preferred to fewer, but it does not necessarily follow that raising the output of a particular industry is always desirable. If the economy is at full employment, for example, increased production in one area implies decreased production elsewhere; and there is a question whether the *allocation of resources* is improved or worsened by such a change.

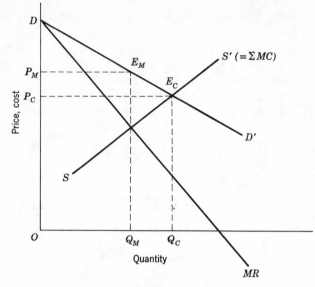

Figure 1.5

qualifications to this comparison, but, setting these aside for the moment, it may be seen that this conclusion is not in itself terribly strong or surprising. It states only that pure competition provides goods to the market on somewhat more generous terms (from the consumer's point of view) than does pure monopoly. It does not, however, tell us directly whether the competitive solution is an extraordinarily "good" one, or the monopoly solution an extraordinarily "bad" one; nor whether the difference between the two is significant. The simple comparison in other words does not really provide very extensive information, although it does lay the basis for a presumption in favor of competitive as compared to monopolistic markets.

D. Competitive Optimality

The economic case for competition can be put in somewhat stronger terms. Generally it can be shown that the competitive outcome is not merely better than that of pure monopoly, but is in some sense the *best possible* from society's viewpoint. To demonstrate this proposition it is necessary to say something about the meaning of "best possible" situations, and then to indicate how competitive markets yield such situations.

Welfare economists have devoted much effort to the definition of *optimal* and *efficient* positions for society. The first question that arises here is, *who* is to judge the goodness or badness of alternatives? The usual approach to this question assumes that choices among alternatives can be made only by the individual(s) affected. If we wish to know, for example, whether a change improves or damages the welfare of an individual, we must ask him or examine that part of his behavior that reveals the answer. No one else can tell us what is best for that person.[8]

Once it is accepted that individuals are to judge their own welfare, the pertinent task is to define the welfare of that *collection* of individuals who comprise society. The definition of social welfare is complicated by the fact that individuals are likely to regard alternatives differently. Let us suppose that society has two alternatives: *A*, which involves the production of more guns and less butter; and *B*, which involves fewer guns and more butter. It is highly probable that some individuals in a society will prefer *A* while others prefer *B*. How are we to say which alternative is socially preferable?

This question is a very old one, but it has never been resolved in an entirely satisfactorily way. There are, of course, some practical methods of solution. If the choice is between more guns and more butter, we might vote in order to determine which alternative the majority prefers. It has been shown by Arrow,[9] however, that simple voting procedures generally violate one or more accepted conditions for democratic choice. In addition, the principle of majority rule itself may be subject to question; for example, if opinion on the guns-and-butter issue is divided evenly, but one group is passionately concerned while the other is almost indifferent, should we not take account of this information as well? Perhaps we should, but there are great difficulties in measuring objectively the intensity of individuals' feelings.[10]

---

[8] The alternative to this approach is to assume that an individual's welfare can be meaningfully defined by an external arbiter (e.g., the government). Although such an assumption will be repugnant to many, it is interesting to note that even a democratic society adopts this principle at certain times.

[9] Kenneth J. Arrow, *Social Choice and Individual Values*, Cowles Commission Monograph No. 12, Wiley, New York, 1951.

[10] One possibility is that intensity be measured by willingness to pay. We might, for example, ask the progun and probutter groups to state how much they would pay to have the decision in their favor (this is, after all, the way in which market decisions are made). The trouble here is that we are measuring not only intensity of feelings but the distribution of income and wealth as well. The decision is likely to be won by the group with the most funds, not necessarily a desirable outcome unless we are convinced that the distribution of funds was initially "correct."

The difficulty in making interpersonal comparisons is such that we often seek to avoid the problem. It is extremely useful (albeit somewhat confining) to analyze situations in which conflicts of preference do not arise. We may proceed under the Pareto criterion,[11] which states that any change is an improvement if it makes one or more individuals better off while making none worse off. A change that helps some but hurts others is not necessarily bad, but *it cannot be evaluated* by this approach. Extending the same criterion, it follows that we have an optimal situation when no further improvement is possible. The *Pareto optimum* is thus defined as a situation in which the well-being of one or more individuals can be improved only by harming the position of another or others.

We have said so far that the definition of a welfare optimum may encounter the perhaps insoluble problem of conflicting desires among individuals. To avoid this we turn to the Paretian notion of optimality. It now remains for us to see what specific conditions are implied by Pareto optimality, and to define the role of competition in relation to this concept of an economic welfare optimum.

1. THE OPTIMALITY CONDITIONS

Our definition of a welfare optimum states in effect that we cannot rearrange goods or resources in such a way that we help someone without hurting someone else. Under what circumstances will this be so?

(a) Condition 1: Optimal Distribution of Goods between Consumers

We may start by considering a simplified economy in which there are two goods produced (X and Y), and two consumers (A and B). Figures 1.6a and b show the indifference maps of consumers A and B respectively. Each indifference curve represents combinations of goods X and Y among which the consumer is indifferent; higher indifference curves imply more utility (satisfaction) for the consumer since, by assumption, more goods are preferred to fewer. In Figure 1.6c consumer B's indifference map has been rotated so that the origin is now in the northeast corner rather than the southwest, and it has been superimposed on the indifference map of consumer A. This is the famous Edgeworth box diagram. We assume that the initial endowment of goods is defined by the axes of the box; in other words, there exists quantity $O_A Z$ (or $O_B W$) of good X and quantity $O_A W$ (or $O_B Z$) of good Y. Any point within the box is

[11] Vilfredo Pareto, *Manual d'Economie Politique*, second edition, Girard, Paris, 1927.

practical in the sense that it divides the goods actually in existence between the two consumers.

Where should the consumers locate for optimum welfare? Consider a point such as i, at the intersection of one of A's and one of B's indifference curves. Goods X and Y could be reallocated (exchanged) in such a way that A remains on the same indifference curve but B moves to a higher curve—point g; or so that B remains on his same curve while A moves to a higher one—point f; or so that both move to a higher curve—

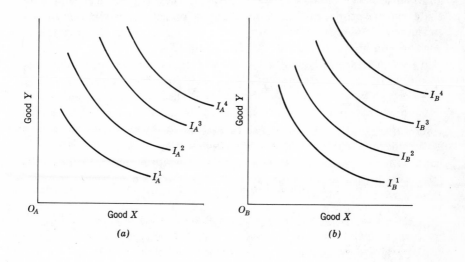

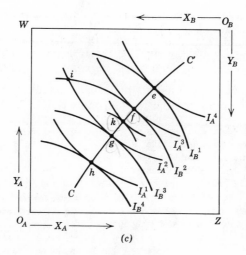

Figure 1.6

point k. Point i is therefore nonoptimal in the Pareto sense; an improvement for one consumer that does not harm the other is still possible.[12] It is, in fact, easy to see that any point in the box that is not a point of tangency between an I_A and an I_B is nonoptimal. At the points of tangency, represented by the *contract curve, CC'*, mutual improvement (or an improvement for one consumer that does not hurt the other), is impossible. The contract curve thus represents optimal points. It is, of course, true that consumer A would prefer a point such as e to a point such as h, while B's preferences are the reverse; yet *every* point on the curve is optimal in that a move away from it must hurt one of the consumers.

The condition for optimal distribution of goods among consumers also may be expressed as:

$$\frac{MU_{XA}}{MU_{YA}} = \frac{MU_{XB}}{MU_{YB}} \tag{1}$$

where MU_{XA} is the marginal utility of good X to consumer A, MU_{YA} is the marginal utility of good Y to consumer A, and so forth. This condition states that the *marginal rate of substitution* between the goods (the ratio of their marginal utilities) must be the same for each consumer. If this were not the case, the consumers could improve their position by exchanging goods. The consumer who values X highly relative to Y could trade some of his Y to the consumer who values Y highly relative to X. Only when the utility ratios are the same for both consumers, is such a mutually beneficial trade impossible.[13]

(b) Condition 2: Optimal Allocation of Inputs in Productive Uses

The second optimality condition concerns the allocation of inputs among productive uses. Consider first the case in which there is a single input, i, that can be used in the production of goods X and Y. This input must be employed in such a way that its marginal product in the production of X equals its marginal product in the production of Y. Were this not

---

[12] As is an improvement for *both*.

[13] In terms of the box diagram, the slope of each consumer's indifference curve represents his marginal rate of substitution between the two goods. This is easily seen once it is recalled that an indifference curve is a curve of constant *total* utility. As one moves along any curve, then, the utility gained from additional units of X is precisely offset by the utility lost from decreased units of Y. Thus, $\Delta X(MU_X) = \Delta Y(MU_Y)$, and, $\Delta Y/\Delta X$ (the slope of the curve) $= MU_X/MU_Y$ (the marginal rate of substitution between X and Y). But at points of tangency between the consumers' indifference curves, the slopes and thus the marginal rates of substitution are the same for each consumer. Accordingly, it is at such points—that is, on the contract curve—that the optimality condition for distribution is satisfied.

the case, society could clearly benefit by transferring some of i into the use yielding the greater marginal (social) product.

This condition can be generalized to cases in which more than one input exists. If two inputs, i and j, are useful in the production of goods X and Y, optimal utilization of inputs requires that the *ratio* of the marginal physical products of i and j in the production of X be the same as the ratio of their marginal physical products in the production of Y. That is:

$$\frac{MP_{iX}}{MP_{jX}} = \frac{MP_{iY}}{MP_{jY}}$$

(2)

If this equality is not satisfied, one input is *relatively more efficient* in the production of one output (and the other input is thus relatively less efficient in the production of the same output). It will thus benefit society to divert more of the first input into its more efficient use (and similarly to divert the less efficient input from that use). This will permit society to expand the production of one output and hold constant the production of the other output at a constant level of resource use.[14] Only when the marginal product ratios are the same can society not gain by reshuffling its inputs among competing uses.[15]

(c) Condition 3: Optimal Amounts of Output

The first two optimality conditions ignore the question of appropriate output quantities. Condition 1 assures that whatever is produced will

[14] The argument is not entirely obvious, and an example may be helpful. Suppose we have

$$\frac{MP_{iX}}{MP_{jX}} = \frac{30}{10} \qquad \frac{MP_{iY}}{MP_{jY}} = \frac{10}{5}$$

The marginal product ratio of the inputs in the production of X exceeds their ratio in the production of Y. Suppose that we now transfer one unit of i from production of Y to production of X, and also transfer two units of j from production of X to production of Y. The production levels of X and Y change as follows.

X: rises by 30 when a unit of i is added ($MP_{iX} = 30$)
    falls by 20 when *two* units of j are removed ($MP_{jX} = 10$)
    Net production rises by 10.
Y: rises by 10 when *two* units of j are added ($MP_{jY} = 5$)
    falls by 10 when one unit of i is removed ($MP_{iY} = 10$)
    Net production is unchanged.

By shifting inputs we have raised the production of X and held constant the production of Y, while using the same (input) resources. Readers may verify that such a change is possible whenever the marginal product ratios of the inputs are unequal in different productive uses.

[15] Readers should observe that Condition 2 is structurally and conceptually similar to Condition 1, and might be portrayed in terms of a similar box diagram.

be divided among consumers in an efficient way; Condition 2 assures that the production of any outputs will be carried on efficiently. We now come to the important task of defining appropriate output levels, *given* that distribution and production of that output are efficient.[16]

In the example of an economy that produces one commodity, X, optimal output requires simply that the marginal utility of X be equal to its marginal cost $(MU_X = MC_X)$.[17] If $MU_X > MC_X$, society can benefit by producing more of X; additional units would be worth more, in society's opinion, than they cost to produce. If on the other hand $MC_x > MU_x$, it would be beneficial to produce less; the marginal cost of some units of X now exceeds their marginal value. Unless the equality is satisfied, then, society can benefit by altering its production level.

Consider the case in which more than one commodity is produced. Optimal output for any pair of commodities, X and Y, requires that the commodities be produced in quantities such that

$$\frac{MU_X}{MC_X} = \frac{MU_Y}{MC_Y} \tag{3}$$

That is, the ratio of marginal cost to marginal utility must be the same for each commodity. If the ratios were unequal society could benefit by producing more of the good that yields the higher marginal utility per unit of marginal cost. Only when the ratios are equal is output optimal in that no such improvement can occur.

This important condition also can be discussed in terms of the *transformation curve* (sometimes called the production possibility curve), TT' in Figure 1.7. Curve TT' shows the quantities of commodities X and Y that can be produced by utilizing fully the resources and technology of the community. The curve is concave (it has an increasing absolute slope), reflecting the imperfect substitutability of factor inputs.[18]

The slope of the transformation curve, known as the *marginal rate*

[16] In other words Condition 3 assumes the satisfaction of Conditions 1 and 2. The idea of an optimal output would make little sense if production or distribution were inefficient.

[17] It should be noted that we are talking in terms of marginal utility and marginal cost as *society* evaluates them. For the present, it is assumed that there are no troublesome discrepancies between social and private evaluations.

[18] That is, some resources are relatively more efficient in producing one commodity than the other. At a point on TT' involving the production of much Y and little X it is possible to increase the production of X without giving up much Y by diverting resources that are inefficient in the production of Y. Similarly, when little Y and much X are produced, the production of more X will involve a greater sacrifice of Y because it is now necessary to divert resources that are relatively efficient in the production of Y.

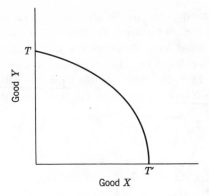

Figure 1.7

of transformation, has an important economic meaning. It is evident that the slope tells us the amount of either good that must be sacrificed in order to obtain a unit of the other good. If, for example, we wish to know what is involved in obtaining one more unit of X at any point, we simply move one unit along the X axis and see how much Y has been lost. It can be shown that the slope also represents the ratio of the marginal cost of good X to the marginal cost of good Y. That is,

$$\frac{\Delta Y}{\Delta X} = \frac{MC_x}{MC_y}$$

Although we shall not bother to demonstrate this identity in a formal way,[19] it should appear to make sense intuitively. In stating how much of one commodity must be given up to obtain a specified increment in the other we *are in effect stating the marginal cost of one commodity in terms of the other.* The slope of the curve, however, gives us this information in two ways: we can read MC_X at any point in terms of Y, and can also read MC_Y in terms of X.

Condition 3 will be satisfied, then, if the slope of the transformation curve (the marginal cost ratio between X and Y) is equal to the marginal utility ratio between X and Y (the marginal rate of substitution). We

[19] The demonstration consists in showing that the slope is equal to the ratio of the marginal products of any input, i, in the production of two goods, X and Y; and that this ratio implies the marginal cost ratio, MC_x/MC_y. It is, incidentally, a convenient way of showing also that Condition 2 requires that the economy operate on the transformation curve—that is, that this curve represents efficient points of production. For a full demonstration, see, for example, Kelvin Lancaster, *Introduction to Modern Microeconomics*, Rand McNally, Chicago, 1969, pp. 265 ff.

have already shown (in footnote 13) that the marginal rate of substitution is defined by the slope of a consumer's indifference curve. If we superimpose a consumer's indifference map on the transformation curve, as in Figure 1.8, we see that the consumer's equilibrium position is at a point of tangency between an indifference curve and the transformation curve. At point E in Figure 1.8 the consumer has attained the highest

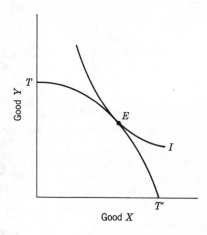

Figure 1.8

level of satisfaction permitted by society's production possibilities. The consumer's marginal rate of substitution, MU_X/MU_Y, is here equal to the marginal rate of transformation, MC_X/MC_Y. We know that if Condition 1 (optimal distribution) is satisfied, MU_X/MU_Y is *the same for all consumers;* thus, if we are willing to equate all consumers with "society," we again have Condition 3:

$$\frac{MU_X}{MC_X} = \frac{MU_Y}{MC_Y} \tag{3}$$

(d) Summary of Conditions

The conditions discussed above define an optimal situation in the Pareto sense. If the distribution of outputs, allocation of inputs, and determination of output levels satisfy the three marginal conditions, there is no way to rearrange economic activities so as to help some individuals without harming some other or others.

2. THE ROLE OF COMPETITION

It now remains to be seen that competition will yield an optimal economic result. This proposition can be demonstrated specifically with reference to the three marginal conditions.

It is easily seen that Condition 1 will be satisfied by any pricing system that sets commodity prices at the same levels for all consumers. A utility-maximizing consumer equates (in equilibrium) the ratio of marginal utility to price for each item he consumes.[20] If all consumers pay the same prices for commodities X and Y, each must act so that his marginal utility ratio, MU_X/MU_Y, is equal to the *same* price ratio, P_X/P_Y. Therefore every consumer's marginal utility ratio (or marginal rate of substitution) is the same. Since a competitive market offers goods to all at the same prices, it satisfies Condition 1; and it is interesting to note that this condition will be satisfied for any arbitrary set of prices, so long as those prices are fixed at the same levels for all consumers.

Condition 2 is similarly satisfied by a competitive system (or by any system that fixes all input and output prices at the same levels for all producers and consumers). This condition provides that the ratio of the marginal products of two inputs in the production of one good must be the same as their ratio in the production of another good. We know, however, that a profit-maximizing firm whose input and output prices are fixed must hire each input to the point at which its price is equal to the value of its marginal product.[21] If input and output prices are fixed at the same levels for all firms, each firm will pay the same amount for any given input, and the value of any given input's marginal product must be the same in all uses.

This implies that for any input i,

$$MP_{iX} = MP_{iY}[22]$$

---

[20] That is, he must act so that, for commodities X and Y, $MU_X/P_X = MU_Y/P_Y$. Were this not the case, more utility could be gained by switching some purchases to the commodity yielding the higher marginal utility per unit spent.

[21] If the value of the marginal product exceeds the input price, the firm is foregoing profitable units of the input; if input price exceeds the value of the marginal product, the firm has hired some unprofitable input units.

[22] We have already said that the *value* of the marginal product of any input must be the same in all uses. With fixed output prices, however, the value of the marginal product of an input is simply its marginal *physical* product times output price; and the marginal physical product is the value of the marginal product divided by output price.

and for any other input j,

$$MP_{jX} = MP_{jY}$$

It then follows directly that

$$\frac{MP_{iX}}{MP_{jX}} = \frac{MP_{iY}}{MP_{jY}} \tag{2}$$

The assumption that all input and output prices are fixed at the same levels for all firms and consumers thus implies satisfaction of Condition 2; and such an assumption is again embodied in the model of a competitive market.

Condition 3 states that the marginal rate of substitution between goods X and Y (MU_X/MU_Y) must equal the marginal rate of transformation between the two goods (MC_X/MC_Y). We know that utility-maximizing consumers will equate the marginal rate of substitution between any pair of goods with the price ratio of the goods: $MU_X/MU_Y = P_X/P_Y$. But, as we also have seen, firms *in pure competition* will produce any product to the point at which its marginal cost equals its price. Thus

$$MC_X = P_X, \quad MC_Y = P_Y, \quad \text{and} \quad MC_X/MC_Y = P_X/P_Y$$

At this point we have said that the marginal rate of substitution between X and Y and the marginal rate of transformation between X and Y will, under competitive conditions, be equal to the ratio of the prices of X and Y. Assuming once again that P_X and P_Y are fixed uniformly, this means that the marginal rate of substitution is equal to the marginal rate of transformation; that is,

$$\frac{MU_X}{MU_Y} = \frac{MC_X}{MC_Y}, \quad \text{and} \quad \frac{MU_X}{MC_X} = \frac{MU_Y}{MC_Y} \tag{3}$$

Condition 3 is thus satisfied.[23]

3. SUMMARY

The arguments outlined above indicate that the Pareto optimality conditions are satisfied by an economic system in which:

a. **The prices of all inputs and outputs are fixed at the same levels for all producers and consumers.**

[23] Strictly speaking, it must also be assumed that all markets are cleared, that is, that there are no excess supplies or demands. Were this not so, consumer equilibrium might be defined at a nonattainable point outside the transformation curve. Its meaning (if any) would then be questionable.

b. Producers seek maximum profits and consumers seek maximum utility.

c. Firms produce to the point at which the price of any product is equal to its marginal cost.

d. All markets are cleared.

Since circumstances (a) through (d) hold for competitive markets, we may conclude that the result of a competitive system is a Pareto optimum.[24]

Referring back to Figure 1.6c, it will be recalled that there are many Pareto optima. We have demonstrated that competition guarantees a Pareto optimum, but we have not shown the obverse: that any Pareto optimum must be the result of competition. We shall not demonstrate this proposition, but it is important to note its validity under certain assumptions. It is true that (under appropriate convexity conditions) any Pareto optimum can be a competitive equilibrium for some distribution of income. In other words, competition is a *necessary* as well as a sufficient condition for Pareto optimality. Other market forms, including monopoly, cannot produce an optimal result.[25]

The caution with which the notion of Pareto optimality must be treated should be emphasized again. Some economists have gone so far as to state that we ought not to speak of Pareto *optimality* but rather of Pareto *efficiency;* the argument here is that the word optimal connotes desirability in a broad sense that is not justified by the Pareto conditions. What we have described above is a system of unique efficiency, but we have also noted that many efficient points exist. Some efficient points would undoubtedly be considered by society to be more desirable than others; and some Pareto optima might be judged *worse* than some non-optima. We have ignored such judgments because there is no objective way to approach them. Nevertheless, it is important to recognize the limitations to the definition of optimality that we have employed.

E. Implicit Assumptions in the Demonstration of Competitive Optimality

The conclusion of competitive optimality rests on a number of assumptions, some of which have not yet been stated explicitly. It is possible

[24] Conditions (a), (b), and (d) might hold as well in other kinds of markets.

[25] Readers may verify this conclusion in a casual way by examining the implications of pricing above marginal cost (a monopoly characteristic) for Condition 3.

that certain of these assumptions may restrict the analysis in an important way; thus they bear brief discussion.

1. NO EXTERNALITIES IN CONSUMPTION

We assumed implicitly in the above analysis that any individual's enjoyment of consumption is independent of the consumption patterns of others. That is, we assume that the individual consumer's satisfaction depends purely on his own consumption; he derives neither pleasure nor displeasure from what others consume.

The necessity for this assumption is obvious. Suppose, for example, that consumers are envious of one another. A rearrangement of society's output that apparently increases the satisfaction of some, while leaving others as well off as before, could *not* then be said to be Pareto desirable. Why? Most simply because those who are left "as well off as before," in terms of their own consumption patterns, are now envious of those who have more. The more general difficulty is that if satisfaction is influenced by the consumption of others there is no way to define optimal or equilibrium positions for consumers in terms of their own experience. Accordingly, we could not move from statements about individual preferences among combinations of goods to statements about the preferences of all individuals—that is, of society. We might be forced to say, for example, that although every individual is as well off as possible (given relevant constraints), the community as a whole is *not* as well off as possible. It is this kind of complication that we seek to avoid by assuming that an individual's satisfaction in consumption is determined solely by his own experience.

2. NO EXTERNALITIES IN PRODUCTION

A very similar assumption about the absence of externalities is included in the production side of the analysis. It will be recalled that the marginal rate of transformation (slope of the transformation curve) represents the marginal cost ratio between two goods, as seen by the producers of those goods. It was shown that if this ratio were equated with the marginal rate of substitution in consumption, output levels of the two goods are Pareto optimal for the community as a whole. The marginal rate of transformation was thus taken to represent the marginal cost ratio between goods X and Y *both* for the producers of those goods *and for the community*. It was assumed implicitly that society's calculation of marginal costs is the same as the calculation made by private business firms (producers). If this were not so, the equation of society's marginal rate of substitution with the producers' marginal rate of transformation would not be socially optimal.

In more familiar language, we have assumed that marginal social costs and marginal private costs are identical. If this is not the case, an externality in production exists, and the optimal or equilibrium behavior of private producers will not coincide with the optimum for society. Suppose, for example, that a power company pollutes the atmosphere in the process of producing electricity. From society's viewpoint, air pollution is a cost associated with electricity production; yet the power company is most unlikely to consider such a "cost" in its own profit calculations. In this particular instance there is an external diseconomy in the production of electricity, and unless the producer can somehow be compelled to take account of it, it is likely that it may undertake too much production—from the viewpoint of social opti-mality.[26] (One solution to this problem, incidentally, would be to tax the producer by the amount of the external cost that he imposes on society.)

Examples of externalities in production are familiar. An educational system, for example, is likely to benefit society above and beyond those benefits that accrue directly to the educated individuals. The willingness of individuals to pay for education is based on the private benefits they expect to receive; but it cannot very well reflect social benefits (e.g., the political stability of an educated nation). The important aspect of such externalities is that the competitive market mechanism breaks down as the servant of society. If the measurement of benefits and costs by firms differs from that of society, the equilibrium toward which the firms tend need not correspond to society's best interests.

Competitive optimality, then, requires the absence of external effects, but external effects are common in reality. The direct implication is that even when all the requisites of pure competition are met there may be instances in which it is not a socially appropriate form of market organization. Or, alternatively, it may be that society can superimpose a system of rewards or penalties in order to render the competitive market socially appropriate. This qualification is of practical importance because it implies that, even in areas in which a market can function, competition may not lead to socially optimal results.

[26] The case of an external economy exists when the private benefit or profit that may be gained through economic activity is *exceeded* by the social benefit. Here a gain external to the private producer exists, and too *little* of the relevant good or service will be forthcoming from society's standpoint.

3. INCREASING COSTS WITHIN A
RELEVANT PRODUCTION RANGE

A fundamental assumption in the analysis is that costs of producing various commodities turn up fairly quickly—that is, that a firm operating under a given technology encounters increasing production costs at relatively low output levels. Stated in reverse, the assumption is that economies of large-scale operation are not so great that firms will be unable to reach equilibrium (profit-maximizing) positions and remain small relative to the market.

Consider a firm in pure competition. The firm attains an equilibrium level of production at which marginal cost and marginal revenue are equated, provided also that MC cuts MR from below. So long as the marginal costs of production begin to rise at low production levels, the firm can reach an equilibrium at a relatively small size. Suppose, however, that production in a particular industry is characterized by significant economies of scale. That is, individual firms can continue to lower unit output costs by producing much larger quantities, possibly because more efficient production methods can be utilized in larger operations. The position of the firm then can be illustrated by Figure 1.9a, in which marginal costs do not turn up within the output range under examination. Two points are obvious. First, there exists no equilibrium position for the firm within this range. Second, the firm as a seeker of maximum profits must attempt to grow, since more production in this situation implies higher profits. Presumably if the firm expands output to a high enough level, marginal costs *will* turn up and equilibrium will be approached. In the long run this expectation follows from the proposition that at some size economies of large scale are exhausted and diseconomies of scale set in. The diseconomies are usually associated with the administrative and managerial difficulties that arise in very large business complexes.

The firm may thus grow and find a level of output such that further expansion would be unprofitable. *But in doing so it may become so large relative to the market that it attains a degree of power over price.* This possibility is illustrated in Figure 1.9b, with the firm's pricing power reflected in its now downsloping demand curve DD'. What has happened is that the firm, seeking its best-profit position, has abandoned the status of an insignificantly small competitor. It has not necessarily done so through any excessive or illegitimate attempt to monopolize the market. Quite the contrary, it is the underlying cost conditions of the market that have impelled this growth. In such an industry it is probable that small,

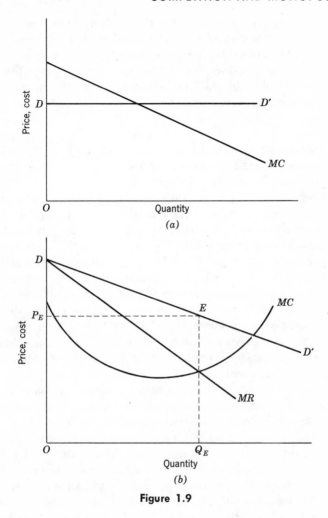

Figure 1.9

"competitive-sized" firms cannot survive. Moreover, to the extent that unit costs are lower at high production levels, the large firm is a technically more efficient entity, although it becomes a partial monopolist in attaining the efficient level.

The case of significant economies of scale, then, may be characterized as one in which competition becomes technically impossible and, under an efficiency criterion, undesirable. The demonstration of competitive optimality implicitly assumes away this kind of complication. In discussing competitive equilibrium we assume that the competitive equilibrium is in fact a meaningful result. Industries containing cost structures that will not support a large number of small firms obviously are not amenable to the usual comparison; or, more precisely, the comparison is not a useful one. For although it remains possible to define a market result akin to the purely competitive, the industry is not capable of generating such an outcome.

4. COMMUNITY PREFERENCES INDEPENDENT OF THE FORM OF MARKET ORGANIZATION

A further assumption implicit in the earlier analysis is that the preference patterns of individuals are not altered by changes in market organization. In other words, society's evaluation of alternative output combinations is assumed to have nothing to do with the shape of the markets in which those outputs are produced. Should a previously competitive industry become monopolized, this will not affect consumer preferences.

The purpose of this assumption should be clear. If the advent of monopoly, for example, were to change consumer likes and dislikes, there would be no way to compare (even hypothetically) the goodness of allocation at competitive and monopolistic points. The problem would be akin to that of trying to compare the well-being of two individuals (or groups) with different tastes.

The purpose of the assumption may be clear, but once again it is subject to some question. Characteristically, many industries whose firms possess some market power do exert considerable effort to affect demand conditions—that is, to alter consumer preferences. Advertising and product differentiation through other means are familiar examples of this effort. Quite possibly, then, a community's evaluation of a commodity is *not* independent of the type of market in which the commodity is produced. This possibility, however, is not easily verifiable, and in any case cannot be taken into account within the standard analytical framework.

5. SOCIETY'S PRODUCTION POSSIBILITIES INDEPENDENT OF THE FORM OF INDUSTRIAL ORGANIZATION

One of the most controversial assumptions relevant to the conclusion of competitive optimality is that utilization of resources is equally efficient in a technical sense under competition and monopoly. The conclusion that competition is the best allocator of resources *for a given technology* fails to take account of the possibility that a monopolistic industry may employ productive techniques different from those of its competitive counterpart.

One of the most important advocates of this possibility was Schumpeter,[27] who argued that the invention and introduction of new products and processes is centered in the large, typically monopolistic or semimonopolistic firm. To the extent that this is so, new innovations and technology will be more likely to occur in monopolistic than in competitive industry. Accordingly, a comparison of monopoly with competition at a fixed technological position systematically understates the social contribution of the former. Diagrammatically, the Schumpeterian contention may be illustrated as follows. The competitive market produces at a point such as E_C in Figure 1.10, where short-run marginal

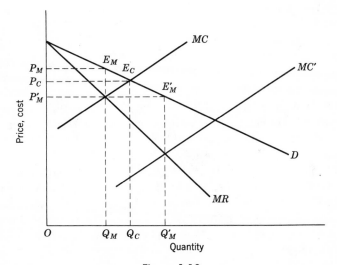

Figure 1.10

cost equals price. If this industry were monopolized, the ordinary expectation would be a price increase and output decrease to point E_M. However, if the monopolist in such an industry introduces cost-saving innovations, the entire marginal cost curve may fall to some level MC'. If the curve falls far enough, the monopolist may actually produce more at a lower

[27] Joseph A. Schumpeter, *Capitalism, Socialism and Democracy*, Harper & Bros., New York, 1950.

price (point E'_M) than the original competitive industry, even if the monopolist fully exploits his market power!

The same idea can be presented in terms of the industry long-run average cost curve AC in Figure 1.11. The unique quality of competitive

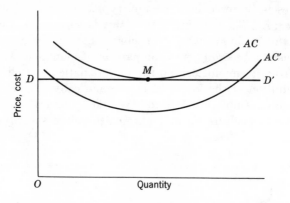

Figure 1.11

efficiency is shown by production at minimum average unit cost, point M; only at such a point can the competitive firm reach a long-run equilibrium. But if monopolistic innovation shifts AC downward to AC', production may occur at a lower average unit cost (anywhere on AC' below DD'), even though it does *not* occur at the minimum average cost point of AC'.

The assumption that society's production possibilities do not respond to changes in the form of industrial organization is not strictly necessary to the analysis described above. Competition is Pareto optimal regardless of whether this assumption holds. The Schumpeterian contention is, rather, that society may achieve more desirable levels of production under monopoly than under competition, although such points might turn out to be nonoptimal in the Pareto sense.[28]

It is of course possible that society will remain worse off under monopoly, even if the monopoly innovates; the benefits of innovation may not outweigh the costs of monopolistic exploitation, and as long as they do not the community's position will deteriorate when monopolization occurs. The Schumpeterian hypothesis thus need not be interpreted as postulating the *inevitable* superiority of monopoly, although Schumpeter

[28] This point may be illustrated with reference to transformation curves. Suppose that the consumer is initially at E, the point of tangency between indifference curve I and transformation function TT. If the transformation function shifts outward to

himself may have intended to suggest this conclusion. The troublesome implication may be rather that the standard comparison of competition with monopoly is *irrelevant* for many problems posed by a dynamic world in which productive techniques are subject to continual change.

6. THE STATIC COMPARISON AND DYNAMIC CONSIDERATIONS

Many of the difficulties that arise in attempting to compare competitive and non-purely competitive results can be discussed in terms of a static versus a dynamic approach. Although the definition of these terms suffers from a degree of ambiguity,[29] they are helpful in discussing a very basic problem of economic analysis. The problem arises because, in complex economic systems, many things are changing at once. It thus becomes extremely difficult to isolate the effects of changes in a single variable. If we wish to examine the influence of a factor X_1 on some other factor Y, we can of course look at the way in which Y changes as X_1 changes. But if the behavior of Y also is influenced by factors $X_2, X_3, \ldots, X_n$, these other factors must somehow be taken into account.

$T'T'$—which is what Schumpeter argues may happen under monopoly—the consumer might find himself at a point such as n. It is true that the consumer now suffers from monopolistic distortion in that he has not attained the best possible position on $T'T'$; yet he is on a higher indifference curve, I', than he was before.

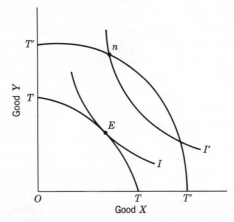

[29] For a thorough and interesting discussion of alternative interpretations, see Fritz Machlup, "Statics and Dynamics: Kaleidoscopic Words," *Southern Economic Journal*, **26**, October 1959, pp. 91–110.

This kind of problem may be circumvented conceptually by confining the analysis of some problems to a moment in time. Various influential elements that are known to change over time are thus "frozen," and the consequences of a change in a single factor may be analyzed, in a sense, before the others have a chance to catch up. This is in effect a *static* approach, and is very familiar in the form of *ceteris paribus* assumptions in economics. (In drawing a demand curve, for example, we examine the effect of price changes on quantity demanded at a moment in time, assuming that all other factors that might affect demand are constant.)

The comparison between competitive and non-purely competitive market results utilizes such a static approach. If we were simply to compare the results of different markets, we would observe discrepancies resulting from a variety of factors. The question in which we are interested, however, is: what difference in market solutions is attributable purely to the *difference in the organization of the markets?* In order to abstract from other influential factors we assume that these elements—for example, distribution of income, the tastes of the community, and technology—are fixed. If these factors were allowed to vary, we could no longer observe the "pure" distinction in which we are interested.

It is the assumption of constant or fixed technology that offers the most difficulty. For not only is it likely that technology will vary through time—a likelihood also associated with the other factors assumed constant—but there is an argument that changes in the organization of the market will cause it to change in a consistent way. Suppose for the moment that the Schumpeterian contention is correct in its extreme form; that is, large monopolistic firms so expand the frontiers of technology that a community is in some sense better off when competitive industries are monopolized. This fact does not challenge the logical validity of the static conclusion that competition is superior, but it may suggest that the fixed-technology assumption of the static approach so restricts the analysis as to render its conclusions uninteresting. We might argue, for example, that the static result, although correct in its own terms, is less relevant to certain of the policy problems in which we are ultimately interested than a dynamic approach that allows for change in elements such as technology.

This discussion is not intended to question the conclusion of competitive optimality, for challenges such as Schumpeter's have not yet been shown to represent more than plausible speculation. The point is rather that selection of an appropriate methodology in economic analysis often involves conflicts. For example, we may be forced to use more restrictive assumptions than seems desirable, simply in order to derive meaningful comparisons. But the conclusions that follow from these comparisons are then tied to the assumptions as well, with the result that their general applicability may be in doubt. The conclusion that competition yields a welfare optimum cannot really be questioned on logical grounds; what may be questioned is, then, not the rightness or wrongness of the conclusion, but its relevance to various problems of policy.

F. Competitive Optimality Reconsidered

The conclusion of competitive optimality sometimes is challenged on the grounds that it is unrealistic. If unrealistic is taken to mean that pure competition is not likely to exist in the real world, then the challenge is a relatively empty one. Competition serves as a standard because of its relation to Pareto optimality. It takes on *normative* significance, which is simply to say that it has something to do with the way things *ought* to be. The question of whether competitive markets are in fact to be found in reality is thus quite irrelevant.

A more pertinent challenge, sometimes couched in terms of realism, concerns the qualifications that are placed on the analysis by the assumptions discussed above. It is important to note that realism is not the basic issue here. Some of the assumptions employed in the analysis of competition are, to be sure, inaccurate descriptions of the world as it is. Certainly it would be desirable to discard all inaccuracy and pursue wholly realistic theories; yet if this were easily accomplished the very need for the theories would be called into question. The kinds of analytical constructs, or models, that we consider are useful precisely because they permit us to analyze, in simplified form, situations of enormous complexity. Realism is necessarily lost in the process, but this is in effect the price that must be paid to reduce some problems to manageable proportions.

If realism itself is not the issue, however, we are still left with an important question: have the assumptions of the analysis so restricted its applicability that its conclusions are of little interest in a dynamic world? A tentative answer to this question is no. The idea of competitive optimality retains real implications, again partly in a normative sense. The limitations imposed by the assumptions do create difficulties; and these in turn make it difficult to proceed directly from analytical conclusions to policy implications. The result is that highly significant questions are raised that cannot be answered on the basis of further theorizing; ultimately we must seek out empirical clues. Theoretical conclusions may thus fail to answer policy questions; more importantly, however, they may assure that the appropriate questions are asked.

Monopolistic Competition: The Chamberlin Contribution

For many years economic theory centered on the "exclusive and opposite" cases of pure competition and pure monopoly—the market extremes. Some analysis in the nineteenth century had focused on duopoly, but had not been widely pursued, perhaps because of the highly simplified and somewhat naive nature of the models proposed. In 1932, however, a book appeared that has redirected the attention of economists to this day. This was the work of Chamberlin expounding the theory of "monopolistic" competition.[1]

The term *monopolistic competition* is accurate in describing the thrust of the Chamberlin innovation. Monopolistic competition is a form of industrial organization in which elements of competition and monopoly coexist. Stated differently, it is a form of competition subject to market imperfections. These imperfections alter the nature of the equilibrium solution so that it is distinct from both the purely competitive and the purely monopolistic solutions. The end result is a kind of in-between outcome that should engender interest if only because imperfect markets

---

[1] Edward H. Chamberlin, *The Theory of Monopolistic Competition*, Harvard University Press, Cambridge, 1932. Page references in the footnotes that follow are to the 7th edition, 1958. A distinct but related work by Mrs. Joan Robinson appeared at about the same time: *The Economics of Imperfect Competition*, Macmillan, London, 1933.

seem to be the rule in the modern economy. The polar extremes of pure competition and pure monopoly are rarely, if ever, visible in the real world. It is true that some agricultural and financial markets seem to approximate pure competition, whereas a narrow definition of a market or industry may disclose some cases that are similar to pure monopoly.[2] Relatively few markets, however, fall within these categories.

The notion of monopolistic competition may be seen to follow from the observation that one particular market imperfection is almost universal: *product differentiation*. There are almost no markets in which consumers fail to make any distinction whatever among different sellers. All aspirins, for example, may be the same physically, but consumers nevertheless seem to believe that differences exist, and aspirins are thus differentiated within the *economic* meaning of the term. Similarly, at the retail level the same products often are sold in different stores. If consumers have a preference for some stores over others—whether this preference arises by virtue of the services offered by the stores, the availability of parking, the personalities of the salespeople, locations that make some stores more convenient, or anything else—then such products are differentiated. In Chamberlin's words,

A general class of product is differentiated if any significant basis exists for distinguishing the goods (or services) of one seller from those of another. *Such a basis may be real or fancied*, so long as it is of any importance whatever to buyers, and leads to a preference for one variety of the product over another.[3]

If true homogeneity is rare, it also is difficult to find cases that meet the pure monopoly condition of "no close substitutes" for the product in question. Without quibbling over the meaning of closeness in substitution, it may be observed that consumers generally have some alternatives to a given commodity. One product may be preferred to another, but the seller of the preferred commodity rarely has the kind of leeway commonly attributed to the pure monopolist. If he attempts to raise his price much above that of an acceptable substitute, a large portion of his customers may desert him. This means that a seller who has some power over price may still face a relatively elastic demand for his product. An increase in his price, *the prices of other goods remaining constant*, may well induce a relatively large decrease in purchases.

---

[2] If the market is defined narrowly enough, any firm may be said to have a monopoly of its own product (General Motors, for example, has a monopoly on new Chevrolets). Very few instances of monopoly under broader definitions are seen, however. Exceptions may include some patented items, although the term market may be considered too inclusive here as well.

[3] *Op. cit.*, p. 56; italics added.

A. The Simple Analysis: The Firm in the Short Run

Consider the Chamberlinian case in which a relatively large number of firms sells somewhat differentiated products. Again, the precise degree of difference or closeness should not be a stumbling block in the initial analysis. The products are ordinarily assumed to be substitutes, that is, capable of performing the same function yet distinct in consumers' minds. Since the products are distinct, each firm faces a downward-sloping demand curve, such as d in Figure 2.1a. It is likely that the presence of close substitutes will cause this curve to be relatively elastic. That is, a small price increase may drive away a relatively large number of customers, whereas a small decrease will substantially increase sales, assuming in both cases that the prices of substitute goods remain unchanged. This elasticity may be reflected in a rather flat or shallow slope, although it is rather dangerous to guess about elasticity values by inspecting the slope of a curve.

The short-run analysis of the firm in monopolistic competition is precisely the same as that of the pure monopolist. The firm will produce at the point at which marginal cost equals marginal revenue, and will charge the price that the demand curve accepts for such a quantity (quantity Q and price P in Figure 2.1a). This is in effect a monopoly price, which may enable the firm to earn an excess, or above-normal, profit. In order to determine whether the firm actually earns profits in the short run, however, the average total cost curve must be specified.

B. The Simple Analysis: The Firm in the Long Run

The long-run situation of the firm is altered by the possibility that new firms will enter the market. Assuming free entry, as Chamberlin does, above-normal profits in the short run cannot persist. New firms will be induced to enter and will produce differentiated products that are closely substitutable with those already marketed. As in the case of pure competition, this will have the effect of depressing the demand curves faced by established firms. The curves will retain their negative slope, because product differentiation continues; but the firms, which had been earning profits, will now find that they are unable to sell as much at any price.

The process of entry will continue so long as excess profits exist,

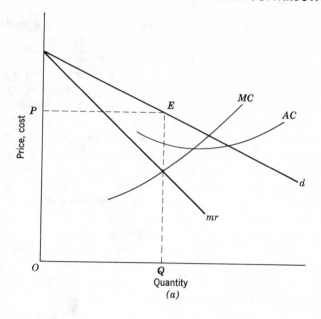

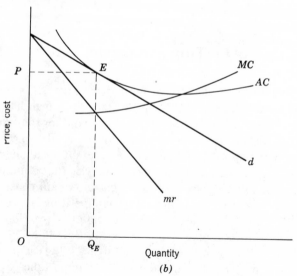

Figure 2.1

and firms will ultimately reach a long-run equilibrium at a point such as E in Figure 2.1b. That is, so long as price exceeds average cost, profits exist and entry continues. Entry ceases only when price is driven down to the level of average cost—that is, when a zero-profit position has been effected. In Figure 2.1b the firm continues to produce at a level of marginal cost—marginal revenue equality. However, the demand curve has been sufficiently depressed that the price the firm can obtain for this optimal output no longer exceeds its average cost of production. Price equals average cost, and total revenue just covers total cost.[4]

This zero-profit condition for the firm in the long run is obviously similar to the long-run equilibrium condition for the firm in pure competition. There is, however, one important difference. Production under monopolistic competition does not occur at a point of minimum average cost. Diagrammatically, as long as there is *any* negative slope in the firm's demand curve, zero-profit equilibrium can be attained only at some point to the left of minimum AC. It is for this reason that monopolistic competition is sometimes referred to as an inefficient form of industrial organization, one that implies a persistent excess capacity for firms.

C. Equilibrium of the Firm and Group

A point of interest in monopolistic-competition analysis is the nature of the demand curve confronting the firm. Since each firm has rivals that produce closely substitutable commodities, demand for the firm's product will depend partly on the prices charged by the rivals. Accordingly, the firm's demand curve must embody some assumption about the way in which rivals' prices behave. In the usual analysis the assumption attributed to the firm is that prices of other goods remain constant at their original level. The firm in monopolistic competition expects, in other words, that if it alters its price there will be no price reaction on the part of rival sellers. This is a plausible supposition as long as each firm individually is small relative to the market, for if this is the case a price change by a single firm may not be an event of great importance to the others. As we have noted, the firm's demand curve under this assumption will be an elastic, probably flat, curve such as dd in Figure 2.2a.

Given an elastic curve such as dd, however, it is quite conceivable

---

[4] Once again it should be considered that some "normal" profit is included in the costs of production for the firm.

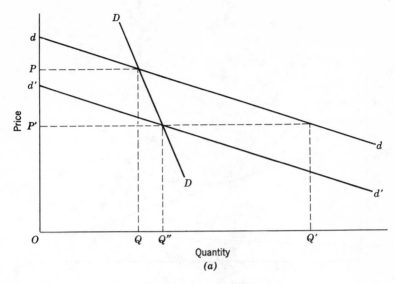

Figure 2.2 (a)

that firms may be induced to attempt price cuts, the reasoning for each being, "If I cut my price a little I may greatly increase my sales."[5] But if *all* or many firms should actually cut prices, *dd* is no longer the relevant demand curve for any individual firm. This curve was drawn on the assumption that the prices of substitute goods remain constant. With the prices of substitutes falling, no single firm will gain as much in sales by cutting its own price. The pertinent demand curve now becomes a curve such as *DD* in Figure 2.2a, reflecting the less elastic demand conditions facing each firm when the prices of all firms move together. The individual firm under this condition will neither gain as much when it cuts prices, nor lose as much when it raises prices, as it would with rivals' prices constant.

As the juxtaposition of the *dd* and *DD* curves in Figure 2.2a indicates, the nature of rivals' behavior makes a substantial difference to the firm in an imperfectly competitive market. The firm facing demand curve *dd* may decide to lower its price from *P*, the prevailing market price, to some level such as *P'*. The firm's expectation is that its sales

[5] Note, however, that an elastic demand curve need not indicate that a price reduction is profitable; the firm must still look to its costs of production.

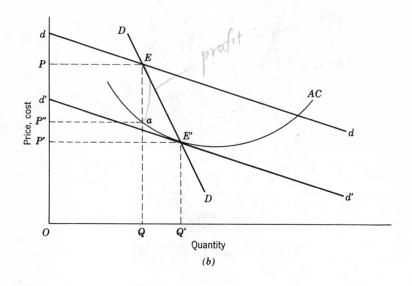

(b)

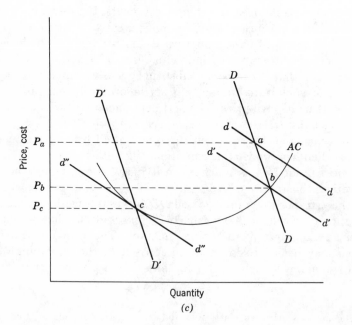

(c)

Figure 2.2 (b, c) Continued.

quantity will increase from Q to Q', but if other firms also lower their prices to P', the actual sales increase for the single firm will be only from Q to Q''. If, after moving from PQ to $P'Q''$, the firm maintains its expectation of rivals' prices constant, it will now confront an anticipated demand curve such as $d'd'$. That is, the firm's dd curve *shifts down*. The firm is disappointed in its original estimate of the sales increase that would follow a price cut, but it still believes that rivals' prices will not respond to its own future price changes. It thus continues to anticipate a relatively elastic demand curve at the lower (P') price level.

The dd and DD curves also provide an apparatus for distinguishing two types of adjustment in monopolistic competition. Suppose that an "optimal" or "appropriate" number of firms exists initially. Individual firms may be charging a price such as P in Figure 2.2*b*. At P, each firm is earning a net profit of Ea per unit (PP'' aE *in toto*). Under the assumption that rivals' prices will remain fixed, each firm may experiment with a price reduction. But when all firms reduce price the dd curve confronting each firm individually shifts down along DD, the relevant demand curve when prices move together. Ultimately, an equilibrium price such as P' is established. At this price, $d'd'$ is tangent to AC at the point at which DD intersects AC. Equilibrium is thus achieved by a given group of firms, and it is seen that some tendency toward equilibrium may exist in monopolistic competition apart from entry or exit.

It must be emphasized, however, that so long as the group is not "optimal" in number, entry and exit remain the crucial long-run adjustment mechanism. Consider the case in which the size of the group is initially nonoptimal. There will be no common price that would establish a stable zero-profit equilibrium. Such an instance is illustrated in Figure 2.2*c*, in which dd and DD are the original demand curves and P_a is original price. A zero-profit position might be reached at point b (price P_b) as firms, attempting price cuts, find that their dd curves shift down along DD. But b is not an equilibrium, for each firm will calculate that it would be better off *raising* its price and moving back along $d'd'$ to a profitable position (price in excess of average cost). The attainment of an equilibrium in this case requires a change in the size of the group, specifically entry of new firms that will shift DD to the left.[6] Eventually, DD must shift to some position such as $D'D'$, at which equilibrium for the firm and group are possible at a point such as c (with associated price P_c).

---

[6] Entry of new firms will serve to depress, or shift to the left, both the DD and dd curves; this simply reflects the fact that the demand curve facing each firm under either pricing assumption will fall as more firms enter the market.

D. Some Difficulties with the Analysis

Monopolistic competition analysis encounters a number of complications that have not yet been mentioned. One of these stems from a remarkable coincidence that may have been noticed in the preceding discussion. This is the fact that we apparently are able to let dd and DD represent the relevant demand curves for *any* firm; and are similarly able to let AC represent the average cost curve for *any* firm. This striking fact simply reflects the assumption—which Chamberlin himself terms "heroic"—that each firm in the group faces identical cost and demand curves. This means, in effect, that every firm is precisely the same size (it produces similar amounts at similar prices), and that the demand for commodities produced by the group is somehow "evenly" distributed among the differentiated sellers.

It may appear that these uniformity assumptions are extreme. Once again, however, the relevant question is not whether the assumptions seem to be realistic in some subjective sense, but rather whether we learn anything of importance under the specified conditions. An examination of monopolistic competition theory under alternative assumed conditions is beyond the scope of this discussion. It is worth considering, however, one important objection to the uniformity assumptions that has been raised by Stigler. He states:

How can different products have uniform costs and demands? The quantity axes of the various product diagrams are simply not the same: one measures [for example] three-room apartments, another four-room houses, and perhaps still another restaurant meals (an excellent substitute for a kitchen).[7]

In other words, how can it be stated that the demands for, and costs of, "different" products are "the same"? A demand for X units of a three-room apartment is not the same thing as a demand for X units of a four-room house, even if an identical number of units of each is demanded at the same price. What Stigler is pointing out is that the uniformity assumption *is not meaningful* when applied to a group of nonhomogeneous products. Accordingly, the precise meaning of the analysis based on the assumption becomes subject to question.

A further difficulty with monopolistic competition analysis is the very vague character of the Chamberlinian "group." Strictly speaking,

---

[7] George J. Stigler, "Monopolistic Competition in Retrospect," in *Five Lectures on Economic Problems*, Macmillan, New York, 1949, pp. 12–24.

the analysis can proceed without a careful definition of the group. That is, the reasoning and conclusions of monopolistic competition theory can be explained almost entirely in terms of the firm, without delineating specifically the group of which it is a part. It is nevertheless helpful to specify a meaningful definition of the group, or at least to determine whether such a definition is possible. At this point, however, a number of common market-definition problems arise.

All that we know about the Chamberlin group is that it consists of a large number of uniform firms producing differentiated, but substitutable, products. This would present no great difficulty if the line between substitutes and nonsubstitutes were clear, but such is rarely the case. What is especially troublesome is that, for any defined product group, some "outside" products are likely to exist that are substitutes for some, but not all, of the products within. What, then, is the appropriate definition of group? If it is broadly defined, so as to encompass some outside products, the group will contain some products that are not substitutes for one another. Yet, if narrowly defined, it will exclude products that may be very close substitutes for some of its constitutent items. It is easy to conceive of a spectrum of products, $X_1, X_2, X_3, \ldots ,$ X_n, such that any given item is a close substitute for those lying near it on the spectrum but is not a good substitute for items lying farther away. X_5 may be an excellent substitute for X_4 and X_6, a fairly good substitute for X_3 and X_7, but a rather poor substitute for X_1 and X_9. An example might be a market in which sellers of physically identical products are differentiated by location. If the sellers are, say, spaced at equal intervals, consumers located in various parts of the market will prefer the sellers nearest to them. Each seller will provide a good substitute product for those sold by the nearest rivals, but a less satisfactory substitute for the products of more remote rivals. There is no obvious cutoff point that would define the group in this setting. The group might be considered to consist of firms 1 through 5, 1 through 10, 6 through 20, 1 through n, or any other segment of the spectrum; each definition would appear equally appropriate or inappropriate.

This kind of market-definition problem is extremely common. The decision as to what product lines should be included or excluded from a grouping is rarely easy, and the practical compromises that are reached are often unsatisfactory. In the case of monopolistic competition the difficulty is at least potentially significant. Although the analysis focuses on the firm, it also presupposes a meaningful idea of the group. As Chamberlin defines it, the group possesses characteristics that are comprehensible; its meaningfulness, however, is compromised by the inherent—and perhaps insoluble—difficulty of definition.

E. Evaluating the Contribution

The nature of the Chamberlin contribution has been a topic of lively discussion among economists.[8] Although the applicability of specific aspects of the theory is quite limited, the significance of the theory is widely recognized. Monopolistic competition theory is important not so much as a prototype of actual markets as for the approaches to market analysis that it has helped to stimulate.

Competition and monopoly are no longer viewed as mutually exclusive, either-or characteristics. It is recognized not only that most markets combine elements of the two extremes, but also that *the analysis of the extremes may be a wholly inadequate tool* for dealing with the combined cases. The attention economists in recent decades have devoted to oligopoly is in no small part owed to the theory of monopolistic competition. Ultimately, it is the opening of such new avenues that may be judged Chamberlin's most important contribution.

[8] For a range of interesting evaluations, see Robert E. Kuenne (Ed.), *Monopolistic Competition Theory*, Wiley, New York, 1967.

3

Oligopoly

The term oligopoly is applied to markets in which a few relatively large firms sell similar or identical products. Many industries in the United States—those that are dominated by a few sellers—fall within this category. Numerous smaller firms may exist in the oligopolistic market, and the dividing line between oligopoly and other market forms may be difficult to determine; most frequently, however, a market is termed oligopolistic when the bulk of its output and sales is accounted for by a small group.

The primary characteristic associated with this condition of "fewness" in the market is known as *mutual* or *conjectural interdependence* among firms.[1] In simplest terms this means that any oligopolistic firm is influenced by the behavior of its rivals, and that its own behavior in turn influences those rivals. The firm, then, must consider not only what its opponents happen to be doing at the moment, but also the way in which rivals may respond to its own actions.

Mutual interdependence introduces a severe complication into the analysis of firm and industry behavior. In any market setting a firm must have some notion of relevant magnitudes such as cost and demand in order to determine its most profitable policies. That is, any firm seeking to maximize profits must know something about the demand conditions it faces, and, as we have seen, such knowledge presupposes knowledge

[1] The significance of this element is such that some economists prefer to define oligopoly as the condition of mutual interdependence rather than in terms of the number and relative size of firms.

of the prices that other firms charge. The oligopolistic firm is not unique, then, in its dependence on the actions of other firms; many firms' demand curves are affected by the prices of others. What is unique to the oligopolist is that the actions of rival firms both affect *and are affected by* him; the situation is circular. Consider an oligopolistic firm, A. The optimal pricing policy for A cannot be defined until it is known (or some reasonable assumption can be made about) what a rival oligopolist, B, will do; A's best policy depends on B. But, by precisely the same token, B's best policy cannot be defined without knowledge of A's policy; B's best policy depends on A.

The analytical difficulty of this situation is manifest. In order to determine his best price A must calculate what B's price is likely to be. But B's price depends on his calculation of what A is likely to do. To make some estimate of B's behavior, then, A must figure out what B expects him to do; B's position is precisely the same: his estimate of A's behavior must encompass some guess about the way in which A expects him to act!

The oligopoly situation is thus akin to a guessing game. Presumably there is a reward to outguessing one's opponent(s). A particular policy adopted by an oligopolist may be extremely profitable if it surprises his rivals, but unprofitable if it is anticipated. This type of game, however, may be played in many ways, and for this reason the outcome is most difficult to predict.

Oligopoly, then, contains a far greater element of uncertainty than do any of the markets we have discussed previously. Unlike a pure monopolist, the oligopolist does have rivals to worry about; and unlike a competitive firm, the oligopolist's optimal policy is not dictated unambiguously by the workings of an impersonal market. There is a similarity between oligopoly and monopolistic competition in that the firm in both markets has meaningful rivals. But the oligopoly firm may not be able to assume, as does its counterpart in the Chamberlin model, that rivals are indifferent to its policies.

To maximize profits the oligopolist must do what any other firm would do: produce to the point of marginal cost—marginal revenue equality and charge the highest price that the market is willing to pay for that output. The complication, however, is that the oligopolist's demand curve *cannot be specified* without knowledge of opponents' behavior. The amount the firm can sell at any price will depend on such variables as the prices that rival firms are charging for their products, and the demand curve confronting the firm may assume very different positions and shapes under alternative assumptions about opponents' price policies.

Oligopoly-type situations frequently are encountered outside the realm of economics and business. In a football game, for example, the best offensive play may depend on what the defense anticipates, and vice versa. A pass may be the best play if the defense expects a run, but if the pass is anticipated it may turn out to be the worst offensive policy.[2] Military situations in which limited resources must be employed to defend and attack targets are similar in nature; the defenders' chances are heightened if he can figure out which targets are likely to be attacked; whereas the attacker's chances improve if he can calculate which targets will be defended. It is not necessary, however, to look beyond our modern market system for examples of oligopolistic conflict.

Although any yardstick used to classify an industry as an oligopoly is necessarily arbitrary, it is easy to cite numerous manufacturing industries—steel, aluminum, automobiles, cigarettes—in which a few firms account for a large proportion of output. Our interest in explaining the behavior of oligopolistic industries and the firms that comprise them is very strong, if only because so much of our national output is produced and sold under such conditions. Unless it is possible to specify some expectations about the behavior of these industries, we may be relatively helpless when it comes to evaluating their economic desirability and suggesting appropriate public policies.

It may appear at first glance that the oligopoly problem is unmanageable—that is, beyond analysis. Optimal behavior for the firm depends on rivals' behavior, or, perhaps more accurately, on the firm's estimate of rivals' behavior. Because this is true for *every* firm, the process seems to lead nowhere. The range of possible actions the firms may view as optimal obviously may be very wide, and this is the crux of the oligopoly problem.

Although few economists are likely to argue that the present state of oligopoly theory is a happy one, there are some means by which the problem may be reduced at least to semimanageable proportions. It is possible to specify a number of simple behavioral reaction or response patterns, and to trace their implications. This yields some initial notion of the range of possible oligopoly outcomes; as will be seen, however, the range is so broad as to be of little use by itself. What is required is some definition of those behavior patterns that, if not universal, may seem sufficiently reasonable to point in the direction of the most probable market solutions. The task is difficult and involves consideration of several basically discrete approaches. It is worth remembering through-

[2] Of course the outcome of a football game may turn largely on the ability of the players, just as the outcome of a market contest may depend on who produces the best goods. In both instances, however, we could say that strategic considerations may make a difference for any given level of performance.

out that no single approach or specific version of an approach is offered as an explanation of the way *all* oligopolists behave at *all* times.

A. The Classical Duopoly Approach

The oldest approach to oligopoly analysis is embodied in the classical models of duopoly. The duopoly model—involving a *two*-firm rather than several-firm market—is primarily a simplifying device. The results of the models need not depend on the existence of precisely two firms, but rather may hold in a general way for all markets in which the number of firms is small. The process of generalizing from the two-firm to n-firm case, however, may be troublesome, and some qualifications of the results may occur.

Characteristically, the classical duopoly models depend on assumptions of extremely simple, perhaps naive, behavior on the part of market rivals. The duopolists are generally assumed to act as profit maximizers, but their expectations of how their opponent will respond to their own policies tend to be both simplistic and persistent.

1. A NAIVE EXAMPLE: THE MACY'S-GIMBELS MODEL

It is conceivable that oligopolists, at least over relatively short periods, will price according to rules of thumb. One of the possibilities that could follow from the adoption of short-sighted rules is illustrated by a simple construct called the Macy's-Gimbels model.[3] Without treating the two firms' costs or demands explicitly, suppose that duopolists Macy's and Gimbels adhere to the following pricing rules:

Macy's: will match Gimbels price.
Gimbels: will undercut Macy's price by 20 percent.

The implication of these policies may be traced by constructing reaction patterns or curves for both firms, as in Figure 3.1. On Macy's reaction curve, R_M, we can read for any price set by Gimbels the price with which Macy's reacts; similarly, Gimbels' reaction curve, R_G, tells us the

---

[3] The relation of this construct to more elaborate duopoly models will become clear shortly. I am indebted to Richard Quandt for this particular example of duopoly naivete.

price with which that company reacts to any price set by Macy's. In Figure 3.1 R_M is a 45° line from the origin, indicating that, for any Gimbels price p_G, Macy's responds with the same price p_M (the scale on the Macy's and Gimbels' price axes being identical). Gimbels' reaction curve, R_G, is also a straight line through the origin, but it lies (20 percent) beneath R_M at all nonzero points. This indicates that for any positive price set by Macy's, Gimbels responds with a price that is 20 percent lower.

Suppose that the companies initially are at a point such as a in Figure 3.1. Here Macy's and Gimbels are charging identical prices,

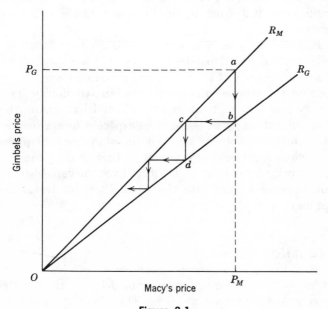

Figure 3.1

P_M and P_G respectively. Gimbels, following its pricing rule, will not remain at P_G, but will cut price by 20 percent, moving the duopolists to point b. But now Macy's, following its pricing rule, will match Gimbels' lower price, with the resulting combination at point c. The pricing path is now clear. Macy's price always will be undercut by Gimbels; Macy's then will match Gimbels' price cut, and Gimbels will cut again. If each company adheres to its pricing rule—that is, remains on the specified reaction pattern—the ultimate result is that both firms will charge a price of zero! No matter how low Macy's price falls, Gimbels will under-cut; but no matter how far Gimbels undercuts, Macy's will match.

This strange result can be explained only by the failure of the duop-olists to realize what is happening to them. Each firm is reacting to the other, but is apparently proceeding as if it does not expect the other to react to its own price initiatives. In fact, each firm's reaction pattern is irrational *in light of the other's policy*.[4] Either firm would do better if it were to select a best (most profitable) price that it could maintain *after the predicted reaction* of the other. Gimbels could reason: "Macy's always will match our price; *given* that they will do so, what price will yield us the highest profit?" Similarly, Macy's could determine its best price, *given* that Gimbels will charge 20 percent less. For either firm to act so implies that it discards its reaction curve in Figure 3.1 and adopts some different policy.

The duopolists in this case come to disaster by effectively ignoring part of the mutual interdependence problem. Each rival recognizes his dependence on the price of the other, and therefore reacts; but each fails to realize that the other also is reacting to him. Obviously the firms are making very poor use of their experience, and it is reasonable to ask whether intelligent oligopolists could be expected to act in this fashion. In general, they probably do not, yet there are cases of price warfare that may reflect a process very similar to that of the Macy's-Gimbels' model. Such price wars tend to be short-lived; nevertheless the model does provide some insight into the possibilities for instability in oli-gopolistic markets.

2. THE COURNOT MODEL

The best known of the classical duopoly models is that presented by the French economist Cournot in 1838.[5] The Cournot model, originally couched in an example of owners of two adjacent mineral springs, employs the following assumptions:

1. There are two sellers of a homogeneous product.
2. Each seller has identical marginal costs, which for simplicity are assumed to be zero.

[4] Suppose that each firm had utilized a policy of matching the other's price. Here the two reaction curves would coincide, since each would be a 45° line through the origin, and *any* market price—however established—would tend to persist.

[5] Augustin Cournot, *Researches into Mathematical Principles of the Theory of Wealth* (1838), translated by N. T. Bacon, 2nd edition, Macmillan, New York, 1927.

3. The market demand curve is fully known to both sellers, and for simplicity is assumed to be linear.
4. The sellers are output adjustors rather than price adjustors.
5. Each seller believes that the other will continue to supply to the market whatever amount of the product he is currently supplying.

The final assumption is crucial to the workings of the model, and it appears similar to the naive assumption employed by Macy's and Gimbels. Each duopolist in effect concludes that the other is insensitive to his policies: "I will react to your policies, but assume that you do not react to mine."

The usual presentation of the Cournot model is shown in Figure 3.2. Suppose that seller A enters the market first. His most profitable output

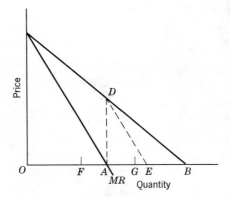

Figure 3.2

level will be OA (which is equal to $\frac{1}{2}OB$), a quantity that equates marginal cost—here zero—with marginal revenue. This is the ordinary monopoly result, although the zero-marginal-cost assumption is a bit unusual. When seller B enters the market, however, he expects A to continue supplying OA regardless of what he may do. Given this expectation, B sees as his relevant demand curve segment DB, that portion of the total market demand not served by A. Accordingly, B will produce quantity AE (equal to $\frac{1}{2}AB$ or $\frac{1}{4}OB$), a point of marginal cost—marginal revenue equality for his defined demand curve. Seller A must now reassess his position. Quantity $AE(\frac{1}{4}OB)$ is being supplied by seller B. Proceeding under the assumption that B's output will be maintained at this level, A will offer his new optimal (profit-maximizing) quantity, in this case $\frac{1}{2}(OB - AE)$ or $\frac{1}{2}(\frac{3}{4}OB)$.

The adjustment process is wholly repetitive. Each seller, assuming his rival's output to be fixed, will produce the amount that maximizes his own gain. This amount will always equal one-half of OB minus the rival's current output.[6] Thus, in the first stage, A supplies $\frac{1}{2}OB$. In stage 2 B supplies $\frac{1}{2}(OB - \frac{1}{2}OB)$, or $\frac{1}{4}OB$. Similarly, in stage 3 A supplies $\frac{1}{2}(OB - \frac{1}{4}OB)$, or $\frac{3}{8}OB$. Continuing the process, total output eventually will approach $\frac{2}{3}OB$ (OG in Figure 3.2), with each seller supplying an equal amount, $\frac{1}{3}OB$ (OF in Figure 3.2).[7] Such a result stands in obvious contrast to both the monopoly (quantity OA) and competitive (quantity OB) outcomes.

A Cournot-type result also can be portrayed in terms of price-reaction curves, as shown in Figure 3.3. If sellers A and B are price adjustors,[8] all other assumptions remaining the same, each can calculate his optimal price response to any price set by the other. Should A set price P_A in Figure 3.3, for example, B may set his price at P_B as the response that yields him the highest profits compatible with P_A. A will now react with price P'_A, and B will response with P'_B as the duopolists grope toward point E. The reaction curves[9] of A and B, R_A and R_B respectively, inter-

---

[6] This follows from the fact that the marginal revenue curve associated with any linear demand curve bisects horizontal lines drawn from the price axis to the demand curve. (See, for the proof of this proposition, Joan Robinson, *The Economics of Imperfect Competition*, Macmillan, London, 1933, pp. 29–30 in the 1959 reprinting.) For the zero-marginal-cost situation of the Cournot model, the marginal revenue curve will intersect the horizontal axis—and become equal to marginal cost—at a point halfway between the origin of the firm's *relevant* demand curve and the point at which that demand curve cuts the horizontal axis. That is, each firm's profit-maximizing output always occurs at the midpoint of its demand curve, where its demand curve is defined as that portion of the market demand curve not served by the opponent. It may be noted that the optimal position is also, in the zero-marginal-cost case, a *revenue-maximizing* position.

[7] Total output will be $OB(1 - \frac{1}{2} + \frac{1}{4} - \frac{1}{8} + \frac{1}{16} \cdots) = \frac{2}{3}OB$ ($= OG$ in Figure 3.2). Output of seller A will be $OB(1 - \frac{1}{2} - \frac{1}{8} - \frac{1}{32} \cdots) = \frac{1}{3}OB$ or ($\frac{1}{2}OG$). Output of seller B will be $OB(\frac{1}{4} + \frac{1}{16} + \frac{1}{64} \cdots) = \frac{1}{3}OB$ or ($\frac{1}{2}OG$) ($= OF$ in Figure 3.2).

[8] There is a difficulty in portraying Cournot duopolists as price adjustors since, with homogeneous products, the market should shift entirely to the low-price seller. Strictly speaking, this paragraph does not describe price *adjustments*, but rather the price *behavior* implied by the quantity adjustments of Cournot duopolists.

[9] The reaction patterns are derived by examining each firm's profit indifference curves—that is, the price combinations charged by the two firms that yield the same profits. The optimal response to any price charged by the rival firm is that price that places the duopolist on the highest profit indifference curve attainable. See William J. Baumol, *Business Behavior Value and Growth*, Harcourt, Brace, New York, revised edition, 1967, pp. 17–18.

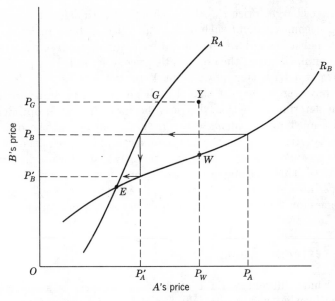

Figure 3.3

sect at E, a Cournot equilibrium. At such a point there is no tendency to change, for each seller is already charging the price that maximizes his profits, given the price of his rival.

This equilibrium, however, still depends on myopic behavior by both duopolists. It is a satisfactory solution only so long as each firm believes that the price charged by the other will persist no matter what he does. Should either duopolist awaken to the fact that his rival is responsive, he can do better than point E. Instead of reacting to B's price as if it were fixed, A may, for example, react to B's entire reaction curve. That is, A may choose the price that yields him the highest profit *after* B *responds* according to the pattern of R_B. A may choose the most profitable point for him on R_B and price in such a way that B responds by going to that point. In Figure 3.3 A's most profitable position on R_B might be a point such as W; if so, A would set his price at P_W since B's reaction, now anticipated by A, will place the firms at W. Of course duopolist B may be the one to awaken. He may choose some price, such as P_G, that will cause A to respond in such a way that the duopolists wind up at B's preferred position, for example, a point such as G.

If either of the duopolists becomes sophisticated in this fashion, the market solution moves to G or W. But suppose that *both* become sophisticated. If A charges price P_W and B charges P_G, the effective price combination becomes a point such as Y, which lies off both reaction curves. Each duopolist has indeed abandoned his original response pattern based on the assumption that the opponent's price was fixed. It is possible that each firm will be better off at point Y than it was before. There is no reason, however, to expect that Y will be an equilibrium position. In order to determine whether the price he now charges is optimal, each duopolist must again calculate the response pattern of the other. The Cournot solution thus breaks down under sophisticated behavior, and it is not possible to show where an alternative equilibrium lies, or even if one exists. This sort of complication is endemic to oligopoly generally. Solutions are attainable under simplistic assumptions,[10] but more realistic assumptions may do little to implement a more useful analysis.

3. THE BERTRAND MODEL

A somewhat different variant of duopoly analysis was suggested by Bertrand in what was apparently a mistaken and confused criticism of Cournot.[11] Bertrand's notion of duopoly is similar to Cournot's, but postulates price-adjusting rather than output-adjusting rivals. In the Bertand process each duopolist, acting on the assumption that his rival will maintain his present price, cuts his own price to a lower level. Since products are again assumed to be homogeneous, the low-price seller takes the entire market; but each seller is in turn undercut by the other. This price-cutting process continues, and ends only when price is reduced to the level of marginal cost—that is, only when a *competitive* market outcome is established!

It is sometimes pointed out that the difference between the Cournot and Bertrand models lies simply in the difference between price- and output-adjusting rivals. This is correct, yet it may not be obvious why such a distinction in the adjustment variable should produce different market results. The reason becomes clear when it is noted that the Cournot duopolist, in supplying some given quantity for any period, is inherently limiting the portion of the market that he can capture. The

[10] Some sophisticated observers of business behavior, however, might argue that the simple assumption here is less outlandish than it may seem. Baumol, for example, states ". . . in practice, management is often not deeply concerned with . . . elements of interdependence in its day-to-day decision-making." *Ibid.*, p. 13.

[11] Joseph Bertrand, "Theorie Mathematique de la Richesse Sociale," *Journal des Savants*, Paris, September 1883, pp. 499–508; and *Bulletin des Sciences Mathematiques et Astronomiques*, 2nd Series, Vol. VII (Paris, November 1883).

Bertrand duopolist, on the other hand, offers a (low) price at which he can capture the *entire* market—that is, all consumers will want to switch to him at that price, removing whatever sales his rival had previously enjoyed. It should be evident that in these contrasting cases the Bertrand price adjustment will be a different and more volatile process. It involves larger swings within the market and a continuing inducement for the swings to persist. The process is limited only by its ultimate unprofitability.

4. THE EDGEWORTH MODEL

The Edgeworth duopoly model differs from those of Cournot and Bertrand by introducing a relevant limitation on the productive capacity of the rivals.[12] Like Bertrand's duopolists, Edgeworth rivals are price adjustors, each of whom believes the other's price will be maintained. Cost conditions for the two competitors are assumed similar (zero marginal cost is assumed for simplicity), and the products sold may be considered homogeneous.[13] As illustrated in Figure 3.4, the Edgeworth process is initially similar to that of Bertrand. Price is measured vertically on axis OD; DD represents the demand curve for seller A; and DD' the

[12] F. Y. Edgeworth, "Le teoria pura del monopolio," *Giornale degli Economist,* **XV** (1897). The original article was reprinted in English as "The Pure Theory of Monopoly," in Edgeworth's *Papers Relating to Political Economy*, Macmillan, London, vol. I, 1925, pp. 111–142.

[13] The products could be treated as similar but nonhomogeneous. However, this would require a simplifying assumption about the distribution of demand among the sellers.

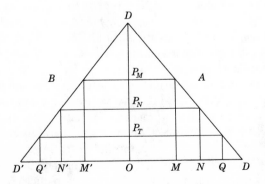

Figure 3.4

demand curve for seller B. The production constraints (i.e., the maximum outputs that can be produced) here are assumed to be OQ and OQ' for A and B respectively. Initially, A may enter the market and set monopoly price P_M, at which OM units are sold. When seller B enters the market, he could simply match A's price, making equivalent sales of OM'. But B has a more profitable course of action under his assumption that A's price will not change: he can undercut A by a relatively small amount, taking away most or all of A's sales; a small price reduction is thus expected to yield a large sales increase. Whether B gets all of A's customers at a lower price such as P_N will depend on whether he runs into his production constraint. If he does not, he can supply his maximum output at P_N, with seller A getting the residual (those customers whom B cannot supply).

Once B sets a price, however, A's calculation is precisely the same: *he* can now take away a substantial portion (if not all) of B's sales by cutting his price a bit. This process continues, much as it does in the Bertrand case, to some point. Each seller cuts his price on the assumption that his rival's price will not change, each price cut carrying with it the expectation of a substantial sales increase. This process ends, however, and is in fact reversed, by the output limitation. As price falls via the successive undercuts, sales by the two rivals are enlarged (as the demand curves indicate, more can be sold by each at lower prices). At some price, however, the output constraint is such that a further price cut cannot lead to increased sales. Suppose that at price P_T in Figure 3.4 seller A is supplying his maximum output, OQ. It is evident that at this point seller B has no reason to cut his price further. He too can dispose of his maximum output, OQ' at price P_T, and cannot benefit by offering the same quantity at a lower price. But there is another option. Rather than being content to sell his entire output at P_T, seller B may rationally calculate that he would earn higher profits by *raising his price* to the monopoly level, P_M, and selling a smaller quantity, OM'. Seller A has, after all, disposed of his entire output at P_T, and, assuming that A's policy will not change, B's best strategem is to behave as a monopolist in the "remaining" portion of the market.

Actually, so long as each rival is expected by the other to maintain his price, this type of calculation may well become relevant before the maximum output constraint is reached. At any price, each rival must ask himself: "Am I better off undercutting and receiving an increased sales volume, or would it be more profitable to raise price and accept smaller sales?" As price becomes lower and output larger, each rival's potential sales gain from a further price cut is reduced. Thus, as price falls, the option of a price *increase* becomes progressively more attractive.

Undercutting is profitable so long as a modest price drop implies large sales gains; but when the output constraint intervenes, so that a price cut no longer is expected to produce large sales increases, the cutting policy becomes relatively unattractive.

Some reflection should indicate that the diagrammatic presentation of the Edgeworth model is not satisfactory. Each duopolist is at some points making decisions on the basis of "his own" demand curve (*DD* for *A* and *DD'* for *B* in Figure 3.4). Yet at other points—those at which either duopolist considers how much in sales can be taken away from the other—decisions seem based on *both* demand curves, that is, on the combined market demand. This peculiarity suggests that the market is segmented when both duopolists charge the same price; but that either duopolist can capture the entire market with a price cut.[14]

The Edgeworth process also can be portrayed in terms of price-reaction curves, as shown in Figure 3.5.[15] *A*'s reaction curve, R_A, indicates that

[14] It should also be noted that the assumption of a maximum attainable output by each duopolist is really not acceptable in the long run. There is no reason why the duopolists could not ultimately expand their scales of operation so as to produce larger quantities.

[15] This does not, however, mitigate the problems suggested above.

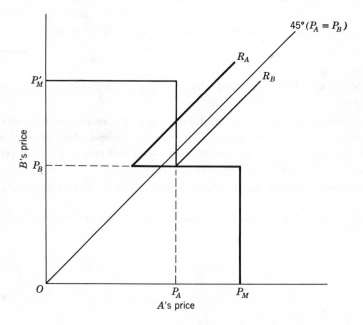

Figure 3.5

when B sets relatively high prices, A's best response is a slightly lower price (this is the price-cutting range). At some point, P_B, however, A's response changes entirely. Instead of reacting to further reductions in B's price (P_B) with slightly lower prices, A's response is a *rise* to the monopoly level P_M. B's reaction curve is similar. Both patterns are discontinuous, the discontinuity occurring for each at that price set by the other beneath which further cuts become unprofitable. The reaction curves have no common point of intersection. There is thus no combination of prices that would tend to perpetuate itself, that is, no determinate equilibrium position. In the Edgeworth case a perpetual movement of prices is implied: prices fall through successive undercuts, rise to the monopoly level, and once again begin to fall.

5. THE HOTELLING MODEL

The development of duopoly theory along the Bertrand-Edgeworth line suggested an element of inherent instability in markets populated by few sellers. A construct presented by Hotelling in 1929 challenged the idea that instability is a general characteristic of duopoly.[16] The Hotelling model is less interesting in its specifics than in its general approach and conclusions about stability. The following assumptions are employed:

1. Sellers A and B offer a physically identical product that is differentiated only by the location of the sellers.
2. Specifically, A and B are located as in Figure 3.6, along a linear market of length L. The market consists of four segments: x and y lie between sellers A and B; seller A is located between seller B and segment a; and seller B is located between A and segment b.
3. Consumers are uniformly distributed along the market, and each consumer

[16] Harold Hotelling, "Stability in Competition," *Economic Journal*, XXXIX, 1929, pp. 41–57.

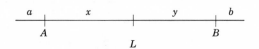

Figure 3.6

makes a given purchase per time period. Demand is thus perfectly inelastic, the quantity sold being assumed invariant to price.

4. Each buyer must transport his purchase home at a cost of c per unit distance.

The Hotelling duopolists have price discretion, but if either is to make any sales his price must not exceed that of his rival's by more than the cost of transportation from the rival's location to his own. This means, for example, that A's price, p_1, cannot exceed B's price, p_2, by more than $c(x + y)$; similarly, p_2 cannot exceed p_1 by more than $c(x + y)$. Given this constraint, A and B will price in such a fashion that A serves market segment a and B serves b. The portion of the market that lies between A and B is then divided into segments x and y, in such a way that A serves x and B serves y. The actual lengths of these intermediate segments will depend on the prices p_1 and p_2, that A and B adopt. At the point of division between x and y, however, purchasing from A or B is a matter of indifference to the consumer. Because their commodities are differentiated only by location, implying a difference in delivered prices, it follows that at the dividing point delivered prices are identical. A's price plus transportation cost equals B's price plus transportation cost. That is,

$$p_1 + cx = p_2 + cy \tag{1}$$

Moreover:

$$L(\text{the length of the market}) = a + x + y + b \tag{2}$$

Hotelling's procedure at this point is simply to show that these equations imply determination of equilibrium prices (and quantities). The model always yields a determinate and stable solution.[17] What is of major interest is the reason that led Hotelling to a conclusion so different from those of Edgeworth and Bertrand. The basis of Hotelling's position is that large, sudden switches of consumers from one seller to

[17] The demonstration is as follows. Equations 1 and 2 are solved,

$$x = \frac{1}{2}\left(L - a - b + \frac{p_2 - p_1}{c}\right)$$

$$y = \frac{1}{2}\left(L - a - b + \frac{p_1 - p_2}{c}\right)$$

Profits are defined:

$$\mathrm{II}_1 = p_1 q_1 = p_1(a + x) = \tfrac{1}{2}(L + a - b)p_1 - \frac{p_1{}^2}{2c} + \frac{p_1 p_2}{2c}$$

and:

$$\mathrm{II}_2 = p_2 q_2 = p_2(b + y) = \tfrac{1}{2}(L - a + b)p_2 - \frac{p_2{}^2}{2c} + \frac{p_1 p_2}{2c}$$

(For remainder of footnote see next page)

another, as depicted by Bertrand and Edgeworth, are not characteristic of markets. Hotelling would expect a price cut to attract a few consumers at the margin to the price cutter, but not to greatly multiply the price cutter's sales or to eliminate those of his rival. So long as the "gradualness" of consumer switching is maintained, according to Hotelling, market stability is likely. Only when it is assumed that all consumers move instantaneously to the low-price seller does the market take on an element of severe instability and possibly an indeterminate solution. This argument is also of interest in explaining differences between the Cournot result on the one hand and Bertrand and Edgeworth on the other. Cournot, by assuming quantity rather than price to be the rivals' adjustment variable *inadvertently* imposed a kind of stability on his market. One rival, by adjusting his quantity, could not remove most or all sales from the other. The quantity-adjustment process in a sense concedes a portion of the market to the rival and therefore precludes policies designed to capture the entire potential sales.

A further point of interest in the Hotelling model is the long-run implication for seller location. In the short run, with location fixed, price is the strategic variable in the search for maximum profits. In the long run, however, location is variable, and the tendency of sellers to adjust location may be socially undesirable. The socially optimal location A and B would occur at the quartile points of market L. Transportation costs would here be minimized, with no consumer more than $\frac{1}{4}L$ away from a seller. The tendencies of the sellers, however, will be different. Both A and B may be expected to move toward the midpoint of L in an attempt to expand their sheltered markets (a, lying to the left of A, and b, lying to the right of B). If followed, these tendencies may imply a highly inefficient location set from society's point of view.

The profit expressions are then maximized:

$$\frac{\partial \Pi_1}{\partial p_1} = \frac{1}{2}(L + a - b) - \frac{p_1}{c} + \frac{p_2}{2c} = 0$$

and

$$\frac{\partial \Pi_2}{\partial p_2} = \frac{1}{2}(L - a + b) + \frac{p_1}{2c} - \frac{p_2}{c} = 0$$

From this is obtained the equilibrium prices:

$$p_1 = c\left(L + \frac{a - b}{3}\right) \qquad p_2 = c\left(L - \frac{a - b}{3}\right)$$

Similarly, equilibrium quantities are obtained:

$$q_1 = a + x = \frac{1}{2}\left(L + \frac{a - b}{3}\right) \qquad q_2 = b + y = \frac{1}{2}\left(L - \frac{a - b}{3}\right)$$

6. THE KINKED DEMAND CURVE

An alternative explanation of stability in oligopoly is the familiar kinked demand curve, as shown in Figure 3.7.[18] Oligopolists are here assumed to reason that their rivals will generally match decreases but not increases

[18] The kinked demand curve was first presented by Paul M. Sweezy, "Demand Under Conditions of Oligopoly," *Journal of Political Economy*, **XLVII**, August 1939, pp. 568–73.

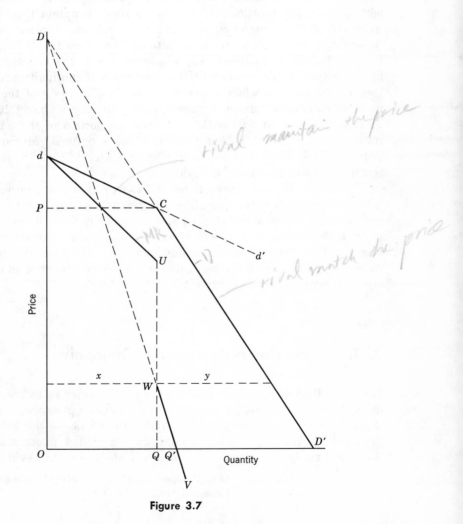

Figure 3.7

from the existing market price. Consequently, each oligopolist expects that if he cuts price below the existing level others will follow and the resulting sales gain will be relatively small. If, however, he raises price, competing firms will refrain from raising theirs, and the sales loss will be relatively great. Under the circumstances neither a price increase nor a price decrease presents an especially attractive prospect to the seller. A market price, once established, thus tends to perpetuate itself, and oligopoly prices may generally prove to be sticky.

Diagrammatically, the demand curve is kinked at point C in Figure 3.7, so that declines below price P result in relatively small quantity increases, while rises above P lead to large quantity decreases. Curve dd' portrays the firm's anticipated demand if rivals maintain their prices, while DD' is the demand curve relevant if rivals match price changes. Accordingly, the demand curve as "actually" envisioned is dCD'. Above C it reflects the nonmatching expectation, below C the matching. The firm's marginal revenue curve, $dUWV$, acquires a discontinuity at output level Q (the point at which demand is kinked). Thus, even if the firm's marginal cost curve shifts, a new equilibrium price may not be established. The curve may shift within the discontinuous portion of the marginal revenue curve, implying that price P remains optimal. Moreover, if demand should shift, it is not clear where the kink will now arise. Conceivably it may be at the same price.

The kinked demand curve theory explains why a price, once established, may persist. It does not, however, tell us anything about how the price was initially established. We know *why* and *how* the kink occurs, but we cannot predict *where* it will occur (to state that it occurs "at the market price" begs the real question: how was this price arrived at)? Accordingly, the kinked demand curve is not a full explanation of oligopoly price behavior, and its interest is rather limited.

B. The Game Theory Approach to Oligopoly

The second major approach to oligopoly is the theory of games, introduced by a mathematician, von Neumann, and an economist, Morgenstern.[19] Game theory attempts to investigate and define the nature of "rational" (optimizing) strategy in situations of conflict among mutually dependent rivals. Its relevance for oligopoly analysis is thus evident, for

[19] John von Neumann and Oskar Morgenstern, *The Theory of Games and Economic Behavior*, Princeton University Press, Princeton, N.J., 1944.

it is precisely the problem of oligopoly analysis that the outcome depends on the (uncontrollable) behavior of rivals. If a rational strategy or course of behavior could be specified for such situations, it might be possible to say a great deal about actual outcomes in markets populated by rational competitors.

The theory of games is not restricted to examinations of the marketplace. A game is defined simply as a situation in which two or more individuals (players) compete, the outcome being influenced by the actions that each adopts. The setting can be a child's game, an oligopoly market, a poker game, or a war; some of game theory's most useful applications have in fact come in the area of military strategy. Each game may be characterized in several ways, for example, according to the number of players and the way in which the outcome responds to alternative modes of behavior. Certain original data comprise the rules of the game, and each player has a set of possible actions—a strategy—corresponding to all circumstances. It is assumed in analyzing the game that all strategies are completely known by the players. That is, each player knows all possible courses of action open not only to him but to his rivals as well. Given these circumstances, it is possible to explore strategic procedures in simplified cases.

1. THE TWO-PERSON, ZERO-SUM GAME

The simplest category of game is described as two-person, zero-sum. There are two rivals, and the outcome of the game is such that "my gain is your loss." In a poker game, for example, the winnings of one player equal the losings of the other, and the combined winnings and losings under all circumstances *sum to zero*. Another way of describing such games is *strictly adversary*. The players will rank alternative outcomes in precisely reverse order ("my best outcome is your worst," etc.), and one may do as well as possible only by assuring that his rival does as poorly as possible.

In an economic context the two-person, zero-sum game may be illustrated by duopolists competing for shares of a market.[20] The strictly adversary nature of the game is obvious. Every percentage addition to the market share of duopolist A implies an equal subtraction from B's share, and vice versa. The best outcome for one (100 percent of the market) is the worst (0 percent) for the other, and the optimizing process for each implies minimization of the opponent's gain. Suppose now that

[20] In this case the game should actually be defined as *constant*—rather than *zero*-sum, since the combined payoff of the players always equals 100 percent. The analysis, however, is essentially the same.

each player has three possible strategy moves. These may involve altering price, advertising, or any other relevant market variable. Each pair of strategies chosen by the two duopolists will determine a particular division of the market between the two. The nine possible outcomes are shown in terms of A's market share in Table 3.1. This table is called A's payoff

Table 3.1

A's Payoff Matrix

| | | B's Strategy | | | |
		1	2	3	Row Minimum
A's Strategy	1	45	30	20	20'
	2	50	75	10	10
	3	85	5	15	5
	Column Maximum	85	75	20*	

matrix, and shows the outcome of the game for A under any pair of strategy moves employed by A and B. If, for example, A selects his strategy 3, and B chooses his strategy 2, A's resulting market share (his payoff) is 5 percent. The information summarized in the matrix could as easily have been portrayed in terms of B's payoff, and B's payoff matrix can be constructed by subtracting A's payoff under each strategy pair from 100 percent. Given this information, each duopolist knows his alternative payoffs for any strategy he selects. A knows, for example, that if he selects his strategy 2, he will obtain 50 percent, 75 percent, or 10 percent of the market, depending on what B does.

2. THE MAXIMIN AND MINIMAX STRATEGIES

How might the players in this game proceed? One possibility is that each will be exceedingly pessimistic in his estimate of the ultimate market division. Each duopolist may reason that, whatever strategy he adopts, his opponent will react optimally—that is, the opponent will always choose the strategy that "maximizes his share of the market and minimizes mine." Suppose that duopolist A proceeds under this assumption.

Which strategy should he select? Referring to A's payoff matrix, we see that if A selects his strategy 1, the worst outcome for him is a 20 percent market share (if B selects his strategy 3). If A chooses 2, the worst outcome is a 10 percent share (under B's strategy 3); and if A plays strategy 3, the worst result is a 5 percent share (under B's strategy 2). These worst outcomes are represented by the minimum value in each row of A's payoff matrix, the *row minima*.

Choosing under the assumption that rival B will react optimally— so as to inflict the worst outcome on A—duopolist A should seek the "best" among the three "worst" results. He should choose his strategy 1 on the ground that, after B retaliates optimally, A will be better off than he would be otherwise. By choosing strategy 1, A assures himself of a 20 percent market share (which he in fact expects), rather than the expected 10 percent under strategy 2 or the 5 percent under 3. A, in other words, selects the maximum of the minimum values under each strategy, the highest of the row minima. This maximization of the minimum payoffs is called A's *maximin* strategy.

Duopolist B can proceed in precisely the same fashion, assuming that, regardless of his strategy, A will retaliate optimally—in the best way for A but the worst way for B. Examining the payoff matrix again, we can define B's worst outcome under each of his three strategies as the *highest* market share obtainable by A. B's worst outcome, then, is the highest number in each of his three strategy columns. For B's strategy 1, the worst result is an 85 percent share for A; for strategy 2, the worst outcome is 75 percent for A; and for strategy 3, the worst is a 20 percent share for A. That is, the worst that B can do under any strategy is represented by the maximum payoff to A in that strategy column. Since B expects A to do his best, thus inflicting the worst result on B, B should select his strategy 3. This limits A's market share to 20 percent at most, whereas A could obtain 75 percent if B plays his strategy 2, or 85 percent if B plays 1. B, in other words, chooses the *lowest* among A's *maximum* payoffs, the *minimum* of the *column maxima*. In choosing the best of *his* worst outcomes, B plays what is called his *minimax* strategy, he minimizes A's maximum payoff.

The maximin-minimax strategy combination leads A to play his strategy 1 and B to play his strategy 3. The outcome, as shown in A's payoff matrix, is a 20 percent market share for A (thus an 80 percent share for B). At first glance it might appear that this division of the market would be unsatisfactory, especially for A. In fact, however, each duopolist has done as well as he possibly could! Each has succeeded in optimizing his own outcome, given the strategy adopted by his rival.

Neither can do better, and the game finds an equilibrium solution in that neither will now tend to readjust his strategy.[21]

The equilibrium solution of the game emphasizes important qualities of the maximin-minimax strategies. The maximin (minimax) is the best possible course of action against an opponent who pursues the minimax (maximin) strategy. In the example above, the maximin strategy employed by A has assured him a market share of *no less* than 20 percent. At the same time, B's minimax has assured him that A will obtain *no more* than 20 percent. Each rival has succeeded in protecting himself from the possibility of less desirable outcomes, and the maximin-minimax approach obviously serves as an effective sheltering device. Despite the degree of safety offered by the maximin (minimax), however, it may be a decidedly inferior strategy against an opponent who does *not* employ a minimax (maximin). Suppose that duopolist B had (rashly) pursued his strategy 2 above, perhaps lured by the possibility of confining A's market share to 5 percent. A, playing his maximin (strategy 1), would obtain 30 percent of the market; yet if A had played his strategy 2 instead, he would have captured 75 percent. Given that B does *not* pursue a minimax, A's maximin may *not* be an optimal strategy. Indeed, it may turn out to be an exceedingly poor course of action.

3. MIXED STRATEGIES

The type of equilibrium solution described above is not found in all games. In fact, the payoff matrix will have an equilibrium or saddle point only if the maximum of the row minima happens to be the same as the minimum of the column maxima, an entirely fortuitous circumstance. Table 3.2 illustrates a case in which no saddle point exists. A's payoff matrix again shows the share of the market that A will obtain under alternative pairs. Here A's maximin strategy is 2, which assures him of no less than 50 percent of the market. B's minimax is his strategy 1, which assures that A will capture no more than 70 percent. If both duopolists pursue such policies, they will end up at strategy combination (2, 1), at which A has 50 percent of the market. Although this will please B (who was acting to prevent A from obtaining more than 70 percent), it is obviously a less pleasing result for A. Had A *not* played his maximin,

[21] Games containing such an equilibrium solution are said to be *strictly determined* The equilibrium is sometimes referred to as a *saddle point* because of its resemblance to a saddle in a three-dimensional diagram of A's payoffs under the various strategy pairs. The saddle point is a maximum in one direction and minimum in the other, with a valley (or saddle) going one way and a hill going the other.

Table 3.2

A's Payoff Matrix

		B's Strategy		Row
		1	2	Minima
A's	1	70	20	20
Strategy	2	50	90	50'
	Column			
	Maxima	70*	90	

and pursued his strategy 1 instead, he would have taken 70 percent rather than 50 percent; that is, his maximin is no longer an unambiguously ideal strategy. The choice of strategies is no longer a simple matter, although it is conceivable that the two rivals will continue to play it safe and pursue their maximin-minimax.

In such a nonequilibrium situation it is obviously important for each duopolist to prevent his rival from guessing in advance what his strategy will be.[22] There are of course various precautions that might be taken. One possibility, ingenious in its simplicity, is to choose one's own strategy in a random fashion. The duopolist may reason that his opponent is a clever fellow who has a good chance of outguessing him in the "I know that he knows that I know . . ." situation. The opponent's cleverness may be effectively neutralized by making the strategy decision a matter of chance. The duopolist might, for example, choose between strategies 1 and 2 by tossing a coin, a procedure that gives him an equal chance of selecting each. Or he might load the odds so that the probability of his selecting one strategy is relatively high.[23] This method of selection is known as a *mixed strategy*, since the player is in effect choosing a combination of alternatives weighted by some probabilities.[24]

The importance of the mixed strategy is that it may succeed in

[22] If, for example, A should choose strategy 1, he will do poorly (20 percent of the market) if B, anticipating this strategy, selects his strategy 2. If B were ignorant, however, he might play his strategy 1, resulting in a 70 percent market share for A. Similarly, B can expect to make out poorly if A guesses which strategy he will employ.

[23] Any number of devices can be used to weight the probabilities in desired fashion. One simple method is to use a spinner, assigning to each strategy that portion of the 360° circumference appropriate to the desired probability. If the strategies are to receive probabilities in a 3:1 ratio, 270° of the circumference would be assigned to the high-probability strategy, and 90° to the low-probability strategy.

[24] In contrast, a simple maximin or minimax is called a *pure* strategy.

providing a more favorable expected outcome than could be obtained through the pure maximin. In order to demonstrate this we may begin by supposing that duopolist A adopts a mixed strategy, which gives him (1) a 0.75 probability of choosing his strategy 2, and (2) a 0.25 probability of choosing strategy 1. If we let the numbers in A's payoff matrix represent the utility (or subjective value) of each outcome, rather than simply the market share,[25] we can then calculate the expected value in utility terms of the mixed strategy. The expected utility of A's strategy, defined simply as the utility of each outcome multiplied by its probability, is calculated as follows:

1. If B employs his strategy 1, A's expected value is $\frac{1}{4}(70) + \frac{3}{4}(50) = 55.0$.
2. If B employs his strategy 2, A's expected value is $\frac{1}{4}(20) + \frac{3}{4}(90) = 72.5$.

A's expected value in each case exceeds the 50 that A could assure himself by playing his maximin (pure strategy 2). It is in this fashion that the mixed strategy improves his expected outcome. What duopolist A has done in effect, is to give up the security offered by the maximin strategy in return for the higher expected value of gain under the mixed strategy. A has left himself vulnerable to the worst outcome, a contingency that the maximin would have avoided. But in doing so, he has improved his expectation of what the actual outcome will be. A similar course of action is open to B.

Certain aspects of mixed strategies are beyond the scope of this discussion. We will not, for example, examine the theory of *optimal* mixed strategies, or the fundamental theorem of two-person, zero-sum game theory, which states that a saddle point will always be determined by mixed-strategy combinations even if there is none implied by the pure-strategy combinations.[26] The point of the present discussion is more limited: it is simply that in certain cases, it may pay players to abandon the extremely conservative maximin-minimax strategy for a far bolder approach.

[25] The reason for doing this is that the subjective value of a percentage of the market may not be constant; for example, a 50 percent share may not be regarded by a duopolist as "twice as good" as a 25 percent share or "half as good" as 100 percent. With such discrepancies, the duopolist presumably will make decisions in accordance with *his subjective evaluation* of the alternative outcomes rather than the simple market share numbers attached to each.

Once we speak in terms of utility payoffs, incidentally, the zero-sum nature of the game is no longer clear. To state that we have a zero-sum game would require interpersonal comparisons that we have previously been unwilling to make (see Chapter 1).

[26] Several lucid discussions are available, such as Baumol, *op. cit.;* and R. Duncan Luce and Howard Raiffa, *Games and Decisions*, Wiley, New York, 1957.

4. MORE COMPLEX GAMES

The zero-sum, two-person game that has received such extensive attention and analysis is the simplest of situations. Matters become more complicated if the combined payoff to players is a nonconstant sum. In duopoly, for example, the market shares always sum to 100 percent, but it is likely that the strategies adopted may alter the size of market sales and associated profits. If we consider profit- or sales-maximizing rivals in such a situation, the game is *nonconstant sum*, and here the variety of outcomes may be considerably enlarged. Possibly it will pay rivals to cooperate, say, to adopt strategies that result in increased total sales regardless of how the larger pie is now divided. If cooperation does not pay, the strategic calculations of the duopolists may be much more complex than in the constant-sum game, and may result in different courses of action.

One interesting possibility, illustrated by a famous example known as the *prisoner's dilemma*, is that rivals may act to mutual *dis*advantage. In the example two prisoners are questioned separately about their involvement in a crime. The prisoners cannot communicate with each other, and each is told the following:

1. If you both confess, you will receive an appropriate penalty.
2. If neither of you confesses, you will go free.
3. If you confess and the other prisoner does not, you will go free and receive an added reward.
4. If the other prisoner confesses and you do not, you will receive a particularly severe penalty.

These rules may be translated into a payoff matrix for A and B, as shown in Table 3.3. A's indicated strategy is to confess, since this will

Table 3.3

Payoff Matrix for (A, B)

		B's Strategy	
		Confess	Don't Confess
A's Strategy	Confess	(−1, −1)	(+2, −2)
	Don't Confess	(−2, +2)	(+1, +1)

leave him better off regardless of what B does. But B's preferred strategy is also to confess, for the same reason. Both prisoners may thus confess and suffer the consequences, even though it would have been mutually desirable for neither to do so! This sort of dilemma may seem more appropriate to grade-D gangster movies than to economics. Its relevance for the analysis of certain oligopoly situations is direct, however, and will be seen in later discussions of collusive behavior.

An even more serious complexity is introduced in games that contain more than two players. Such situations, called n-person games, provide a wide range of possibilities, some of them very unwieldy. In addition to some of the earlier alternatives, the n-person game may result in coalitions, that is, the cooperation of some group or groups of players against other groups or individuals. Formal analysis of n-person situations is not nearly so well developed as that of the simpler cases. Moreover, the simple-case analysis is not capable of generalization to the more complex forms, which are in some instances far less stable.

5. GAME THEORY AND OLIGOPOLY ANALYSIS

The application of game theory to oligopoly analysis encounters several difficulties even in its simplified forms. An initial problem is the full-information requirement. It seems unlikely that many market situations would arise in which rivals are completely knowledgeable not only about their own possible strategies, but also about those of their opponents. Yet it is evident that the types of strategy suggested by the theory require information about all relevant combinations, and are not directly applicable when ignorance obscures some possibilities.[27]

Further objections to game theory as a tool of market analysis have to do with the kind of psychology required by the prescribed strategies. It has been argued that business managers are simply too optimistic to adopt the conservative, play-it-safe outlook of the maximin-minimax procedure. At the same time, it is suggested, few managers are so amenable to risk taking that they would actually be willing to allow their own decisions to rest on a random choice, as required by the mixed-strategies cases.[28] These criticisms do not challenge the rationality of

[27] A separate but closely related branch of analysis known as *decision theory* suggests criteria that might be adopted when knowledge is more limited. See Luce and Raiffa, *op. cit.*, Chapter 13.

[28] It is difficult to envision a corporation executive calling for the spinner when an important policy decision is at hand, and then spinning it to reach the decision. This whimsical example, however, misses the main point: the executive may have neither the knowledge nor the disposition to rely on any random-choice procedure, no matter how dignified it may be.

the strategems suggested by the theory of games; rather, they argue that these approaches to decision making assume a disposition that decision makers in business are unlikely to possess.

A final problem with game theory is that the minimax-maximin strategy approach is rational only under certain conditions. As we have noted, the strategy may be undesirable against an opponent who is pursuing some other strategy. Accordingly, there may be no good reason for anyone to adopt such a course unless he is certain that his opponent does the same thing. And should anyone experiment with a deviation from the minimax-maximin, there may be no rational incentive ever to return to it.

Even without such possible shortcomings, game theory has not succeeded in defining specific outcomes for all situations of conflict. It has so far proved impossible to suggest determinate solutions for many of the more complex cases. For this reason it must be said that game theory has failed to define a rational strategy that is directly applicable to the wide variety of oligopoly situations. Aspects of oligopoly behavior that puzzled economists before the appearance of *Theory of Games and Economic Behavior* in general remain puzzling today. But if game theory has failed to provide *the* solution to the oligopoly problem, it has nonetheless laid the foundation for a novel approach to strategy under mutual interdependence, and has thus expanded the horizons of oligopoly analysis. Its major impact in economics ultimately may turn out to be that it has led analysts to think in somewhat new terms about the interdependence problem.

C. The Collusion Approach to Oligopoly

In *The Theory of Monopolistic Competition* Chamberlin[29] suggested that Cournot duopolists, recognizing their interdependence, would adjust output levels so that total market supply reached only the monopoly level (OA or $\frac{1}{2}OB$ in Figure 3.2). The duopolists would share equally in the monopoly reward, each doing better than he would under the conventional Cournot process in which interdependence is never fully recognized. This suggestion illustrates a third group of solutions in oligopoly analysis that may be broadly termed collusive. This approach assumes that mutually dependent firms are aware of their situation, and reasons that they may rationally agree to avoid the various competitive

[29] E. H. Chamberlin, *The Theory of Monopolistic Competition*, Harvard University Press, Cambridge, 7th ed., 1958.

processes that might otherwise characterize the small-group market. Certainly many of these processes imply highly undesirable results for the firms involved. This is especially true of any type of price warfare or market instability, as in the Macy's-Gimbels and Bertrand-Edgeworth situations; yet even in cases that do not involve such obviously damaging consequences the likely outcome of unrestricted competition may fall short of what concerned firms would consider optimal. In such circumstances concerted or cooperative action by firms may be far more attractive than unlimited competing behavior.

The collusive approach to oligopoly is in many ways an appealing one to analysts. It is clearly desirable for participating firms who avoid potentially disastrous competitive processes. Moreover, "collusion" in the broad sense need not imply a formal or explicit conspiracy that would violate existing antitrust laws. Rather, it may take the form of a purely tacit understanding among competitors, such as an unwritten, unspoken agreement to avoid mutually disadvantageous policies such as price cutting. In addition to its plausibility on this basis, casual observation of American industries indicates that collusion, both tacit and overt, is a rather common event. Government prosecution of price-fixing conspiracies is frequent and unsurprising, save perhaps among the accused companies. Pricing patterns among competing products are often so uniform as to create suspicion (although not proof) that some kind of tacit agreement is operative. Indeed, active price competition may be the exception rather than the rule in oligopoly today. Thus collusion in the broad sense is not only a reasonable approach to oligopoly on a priori grounds; it is also an apparent fact of life.

Finally, the collusive framework offers an extremely simple means of treating oligopoly behavior. Analysis of the behavior of a cohesive group of firms is almost bound to be more straightforward than that of competing elements within a group. In the cohesive or cooperative case the group may in effect behave as a single unit. If so, the problem of oligopolistic interdependence per se no longer exists. Firms need not take account of their opponents' likely response to policy moves because both the original moves and the countermeasures are defined by the general understanding. Before concluding, however, that this approach is ideal in its plausibility, realism, and smplicity, it is necessary to spell out in greater detail precisely what the meanings of collusive oligopoly may be.

1. OUTRIGHT CONSPIRACY

Consider a small group of firms (oligopolists) whose managers are fully aware of their mutual interdependence. These managers will almost certainly recognize that vigorous and unrestrained price competition may not be in their interest individually. Even if the oligopoly manages to avoid a truly disastrous course of behavior, it is quite possible that the market outcome will prove unsatisfactory to firms, in that suboptimal (non-profit-maximizing) prices and quantities will be determined. In the absence of obstacles such as the antitrust laws an explicit pricing agreement may appear to be the logical course of action. If firms agree to a cooperative pricing policy, they should be able to set prices much as if they were a single-firm monopolist. That is, they can choose the price that maximizes total profits of the group and adhere to it so long as it remains appropriate.

In the simplest possible case we may assume that the cost curves of all firms are identical, as are their anticipated demand curves, under both collusive and competitive behavior. The setting of price by the collusive group, sometimes called a *cartel*, then proceeds in the manner of a monopolist, as shown in Figure 3.8. Group output is determined at quantity OQ',

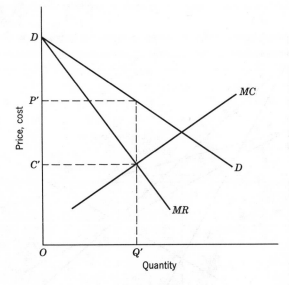

Figure 3.8

the level corresponding to intersection of the industry marginal cost and marginal revenue curves, MC and MR respectively. OP', the price that the market will pay for quantity OQ', results. As we have assumed identical cost and demand curves for all firms, this price-quantity combination should prove satisfactory to each. That is, the price not only maximizes joint profits for the group, but is also the maximizing price for every individual firm.

This simplified example represents the ideal collusive situation, yet even here it is easily shown that peculiar conditions exist that may threaten the stability of the result. It is true that under collusion each firm is better off than it would have been in a competing situation, and in this sense, every firm has a stake in making the collusive agreement work. That is, if unrestricted competition is the alternative to collusion, each and every participating firm will be motivated to adhere to the agreement. There is, however, a third alternative that creates complications. This is the possibility that an individual firm may depart from the agreement by cheating on its own price (cutting it), while all other firms remain in collusion. From the viewpoint of any given firm this may well be the most profitable of the alternatives.

This condition is demonstrated in Figure 3.9. Curve DD' is the firm's demand curve, under the assumption that all firms charge the same price, that is, that their prices move together; and DMR is the associated mar-

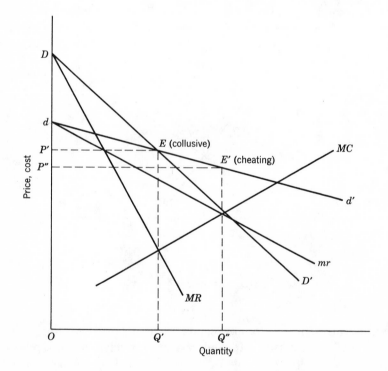

Figure 3.9

ginal revenue curve. MC is the firm's marginal cost curve, and point E is the firm's equilibrium price-quantity combination, which, under our assumptions, is the combination actually established by the collusive group. Curve dd' represents the firm's demand, *given that all other firms charge the agreed-on price, P'*. (It may be noted that curves DD' and dd' are much the same as the analogous curves confronting the firm in monopolistic competition and in the kinked demand case.) Should the firm decide to cut price, while all other firms adhere to the pricing agreement, it can expand sales to level Q'' at price P''—that is, it can attain equilibrium combination E'. This is likely to be a tempting course of action, since the firm probably faces an extremely elastic demand situation. That is, it could obtain a large sales increase with a relatively small price cut, so long as rival firms stick to the (higher) collusive price. This is not to imply that cheating on collusive price agreements is always profitable for an individual firm. It may be possible to construct situations in which the position of the cost curves is such that the firm remains better off sticking to the agreed-on price. Moreover, cheating is a risky maneuver that the firm may not regard as worthwhile if it is likely to be discovered and punished by the collusive group. The demand curve dd' shows the prices at which the firm may sell various quantities if it cheats *and gets away with it*. To the extent that firms do depart from collusive agreements, the collusive result may not be a stable one.

The potential instability of collusive agreements is also demonstrable in terms of the payoff matrices shown in Table 3.4. For any competing

Table 3.4

Payoff Matrix for (A, B)

		B	
		Colludes	Competes (Cheats)
A	Colludes	(150,150)	(0,200)
	Competes (Cheats)	(200,0)	(100,100)

firms, A and B, within the group, the matrices show that collusion by both is preferred to active price competition by both. Yet each firm does still better if it competes (cheats) while the opponent colludes (adheres to the agreed-on price). If A and B are faithful to their collusive agreement, each receives a payoff of 150, whereas if both actively compete, each receives only 100. If, however, A cheats while B colludes, A's payoff is 200 and B's is zero; similarly, should B cheat and A collude, B receives a payoff of 200 while A receives zero.[30] Under the circumstances, it might be expected that any firm such as A will cheat. If it does so, and B does not, it will receive 200. But beyond this, A's cheating protects it against the undesirable situation in which it remains faithful but B cheats. B's reasoning, however, may be exactly the same, in which case it also will cheat. Thus A and B may wind up competing, even though collusion would have been mutually preferable. It is thus apparent that there may exist in collusive oligopoly a condition precisely analogous to the prisoner's dilemma. It should not be concluded that such a situation is inevitable, however. If the payoffs associated with both firms competing are very low, or if cheating is likely to be discovered, each may choose to take its chances with the collusive course. The purpose of this illustration is simply to point out that even under the most perfectly simple conditions for collusion the stability of the agreement is not assured.

The probability of unstable or ineffective collusion is increased when the simplifying assumption of uniform costs is dropped. It is intuitively obvious that a group of firms operating under substantially different cost conditions is unlikely to view a single price as ideal. Given similar demand curves, high-cost firms will prefer higher prices. The question, then, is whether the price that maximizes group profits will prove acceptable to all firms. Actually this question may be appropriately posed in a slightly different form: granted that all firms agree on the price that maximizes joint profits, will such a price lead to satisfactory *allocation of sales and profits* among the firms?

In Figure 3.10a an optimal cartel price, OP, is illustrated. This is in effect a pure monopoly price, for it is the price that consumers are willing to pay for output OQ, that quantity at which cartel marginal cost equals marginal revenue. The marginal cost curve for the cartel is derived from the marginal cost curves of constituent firms; if the firms obtain inputs in perfectly competitive markets, the cartel curve will be the simple summation of the individual curves. The marginal revenue curve is associated with the industry demand curve.

The cartel has determined that it will maximize its profits by producing output OQ and charging price OP. But how are the various mem-

---

[30] Obviously this is *not* a constant-sum game. If both rivals compete, their *combined* payoff is 200; if both collude, the combined payoff is 300; and if one competes and one colludes, the payoff is again only 200.

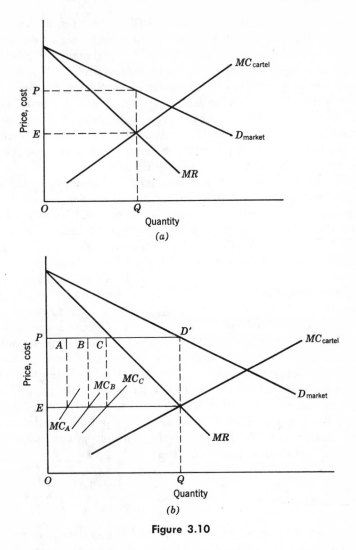

Figure 3.10

ber firms to share the output and receipts? To arrive at total output
OQ each firm must produce to the point at which its marginal cost
equals the value of cartel marginal cost–marginal revenue equality, OE in
Figure 3.10a and b. Figure 3.10b illustrates a division of sales in a three-
firm cartel. Firms A, B, and C are assumed to have marginal cost curves
MC_A, MC_B, and MC_C respectively; producing to the point at which
marginal cost equals OE, the firms will turn out quantities PA, PB,

and PC, these quantities summing to PD' or OQ, the optimal cartel output. The difficulty with this arrangement is that a high-cost firm such as A will find that it is supplying a relatively small amount, while lower-cost firms may enjoy the bulk of market sales and profits. High-cost firms thus may regard their *share of the market* under the cartel price—rather than the price itself—as unsatisfactory, and it is not surprising that one of the major problems in cartel-type agreements has in fact been allocation of the market.[31] Various market-dividing schemes have been employed, but the task of providing each firm with a satisfactory share of sales over an extended time period is difficult.

The problems associated with outright conspiracy are, then, significant. Even if a market price acceptable to all firms is established, the temptation to cheat may be strong. However, the establishment of satisfactory price-quantity combinations for all firms may itself be far from easy. When we add to this the realistic qualification that outright conspiracy among competitors in the United States is illegal, it is easy to understand why "perfect collusion" may be a rare event, if it occurs at all. This does not mean that the collusion approach to oligopoly should be dismissed. It must be recognized, however, that collusion is not an entirely simple and unambiguous event. We cannot assume that oligopolists band together and behave precisely as a joint monopolist, thus reducing the oligopoly problem to that of monopoly. Something like this may occur at times, but the dangers of oversimplification in most instances should be manifest. If outright conspiracy and cartels are facts of life, as indeed they are, then so too are the instability and continual breakdowns of such arrangements. The fundamental problem is that what is best for the whole—the collusive group—may not be best for each constituent part—the firm.

2. PRICE LEADERSHIP

Rather than resorting to outright collusion, oligopolists may choose to follow informally the policies set by a single firm, the *price leader*. A price charged by the leader becomes a signal for other firms to follow. This type of arrangement has at least two advantages for firms. First, it is extremely simple, mitigating the need for formal and perhaps elaborate agreements with repetitive negotiations. Second, and perhaps equally important, price leadership is far more likely to be legal than is

---

[31] It should be noted that firms would share the market equally if their marginal costs were identical.

any form of overt conspiracy. Although standards of legality change over time, antitrust policy in the United States has been consistent in treating formal collusion more stringently than informal practices.

Analytically, price leadership has the same sort of appeal that any type of collusion possesses. It is simple, and is again realistic in the sense that it seems to exist widely. Rather than attempting to explain oligopoly behavior by analyzing the complex interrelationships among firms, price leadership focuses on the behavior of a single firm. All rivals are assumed to have the same simple response pattern: they match whatever price is set by the leader. The plausibility of price leadership is unquestioned, yet the fact that a group of firms adopts this *pricing mechanism* does not by itself tell us much about the *nature of the price* that will be established. The actual price will depend not merely on the existence of the leadership practice, but also on *which firm* emerges as the leader and what pricing rules it follows. Three frequent suggestions about the type of leadership patterns that are likely to emerge may be considered.[32]

(a) Dominant-Firm Leadership

One possibility is that the leadership function will be assumed by the dominant firm in the market. This seems likely if there exists a firm so powerful in depth of resources that smaller rivals are reluctant to compete with it. Whatever price the dominant firm sets is accepted by the remainder of the industry, and the firm becomes a leader by default; that is, it leads because all others insist on following. In this situation the smaller firms accept the price of the leader as given in precisely the same way that firms in pure competition accept a market-determined price. That is, they do not attempt to find a more desirable price, but simply proceed to produce and market as much as is profitable at the given level. The immediate question then is, where will the dominant firm set price?

It may be that the firm will pursue a live-and-let-live policy, acting benevolently in the hope that its (partial) monopoly power will not attract the attention of antitrust authorities. If it does so, the dominant firm will price (and produce) in such a way that the smaller group of rivals can sell all that they wish at that price. Such a policy is illustrated in Figure 3.11. Here DD' is the market demand curve, MC_h is the marginal

---

[32] Most of the basic ideas discussed in the next three sections are to be found in the following original works: Kenneth E. Boulding, *Economic Analysis*, Harper, New York, revised edition, 1948, pp. 582 ff.; Jesse W. Markham, "The Nature and Significance of Price Leadership," *American Economic Review*, **XLI**, December 1951, pp. 891–905; George J. Stigler, "The Kinky Oligopoly Demand Curve and Rigid Prices," *Journal of Political Economy*, **LV**, October 1947, pp. 432–49.

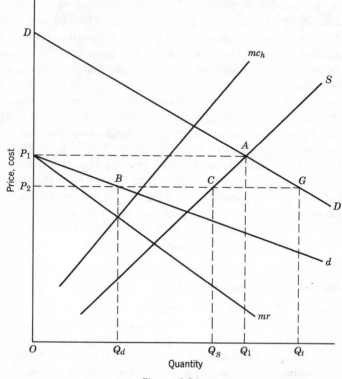

Figure 3.11

cost curve of the dominant firm, and S is the supply curve of the smaller firms (the summation of their marginal cost curves). Since it is going to allow rivals to sell as much as they wish, the dominant firm can derive its own relevant demand curve by subtracting the output that smaller rivals will produce at any price from the quantity demanded by the market at that price. For example, at price P_1 smaller firms will supply quantity P_1A, the entire amount that the market demands; therefore, the dominant firm's residual demand is zero at this price. At price P_2 small firms will supply quantity P_2C, but the market demands quantity P_2G; the dominant firm thus defines its own demand at this price as CG ($= P_2B$), and a second point on its own demand curve is defined. The dominant firm derives its demand curve, P_1d, as the quantity demanded by the market at any price *less* the quantity that the smaller firms will supply at that price. The marginal revenue curve associated with this demand curve is *mr*.

In Figure 3.11 the dominant firm will produce at the point of intersection between mr and mc_h, charging its profit-maximizing price, P_2. Smaller firms will supply P_2C (or OQ_S) = BG (or Q_dQ_t), as indicated by S. Thus the market price-quantity solution is determined at point G, involving price P_2 and output OQ_t. In this example the smaller firms actually produce more than the dominant leader; however, the analysis would proceed similarly if we allowed the large firm to have the bulk of sales (this would simply mean that mc_h lies below and to the right of S).

This particular outcome assumes that the dominant firm is a benevolent monopolist. The firm maximizes profits, but only after imposing on itself the condition that its smaller competitors must do relatively well. How likely such a policy may be is a matter of speculation. In fact the example presented is a rather extreme case in that the firm's dominance and benevolence are both assumed to be complete.

(b) Low-cost Firm Leadership

A slightly different variant suggests that the price leader may be the low-cost firm in the industry. There is, incidentally, no reason why a low-cost firm might not also be the dominant firm. Since the optimal price for such a firm will be lower than the optimal price for any rival, the low-cost firm may be in a position to impose its will on the industry. The question again becomes, what pricing policy will it follow? The firm may behave as a conventional maximizer of its own profits, in which case a suboptimal price for other firms is implied; or it may adopt a more communal attitude, seeking a policy that is more acceptable to other firms.

(c) Barometric Firm Leadership

A third possibility is that the price-leadership function will be assumed by any firm that acts as a good barometer of market conditions. It may be that a firm known for its ability to read the market will become the *de facto* leader simply because rival firms respect its pricing decisions. There is again no reason why the barometric firm also might not be a dominant or a low-cost firm. The barometric leader will maintain its leadership only so long as its decisions prove satisfactory to rivals. Such a firm may pursue a group-oriented policy, designed to maintain its own position; or it may act purely as an unconstrained profit maximizer, in which case the leadership function could shift among firms. Indeed, price leadership does not necessarily imply that the same firm acts as leader over prolonged periods. In the barometric case it is possible that different firms will assume leadership as alternative policies are tried out by the industry. This is not to imply, however, that frequent pricing experiments will occur. Quite the contrary; prices are notoriously rigid (or stable) in many industries characterized by such leadership.

(d) Summary

These examples of price leadership may characterize the actual pricing mechanisms of numerous oligopolistic markets. Frequently the price leader may be caught in a conflict between maximizing his own short-run profits, and acting as a maximizer in behalf of the industry.[33] Presumably the market outcome will depend on which course is chosen, in addition to which firm leads, and here an obvious weakness in the leadership analysis is evident. For all its apparent realism, price leadership, as a view of what really goes on in oligopoly, does not yield conclusions much more specific than those following from the general view that oligopoly is collusive.

It is not price leadership that *creates* collusive conditions in oligopoly. Rather, it is the *symptom* of a noncompetitive set of conditions, the result, but not the cause, of monopoly power. As such, the significance of price leadership should not be overstated. It is a device that may explain the conduct of numerous industries. If we wish to know how, in a purely mechanical sense, oligopoly pricing decisions are made, leadership may be as good an answer as we currently have. But if we wish to inquire into the quality of the market performance that arises from this mechanism, the answer is far less satisfactory. Virtually any result possible under collusive oligopoly could be reached via price leadership. Different examples of leadership may reflect different sets of circumstances, with quite different implications for firm and market performance.

3. INFORMAL AND SPONTANEOUS COLLUSION

Collusion in oligopoly often may occur without anything so formal or overt as an explicit agreement or recognition of a price leader. Consider, for example, a market in which all firms consider price competition to be potentially dangerous. There is no need for such firms to agree to refrain from competing in price. They may simply refrain "independently," as a matter of self-interest. Such conduct patterns are sometimes referred to as quasi-agreements or agreements to agree.[34]

---

[33] The latter course of action does not necessarily mean that we must abandon the traditional view of the firm as a profit maximizer. Rather than concluding that the firm no longer seeks maximum profits, we might argue that it seeks the maximum *subject to certain constraints or limitations*, e.g., that it cannot price so as to eliminate all competitors.

[34] See William Fellner, *Competition Among the Few*, Knopf, New York, 1949, especially Chapters I and VII.

Spontaneous collusion is likely to develop as the result of a trial-and-error process. In a Cournot-type market, for example, each rival may begin by assuming that its competitors' policies are fixed. After some experience with quantity adjustments, however, the oligopolists are likely to recognize that the policies of rivals are not fixed, but respond to their own behavior. The rivals may then experiment with different quantities, discarding those that are mutually unprofitable, and groping toward the monopoly result. Similarly, price-adjusting oligopolists may experiment with alternatives separately but interdependently. If their products are homogeneous, prices will tend to converge at a single level. As individual firms try out new levels (and prices converge at each), they are likely to discard those that prove to be unprofitable, and will move toward increasingly profitable levels and a monopoly result.

Purely informal collusion, like other collusive conduct, may lead to alternative market results, and will be subject to the same kinds of imperfection and variation in effectiveness. Indeed, in a market characterized by relatively many firms and frequent entry and exit, informal procedures that lack means for discipline may be rather impotent. There is also likely to be some limit to the scope of such arrangements. Spontaneous collusion presupposes objectives that are obvious to all participating firms. Any coordinated policies involving nonobvious restraints on competition, or requiring subtle and precisely coordinated moves, would be difficult to effect without a more highly structured arrangement. This is not to say, however, that informal procedures cannot work well in relatively simple situations. When firms are very few and when the objective of cooperation is evident, such arrangements may be very effective.

The pertinent question once again is what market results are likely under this particular type of market conduct. It seems probable that price rigidity—at least downward—will result. Firms that fear active price competition would want to avoid any action such as price cuts that might precipitate price warfare. Beyond this, however, it is difficult to specify the likely results. Firms might wish to move the market price toward a pure monopoly level, and some such result is certainly possible. Whether this actually happens will depend largely on the degree of certainty with which price adjustments can be made. If conditions permit all firms to see readily which adjustments are mutually beneficial, the likelihood that the industry will approach monopoly performance may be relatively high. If the benefits of adjustments are less visible (without overt communication or negotiation), the industry may still succeed in preventing vigorous price competition, but it is less likely to be able to move price so that something like a monopoly result is forthcoming.

4. SUMMARY

The collusion approach to oligopoly behavior may be the most realistic in terms of market conduct, but it seems to offer more than it produces in terms of market performance. Collusive conduct allows oligopolists to take advantage of their joint market power. It is therefore likely to move market performance closer to that of pure monopoly than it otherwise would be. It cannot be assumed, however, that oligopoly performance will be *identical* with, or very close to, that of monopoly.

None of the specific collusive procedures—outright conspiracy, price leadership, or informal collusion—really mitigates the problem of indeterminate solutions in oligopoly, for both the goals of agreements and their effectiveness need to be specified. Sophisticated oligopolists often do act collusively in the sense that they take full account of mutual dependence and seek to avoid the worst outcomes. But the precise implications of this conduct for market solutions are not at all clear. Neither the nature of the price that is determined nor the stability of adopted arrangements can be predicted confidently simply by invoking the term collusion.

D. Conclusions

The current state of oligopoly theory, as this brief survey should indicate, is unsettled. Mutual interdependence permits a wide variety of solutions, none with any particular claim to universality. The fundamental difficulty of oligopoly analysis is that the meaning of optimization or maximization for the firm is obscure. There is no such thing as a best course of action unless the actions of rivals are specified; but the specification of rivals' behavior is similarly impossible until *their* rivals are known to act in specified ways. Oligopoly models have proliferated, and there exist at least as many market solutions as there are assumptions about firms' response patterns.

The difficulty, however, is not simply that there are many possible solutions. In a real sense it might be argued that there can exist *no* solution to the basic oligopoly problem. *Any* solution that can be proposed has the property that it is rational for one rival only if it is also rational for the other(s); and any deviation or experimentation on the part of rivals may lead them away from the "solution" with no tendency to return.

Efforts to solve the oligopoly problem have produced some impressive intellectual achievements; but the problem remains. A number of writers, such as Peck,[35] have suggested that at least in some specific cases the reality of oligopoly is simpler than the theory. Firms may eliminate or neutralize some problems of mutual interdependence by adopting a collusive framework. Many uncertainties of price response and counterresponse then evaporate because they are ruled out by the collusive group. As we have noted, however, the realistic simplicity of collusion may extend only to the conduct of oligopolistic firms without doing much to pin down resulting market performance. The collusive approach does contribute the valuable suggestion that oligopoly behavior may "rationally" tend toward joint profit maximization, but we are left with the need to ascertain how strong or weak such tendencies may be. We have not yet found *the* answer to oligopoly behavior. As Baumol has put it, "Perhaps the most remarkable failure of modern value theory is its inability to explain the pricing, output and other related decisions of the large, not quite monopolistic firms which account for so large a proportion of our output."[36]

[35] Merton J. Peck, *Competition in the Aluminum Industry, 1945–1958*, Harvard University Press, Cambridge, 1961.

[36] *Business Behavior, Value and Growth, op. cit.*, p. 13.

4

The Theory of the Firm: Alternatives to Profit Maximization

The more orthodox theories we have discussed so far have either explicitly assumed profit maximization to be the objective of the firm, or have been readily adaptable to this assumption. Many writers in recent years, however, have questioned the adequacy and usefulness of profit maximization as an explanation of business policy. This questioning of the treatment of the firm is important to consider, for it raises basic questions. Certainly if it could be shown that firms generally are trying to do something other than maximize their profits, the conclusions of much of traditional market theory would need to be re-examined.

It is important initially to understand something about what is and is not meant by the profit-maximization assumption. It does *not* mean, for example, that all firms are at all times producing precisely to the point at which marginal cost equals marginal revenue, and are charging precisely the maximum price that the market will bear. It does not even mean that the pursuit of short-run profits is so singleminded that all other considerations become irrelevant to the firm. What the profit-maximization assumption does mean is: *first*, that business firms desire to earn as large a profit as possible, given the conditions and constraints under which they operate; and, *second*, that pursuit of this largest possible profit is the dominant objective of the firm, and that, accordingly, the most meaningful way of characterizing the firm's behavior is profit maximizing.

Viewed in these terms the profit-maximization assumption may not be quite the rigid statement that some students of economics would believe. Indeed, firms that seek maximum profits over some time horizon do not necessarily act as maximizers in the short run. A company that is breaking into a new market, for example, may find it profitable in the long run to charge an initial price that does not maximize short-run profits. A submaximum price may gain exposure for the firm's product that will eventually more than compensate the immediate sacrifice of profits.

Similarly, a firm that operates under various constraints may nevertheless be maximizing profit. We have noted in Chapter 3 the example of a dominant company that sets a price that will keep its rivals in business. Such a firm is indeed maximizing subject to the constraint that it cannot select a price that drives competitors from the market.

Obviously it is the information a firm has, including the constraints under which it must operate, that determines the precise nature of profit-maximizing behavior. Such information is extremely difficult to obtain, yet, unless we can somehow take account of it in constructing the firm's cost and demand functions, it may be impossible to determine objectively whether maximizing behavior is being observed.

At the outset, then, some of the more naive challenges to the assumption that firms are profit maximizers can be dismissed easily. The assumption cannot be rejected merely because the precise maximizing position is difficult for an objective observer to define, or because the maximum at which the firm can aim is constrained by other factors. Similarly, the maximization assumption cannot be invalidated by observing that firms have trouble maximizing—that is, that they may not actually attain maximizing positions at any moment.

A serious challenge to profit maximization rather must demonstrate that firms consistently pursue policies that *conflict* with maximum profits, given relevant uncertainties and constraints. It must, in other words, argue that there is *some other goal* (or goals) that systematically prevents firms from moving in the directions that the traditional assumption implies. This sort of argument is considerably more difficult to construct than one that simply cites the ways in which firms may fail to *achieve* a maximum-profit objective.

It is worth noting that in purely competitive markets the question of a firm's motivation does not really arise. The market itself enforces a zero-profit condition that is in effect profit maximization. The motivation of firms becomes a meaningful issue only when there exists some discretion in behavior. Accordingly, the profit-maximization discussion is applicable in a strict sense only to markets in which firms exert some degree of monopoly control.

A. Maximum Profits and Business Managers

Some objections to the idea of profit maximization have been based on observations of the psychology of business managers who determine the policies of firms. A common argument begins by noting that at a time when these managers, or *entrepreneurs*, were also the owners of their companies, profit maximization presumably *was* a plausible goal. However, the argument continues, in a modern economy owners and managers tend to be different individuals; the managers are salaried employees whose task it is to determine the policies of companies owned by someone else.[1] This well-documented observation poses an obvious problem. Since managers no longer directly receive the profits earned by their companies, perhaps their interest in maximizing those profits will wane; profits may be pursued with diminished enthusiasm, and the personal motives of managers may be substituted for the profit motive. This may, of course, displease the stockholders who own the firms in question, but stockholder control over the policies of management is notoriously weak, and may be exercised only in extreme situations.

These observations form the basis of a familiar questioning of the profit-maximization assumption. According to this line of argument there is no especially good basis for assuming that firms maximize profits when the men who manage the firms may have little incentive to do so. Moreover, speculation about the actual motives of business managers has tended to support a skeptical attitude toward profit maximization. Presumably business executives are a reasonably normal group, subject to the usual human desires. As such, they may seek power, prestige in the business world, and the respect of the larger community. Many observers contend that there is nothing in these desires that would cause them to promote profit-maximizing policies, and much that might not.

Cogent as these observations may be, there are several reasons for thinking that the profit-maximization assumption is not rendered

[1] The pioneering work in bringing to light the divorce of ownership and management is by Adolph A. Berle, Jr., and Gardiner C. Means, *The Modern Corporation and Private Property*, Macmillan, New York, 1932.

implausible by the nature of managerial motivation. First, it may be inaccurate to suppose that the personal motivations mentioned have any effect whatever on the policies of firms. There are certainly restraints on the actions of managers, and it is unlikely that any executive, however impotent his stockholders might be, or whatever his state of mind, could easily pursue policies inimical to the profit interests of his company over an extended period of time. Personal motivations may have little to do with corporation policies.

Even if we are willing to accept the contention that individual psychology has a bearing on business decisions, however, this does not necessarily argue against the profit-maximization assumption. In the first place, human traits such as vanity and the desire for power cannot readily be shown to be systematically incompatible with profit maximization. It cannot be casually concluded, in other words, that profit maximization requires individuals to act in conflict with their nature; to the contrary, observation might suggest that high-level business executives develop intense loyalty to their companies, and that an important motive becomes to do what is best for the firm. It is conceivable that the personal motives of business managers *do* stimulate a search for higher profits; to the extent that a company's profits measure the success of its managers—and to the extent that personal motives are satisfied by attaining professional success—the assumption remains plausible.

In addition, executive compensation is in many instances tied to the profits of the firm. Stock options, for example, are a common form of supplementary compensation in large companies. Since stock prices depend on company profits, the executive's reward may vary directly with profit performance. Although such schemes are far from universal, it could be argued that the owner-manager dichotomy has been overcome in many large companies. There may also be some direct risk for an executive who consistently fails to maximize profits. Suboptimal performance could induce a takeover bid by a corporate "raider" who sees unexploited profit potential in the firm; if so the manager responsible for submaximization might well find himself out of a job.

To conclude that personal motivation interferes with profit maximization as the objective of the firm, it would be necessary to pursue one of two arguments: either personal factors cause business managers consistently to pursue something other than maximum profits (perhaps a maximum growth rate or sales volume); or these factors introduce a nonsystematic, disorderly distortion of business policies. The position that some objective other than profits may become the dominant motive of the firm is supported by a number of economists, but not on psychological grounds. Baumol, for example, argues that firms are more interested in sales revenue than profits, but this argument (which will be discussed later) is the result of observation and not the conclusion of a psychological hypothesis. The second position is essentially a counsel of despair. If business policies are influenced in a nonsystematic way by personal feelings, there is no way of determining what these policies are in general likely to be. We might be reduced to saying, for example, that a firm will act one way if its president has had a good breakfast, and another way if the toast was burned.

Ultimately, the profit-maximization framework cannot stand or fall on statements about individual psychology. The primary test of an economic theory based on a profit-maximization assumption must continue to be its usefulness in predicting and explaining events, and not merely the subjective realism of the assumption employed.

B. Acceptable Profit Levels: "Satisficing"

One specific alternative that has received wide attention is the possibility that firms may aim for a satisfactory or acceptable rather than a maximum level of profits. The goal of firms is assumed to be not maximization of profits, but *satisficing*. At least two distinct reasons have been offered in support of a satisficing assumption. Simon has argued that the requirements of maximization in a complex and uncertain world are so immensely difficult that the goal is abandoned in favor of a more definable target.[2] That is, faced with an impossibly difficult problem—the maximization of some quantity such as profit—business firms may attempt *not* to solve the problem (for it is really insoluble), but to substitute another, more soluble task, the attainment of a *satisfactory* outcome.

A second argument for the satisficing assumption, discussed by Cyert and March,[3] is that there may be factors in the firm *as an organization* that work against maximization as a goal. There is no single organization theory of the firm, as such, but the important general principle is that the firm as an organization is distinct from individuals within it who are responsible for setting policy. The behavior of the organization reflects the coordination of efforts by individuals and groups of individuals

[2] Herbert A. Simon, "Theories of Decision-Making in Economics and Behavioral Science," *American Economic Review*, **XLIX**, June 1959, pp. 253–83.

[3] See R. M. Cyert and James G. March, "Organizational Factors in the Theory of Oligopoly," *Quarterly Journal of Economics*, **LXX**, February 1956, pp. 44–64; and *A Behavioral Theory of the Firm*, Prentice-Hall, Englewood Cliffs, N.J., 1963.

within, but the transition may not be simple. Moreover, the policies adopted by organizations reflect not only the interaction among individuals, but also the influence of the organization itself on those individuals.

Simon and Cyert and March are criticizing the traditional *normative* theory of the firm, which bases predictions on statements of what the firm *ought* to do under an assumption of rationality—that is, profit maximization. They propose instead a *behavioral* theory that would specify what firms *actually* do. In order to achieve this, they argue, we must discover a great deal more about the processes by which organizational goals are adopted and modified, and about the ways in which organizations go about measuring relevant magnitudes. The claims of the satisficing school are not only argued logically, but are buttressed by some empirical evidence as well. Cyert and March have shown, for example, that good predictions of some business decisions follow from their framework.

There can be no doubt that the behavioral theorists have raised legitimate and troublesome questions about the traditional treatment of the firm. It is less clear, however, that the satisficing criterion is itself a much superior foundation for treatment. We might postulate that firms do not seek to maximize, but rather set profit *targets.* The question then becomes: what is the nature of these targets? Even if it is agreed that the firm's decision makers think in terms of pricing for acceptable returns, what determines the meaning of "acceptable"? At the moment there is no single answer. An acceptable or satisfactory profit level can be defined in various ways, and it is even possible that firms might consider *maximum* profits to be the *acceptable* goal.[4] Models assuming satisficing or target-return pricing, then, may not imply a single specific alternative to profit maximization. Indeed, it is not inevitable that market results of satisficing differ significantly or at all from profit maximizing, although the calculus of the firm's decisions may be changed.

The empirical status of maximizing and satisficing is ambiguous. It is extremely difficult, on one hand, to deduce much about the policy principles of firms purely from objective data such as prices, quantities produced, and profit rates. On the other hand, however, there are numerous and well-known pitfalls in attempting to ascertain decision rules by interviewing business executives. A major empirical study, published by the Brookings Institution in 1958, utilizes extensive interview data. Here

---

[4] For some pertinent suggestions, see Richard H. Day, "Profits, Learning, and the Convergence of Satisficing to Marginalism," *Quarterly Journal of Economics*, LXXXI, May 1967, pp. 302–11.

[5] A. D. H. Kaplan, Joel B. Dirlam and Robert F. Lanzillotti, *Pricing in Big Business*, Brookings, Washington, 1958.

the findings of the authors lend little conclusive support to either the maximizing or satisficing hypotheses as useful frameworks for exploring firms' pricing policy. The study finds "some clustering around a norm of target return pricing," but concludes that firms are in fact so wide of this mark that target returns cannot be considered "a master key" to pricing policy.

C. Sales Revenue Maximization

Baumol has proposed that firms seek not maximum profits, but maximum sales revenues subject to some minimum profit constraint.[6] That is, the goal of the firm is defined as attainment of the largest possible sales revenue, subject to the limitation that profits not fall below a specified level.

Baumol's hypothesis, which he associates with large, oligopolistic enterprises, is drawn from his experience as a consultant to business firms. His evidence is admittedly subjective and "impressionistic," but the case he makes is a cogent one. Baumol notes that trends in sales and profits are not entirely independent, but his argument is more than a statement that higher sales may be the means to higher profits.[7] Specifically, he points out that managers seem to evaluate the state of their businesses in terms of sales trends, with profits mentioned as an "afterthought." He notes that executive salaries are more closely related to the size of an enterprise than to its profitability (an observation that may require qualification as supplemental compensation systems tied to profits become more common). Baumol argues further that the pricing rules of thumb and policy deliberations he has observed are fundamentally consistent with sales-revenue maximization. Managements, he believes, are primarily concerned with expanding sales once they are reasonably confident about achieving their usual rate of return on investment.

The sales-revenue maximization hypothesis would carry no precise

---

[6] William J. Baumol, *Business Behavior, Value and Growth*, Macmillan, New York, 1959; Harcourt, Brace, New York, revised edition, 1967.

[7] Franklin M. Fisher has suggested that most of Baumol's evidence is consistent with the alternative hypothesis that firms maximize short-run profits subject to a minimum sales or market-share constraint. The idea here is that the relationship between short-run and long-run maximization is somewhat obscure, and that firms pursue short-run profits unless they have some indication that this will cause a deterioration in their long-run position. See his review of Baumol, *Journal of Political Economy*, LXVIII, June 1960, pp. 314–15.

implications without some explanation of the minimum-profit constraint. What profit level is "acceptable" or "usual"? Unless we can specify it, the meaning of revenue maximization subject to this profit constraint will be, at best, unclear. Here Baumol refers for an answer to the capital markets. Firms that hope to sell securities in the future must consider that the marketability of future shares depends on the profits of the enterprise. As Baumol puts it, "Its [the firm's] minimum earnings must supply funds sufficient to pay dividends, and to reinvest in such amounts that the combination of dividend receipts and stock price rises can remunerate stockholders adequately."[8] In other words, the minimum acceptable profit is a level that permits the firm to remain competitive in marketing its own securities. And the firm is competitive when its payments to stockholders—both directly through dividends and indirectly through capital appreciation—are sufficient to keep its securities salable in contest with the securities of other corporations.

The behavior of the sales-revenue maximizer may be viewed in straightforward fashion once it is noted that Baumol also assumes that oligopolistic interdependence is ignored in day-to-day decisions. That is, the construction of a firm's revenue functions is not complicated by considerations of how rival firms will react. Given that the firm confronts a defined demand (average revenue) curve, its sales-maximizing policy will be as follows: it may produce to the point at which elasticity of demand is unity, that is, the point at which marginal revenue equals zero. This point, S in Figure 4.1, yields an unconstrained maximization of revenues (since any less production would forego positive marginal revenue, while any more would imply negative marginal revenue and a subtraction from total revenue). If the firm at this point is earning an acceptable profit it has achieved equilibrium. Should this sales-maximizing point, however, carry with it an unacceptable rate of return, the output level must be altered so that an acceptable profit is achieved. The firm will then come to a constrained equilibrium at some point on curve D between points S and P in Figure 4.1; it will not be maximizing revenue in an absolute sense, but it will be obtaining the largest possible revenue consistent with its minimum profit requirement.

Sales-revenue maximization implies a number of interesting characteristics for firm behavior. Generally, the output of a revenue maximizer will exceed that of a profit maximizer, and the associated price will tend to be lower. This point is easily seen once it is noted that the profit-maximizing output must occur within the elastic portion of the firm's demand curve. This is so because the profit maximizer equates marginal

[8] *Op. cit.*, first edition, p. 51.

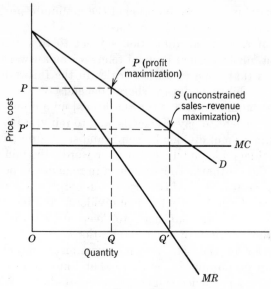

Figure 4.1

cost and marginal revenue at some positive value, and positive marginal revenue implies demand elasticity greater than unity.[9] The unconstrained revenue maximizer, by producing at the point of unitary demand elasticity, will necessarily supply a larger output. In Figure 4.1 profit-maximizing output occurs at an output level such as OQ, and revenue maximizing at a level such as OQ' ($MR = 0$). Invariably the unconstrained revenue maximizer produces to the right of the profit maximizer. If the revenue maximizer is constrained, however, it will most likely produce at some point between OQ and OQ'. Only if the minimum profit acceptable to the firm is identical to the firm's maximum profit will the revenue maximizer prove to be as restrictive a producer as the profit-maximizing firm. By similar token, any increase in the acceptable profit level itself would be expected to result in a restriction of output relative to that which had been produced before.

A further important implication of sales-revenue maximization is that prices (and outputs) will respond to changes in overhead. Under the traditional profit-maximizing assumption, changes in fixed cost will not lead to price revisions, since no marginal factors are affected in the

---

[9] If demand is elastic, a price decrease of X percent will call forth a quantity increase greater than X percent. Accordingly, total revenue (PQ) will rise, and marginal revenue—defined as the increment to the total—is positive.

short run. That is, the marginal cost and marginal revenue curves remain intact, and the most profitable point of production therefore is not altered. If a firm maximizes sales revenue, however, a change in such costs, which alters actual profits, could lead to some price response. If, for example, a firm that is earning precisely its minimum acceptable profit experiences an increase in overhead, it will need to respond with a restricted output and higher price in order to get back to an acceptable profit position. It will, in other words, act to recoup some of the profit previously foregone in the quest for higher revenues. Similarly, a tax imposed on the firm may lead to short-run price and output changes even though the tax is not of such a nature as to affect the maximum-profit position. These particular implications of sales-revenue maximization would explain a group of phenomena thought to be quite common but that cannot be readily accounted for by the more orthodox assumption.

D. Further Suggestions on Firm Behavior

An extensive literature on the behavior of the firm contains numerous hypotheses. Marris has suggested that firms maximize the growth rate of corporate capital subject to the constraint that they must protect against bankruptcy or take-over.[10] Rothschild, noting instances in which companies reinvest in the face of more profitable outside opportunities, has argued that secure (rather than maximum) profits may be the key to business behavior.[11] Scitovsky has proposed that entrepreneurs trade off between money income and leisure time, maximizing neither variable, but, rather some function composed of both.[12]

It is not possible to do justice here to these and many other suggestions about firm motivation and policy. One further argument, however, is well worth mentioning. The debate about profit maximization is in a sense part of a broader controversy over marginal analysis in economics. This controversy reached its height in the late 1940's, when Lester presented empirical evidence to show that marginalism does a poor job of

[10] Robin Marris, "A Model of the Managerial Enterprise," *Quarterly Journal of Economics,* **77,** May 1963, pp. 185–209.

[11] K. W. Rothschild, "Price Theory and Oligopoly," *Economic Journal,* **57,** September 1947, pp. 299–320.

[12] Tibor Scitovsky, "A Note on Profit Maximization and its Implications," *Review of Economic Studies,* **11,** 1943, pp. 57–60.

LEWIS AND CLARK COLLEGE LIBRARY.
PORTLAND, OREGON 97219

explaining economic behavior.[13] Lester presented examples drawn from the labor market that seemed to indicate that relationships between wage rates and employment patterns do not follow the expectations of marginal analysis. Among the responses to Lester's argument perhaps the most emphatic was that of Machlup.[14] Machlup, describing the many potential pitfalls in empirical tests of marginal analysis, noted that such elements as marginal revenue and costs of production are subjective. That is, business firms act on *what they perceive* as the relevant quantities, and not on what is perceived objectively by the calculations of disinterested men.

The distinction between subjective and objective perception is an important one to bear in mind when assessing empirical evidence. From time to time, for example, it has been found that particular firms appear to produce at a point of negative marginal revenue. Such behavior is of course not profit maximizing, but does this sort of evidence justify a rejection of the maximization hypothesis? Possibly it does not. The firm's selection of an output level depends on its view of demand conditions. Conceivably this view encompasses constraints of which the empirical analyst is unaware or has chosen not to include in the firm's demand or cost curve. If this is the case the firm may indeed be maximizing by its own lights, although it may appear to an analyst to be acting suboptimally. Suppose, for example, that a company fears antitrust prosecution if it grows too large. It may rationally price and produce so as to keep its market share below what it regards as the critical level; yet such behavior may appear irrational to an outside observer who is unaware of the antitrust constraint. The troublesome point is that if subjective and objective measures of relevant economic magnitudes are generally very different, the implications of the marginal analysis and the testability of propositions that flow from it will be extremely limited.

The Machlup argument need not be interpreted too strongly. In essence, he appears to conclude only that empirical findings apparently inconsistent with theoretical hypotheses should not lead directly to the scrapping of the analysis. To the contrary, the difficulties and subtleties inherent in formulating hypotheses and their tests are so great that such inconsistencies might well be viewed with suspicion. At the very least, outright rejection of marginalism should not be undertaken

[13] Richard A. Lester, "Shortcomings of Marginal Analysis for Wage-Employment Problems," *American Economic Review*, **36**, March 1946, pp. 63–82.

[14] Fritz Machlup, "Marginal Analysis and Empirical Research," *American Economic Review*, **36**, September 1946, pp. 519–54.

lightly; and at least some of those who reject it may have lacked a thorough understanding of the theory and its implications.

E. Summary: The Status of Profit Maximization

It would be wrong to suggest that there exists among students of business behavior anything approaching a consensus about profit maximization. At least two points, however, might find fairly broad acceptance:

1. Challenges to the profit-maximization hypothesis raise enough troublesome questions to make us cautious in approaching the behavior of the firm.
2. There is at present no single alternative hypothesis that gives us a more useful general approach.

As additional empirical evidence is marshaled, the outlook may change. Possibly some alternative motivational assumption, such as Baumol's, can be shown to imply a generally verifiable type of business behavior. On the other hand, it may be found that profit maximization is a more satisfactory characterization than some would think, once various constraints are taken into account. That is, it may be that when limitations on the actions of firms are drawn into their cost and demand curves, their behavior will appear consistent with maximization of profits.

5

Some Modern Views of "Monopolistic" Markets and the Competitive Norm

As our review of market theory has indicated, traditional economic analysis demonstrates the unique efficiency of competitive market arrangements. Departures from competitive conditions take various forms, but all are associated with nonoptimality of resource allocation. Deviations tend to preclude the attainment of a Pareto optimum, and this central conclusion has produced wide acceptance of the competitive system as a norm or standard of "the way things ought to be."

A competitive standard obviously carries direct implications for public policy. If competitive markets are desirable, there is much that government can do, primarily through antitrust laws, to encourage the appropriate conditions. Even the most cursory examination of present United States markets, however, will disclose that these conditions do not exist. Not only are there very few instances of strictly competitive markets, but in many areas the concentration of market power is extreme. Numerous sectors of the market economy are characterized by what might be called structural oligopoly—a situation in which relatively few firms account for a relatively large proportion of sales and output. Such markets are, in traditional terminology, distinctly noncompetitive or "monopolistic."[1] In view of the competitive norm, it might be expected that current market conditions would provoke a major effort by government to implement more competitive conditions. It is true that both federal and state governments follow broad policies of promoting competition; yet it also is clear that there has been no serious effort to establish a strictly competitive market system.

Why should this be the case? One possibility is that the competitive norm, while it receives generous vocal support, is not really accepted as a basis for policy. Certainly numerous individuals both in and out of government believe that the economic results of American markets in their present form are quite satisfactory and even outstanding. Understandably, such people would be reluctant to alter the conditions that have produced "success." A second possibility, suggested by the virtual universality of noncompetitive conditions, is that pure or perfect competition is generally unattainable. If this is so, the relevance, if not the desirability, of a competitive standard is called into question.

A number of fundamental issues are raised by these observations. Is competition in the strict sense desirable? Is it a possibility? If not, are we better off seeking the maximum possible competition, or might such a policy objective lead to a deterioration in economic welfare? What we now approach is the problem of translating theoretical implications and conclusions into meaningful statements for policy. As will become evident, the translation is neither simple nor straightforward.

A. The Causes of Concentration

In some other world competitive markets might be the rule. Pure or perfect competition would perhaps not prevail in all sectors, but numerous rivals seeking to sell closely substitutable commodities might typify the organization of most markets. Although it is difficult to define what is in fact "typical" of the immensely complex United States market system, the extent to which it departs from even a modified ideal is dramatic. The only areas that seem to approach purely competitive conditions closely are certain agricultural and financial markets. The wheat farmer, for example, cannot influence the price at which he sells; he is simply too

[1] The word monopolistic is used here in the broadest sense. It denotes not only pure monopoly, but any market situation in which firms have some power over the prices they charge. Such firms may be said to have a *degree of monopoly power* or to be *partial monopolists*.

small relative to the market. Moreover, the buyer of wheat does not care (and may well not know) from which farmer he buys. The product is thus truly homogeneous.

If we look at manufacturing industries generally, however, the picture is very different. Production of primary metals, for example, is characterized by an extremely high degree of concentration. Four firms produce about 50 percent of all domestic iron and steel; four (different) firms account for 78 percent of copper production. There are only seven domestic producers of primary aluminum, and six producers of lead. In many large and important markets—notably automobiles, cigarettes, soaps and detergents, tires and tubes, and containers—concentration of production and sales is as high or higher. The representative industries shown in Table 5.1 give some notion of the range and extent of market concentration in 1963. Although these industries cannot reflect fully the structure of the economy, there can be no doubt that concentration is an imposing fact of life. Even when concentration is relatively low, leading firms may exert very substantial influence over price. Entry of new firms is often difficult and product differentiation, which may serve to enhance market power, is widespread. The precise degree of divergence from truly competitive conditions in the American economy is of course hard to define, although substantial efforts to measure such divergence have been made. The problems of measuring competition and monopoly will be discussed in a later section. For the moment, it is sufficient to note the obvious fact that monopoly elements are very widespread.

The immediate question is why this deviation has occurred, for our attitudes toward concentration and the possibilities of remedial policies must depend in part on the causes of the present condition. The most familiar explanation of concentrated market power, mentioned earlier, is stated in terms of efficiency. If large-scale operations are inherently more efficient, that is, able to produce at lower unit costs than smaller units, then large firm size is encouraged. As a consequence, firms in various markets will tend to be large relative to the markets themselves, and this is the essential meaning of concentration.

There can be no doubt that efficiency plays an important role in firm size and market concentration. New and effective techniques can often be brought to bear in the large firm. Specialization can be intensified, with the result that each component of the productive process may be more expeditiously carried out. Moreover, managerial coordination of the varied components may improve with size. The potential for increased efficiency with size, however, is neither limitless nor uniform among firms and industries. Economies of large-scale production, when

Table 5.1

Concentration of Value of Shipments in Selected
Manufacturing Industries, 1963

Industry	Percentage Accounted for by Four Largest Firms	Percentage Accounted for by Eight Largest Firms
I. *High concentration*		
Flat glass	94	99+
Cigarettes	80	100
Motor vehicles and parts	79	83
Primary copper	78	98
Typewriters	76	99
Metal cans	74	85
Soap and other detergents	72	80
Tires and inner tubes	70	89
Photographic equipment	63	76
Distilled liquor, except brandy	58	74
II. *Moderate concentration*		
Flour mills	35	50
Petroleum refining	34	56
Malt liquors	34	52
Metal office furniture	33	50
Meat slaughtering	31	42
Scientific instruments	29	40
Shoes, except rubber	25	32
Bread and related products	23	35
Paints and allied products	23	34
III. *Low concentration*		
Hardwood dimension and flooring	17	22
Men's and boys' suits and coats	14	23
Printing, except lithographic	13	19
Brick and structural tile	12	19
Bottles and canned soft drinks	11	16
Blouses	11	15
Creamery butter	8	14
Dresses	6	9
Signs and advertising displays	5	8

Source: Concentration Ratios in Manufacturing Industry 1963, Report prepared
by the Bureau of the Census for the (Senate) Subcommittee on Antitrust and Monopoly, G.P.O., Washington, 1967.

they exist, are likely to be exhausted and perhaps reversed beyond some size. This suggests that although we can point to economies of scale as a potentially significant factor in size and concentration, we cannot proceed to assume that larger size and higher concentration always imply more efficiency.

The immensely difficult but most relevant question is: in any industry, what size of plant and firm, and what level of concentration, can be justified on efficiency grounds? It should be noted that the efficiency argument for large *plants* is distinct from the argument for large *firms*. It is presumably the technology of the industry that necessitates some level of plant size, whereas for firms the argument centers on the ability of a single management to extract additional economies by somehow meshing the operations of multiple plants. In various industries—for example, automobile manufacturing—the contention that large plants are necessary may be accepted without any implication that the size of existing *firms* is therefore also necessary. It is most likely that the existence of 500 automobile producers would imply much chronic inefficiency, but *it does not follow* from this that companies the size of General Motors, Ford, or Chrysler are desirable for efficiency reasons. Indeed, many such large companies operate their various divisions almost autonomously. This may well indicate that the companies themselves see potential inefficiencies in large size.

An ideal procedure would be to estimate the optimal size of plants and firms for every industry. The extent to which variations from optimality exist could then be seen directly, and conclusions reached about the appropriateness of existing concentration levels. Tentative efforts to define these magnitudes in specific industries have been undertaken,[2] but with somewhat unsatisfying results. The very notion of a unique optimal size, or even a narrow optimal range, may be difficult to defend; estimates rely partially on subjective judgment, and the conclusions reached may be so broad as to be of little help in judging many industries. As the work of Bain demonstrates, estimates of multiplant economies, which are necessary to conclusions about firm size, may be especially difficult to derive.

A further complication in relating concentration to efficiencies arises when we consider that the meaning of efficiency or economy of

[2] For estimates pertaining to selected industries, see Joe S. Bain, *Barriers to New Competition*, Harvard University Press, Cambridge, 1955. George J. Stigler has suggested that optimal size may be defined simply as the size that succeeds by surviving in the market. See his "The Economies of Scale," *Journal of Law and Economics*, 2, October 1958, pp. 54–71.

large-scale operation may be different for the firm than it is for the community in general. It is necessary to distinguish between genuine economies of scale and what are sometimes called *pecuniary* economies. The true economy of scale is a technical expression that relates inputs to outputs in a specific way. If, for example, doubling all inputs causes output to triple, a genuine economy exists. A true economy also might be said to exist when returns to a particular input are increasing; that is, the notion of economies need not be restricted to cases in which the proportion of inputs is maintained and only the scale is changed.

The pecuniary economy, on the other hand, implies that additional output can be produced more *cheaply* even though no technical efficiency may be involved. Suppose, for example, a firm can double its output by less than doubling its *expenditure* on inputs. This may occur because the firm at a larger scale of operation enjoys greater market power and can obtain inputs at more favorable terms. From a technical standpoint such a firm need not be more efficient, and may be less efficient, at a larger size. In society's terms, there is no necessary efficiency implicit in the growth of the firm. The firm itself, however, will almost certainly regard larger size as more efficient, and its inducement to grow will not be diminished by the pecuniary nature of the efficiency.

It appears generally that virtually any inducement to grow could be rationalized by firms on grounds of efficiency, even though no genuine social efficiency is present. If growth offers the prospect of higher profits or a more secure future, the firm may regard it as an obviously efficient proposition. The pertinent question, however, is whether the entirely legitimate objectives of the firm will, if effected, serve the interests of society as well.

If we are to decide, then, what is a socially appropriate market organization in terms of efficiency, we must learn not only what happens to costs of production and profit levels as output increases, but also what portion of this behavior reflects true efficiencies. There is little question that true efficiencies of large size preclude purely competitive conditions in many industries. When production techniques are best developed and exploited by large plants and firms, there would be little point in imposing —by government fiat or otherwise—a regime of small "competitive" units. Because efficiency is an important economic objective, it cannot be ignored in a search for competition.

Public policy would proceed best with greatly expanded knowledge about optimal or efficient levels of size and concentration. Efficiency, however, is not the sole objective of public competition policy. Indeed, some of the most troublesome policy problems arise when efficiency conflicts with some other objective. Expansion of our knowledge of size-efficiency relationships is thus a matter of high priority for the policy maker, but it does not imply the end of policy problems and dilemmas.

B. Schumpeterian Dynamics

Schumpeter's view of the economic system is, as we have noted, very different from that implicit in the orthodox body of market theory.[3] His concern was with innovation in products and techniques rather than with the traditional problem of resource allocation; and he saw as the basic strength of the capitalist system its ability to introduce the "perennial gales" of "creative destruction" that imply change and improvement. Schumpeter attributed this strength specifically to the large, typically semimonopolistic firm. Such firms, according to Schumpeter, are likely to engage in inventive activity for several reasons.[4] First, they have the financial wherewithal to do so. The invention and introduction of new products and techniques often requires extensive financial capital, and possibly the ability to absorb losses over some time period. Even if the inventive process is simple and does not require much research, it may be costly to place new items on the market under conditions that offer a reasonable chance of success. The kind of small, zero-profit firm that exists in pure competition would not, in the Schumpeterian view, have sufficient funds to bring about major changes. Further, Schumpeter argued, a large potential payoff is required to induce inventive activity.[5] Unless a firm can see some prospect of a large, essentially *monopolistic*, reward, it may find little reason to experiment with new developments, which are, by virtue of their untested nature, risky. Finally, Schumpeter noted that although the large firm operates in what are termed non-competitive markets, it is not free from competitive pressures. Such a firm may be very insecure in markets in which it confronts powerful opponents. Accordingly, invention and innovation may be stimulated

[3] Joseph A. Schumpeter, *Capitalism, Socialism and Democracy*, Harper, New York, third edition, 1950.

[4] A distinction is usually made between *invention*, the development of a new product or technique, and *innovation*, the actual introduction of the novelty to the market.

[5] It is interesting to note that the American patent system presupposes precisely the requirement of a large payoff. The assumption of the current system is that invention will be stimulated by granting the inventor a monopoly on his development for a specified number of years. During this period, the inventor may exploit his invention, or may profit by licensing it to others.

by the desire to survive against firms that are similarly motivated. The threat of failure in a market populated by a few innovators is seen as potentially greater than that posed by a market of many small competitors, none of whom are active innovators; and the purpose of innovation in the concentrated market thus may be not monopolization, but simply maintenance of an established position.

The Schumpeterian thesis, as stated in *Capitalism, Socialism and Democracy*, is rather general. His position is that the strength of the capitalistic system lies not in traditional price competition, but in the "true" competition of invention and innovation. Such activity flourishes in imperfectly competitive markets; thus the good performance of the modern capitalistic economy is not a result of adherence to the competitive ideal, but of *divergence* from it. There are of course objections to this position. It can be argued that large firms generally are *not* under severe pressure to innovate, and that smaller firms in more competitive market settings are more likely to be subject to the kinds of pressure that encourage innovation. It also is possible that the large firm, although induced by competitive pressures to "do something," may not concentrate on meaningful or genuine change. Rather than introducing a new product or improving an old one, the firm may decide that it is profitable instead to alter the packaging or styling of the product. Rather than attempting to develop cost-saving productive techniques, it may choose to alter its demand curve by increased advertising.

One of the necessities in evaluating the Schumpeterian hypothesis is a definition and specification of terms. We need to know what is and what is not a true innovation; and we must define more precisely the implied relationship between firm size, degree of market power, and innovation. We need to know more than that a large firm will engage in more inventive activity than a smaller firm. The real question is: *how much more?* It is necessary to determine how inventiveness relates to firm size, and in what patterns. Possibly, for example, firms must attain a certain size before they become active inventors and innovators, but will not respond to *further* size increases with more innovation. These questions are empirical, and the accuracy and significance of Schumpeter's contention must be established by facts rather than speculation.

This discussion cannot deny or confirm the contention that monopoly may be progressive. Rather, it is designed to point out that such a contention does not carry especially strong credentials for acceptance on an a priori basis. If the contention is accepted, it will be because evidence is found to support it, and not because logic demands it. As will be seen in Part II, economists have attempted to marshal relevant empirical information on this issue, with somewhat inconclusive results. For the present, then, it may be wise to reserve judgment, noting that Schumpeter has provided an interesting, but not necessarily convincing, challenge to the traditional conclusion of competitive optimality.

C. Galbraith and Countervailing Powers

Galbraith has offered a different explanation of "good" market performance in an extensively monopolized economy.[6] Galbraith claims that when a small group of firms gains a degree of monopoly control in a market, there is a tendency for similar power to arise in adjacent markets. For example, strong labor unions may arise in opposition to strong management, or a powerful manufacturer may find himself confronted by equally powerful retail buyers. According to Galbraith, the existence of such *countervailing powers* in opposed positions throughout the economy is mutually neutralizing. The power of one monopolistic group is checked, and in a sense cancelled, by that of another. The implications of the Galbraith argument are important, for if monopolistic groups effectively cancel one another's power to exploit, public policy might make an important mistake by attempting to limit the degree of monopoly in the economy. Rather than rendering the economy more competitive, such action could, by enhancing the power of those monopolistic groups that remain, lead to a less desirable situation.

The concept of countervailing power is interesting but must be considered in perspective. As Stigler has pointed out, the empirical case for countervailing power as a general phenomenon is rather weak.[7] It is true that a number of fairly important "adjacent" oligopolies are to be found in American industry, but there is also extensive evidence that suggests the presence of unopposed power concentrations. This is not especially surprising, for Galbraith fails to argue convincingly that countervailing groups are inevitable, or even very likely. The factors that cause or permit concentration to develop in one sector may be absent or substantially different in another. There is thus no compelling expectation that strong groups will *consistently* arise to oppose similar groups in other areas. Moreover, even if the phenomenon were pervasive,

[6] John Kenneth Galbraith, *American Capitalism*, Houghton Mifflin, Boston, second edition, 1956.

[7] George J. Stigler, "The Economist Plays with Blocs," *American Economic Review*, **XLIV**, May 1954, pp. 7–14.

it is not clear that "good" economic performance is the most likely outcome. Galbraith argues that the opposed groups cancel out to the ultimate benefit of the consuming public, but it may be equally probable that these groups act to the detriment of consumers. Union-management bargaining situations in which both sides are powerful, for example, do not seem consistently to produce socially beneficial wage-price behavior.

The idea of countervailing power, then, cannot be used to argue with real confidence that society has an effective automatic check on monopolistic groups. Neither the analytical nor the empirical status of the concept would support such a conclusion. Galbraith's valuable suggestion is rather that the power of monopolistic groups is not always capable of full exploitation. There may exist limitations to the power of even the strongest firms; and these limits ought to be carefully noted in evaluating the social disutility of such companies.

D. Measuring the Extent of Monopoly

The approaches of Schumpeter and Galbraith might be characterized, in simplified fashion, as explanations of why monopoly is good. Their arguments state that deviations from perfect competition do not result in the gross distortions that classical economics would suggest. Even an economy that might be judged substantially noncompetitive would thus not necessarily imply poor performance. A different approach to the question of competitiveness and performance is provided by those writers who in effect refuse to accept the casual judgment that the United States market economy is highly noncompetitive. They have sought rather to define in more systematic fashion the extent of deviations from competition.

Wilcox, for example, has argued that the conclusions following from superficial inspection of industry and product concentration data, are often erroneous.[8] Existing industry and product classifications, according to Wilcox, may give a poor picture of the actual alternatives open to consumers. If these alternatives are understated, the extent of competition within and among markets will be similarly distorted. Moreover, Wilcox argues, the distribution of consumer expenditures indicates that numerous

[8] Clair Wilcox, "On the Alleged Ubiquity of Oligopoly," *American Economic Review*, 40, May 1950, pp. 67-73.

quantitatively important areas—notably housing, food, and clothing—are competitive, or at least unconcentrated.[9]

Other investigators have attempted to derive quantitative estimates of the extent of monopoly in American markets. Nutter, for example, concluded that the percentage of national income originating in "effectively monopolized" industries in 1937 was between 12.9 and 21.1, as contrasted with a figure of 17.4 percent for 1899.[10] Stigler estimates that slightly more than 24 percent of income originated under "monopoly" in 1939.[11] Adelman has concluded that, whether existing degrees of concentration and monopoly are considered high or low, there has been no discernible upward trend since the beginning of the century.[12]

Other economists have attempted to quantify the *effects* rather than the *existence* of monopoly in the United States. Harberger, for example, has estimated that the misallocation of resources caused by monopoly is less than might be thought—about $225 million, or less than $1.50 per capita as of 1953.[13] Harberger examined industry rates of return. Reasoning that above-average returns reflect monopoly misallocation— the devotion of two few resources to the industry in question— he proceeded to measure the adjustments in price and quantity that would be necessary to eliminate such distortions. Assuming unitary elasticity of demand, Harberger found that the "welfare losses" indicated were surprisingly small. The loss, as shown in Figure 5.1, is area E_mAE_c. This is the measure of what society gives up under a monopoly that

---

[9] The Wilcox argument was directed not only at statements citing specific-industry concentration, but also at assertions based on the concentration of wealth within the economy as a whole. The best-known exposition of the general phenomenon is A. A. Berle and Gardiner C. Means, *The Modern Corporation and Private Property*, Macmillan, New York, 1932. Berle and Means found that 49 percent of nonbanking corporate wealth was held by the largest 200 (among a total of 300,000) corporations in 1929.

[10] G. Warren Nutter, *The Extent of Enterprise Monopoly in the United States 1899–1939*, University of Chicago Press, Chicago, 1951.

[11] Adapted from George J. Stigler, *Five Lectures on Economic Problems* (Macmillan, London, 1950). Cited in Richard B. Heflebower, "Monopoly and Competition in the United States of America," in E. H. Chamberlin (editor), *Monopoly and Competition and their Regulation*, Macmillan, London, 1954, pp. 110–40.

[12] M. A. Adelman, "The Measurement of Industrial Concentration," *Review of, Economics and Statistics*, 33, November 1951, pp. 269–96.

[13] A. C. Harberger, "Monopoly and Resource Allocation," *American Economic Review*, 44, May 1954, pp. 77–87. Similar conclusions have been drawn in a study comparing monopolized Canadian industries with their American counterparts; see D. Schwartzman, "The Burden of Monopoly," *Journal of Political Economy*, LXVIII, December 1960, pp. 727–29.

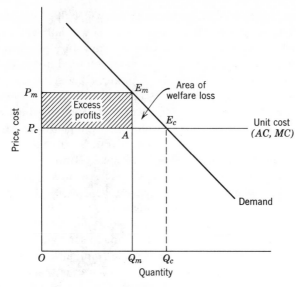

Figure 5.1

locates at equilibrium E_m when competitive equilibrium would have been established at E_c.

Harberger's methodology has been subject to some criticism. Stigler points out that the assumption of unitary demand elasticity is objectionable, since it implies that monopolists produce to the point at which marginal revenue is zero.[14] Under an assumption of higher demand elasticity, the measured welfare loss would increase. Further, Harberger's measure reflects only those monopoly effects that appear as payments to capital; other real distortions are missed. Leibenstein has recently suggested that the most important efficiency loss implied by monopoly may lie outside the traditional resource-allocation area.[15]

Still another clue to the severity of monopoly in the United States is provided by Kaplan.[16] Kaplan calculated the turnover among the 100 largest corporations during the period 1909–1948, and concluded

[14] George J. Stigler, "The Statistics of Monopoly and Merger," *Journal of Political Economy,* **LXIV** (February 1956), pp. 33–40.
[15] Harvey Leibenstein, "Allocative Efficiency vs. 'X-Efficiency," *American Economic Review,* **56,** June 1966, pp. 392–415.
[16] A. D. H. Kaplan, *Big Enterprise in a Competitive System,* Brookings, Washington, 1954.

that it was sufficiently high to discredit the belief that huge firms enjoy secure market positions. The degree of turnover indicated to Kaplan that although a few corporate giants account for a disproportionate percentage of total corporate size, this condition need not imply a similar disproportion in the distribution of power. Precisely what this sort of finding may indicate, however, is open to question. Turnover in the top 100 lists is attributable to various factors, some of which have little to do with the severity of competition. For example, the merger of two firms on the list results in the "disappearance" of one. It would be misleading to conclude that such an addition to turnover reflects severe competitive pressure. Despite difficulties such as these, the Kaplan data raise a further question about the degree of monopoly that has existed and currently exists in the nation's economy.

Taken *in toto*, empirical examinations of competition and monopoly in the United States are inconclusive. Although some may be tempted to conclude that monopoly is a nonexistent or unimportant problem, these studies have left open many questions about the extent and importance of market power concentrations. The studies make an important contribution by forcing us to question the "obvious" interpretations of highly publicized data on firm sizes and market concentration. Perhaps we do not have sufficient evidence to conclude that the economy is extensively monopolistic. In fact, as we shall see in Part II, the measurement of monopoly in specific industries, as well as in the economy as a whole, presents subtle and difficult problems. There is no doubt that most American markets currently deviate from the competitive ideal, but the extent and implication of this deviation are not entirely clear.

E. The "Theory of Second Best"

It is widely accepted that large plants are required by the technology of many industries and that consequently efforts to impose a competitive regime of small firms would be self-defeating. That is, pure or perfect competition is at best an unrealistic objective. Given this limitation, an intuitively plausible statement has also gained currency: if we cannot attain the ideal state of competition, the next best thing would be to approximate it as closely as possible. Public policy in this view ought to work toward attainment of the maximum degree of competition in all markets, even though it will inevitably fall short of perfection. This position is an obviously appealing one: "If we cannot have the whole loaf, let us at least take what we can." It is true that our best efforts often are stimulated by the pursuit of "impossible" goals; why worry that the goal is unattainable if it drives us to do more than we otherwise would?

As is sometimes the case in economics, however, the "obvious" statement has been shown to contain a logical flaw. Recently, much attention has been devoted to the so-called *theory of second best,* a group of closely related ideas whose central points may be summarized as follows: ". . . if one or more of the well-known marginal conditions for pareto optimality cannot be fulfilled, the rest of these conditions are, in general, no longer desirable."[17] [Therefore] ". . . it is *not* true that a situation in which more, but not all, of the optimum conditions are fulfilled is necessarily, or is even likely to be, superior to a situation in which fewer are fulfilled."[18]

In other words, if *all* the conditions for pareto optimality cannot be met, there may be no point in attempting to meet as many as possible. Indeed, the *second best* solution to full attainment of the conditions may turn out to be *abandonment of the other conditions.* As we have seen, perfect competition in all markets satisfies the marginal conditions for a pareto optimum. What the theory of second best implies, then, is that if some monopoly element in the economy is inevitable, that is, if it is impossible to satisfy fully all of the marginal conditions, an attempt to foster "as much competition as possible" may actually be detrimental to economic welfare. Indeed, the second best solution might be attained by allowing *more monopoly* rather than more competition.

The exposition of the theory of second best is largely mathematical, and its central conclusion is not intuitively obvious.[19] We may attempt to illustrate the idea of the theory in the following way, however. The "problem" of monopoly is seen as one of resource misallocation; too little in the way of resources flow to monopolized sectors, and too little is produced. But in a universe, or world, or country—whatever the relevant dimension—that contains both competitive and monopolistic sectors, it also follows that for society to reallocate and arrive at a better welfare position, resources must be *taken away* from competitive sectors. In other words, the resource-allocation problem that we traditionally describe as too few resources in the monopoly sector, can also be described meaningfully as too many resources in the competitive sector.

[17] P. Bohm, "On the Theory of 'Second Best,' " *Review of Economic Studies*, **34,** July 1967, p. 301.

[18] R. G. Lipsey and Kelvin Lancaster, "The General Theory of Second Best," *Review of Economic Studies*, **24,** 1956, p. 12.

[19] For the mathematical exposition, see Lipsey and Lancaster, *ibid.;* and Paul A. Samuelson, *Foundations of Economic Analysis* (Harvard University Press, Cambridge, 1947).

Suppose that in a particular economic system all industries are monopolies. There is an argument that under these circumstances, *no misallocation* will exist! The misallocation of resources is a relative problem. Monopolistic sectors of an economy cannot demand too little unless other, nonmonopoly sectors demand too much. As Baumol puts it, "If each of a number of runners slows down, none of them need come in ahead of the others, and if each industry is weak in its bidding for resources, no lopsided allocation of these resources need result.[20] Viewed in these terms, more competition is not necessarily desirable. The misallocation that we have habitually referred to as a monopoly problem could be called a competitive problem. And if universal competition is the best of all worlds, universal monopoly may be the next best. Indeed, a world of much competition and little monopoly may represent an unsatisfactory situation that would be worsened by increasing the extent of competition, so long as universally competitive markets are not possible.

This essential conclusion of the theory of second best implies that policies that *partially remedy* monopolistic conditions may be worse than no policies at all. Although this implication has received serious attention,[21] it has not led economists generally to advocate the abandonment of procompetitive public policies. One reason for this is that the theory represents a general equilibrium approach that may not be appropriate to many policy problems. According to the theory a change that is good for one segment of the economy may prove to be bad in its ramifications throughout the system.

Public policy, however, most often follows a piecemeal approach in which direct effects on the immediate segment are considered paramount.[22] This approach makes sense if changes in one part of the economy are thought to hold negligible implications for most others. In a sense the question becomes one of defining the relevant system or universe. If various sectors of the economy are independent of each other, there is a strong case for treating each as a separate system, that is, as an isolated

---

[20] William J. Baumol, *Economic Theory and Operations Analysis*, Prentice-Hall, Englewood Cliffs, N.J., second edition, 1965, p. 366.

[21] This attention is attested to by an already extensive literature. For recent discussions, see E. J. Mishan, "Second Thoughts on Second Best," *Oxford Economic Papers* (New Series), 14, October 1962, pp. 205–17; O. A. Davis and A. Whinston, "Welfare Economics and the Theory of Second Best," *Review of Economic Studies*, 32, January 1965, pp. 1–14; O. A. Davis and A. Whinston, "Piecemeal Policy in the Theory of Second Best," *Review of Economic Studies*, 34, July 1967, pp. 323–31; and William J. Baumol, "Informed Judgment, Rigorous Theory and Public Policy," *Southern Economic Journal*, 32, October 1965, pp. 137–45.

[22] See Mishan, "Second Thoughts," *loc. cit.;* Baumol, "Informed Judgment," *loc. cit.;* and Davis and Whinston, "Piecemeal Policy," *loc. cit.*

problem. Although a general Pareto optimum embracing all systems is unattainable, there may be gains in meeting the Pareto conditions in some systems. Even if the sectors in which competition can be effectively induced are related to other, monopolistic areas, the gains may outweigh the losses. As one writer notes, if we desire efficient postal services, we are not as a matter of practical procedure likely to be inhibited by the fact that there may be monopoly in the production of pinwheels.[23]

There is a further difficulty with the idea that universal monopoly may be the second best of all possible worlds. This idea is based on the fact that if all industries are in some sense *equally* monopolistic, the ratio MC/P will be the same everywhere although marginal cost (MC) *exceeds* price (P) everywhere. The Pareto condition that the marginal rate of transformation between any two goods must equal the price ratio of the goods is then satisfied even though price does not equal marginal cost in the production of any good. The difficulty with this argument is seen by viewing leisure as an alternative to the production of any good.[24] The optimality requirement here is the same as it is between any two goods: the marginal rate of transformation (or marginal cost ratio) between leisure, L, and any good, X, must equal the ratio of their prices. Or,

$$MRT_{XL} = \frac{MC_L}{MC_X} = \frac{P_L}{P_X}$$

The "price" of leisure is simply the wage rate, w, thus:

$$\frac{MC_L}{MC_X} = \frac{w}{P_X}$$

But since the wage rate also measures the marginal cost of leisure (the cost of not working is the wage foregone), the price of good X must *equal* the marginal cost of good X for the above ratio of hold. Good X, which is *any* good, must thus be priced *at* marginal cost; that is, it must be produced under competitive conditions.

The theory of second best yields the same sort of implication as the idea of countervailing powers: it is wrong to suppose that more competition is always better than less competition even if universal competition is accepted as the ideal. Second best, however, does not provide an unqualified challenge to competition-promoting policies. Rather, it demands that we consider that policies aimed at one sector of the economy may yield results that are affected by the existence of imperfections elsewhere.

[23] Davis and Whinston, "Piecemeal Policy," *loc. cit.*

[24] For pertinent discussion, see Kelvin Lancaster, *Introduction to Modern Microeconomics*, Rand McNally, Chicago, 1969, pp. 270 ff.

F. Workable Competition

If we accept that pure or perfect competition is an unrealistic and in some circumstances an undesirable policy objective, the question becomes: what kind and degree of competition ought to be pursued? Presumably we should seek the best arrangement that is practically attainable. Rather than chasing perfection, we may aim for a market system that is *workably* competitive. Definitions of workable or effective competition represent efforts to provide a more meaningful and useful policy objective than can be drawn from the competitive ideal.

The notion of workable competition is present in the Chamberlinian view that an intermingling of competitive and monopolistic elements is a fact of economic life.[25] What is workable or effective is not some pure ideal that could never come about, but rather some compromise that includes imperfections. The father of the term workable competition, and the first developer of the idea, was Clark,[26] who noted that competition, which he defined as "rivalry in selling goods," depends on many conditions in the marketplace. As he pointed out, there are so many variables involved that there may be literally hundreds of thousands of combinations, each representing a different competitive state. In approaching workable competition Clark was careful to explain that his concept was not simply a close substitute for perfect competition, but might involve something very different:

One central point may be put abstractly. If there are, for example, five conditions, all of which are essential to perfect competition, and the first is lacking in a given case, then it no longer follows that we are necessarily better off for the presence of any one of the other four. In the absence of the first, it is a priori quite possible that the second and third may become positive detriments; and a workably satisfactory result may depend on achieving some degree of "imperfection" in these other two factors.[27]

Although Clark did not posit a single specific definition of workable competition, he did specify the following factors as prime ingredients: the existence of *uncertainty* about opponents' responses in small-group

[25] E. H. Chamberlin, *The Theory of Monopolistic Competition,* Harvard University Press, Cambridge, seventh edition, 1958.

[26] J. M. Clark, "Toward a Concept of Workable Competition," *American Economic Review*, 30, June 1940, pp. 241–56.

[27] *Ibid.*, p. 242. This statement has led C. E. Ferguson to believe "that Clark was among the first clearly to recognize the theory of second best." *A Macroeconomic Theory of Workable Competition*, Duke University Press, Durham, 1964, p. 27.

markets; a sufficiently steep demand curve that firms can cover their average costs; substitutability among various products; and potential competition as a threat to existing competitors. In later writings[28] Clark stressed that an important element of workability lies in the development within markets of various and improved products, and in the evolution of efficient production methods. He is careful to note, however, that these developments are not themselves sufficient; there must in addition be some force, part of the competitive process, that *diffuses* the benefits of new products and techniques throughout the economy. Moreover, Clark refuses to accept as satisfactory the "secure monopoly" that might perform well only as a matter of "its arbitrary choice."

No brief description can convey the range and richness of the ideas put forth by Clark. In his discussions of workable competition he set forth many of the criteria that today continue to influence thinking in this area. The workability of a competitive situation, he argued, has something to do with the kinds of *result* that the market arrives at. At the same time, competition cannot be fully described in terms of market results. It is a *process*, a struggle among competing units, and should "good" results occur without the struggle, this may not be sufficient to satisfy a workability criterion.

The Clark discussions raise basic questions about the very meaning of competition. Few individuals would disagree with Clark's characterization of competition as a process of rivalry, but there is no obvious or direct way of measuring the process. Even if it is agreed that competition is workable when rivalry is active, the activity is itself an elusive concept; and judgment of it is a subjective and impressionistic task.

One possibility is to consider competition in primarily *structural* terms. That is, we may attempt to describe the state of competition in a market by referring to some organizational characteristics of that market, such as the number and size of firms, the nature of the product, and the obstacles to entry by new firms. The structural approach defines competition indirectly, by describing those market conditions that are expected to influence the competitive process. In a market characterized by a few large firms, high entry barriers, and differentiated products, for example, we would anticipate oligopolistic—or, in broad terms, monopolistic—rivalry. The anticipation may be plausible even if we do not inquire more specifically into the nature of the struggle among the firms.

A second alternative view of competition stresses market results

[28] See, e.g., his "Competition: Static Models and Dynamic Aspects," *American Economic Review*, **45**, May 1955, pp. 453–57; and *Competition as a Dynamic Process*, Brookings, Washington, 1961.

or *performance;* for example, pricing patterns, profit rates, and innovation. Under this approach it can be argued that the proper test of the competitive process is its outcome. An industry should be termed monopolistic (or competitive) when it performs as a monopolistic (or competitive) industry would.

Finally, the suggestion has been made that competition might be defined partly in terms of firms' *conduct.* If the companies in a market make independent decisions, one conclusion about the state of competition follows, whereas an interdependent, perhaps collusive, decision process implies something very different. Focusing on the conduct or strategems of firms may represent an effort to measure the competitive struggle more directly than can be done by examining structure or performance. Although there may at times be visible clues to the severity of the competitive struggle, however, these may be few and far between.

Many writers since 1940 have attempted to formulate standards of workable competition in terms of structure and performance (and, to a lesser extent, conduct) variables. Among those tending toward the structuralist approach are Stigler[29] and Edwards.[30] Stigler proposes that an industry is workably competitive when: there is a considerable number of firms selling closely related products in each important market area; these firms are not in collusion; and the long-run average cost curve for a new firm is not materially higher than for an established firm (i.e., entry of new firms is relatively "easy" or "free"). Edwards presents a more extensive, but essentially similar, listing of workability criteria. What both are suggesting is that competition can be meaningfully described in largely structural terms, with the additional requirement that conduct be noncollusive.

Proposed standards for workable competition are numerous. An exhaustive review of the literature by Sosnick[31] cites, among others, the following common suggestions:

1. Conditions of structure:
    (a) Moderate and price-sensitive quality differentials.
    (b) No artificial handicaps on mobility.
    (c) Adequate access to information.
    (d) Some uncertainty about whether price reductions will be met.

---

[29] George J. Stigler, "The Extent and Bases of Monopoly," *American Economic Review*, 32, May 1942, pp. 1–22.

[30] Corwin D. Edwards, *Maintaining Competition*, McGraw-Hill, New York, 1949.

[31] Stephen H. Sosnick, "A Critique of Concepts of Workable Competition," *Quarterly Journal of Economics*, 72, August 1958, pp. 380–423.

2. Conditions of conduct:
   (a) Firms should not shield permanently inefficient rivals, suppliers or customers.
   (b) There should be no unfair, exclusionary, predatory, or coercive tactics.
   (c) Sales promotion should not be misleading.
3. Conditions of performance:
   (a) Efficiency in operations.
   (b) Promotional expenses should not be excessive.
   (c) Profits should reach levels that reward investment and efficiency and induce innovation.
   (d) Output should be consistent with a good allocation of resources.
   (e) Quality should conform to consumers' interests.
   (f) Opportunities for better products and techniques should not be ignored.
   (g) Conservation should not be disregarded.

These proposed criteria of workable competition are among those mentioned most frequently by writers on the subject. There is, as Sosnick points out, some clustering of proposals, that is, some agreement that certain attributes are relevant. At the same time, there is considerable diversity in the views expressed. Some observers stress workable market structures, while others place a higher priority on performance or conduct. Few have actually suggested, however, that workable competition can be defined adequately within any single category. Many would agree with Sosnick that performance is of ultimate importance in the economy, and that the primary question we ought to ask about competition is: what do we want it to *do* for us? Like Sosnick and Clark, however, few would accept a *pure* performance criterion of workability. As Lewis puts it:

Results alone throw no light on the really significant question: have these results been *compelled* by the system—by *competition*—or do they represent simply the dispensations of managements which, with a wide latitude of policy choices at their disposal, happened at the moment to be benevolent or "smart"? This points up the real issue.[32]

In a sense, then, we demand not only good performance, but good performance for the right reasons. The well-behaved monopolist may, like the benevolent despot, perform splendidly; but if he does so at his own discretion, society cannot be certain that a similarly good record will

[32] Ben W. Lewis, in "The Effectiveness of the Federal Antitrust Laws: A Symposium," Dexter M. Keezer, editor, *American Economic Review*, **39**, June 1949, pp. 706–707, italics in original.

continue in the future. Structure or conduct norms, however, are also not fully acceptable, in part because they may not imply satisfactory performance.

The categories of structure, conduct, and performance are related. Certain market structures are associated with particular patterns of conduct and performance; specific types of conduct bear on performance; and performance may influence both structure and conduct. But these relationships are not necessarily precise and are not well defined. A comprehensive definition of workable competition, even in the broadest terms, is thus difficult to formulate. Certain aspects of structure, conduct, and performance may seem desirable, but the ordering of these aspects by degree of importance and the resolution of conflicts among them present us with difficult dilemmas.

If we attempt to define in more specific terms the market conditions that imply a satisfactory level of competition, further problems arise. Suppose, for example, there is general agreement that innovation is an important aspect of workability; that is, for a market to be judged effectively competitive it must demonstrate an acceptable rate of development and introduction of new processes and products. The first problem is how to measure these magnitudes, but assuming that meaningful observations of inventiveness are possible, a fundamental difficulty remains. This is simply the *assessment* of what is observed. What constitutes a "good" innovative record? Against what standard can it be measured? It is not only conceivable but highly probable that different individuals will evaluate a given set of observations in different ways. The problem of evaluation is one that runs through all criteria of workability. What is meant by a "considerable" number of firms? by an "efficient" productive operation? by "independence" in firm policy making? Without answers to such questions there is no way to form judgments of industries. The most common notions of workable competition, although they specify the relevant *dimensions* of workability, do not generally tell us how acceptable levels of these dimensions are to be defined.

A newer approach to workable competition has been suggested by Markham, who states:

An industry may be judged to be workably competitive when, after the structural characteristics of its market and the dynamic forces that shaped them have been thoroughly examined, there is no clearly indicated change that can be effected through public policy measures that would result in greater social gains than social losses.[33]

[33] Jesse W. Markham, "An Alternative Approach to the Concept of Workable Competition," *American Economic Review*, **40**, June 1950, p. 361.

Markham's view is essentially pragmatic, and contains two important virtues. First, it makes clear that there can be no uniform standard of workability applicable to all industries. What is workable in one set of circumstances may be wholly unacceptable in another. This might mean, for example, that a particular rate of innovation would be satisfactory in an industry in which the state of the arts is not conducive to new developments, but unsatisfactory when existing technology and the nature of products and processes seem to invite innovation.

The second, and perhaps most useful, aspect of the Markham definition is that it requires no subjective assessment of what is good or bad in the structure, conduct and performance of industries. Rather than whether the various characteristics of a market are good, the relevant question becomes: are these characteristics *improvable* by public policy? An industry that everyone agrees is well behaved will not be judged workably competitive under Markham's approach if public action could force it to behave still better. Similarly, an industry that appears to do poorly by accepted standards might be found workably competitive if no public policy offered hope of improvement.

Despite these virtues, newer formulations of workable competition such as Markham's suffer from much the same difficulty that has plagued earlier definitions. Lacking precise and agreed-on criteria, definitions of workability often are tautological; they tend to be redundant, stated in such a way that the definition adds relatively little to the meaning of the term. To say, for example, that workable competition requires a considerable number of firms is not much different from saying that workable competition requires a workable number of firms. As Ben W. Lewis has stated more generally: "Workable competition is competition that works."

The tautological nature of many definitions of workable competition does not mean that the concept is a useless one. In the first place the definitions are not usually *pure* tautology. Specifying the dimensions of workability—number of firms, innovation and profit rates, and so on—is itself an addition to knowledge. It is also possible that in some cases agreement on the ranges of workable values in the various dimensions will be possible. Ultimately, however, the question of what is and is not workably competitive depends on subjective judgments. The notion of workable competition may therefore be useful not so much as a guide—for it cannot easily surmount this dependence—but rather for the questions it *raises*. The idea of workable competition, however vague it may be, makes it clear that those concerned with public policy must decide what is important. Given an imperfect world, there is a need for priorities. We cannot have everything, therefore we must define what it is that we can attain and what we are willing to settle for. Mere invocation of the words workable competition will not provide us with a specific idea of appropriate policies, but the term does help to focus attention on the problems that must be resolved.

G. Summary

Modern interpretations of the market system vary widely in the roles they assign to competition and monopoly, and indeed in the very meanings they assign to these terms. There is general agreement that competition in the strict sense of a pure or perfect market system cannot be achieved, but the status of pure or perfect competition as a norm for public policy is still debated. In the view of some, the competitive norm is not merely an anachronism but a positive danger; it is not simply an unattainable ideal, but one the pursuit of which is likely to leave society worse off.

Certainly the economist's strict definition of competition appears in some ways an awkward device with which to guide a modern and complex economy, almost like trying to build a structure with an incomplete set of parts. It is widely but not universally agreed that the structure would be desirable if it could be completed; but with parts missing it is not clear whether we would be better off with the partial structure or with some different structure that, although not so desirable as the original, could at least be completed. Ought we to aim for perfection everywhere, knowing that this structure will contain many gaps? Or should we build something entirely different?

Competition as a theoretical construct has a clear meaning, but it is evident that the kind of competition toward which we may reasonably aspire in practice is not an unambiguous concept. There is even disagreement as to whether the theoretical construct is relevant to the real world of policy formulation. Under the circumstances it should not be surprising to find that our attitudes toward public competition policy are ill defined.

6

Competition Theory and Policy: Some Implications

Barring Utopia, the basic economic problem of all societies is much the same: human beings need or want more than they can have, and a way must be found to use limited resources to obtain the best level of satisfaction. One framework within which decisions about resource utilization can be made is the private-enterprise system. As we have seen, the rationale for such a system is closely related to the optimality of resource allocation that competitive markets tend to yield. Few individuals, however, would insist on the laissez faire view that such a system is capable of running itself. Evidence of imperfection is abundant, and the vulnerability of the system to distortion and abuse is widely recognized. This is the general rationale for government intervention in economic matters. When the system is abused or does not run smoothly, government as the representative of the people enters to protect society's welfare.

In the United States governmental intervention in the economy takes many forms and is justified by a wide variety of special circumstances. Certain activities (e.g., national defense) are handled by the government because they present problems that are not amenable to market-type solutions. Other activities may be subsidized positively or negatively by government because there is reason to expect that the market will chronically misestimate their benefits or costs (for example, it is thought that the market would underestimate the value of education and thus produce too little; similarly, it would underestimate the cost of air pollution and thus produce too much). Antitrust—or, more precisely, public competition—policy[1] is one of the more inherently conservative forms of governmental intervention. It does not attempt to substitute social preferences for those of the private market, nor does it alter private valuations by subsidization or taxation of activities. To the contrary, antitrust policy is intended to preserve the conditions under which the private market functions best. It is designed to protect an environment in which individual judgment reigns.

Accordingly, the attention of antitrust focuses primarily on areas of the economy in which the market system is thought to be workable. It is obvious, however, that even here market conditions do not conform to a strict competitive ideal, and that public policy has not attempted to implement the ideal. This suggests that for some reason or reasons a clear theoretical conclusion about the desirability of competition has not been capable of straightforward translation into public policy. This difficulty is not surprising in light of challenges to the competitive norm such as those discussed in Chapter 5. In considering the reasons why theory has not provided a clear and detailed blueprint for policies toward competition, it may be helpful to note the following general positions:

1. The theoretical superiority of competition is logically established, but is irrelevant for policy because of the extremely restrictive assumptions under which the conclusion of superiority is reached. Policy makers cannot ignore the potential benefits of monopoly and costs of competition that exist in the real world simply because such ignorance makes abstract analysis easier.

2. The conclusion of competitive superiority is useful for policy in some circumstances, but is limited by the fact that the theoretical apparatus does not tell us enough. We know, for example, that pure competition is preferred to other market forms; but there is little in the theory that would indicate which among numberless imperfect alternatives we ought to prefer.

3. The superiority of competition is established. What is not established is how much this kind of superiority means to us as a society. The problem of translating theory to policy lies not so much in the inadequacies of the theory as it does in our inability to decide what is and is not important.

---

[1] The term "antitrust" is something of a misnomer today. A trust is a legal arrangement that was widely utilized in the nineteenth century by business rivals who wished to avoid competition and to pursue common policies. Statutes designed to re-establish competition and prevent the spread of such arrangements were thus called *antitrust* laws, and the term persists, although the applicability of the laws is much broader.

Each of these positions may have some claim to truth. For various reasons the theoretical superiority of competition does not imply a ready-made prescription for public policies. This failure indicates immediately that the role of theoretical conclusions in policy formulation is inherently limited. For the present, at least, we cannot simply take economic models, plug in real-world values, and expect to derive optimal policies.

What, then, is the role of economic theory in antitrust? Most broadly, the theory contributes a series of data or clues as to what may occur when certain dimensions of firms and markets are altered. That is, the theory associates a number of characteristics with expectations—albeit imprecise expectations—about firm and market behavior. Public policy can in some ways influence these characteristics, and the primary role of economic analysis is to provide predictions about the consequences of alternative policy actions. We know, for example, that behavior depends to some degree on the concentration of power among firms in a market. Accordingly, it should be possible to say something about the behavioral consequences of policies that affect the concentration of power.

There are a number of characteristics in addition to power concentration that may be termed policy variables; that is, they are amenable to policy manipulation. Given some notion of the kinds of goals we would like to attain, it may be possible to define (at least roughly) the policy manipulations that are most likely to be successful. Is the kind of market behavior that we desire, for example, associated with a high degree of market concentration? If so, there are policy moves that will tend to produce the concentration levels that are thought to be appropriate. Does market performance deteriorate when firms conspire? If so, it may be possible through public action to prevent conspiracy from occurring.

In practice, the issues that come before policy makers are likely to be narrower: will the merger of two large steel producers, for example, have a significant impact on the structure of the steel industry? And if so, is the implication for industry performance such that the merger ought to be prohibited?

The role that is envisioned here for economic analysis is both important and limited. It is important in that governments—state as well as federal—continually make decisions that will affect the future organization of markets. Even something as seemingly far-removed as the awarding of defense contracts, for example, may determine the size structure of a defense-oriented industry. In choosing among alternatives, the theoretical apparatus may yield very helpful information about the economic effects that will result.

Limitations on the role of theory arise for two general reasons. The first is that theory alone may not be capable of answering many questions. The merger of the steel companies, for example, could have several effects. It might increase the efficiency of the merged firm; but it might also increase concentration and affect the condition of entry into the industry for new firms. The likelihood of these possibilities and the importance of each are not questions that can be answered adequately on the basis of abstract reasoning. It is necessary to estimate the relevant magnitudes, to lend empirical content to the possibilities suggested by the analysis. The role of theory in antitrust is, then, largely informational; and the information provided tends to be incomplete. The clues and suggestions to be drawn from theoretical constructs are valuable; but those who might expect to derive categorical policy statements are likely to be disappointed.

A second restriction on the role of theory in policy making is that the definition of desired goals cannot be aided by objective analysis. To this point we have referred to *appropriate* or *desirable* policies as if the meanings of the words presented no difficulty. In fact this is hardly the case. If policy goals are well defined, it is still necessary to determine what policies will satisfy the goals, and such a determination may prove to be difficult. The situation is compounded, however, when—as in antitrust —the definition of objectives is itself unclear. There is nothing in economic analysis that can help much with this problem. Our theoretical structures can illuminate the implications of alternative policy moves, or, perhaps more frequently, suggest ways in which we can test for implications. But there is nothing in objective analysis that can tell us what our goals *ought* to be.

The definition of policy goals seems to be especially difficult in antitrust. Broadly speaking, of course, the goals are little different from the general economic and political objectives of society. Antitrust seeks to promote economic progress and efficiency and to protect individual liberty and freedom of choice. Many governmental policies are designed to encourage precisely the same things.

What is unique to antitrust is the lower-order, more immediate objective, which serves as the means to the final ends. The proximate objective is to maintain a competitive market system, in the belief that such a system ultimately yields progress, efficiency, and freedom. But although it is easy to *list* these noble aims, with which no one is likely to disagree, such a listing does not represent a meaningful definition of objectives. A meaningful definition must go beyond general enumeration of goals to: state specifically what is meant by each; and specify the *relative importance* of each.

A hypothetical example may be helpful. Suppose it were agreed that technical efficiency and limitations on economic power are the only goals of antitrust policy. By itself this statement does not tell us very much about what antitrust ought to do. Perhaps there is one set of policy moves that will increase efficiency and another that will increase power limitations. The two goals cannot be simultaneously maximized. If we take steps to advance efficiency we will necessarily ignore other steps that would have limited power. What is the proper mixture of policy steps? There is no way to be sure, so long as we have specified only that we are concerned with both objectives.

Suppose we now go a bit further and specify that efficiency is to be the primary objective. This is more helpful since it tells us that efficiency-increasing moves are to be more heavily emphasized than moves that limit power, but there is still an area of ignorance. We do not yet know *how much more* efficiency is to be stressed relative to power limits. Should we devote 51 percent of our resources to efficiency-promoting policies and 49 percent to policies that limit power? Or is the proper ratio 75–25 or 90–10? The two objectives are competitive in that both require resources. They may also compete in the more direct sense that policies that create efficiency simultaneously increase power (i.e., decrease its limits). In any event, to get more efficiency we must give up some limit on power and vice versa.

In order to pursue the best possible policy we need some further guidance. Specifically, we need to know the following.

1. The actual trade-offs between efficiency and retardation of power; that is, the amount of one that must be sacrificed in order to obtain some specified incremental amount of the other. We must determine, in other words, the price or marginal cost of each characteristic in terms of the other.
2. A more precise statement of our relative preferences. That is, how much is efficiency *worth* to us in terms of lesser restraints on power, and vice versa?

Stated in this way our knowledge requirements are clearly demanding. Indeed, it can hardly be surprising that economic analysis fails to provide a blueprint for public policy. At best, our theoretical framework can do little more than show us what kinds of variables to examine, and to give us an idea of what kinds of relationships to expect. We know, for example, that when economies of scale are important there is likely to be a direct conflict between our interest in efficiency and our interest in restraining power. To get greater efficiency we may have to accept a high concentration of power; but to restrain power we may have to give up efficiency.

This much may be drawn from the theory, but it is now evident that the knowledge we require for policy purposes is much broader. What economics must do to assist the antitrust policy maker is, most basically, to price his alternatives; that is, to specify the price (or cost) of any policy in terms of alternatives foregone. Do we wish more efficiency? Certainly! But this does not necessarily mean that we will pay any price, in terms of increased power or something else, in order to get it.[2] A prime objective of the economist is to define for the policy maker the price of efficiency, or any other objective. This presupposes an ability to predict the effects of policy moves on both the objective in question and its alternatives.[3]

There is no question that economic theory itself cannot provide the necessary information. It should in fact be obvious that the kind of information we lack can be obtained only by measuring relevant magnitudes. Theory may suggest, for example, that high market concentration could imply both an efficiency gain and a welfare loss. If we wish to formulate policies toward a particular market, however, the theoretical suggestion does not tell us what to do. Is existing concentration such that an increase (or decrease) would imply relatively large losses or relatively large gains? There is no substitute for empirical estimates of these magnitudes. For this reason it is necessary to consider in some detail the approaches to and problems of empirical measurement.

[2] The analogy to the consumer should be an obvious one. Perhaps each of us would like to own a new Cadillac. But will each of us buy one? Such a question simply cannot be answered without specifying the price of the car. At current prices relatively few individuals purchase Cadillacs, but imagine the demand for such automobiles if the price were, say, $100! (Of course, there are probably some Cadillac owners who would get rid of their cars if "anyone" could afford to buy one!)

[3] This ability would contribute to knowledge under (1) above; it would not, however, clarify the preference information requirement of (2).

PART II

Empirical Problems and Evidence

The ultimate test of an economic theory is its ability to predict or explain actual events. A theory may be subtle, sophisticated, and even intrinsically interesting, but if it can do nothing to help us understand "the way things are," its usefulness is limited. The usefulness of the body of economic theory discussed in Part I to public competition policy depends to an extent on its ability to meet such a test. This is so if only because the direct inferences of theory for policy are both incomplete and somewhat ambiguous. It would be extremely difficult to formulate a public policy on the basis of our current theoretical understanding of the workings of markets, and there is a clear need for further clues.

A wide variety of empirical methods is employed in testing economic theories. The suggestions of theory are used to explain or predict observed behavior, and attempts then are made to determine whether and in what way the theoretical explanation works. If the explanation does work, the theory is supported or verified. If it does not—and if we are satisfied that our specification of relationships, observations of reality, and methods of testing are correct—it may be considered an invalid explanation, one that is rejected on the basis of the evidence.

There are several steps in the empirical testing process. First it is

131

necessary to select meaningful suggestions from the theory and to formulate them carefully. These suggestions, usually termed hypotheses, are the explanations or predictions of events that we draw from the theory and wish to verify or reject. The hypotheses must be developed into testable propositions, statements that can be measured against observed events. For example, we might make the statement, "Large firms innovate more than small firms." This is a general assertion that needs further specification, but it is potentially testable. What is needed is some measure of firm size and of innovation.

Suppose that the statement had instead been, "Oligopolists charge higher prices than firms in competitive markets." This statement is again testable in principle; however, it may turn out to be a less useful hypothesis in terms of our ability to apply meaningful tests. We could formulate some index of "competitiveness" and "oligopolisticness," apply it to various firms, and examine the prices they charge. But the prices charged depend so heavily on other factors, such as cost and demand conditions, that we may not be able to isolate that part of the price variation that is attributable to the difference in the nature of the markets. The statement is in fact so imprecisely framed that it is not useful. It would be better as, "Oligopolists charge higher prices than they would under competitive market conditions, other factors remaining constant."

Still other statements may not even be susceptible in principle to empirical verification. If we state, for example, "Large firms try harder to maximize profits than small firms," there is probably no meaningful way to proceed, for "trying hard" is not something that can be readily measured in an objective way.

Once a hypothesis is framed in a testable fashion, numerous data problems may arise. Measures of relevant magnitudes may be unavailable. The variables that *are* measurable may be conceptually less than ideal, and a host of measurement difficulties may cause an investigator to question the accuracy of the information that is utilized. A thorny problem in empirical investigation often is involved in the decision as to whether available data are "good enough" to permit meaningful tests of hypotheses. Here an element of subjective judgment may be unavoidable.

A final problem in the process of hypothesis testing is the selection of an appropriate methodology. This refers in part to the problems already noted: specification of the hypothesis and assembly of data.

It also pertains to the type of statistical tests that will be applied to the data. Many methods exist for determining the relationships among two or more variables, and it is necessary to select those that are conceptually appropriate to the problem at hand.

Obviously the subjection of theoretical propositions to empirical tests can be a difficult and tricky job, one that often requires a thorough understanding of statistical techniques. Not the least of the task, however, lies in the initial choice of problems to be studied. It is necessary to develop hypotheses that are not only susceptible to empirical techniques, but are also meaningful and of some general interest. In short, a sound conceptual basis is required. Aimless hunting for correlations among variables is likely to add nothing to our knowledge.

The question of what constitutes an ''interesting'' problem or hypothesis cannot be answered with complete objectivity. In the area of industrial organization interests tend to be policy oriented. The selection of problems for study therefore depends in part on the presence of implications for public competition policy. But what is important for policy in turn depends on what the actual or ideal goals of policy are seen to be. Since individuals hold different views, we should expect some disagreement about what constitute the most pressing empirical questions. It appears, however, that the attention of economists in industrial organization focuses on a rather well-defined subset of problems having to do with the behavior of firms and industries.

This section reviews the nature of measurement difficulties and some of the empirical evidence on firm and industry behavior. It should be recognized—as we stressed earlier—that the role of the evidence is purely informational. It can yield some hints of the economic consequences of alternative policies, but it cannot define for us what an appropriate or ideal policy is.

7

The Conceptual Problem: Deciding What to Measure

There is no scarcity of interesting hypotheses in industrial organization. Economic theory engenders expectations about the behavior of firms and markets that form the basis for many potentially testable statements; and tests of such statements often provide information that is pertinent to public competition policy. The formulation of a testable hypothesis requires initially that variables relevant to the hypothesis be defined. That is, it is necessary to identify the kinds of magnitude that need to be measured in order to examine the validity of the idea in question. Initially the task is largely conceptual, involving specification of what ought to be measured. More practical problems concerning the nature of available data must also be considered; however, it is sometimes useful first to define the ideal measures, and to isolate partially the problem of what measures are actually possible.

What kinds of hypotheses ought we to test? There are of course no rigid rules. In the industrial organization area policy interests may lead most frequently to hypotheses seeking to explain the behavior of firms and industries. An important policy objective is to secure the kinds of economic results that we consider desirable; accordingly, it is necessary to determine what factors are associated with the desirable behavior patterns.

Our theoretical structures are very helpful in this regard. It is clear, for example, that an industry that is competitive in the strict sense is expected to act somewhat differently than one that is monopolistic. Should an industry contain elements of both competition and monopoly—and this is almost always so—expectations about its behavior may be less precise. But even here it may be possible to formulate some expectation in terms of the degree to which the industry deviates from truly competitive or monopolistic conditions. The important point is that the way in which firms and industries function has something to do with the *state of competition* present. Moreover, it is precisely this element of the economy with which our antitrust laws are designed to deal. Other factors will certainly influence performance, but it is the state of competition that stands as a theoretically important determinant that is also amenable to policy control.

The first problem, then, concerns the ways in which the competitive status of an industry can be described and measured. We may expect that competitive and monopolistic industries will perform in different ways, but in order to test specific hypotheses we must be able to decide which industries fit various categories. At the extremes the question may prove to be relatively easy, but for mixed cases, in which elements of competition and monopoly coexist, it becomes more troublesome. What is necessary for the mixed category is a measure or measures of the degree of competition or monopoly present. Clearly, such measures, even if they are perfect, cannot imply the end of our conceptual problems. But if the degree of competition in markets can be described meaningfully, some useful predictions about behavior become possible.

Unfortunately, the measurement of competition and monopoly is not a straightforward problem. No single variable or group of variables is appropriate in all situations. The dimensions of the problem are easily seen if we consider a simple question: What should one look at to determine how competitive (monopolistic) an industry is? The basic question is: What do we mean by a competitive (monopolistic) industry? Referring back to earlier definitions, it can be seen that various answers may exist. The purely or perfectly competitive industry, for example, can be described in alternative ways:

1. As a situation in which no single firm has any control over the terms at which it supplies the market—that is, no power over price.

2. As a situation that yields a particular market *result*: namely, production at minimum average cost, price equality with marginal cost, and the absence of long-run profits.

3. The structural set of conditions that implies situations 1 and 2: a large number of firms, product homogeneity, and free entry and exit.

The alternative definitions of a competitive market suggest three possible ways of approaching the degree of competition or monopoly in an industry. First, we could attempt to measure directly the pricing *power* of constituent firms. A second approach would attempt to measure the *performance* of the firm and market, reasoning, for example, that a monopolistic market is best defined as one that performs as we would expect a monopoly to perform. Finally, a widely utilized approach would measure elements of market *structure*. This would permit some conclusions about the organizational environment in which firms operate, and yield some clues to the degree of market power that is present and the type of performance that may be expected.

As is often true in economics, the desirability of a particular approach depends heavily on the type of problem that is under investigation. Each of the possibilities noted above has a number of general shortcomings, however, that may influence their potential usefulness:

1. Measures of market power—that is, firms' power over price—may be conceptually desirable but practically difficult to obtain. Such measurement often involves definition of firms' demand curves, a task that presents serious problems especially in small-group markets.

2. Measures of market performance are likely to be easier; but *interpreting* what has been measured is extremely difficult; moreover, performance is not usually vulnerable to direct policy control.

3. Measures of market structure are again relatively easy to obtain, although it may be hard to determine what sorts of measures are most appropriate. An important problem with structural measures is that the precision of predictions may be unsatisfactory for many problems; it is not always possible to draw accurate inferences about market power and performance from structural variables.

There is now an obvious quandary. It might be possible to proceed simultaneously on all fronts, and to measure everything that could conceivably have meaning for the state of competition or monopoly. Such a process, however, would at best involve some waste of effort. The immediate problem is where to begin. To answer this question, it is helpful to consider again *why* it is that we are interested in measuring such things as monopoly and competition. From an economic point of view, the significant test of an economy (or of the markets within an economy) is whether it secures for us the sort of results that are desired. This central concern indicates that our ultimate interest must have something to do with economic *performance*. Consequently, our interest in measuring the state of competition and monopoly is, at least in part, performance oriented.

As we have seen, the performance orientation of our interests implies a strong reason to discover what *determines* performance patterns, and especially to identify determinants that are amenable to public policy influence. Since performance is not subject to direct policy control, discussions of competition and monopoly often proceed in terms of market power and market structure. It is here that we may find clues to the nature of performance that will in addition point to the policy approaches appropriate to improving future patterns.

A. Theoretical Indices of Competition and Monopoly: The Power of Firms

The most direct way of measuring the degree of monopoly or competition focuses on the power of firms within relevant industry groupings. In some areas firms have little control over the price they charge. Any deviation from the market-determined level is likely to prove impractical. In such circumstances the firms may be termed *powerless*, a condition in accord with our idea of pure competition. In most markets, however, some leeway exists. Firms can get away with lesser or greater pricing deviations, and are thus said to hold power or control over price—a condition associated with economic notions of monopoly.[1]

The first difficulty in attempting to measure this kind of control is the fact that it is not one-dimensional. That is, there is no *single* magnitude that comprehensively reflects market power. The problem has been compared by Chamberlin to that of measuring a person's health: "Some aspects of health can be measured and others cannot. Among the former we have body temperature, blood pressure, metabolism, weight, etc. But these do not lend themselves to the construction of a *single* quantitative index of health."[2] It turns out that a number of

---

[1] Readers may observe a conceptual difficulty even here, however. For given demand and cost curves there exists (in all likelihood) only one profit-maximizing price. If the firm is a maximizer, it has pricing "leeway" only in the sense that its position is not enforced by the market. That is, the firm's decision to maximize is itself a matter of choice; once this decision is made, however, the firm's appropriate behavior is closely prescribed by market forces.

[2] Edward H. Chamberlin, "Measuring the Degree of Competition and Monopoly," in E. H. Chamberlin, editor, *Monopoly and Competition and Their Regulation*, Macmillan, London, 1954, p. 267.

practical measures, while providing useful clues to the state of monopoly, cannot be taken as definitive statements. Further, there exist measures that are potentially useful but are impractical because of difficulties in quantifying the relevant magnitudes. Economists have expended considerable effort in trying to define meaningful indices of competition and monopoly, and the results, although not fully satisfactory, include several valuable suggestions.

1. SIMPLE MEASURES OF ELASTICITY

The degree of pricing power held by a firm obviously depends in some way on the shape of its demand curve. The most convenient way of characterizing the curve is by its price *elasticity*—that is, the extent to which quantity demanded responds to price changes made by the firm. The price elasticity of demand for a product, X, is defined as

$$\frac{\% \text{ change in quantity demanded of } X}{\% \text{ change in price of } X}$$

The fraction ordinarily has a negative sign, since price *increases* lead to quantity *decreases* and vice versa.[3]

This simple measure of quantity responsiveness to price provides one clue to the pricing power of the firm. The more inelastic (less elastic) the firm's demand curve, the more power or control over price the firm may be said to possess. This is true in the sense that the firm is freer to manipulate its price without regard to implications for the quantities demanded. In the case of a *perfectly inelastic* demand curve, as shown in

[3] To compute the elasticity of a demand curve, the following formula is derived:

$$E = -\frac{\% \, \Delta Q}{\% \, \Delta P} = -\frac{\Delta Q/Q_o}{\Delta P/P_o} = -\frac{\Delta Q}{\Delta P} \times \frac{P_o}{Q_o}$$

Where E is elasticity; ΔQ and ΔP are changes in quantity and price; and Q_o and P_o are original quantity and price. This formula is used to compute the *arc elasticity*, the average elasticity of some segment of the curve. Such a measure may be adequate when the arc in question is relatively small. It is often desirable to compute elasticity for a *point* on a demand curve by examining the response of quantity demanded to an infinitesimally small price change. The formula for point elasticity is:

$$E = -\frac{dQ}{dP} \times \frac{P_o}{Q_o}$$

where dP is an infinitesimal change in price and dQ is the response of quantity demanded.

Figure 7.1*a*, the firm has complete pricing control. Given demand curve *DD′*, it can charge any price it wishes without affecting the quantity it is able to sell. The opposite extreme of a *perfectly* or *infinitely elastic* demand curve—as shown in Figure 7.1*b*—occurs, it may be recalled, in the case of a firm in pure or perfect competition. Such a firm, confronting demand curve *DD′*, faces the ultimate in price sensitivity in that the slightest price increase will result in the loss of all sales.

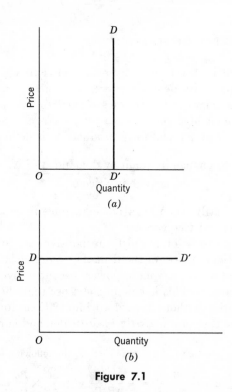

Figure 7.1

Although demand elasticity tells us something about pricing control, it is neither a sufficient nor an especially convenient index of monopoly power when considered alone. In the first place, the elasticity values may not be readily translatable into degrees of monopoly. It is true that in pure competition elasticity is infinite; however, there is no corresponding value for the case of pure monopoly. The monopolist's demand elasticity is simply that of the industry. The firm and industry demand curves are identical. For any firm, price elasticity of demand measures a combination of two factors: industry demand elasticity, a function of consumer preferences for the products of the industry, and the closeness of substitute products outside the industry; and the firm's power within the industry. Conceivably such a hybrid measure may be appropriate for many problems, but it is likely that there will also be instances when our concern is primarily with market dominance, abstracting from consumer preferences and the closeness of other markets.

Measures of price elasticity of demand also ignore certain factors that may be important to the market power of firms. Demand curves are constructed under a *ceteris paribus* assumption that holds constant the prices of other commodities (among other factors). It may be, however, that a firm that has considerable pricing power within its defined market when other things are equal, will nevertheless be affected by changes in the price of other goods. A second type of elasticity measure can be used to describe this sensitivity. This is the *cross-elasticity* of demand, which measures the effect on the quantity demanded of one commodity of changes in the price of another commodity. If we wish to describe the impact on sales of good X when the price of good Y changes, we can examine:

$$\text{Cross elasticity of demand} = \frac{\Delta Q_X}{\Delta P_Y} \times \frac{P_Y}{Q_X}$$

This in effect measures the percentage change in demand for $X (\Delta Q_X / Q_X)$ that results from some percentage change in the price of $Y (\Delta P_Y / P_Y)$.

Measures of price elasticity and cross-elasticity of demand provide a conceptually simple means of looking at the pricing power of a firm. A firm facing an inelastic demand curve may possess—given the absence of high cross-elasticities with other products—considerable leeway in setting its price. On the other hand, a firm whose demand curve is highly elastic—or that sells a product highly cross-elastic with other items— may be closely constrained in its pricing policies by the existence of competing products. These measures are useful. However, it cannot be assumed that they convey all the information relevant to an assessment of degree of monopoly power. Moreover, observation of actual elasticity magnitudes is ordinarily a complex and difficult task.

2. THE LERNER INDEX OF MONOPOLY

Lerner proposed in 1934 a measure of monopoly that is related to price elasticity of demand.[4] Noting that "the mark of the absence of monopoly

[4] Abba P. Lerner, "The Concept of Monopoly and the Measurement of Monopoly Power," *Review of Economic Studies*, I, June 1934, pp. 157–75.

is the equality of price or *average* receipts to marginal cost,"[5] Lerner suggested that monopoly be measured by the extent of divergence of price from marginal cost. Specifically, the Lerner index is defined as:

$$\frac{\text{Price} - \text{Marginal cost}}{\text{Price}}$$

In pure competition price equals marginal cost and the value of the index is zero. The greater the ability of the firm to price above marginal cost, the higher the value of the Lerner index, and the greater the degree of monopoly inferred.

The relation of the Lerner index to demand elasticity is evident when we consider ordinary demand and cost functions. For a given marginal cost curve, the extent to which the price charged by a firm can exceed marginal cost—that is, the vertical distance between price and marginal cost—will have something to do with the shape of the demand curve. Yet price elasticity also has something to do with the shape of the demand curve. It turns out that for firms *in equilibrium*, the index is precisely the reciprocal of the price elasticity of demand,[6] a situation Lerner treats as a special case.

The Lerner index is conceptually appropriate for a wide range of welfare problems. By examining the extent of deviation from optimal (marginal cost) pricing, it serves as a gauge of exercised, as opposed to potential, market power, and measures the social cost or harm of monopoly. Attempts to apply the Lerner index have yielded only limited results,[7] however, largely because of the difficulty of estimating actual cost and demand functions.

[5] *Ibid.*, p. 161.

[6] At equilibrium marginal revenue equals marginal cost; thus the Lerner index can be written $\dfrac{P - MR}{P}$. But it can be shown that price elasticity of demand is equal to $\dfrac{P}{P - MR}$. See, e.g., George J. Stigler, *The Theory of Price*, Macmillan, New York, third edition, 1966, pp. 333 ff.

[7] For an effort to apply the index to the economy as a whole, see M. Kalecki, "The Determinants of the Distribution of the National Income," *Econometrica*, 6, 1938, pp. 97–112. This effort is criticized in R. H. Whitman, "A Note on the Concept of 'Degree of Monopoly,'" *Economic Journal*, LI, June–September 1941, pp. 216–269. An attempt to apply the index to individual industries is provided by John T. Dunlop, "Price Flexibility and the 'Degree of Monopoly,'" *Quarterly Journal of Economics*, LIII, August 1939, pp. 522–533. See also Rufus S. Tucker, "The Degree of Monopoly," *Quarterly Journal of Economics*, LIV, November 1940, pp. 167–169.

3. THE BAIN INDEX OF MONOPOLY

Bain has suggested measuring the degree of monopoly power by referring to the rate of profit,[8] reasoning that the existence of *persistent excess* profits in a market is likely to reflect monopolistic elements. The Bain index is initially appealing because profit data are more readily available than estimates of price elasticity of demand or marginal costs. One difficulty, however, is that excess of pure economic profits are not the same thing as the accounting profits reported by firms. In Bain's words, "accounting profit is 'not all profit' in the economic sense."[9] The former refers simply to total revenues minus allocable current cost minus allocable past cost (depreciation and amortization). To obtain the measure of excess profit, it also is necessary to take account of the normal profit, which Bain defines as the *alternative* or *opportunity cost* of investment, that is, the receipts foregone because business owners' investment cannot earn a return elsewhere. Bain defines accounting profit as $R - C - D$, where R is total receipts, C is current costs, and D is depreciation; economic or excess profit is then

$$R - C - D - iV$$

where V is the value of owners' investment and i is the rate of return this investment could earn if it were not tied up in its present use.

The profit rate is in effect a measure of the deviation of price from average cost, and may thus appear similar to the Lerner index. There is, however, a fundamental difference between the two. The Bain profit index of monopoly is a less certain measure than either the Lerner index or measures of price elasticity. The reason for this relative uncertainty is clear when it is recalled that although a pure or partial monopolist *may* earn persistent excess profits, such profits are not inevitable. The partial monopolist in the Chamberlin model, for example, earns zero excess profits in the long run. More generally, no monopolistic firm can earn better than normal profits if sufficient demand for the product does not exist. There is absolutely no reason why profits would accrue to a monopolist of some product that consumers do not desire. The Bain index is therefore uncertain in the following sense: a high rate of excess profits persisting over a reasonably long period, may well reflect the presence of

[8] Joe S. Bain, "The Profit Rate as a Measure of Monopoly Power," *Quarterly Journal of Economics*, **LV**, February 1941, pp. 271–92.

[9] Joe S. Bain, *Industrial Organization*, Wiley, New York, 1959, p. 365

monopoly power, but the absence of excess profits does not necessarily mean that no monopoly power is present. The index, then, fails to distinguish between some competitive and some monopoly cases. It tells us something about the *likelihood* of monopoly power in an industry, but is not a direct or definitive measure.

4. THE ROTHSCHILD INDEX

A distinctive approach to the measurement of monopoly was offered by Rothschild shortly after the appearance of the Bain index.[10] Rothschild starts with the situation shown in Figure 7.2. The CC' curve is the cost

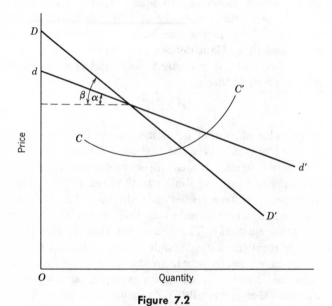

Figure 7.2

curve of a single firm that produces a commodity differentiated from those produced by rivals. Curve *dd'* is the demand curve for the firm's product assuming that prices charged by rival producers are held constant, and *DD'* is the firm's demand curve assuming that rivals' prices respond in

[10] K. W. Rothschild, "The Degree of Monopoly," *Economica*, **9**, February 1942, pp. 24–39.

some consistent way to the price of the firm in question. These curves, termed *species* and *genus* respectively by Copeland,[11] are similar to the dd' and DD' curves presented by Chamberlin. In fact the only difference is that whereas Chamberlin's DD' curve assumes that the prices of all firms move together, Rothschild's DD' assumes that "other firms change their price . . . in the same *or some other* predetermined way. . . ."[12] Rothschild's DD' thus can be the same as Chamberlin's, but it is left open to a wider variety of possible assumptions.

In terms of Figure 7.2, Rothschild proposes the following index of monopoly: $m = \tan \alpha / \tan \beta$,[13] that is, the *slope of dd'* divided by the slope of DD'. In pure competition dd' has zero slope and $m = 0$.[14] In pure monopoly dd' and DD' coincide, and $m = 1$. Between these extremes,[15] the value of m will reflect "the infinite possibilities of a mixture" of monopoly and competition. The distinctive quality of the Rothschild index is its exclusive focus on the strength of the firm within the market. The index does not tell us whether the market is itself strong in the sense that its demand is relatively inelastic. Rather, it tells us how much control of the market the firm has, regardless of the character of marketwide demand. The Rothschild index also is somewhat different in that it measures not the actual effects of monopoly, as do the Bain and Lerner indexes, but the *potential* of the firm for exercising monopoly power. In these respects Rothschild is attempting to measure something different from either Lerner or Bain.

[11] M. A. Copeland, "The Theory of Monopolistic Competition," *Journal of Political Economy*, XLII, August 1934, p. 531.

[12] *Ibid.*, p. 24. Italics added.

[13] For readers unfamiliar with trigonometry, the tangent of an angle β is defined as ac/cd. Thus in the Rothschild example the tangent of each angle is the slope of the associated demand curve.

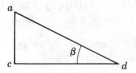

[14] The tangent of α (or its slope) is zero. Thus $m = \tan \alpha / \tan \beta = 0$, regardless of the value of $\tan \beta$.

[15] As Rothschild points out, there are exceptional circumstances under which dd' might have a steeper slope than DD'. Here m would have a value greater than 1, but we need not be concerned with such a possibility.

5. THE PAPANDREOU MEASURES

Papandreou has defined two measures describing monopoly power that are based on modifications of the cross-elasticity of demand.[16] The reason Papandreou rejects a simple cross-elasticity measure is twofold. First, the cross-elasticity of demand will be the same for the pure monopolist as it is for the purely competitive firm. In pure competition nothing that a firm, i, does to its price can affect the sales of any other firm, j. Firm i is too small for its price to have any impact on j, and vice versa. The relevant cross-elasticities are thus zero. But the pure monopolist by definition has no rivals selling substitute commodities. His cross-elasticity with respect to other commodities is therefore also zero. In some sense neither the monopolist nor the competitor has meaningful rivals. The former faces *no* firms selling similar products; the latter faces *so many* firms selling identical products that no single competitor makes a difference. The cross-elasticity of demand thus records these opposite cases as identical.

Papandreou's second reason for rejecting cross-elasticity as an adequate measure of monopoly is that it fails to take account of the firm's productive capacity as a constraint on its ability to take business away from others. The cross-elasticity measures *potential* ability to attract demand units from other firms by lowering price. Papandreou suggests a measure that would qualify this potential by referring to the firm's ability to *supply* these additional units. The firm may be able to attract potential customers away from other firms with a price cut, but if its capacity to expand production is limited this potential magnitude will overstate the threat that the firm poses to others. Papandreou thus proposes a measure called the *coefficient of penetration,* which describes the actual or realizable relative changes in sales of a firm that result from price changes made by other firms.[17] In Papandreou's words, it is "an index of the capacity of firm j to match with supply units the demand units which stand ready to shift to it following its price change."

[16] Andreas G. Papandreou, "Market Structure and Monopoly Power," *American Economic Review,* **39**, September 1949, pp. 883–97.

[17] This index is defined as

$$R_{Q_i P_j} = K_j \left[\frac{P_j}{Q_i} \times \frac{\partial}{\partial P_i} f_i(P_i, P_j, P_{N''}) \right] = K_j N_{Q_i P_j}$$

The term within the brackets is the cross-elasticity of demand for the product of firm i in terms of the price of the product of firm j ($P_{N''}$ represents the "price" of the products of all other firms in the industry). K_j is the factor describing the firm's output limitation.

The coefficient of penetration defines a firm's ability to penetrate the rival's market. Papandreou suggests that this is only half the picture. It is also necessary to define a *coefficient of insulation* that measures the ability of a firm to withstand similar attacks on its market by other firms.[18] Using the two coefficients in conjunction, it is possible to describe various combinations that would imply different degrees of monopoly power. The Papandreou coefficients constitute a real innovation in monopoly measurement. They are, however, subject to the usual difficulties, not the least of which is the problem of finding a way to apply the indexes to actual firms and industries.

6. SUMMARY

The foregoing indexes attempt to measure monopoly by defining in somewhat different ways the degree of market power or discretion possessed by firms. In this respect they may be as appropriate theoretically as any measures designed for this purpose. Yet they suffer from two common problems. The first difficulty, which is conceptual, is shared by virtually all measures of competition and monopoly: they are one-dimensional; that is, they take account of a single aspect of monopoly or competition. The degree of monopoly or competition present in a market, however, is not a simple thing to define, and it is therefore unlikely that any such measure can provide an adequate description.

The second problem with the indexes is more practical. Each requires that values be assigned to one or more variables that are extremely difficult to measure. Even the Bain profit index—perhaps the most amenable to measurement among the group—presents substantial problems. The economic profit rate may be hard to measure if only because valuation of owners' investments and selection of an appropriate interest rate can be treated in various ways.

In view of these difficulties it is unlikely that any of the monopoly indexes would be utilized as a full description of the competitive state of industries. In fact, only the Bain measure has been applied, in modified forms, to large numbers of industries. The indexes nevertheless point to some of the significant factors that ought to be considered in assessments of the degree of monopoly or competition.

[18] As Papandreou notes, a coefficient of insulation was initially proposed in Theodore Morgan, "A Measure of Monopoly in Selling," *Quarterly Journal of Economics*, **LX**, May 1946, pp. 461–63. The derivation of Papandreou's coefficient is somewhat more difficult mathematically than earlier measures, and is omitted here.

B. Structural Indicators of Competition and Monopoly

The structure of a market refers generally to the way in which it is organized; however, the term is sometimes ambiguous. The number of firms in a market and their relative importance, for example, are organizational or structural characteristics. The degree of product differentiation may also appear to be structural; however this element can be interpreted in different ways. To the extent that differentiation can be influenced by firms, it might actually be considered a reflection of performance. On the other hand, to the extent that it is totally beyond the influence of firms and is inherent in the nature of the product, it can be interpreted as an environmental factor that is outside the realm of market organization.

Rather than quibbling over semantic distinctions, however, the meaning of market structure can be defined in a more pragmatic way. It is limited to those elements of organization that are theoretically significant in that they create expectations about market behavior. Indeed, this is precisely the reason for discussing structure. Our various market models are presented in essentially structural terms. (Perfect competition, for example, "means" many small firms, ease of entry, and product homogeneity.) Such models posit chains of causation that originate in these structural conditions. Our attention is, accordingly, focused on those elements that support predictions about the ways in which firms may behave and the market results that may be forthcoming.

1. CONCENTRATION

If we wished to predict market behavior and could observe only one structural fact, that fact would probably be the number of firms in the market. The presence of only one firm would indicate monopoly, a few could denote oligopoly, and many might suggest the possibility of something akin to pure or perfect competition. Although knowing the number of firms in a market is better than having no knowledge whatever, this is obviously a most unsatisfactory clue to the state of competition. Counting firms tells us nothing about their relative positions in the market. An industry that contains several hundred companies may be dominated by a small handful. If so, it might be considered "more monopolistic" structurally than an industry containing fewer firms, in which no single company or small group dominates. What is needed in addition to information on the number of firms is some measure of their *size distribution*, where it is assumed that size is a reasonably good indicator of a firm's position or power within the market. Measures that take account of such information are usually referred to as concentration indexes.

(a) Bases of Concentration Measures

The base of a concentration index is the element that is used to measure the size of firms and markets. If, for example, we take the dollar value of assets, the large firm is one whose asset value is high, and the concentration index will tell us something about the distribution of assets among firms within a defined industry. A variety of bases might be appropriate, and although the values an index yields using different bases may be highly correlated, different bases may give somewhat different concentration rankings of industries. For this reason the choice of a base is an important decision.

(1) **Sales.** Sales revenue is a commonly mentioned base for concentration measurement. The major objection to using sales is that this measure may neglect *intra*firm transactions. If reported figures reflect only sales to outsiders, the base may fail to take account of part of the relevant market activity generated by some firms. Specifically, the size of vertically integrated firms may be understated relative to their true significance in the market, and this understatement may affect the concentration index. It is not clear that counting all intrafirm transactions would be the proper method of weighting vertical integration; perhaps this would overstate its significance. But complete neglect of such activity may produce somewhat inaccurate estimates of firms' positions in markets when there are large differences in degree of integration among companies.

(2) **Employment.** A base that is frequently utilized is employment. Here the size of firms is defined in terms of the number of employees. The employment base may be even less acceptable than sales revenue, for it introduces a systematic bias into virtually any measure of concentration. It is known that the degree of capital intensity (and labor intensity) varies with firm size. Larger firms tend to rely more on capital and less on labor than smaller firms, a fact that may be casually confirmed by thinking of the relative extent of automation in large and small enterprises. In light of this fact an employment base will consistently understate the size of large firms relative to small firms, for the larger organization is likely to employ fewer workers per unit of output. Because concentration measures are heavily influenced by the size of the largest firms, the employment base will understate the degree of concentration. It is also true that the way in which capital and labor intensities vary with firm size differs from industry to industry and from firm to firm. Thus, although the direction of the bias introduced by the employment base is known,

there would be no simple way of adjusting concentration findings for all industries to reflect a truer result.

(3) Assets. Another commonly used base, the value of assets, presents somewhat the opposite problem to that of employment. The size of larger, more capital-intensive firms may be overstated by taking asset value as the measure, and the result may be a general overstatement of concentration. Once again, although the direction of the bias is known, the bias is not so completely consistent that it would permit us to apply a simple adjustment. If the asset base were applied to a group of industries, we would know only that the concentration level of some industries is probably overstated by unknown and varying degrees. There are additional problems with the valuation of firms' assets. Several valuation methods are possible, and to the extent that firms' practices differ, random distortions would be introduced into an asset-based concentration index.

(4) Value Added. Some writers have suggested that value added would be a useful base for measuring concentration. Value added is the difference between cost of materials and sales revenue. It measures, in effect, the difference between the values of the product when it enters the firm and the value when it leaves. Such a measure would be affected by the profit rate of the firm and interindustry differences in the raw-materials component of final value. Even if these problems were not especially troublesome, however, a major difficulty that remains with the value-added base is the paucity of data on value added at the firm and industry level.

(b) The Broad Spectrum of Concentration Indexes

One way of describing the number and size distribution of firms in an industry is simply to list each firm and its share of whatever market base is utilized. Such a procedure would obviously be cumbersome. Although the comprehensive size distribution contains all the information that is relevant to a concentration measure, it could be extremely difficult to characterize this information. Even a relatively short list of firms and their share of the base might in many cases appear to be a hodgepodge. The list could be described adequately by a series of statements, but the task of *comparing* the distribution in different industries would be very difficult. What is needed—and what concentration measures of various kinds provide—is a shorthand method of summarizing the information contained in such listings. The objective ideally is to define a single statistic that tells us something meaningful about the distribution and that also permits comparisons among the distributions of various industries.

(1) The Concentration Curve. The concentration curve is simply a diagrammatic representation of the data contained in a distribution listing. In Figure 7.3 three concentration curves are illustrated. The vertical axis measures the cumulative percentage of the base, here the value of shipments. The horizontal axis measures the number of firms in the industry, where the firms are arrayed from largest (at the left) to smallest. The concentration curve does not itself yield a single statistic that characterizes the distribution; it does, however, permit a number of statements to be made conveniently. From such a curve we can specify any percentage of the base, and see how many firms account for it; or specify any number of firms and see what percentage of the base they possess.

The concentration curve begins at the origin (no firms have zero percent of the value of shipments) and reaches the 100 percent level at the total number of firms in the industry (all firms have all of the shipments). In between the curve *increases* at a *decreasing* rate, except for the special case in which all firms are the same size. In this instance the curve is a straight line, increasing at a constant rate. Generally, short, steep curves reflect high concentration, whereas long, flat curves reflect low concentration. The degree of concentration, however, is not precisely or unambiguously stated by the curves. In Figure 7.3 curves II and III intersect. Which of the industries represented by these curves may be "more concentrated" is not clear, although both are less concentrated than the industry represented by curve I. The two largest firms in industry II have 55 percent of the value of industry shipments, as compared with 45 percent for the top two in industry III. At this point industry II is more concentrated. However, the four largest firms have 79 percent of industry III and 72 percent of industry II, indicating that at this point III is more concentrated.

Concentration curves present a great deal of useful information in a convenient form, and may thus provide an excellent means for initial examination of industry structure. They do not, however, provide the kind of shorthand description that would enable meaningful comparisons to be made among all industries.

(2) The Top-Four Concentration Ratio. The most common concentration index simply gives the percentage of the market base held by the top four firms (or sometimes the top eight or 20). If, for example, it is stated that "the concentration ratio of the widget industry is 55 percent," this simply means that the specified number of firms accounts jointly for 55 percent of the market base. The information conveyed by the top-four ratio is simply that given by the fourth-firm level of a concentration curve.

The ratio is useful because it makes a simple statement about the condition of "fewness" (or "manyness") in an industry, while yielding considerably more knowledge than a simple counting of firms. It is possible to get an idea from the top-four ratio whether a market is clearly

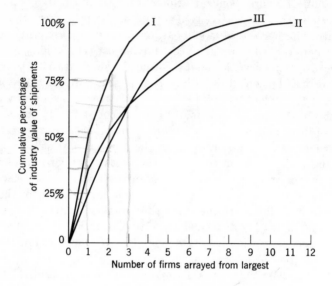

	Industry	
I	**II**	**III**
Firm	Percent of Industry Value of Shipments	Firm	Percent of Industry Value of Shipments	Firm	Percent of Industry Value of Shipments

Firm	Percent of Industry Value of Shipments	Firm	Percent of Industry Value of Shipments	Firm	Percent of Industry Value of Shipments
1	50	1	35	1	25
2	25	2	20	2	20
3	15	3	9	3	18
4	10	4	8	4	16
		5	7	5	10
		6	6	6	5
		7	5	7	3
		8	4	8	2
		9	3	9	1
		10	2		
		11	1		

Figure 7.3

dominated by a small group. The index is also most convenient in that its value is unaffected by relatively insignificant changes in market structure. Entry or exit of firms, for example, does not influence the top-four percentage unless it perceptibly alters the distribution of market shares among existing firms.

A shortcoming of this ratio is that it fails to take account of differences in structure *within* the top group. Table 7.1 shows three industries, each of which has a top-four concentration ratio of 80 percent. Obviously the structural situation in each is considerably different from the others. Industry *A*'s 80 percent ratio is accounted for by four equal-sized firms;

Table 7.1

Industries with Identical Top-Four Concentration But Different Size Structures

	Industry A		Industry B		Industry C	
	Firm	Market Share	Firm	Market Share	Firm	Market Share
	1	20%	1	40%	1	75%
	2	20	2	15	2	3
	3	20	3	15	3	1
	4	20	4	10	4	1
Top four		80%		80%		80%

industry *C* has the same ratio, but is dominated by a single firm; industry *B* lies somewhere between. Possibly we would expect somewhat different behavior from these three industries, but nothing in the simple 80 percent ratio enables us to make distinctions of this kind. The top-four ratio thus neglects a potentially important kind of information: the degree of equality or inequality in firm size within the leading group of firms.

The upper limit of the top-four ratio is 100 percent, attained whenever there are four firms or fewer in the market. The lower limit varies with the number of firms in the market, and is achieved whenever all firms are of precisely equal size. If the market consists of 100 firms, minimum concentration is 4 percent; if it consists of 10 firms, the minimum is 40 percent. The ratio reflects both the number of firms within a market grouping and the inequality of market shares. It is an extremely useful and convenient statistic, despite the fact that it is unresponsive to certain significant aspects of market structure.

(3) The Gini Coefficient. The Gini coefficient[19] is a type of concentration index based on a classic device for measuring distributions, the *Lorenz curve*. The Lorenz curve is illustrated in Figure 7.4. The vertical axis measures the (cumulative) percentage of industry value of shipments, or any other market base. The horizontal axis measures the (cumulative) percentage of firms, where the firms are arrayed from smallest (at left) to largest. With the Lorenz curve constructed in this fashion for

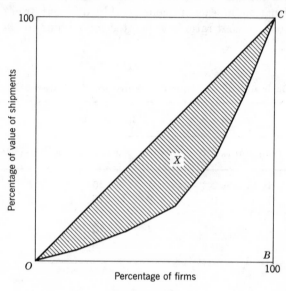

Figure 7.4

an industry, it is possible to select any percentage of firms and read off the percentage of value of shipments they account for; or, alternatively, to select any percentage of value of shipments and read off the percentage of firms that supplies it. The Lorenz curve is obviously similar to the concentration curve; it differs in relating the *percentage* of firms, rather than the number of firms, to the percentage held of the industry base.

The Gini coefficient is a statistic that summarizes the information of the Lorenz curve. It is defined as the area between the Lorenz curve and the diagonal *OC* in Figure 7.4, divided by the area of triangle *OBC*,[20] or:

[19] C. Gini, "Sulla misura della concentrazione e della variabilita dei carattere," *Transactions of the Real Istitute Veneto di Scienze, Lettere ed Arti*, LIII, part ii, 1914.

[20] The Lorenz curve is frequently discrete, i.e., composed of straight-line segments as in Figure 7.4. When the number of firms is large, however, these segments become numerous, and may be smoothed into a continuous curve.

Area X/Area OBC. If all firms in the industry are of the same size, the Lorenz curve will coincide with the diagonal. Ten percent of the firms will have 10 percent of the shipments, 20 percent will have 20, and so forth. In this case there is no area between the curve and the diagonal, and the value of the Gini coefficient is zero. The greater the *inequality* in firm size, the greater the area between the curve and the diagonal, thus the higher the value of the coefficient. In the extreme case in which there is a large number of firms, one of which has virtually the entire value of shipments, the value of the Gini coefficient approaches 1. The coefficient is, then, a measure of *inequality* in distribution.

The weakness of this index is that it does not really measure the condition of fewness in the market. If, for example, the Gini value is zero, this tells us simply that all firms are of equal size. But it does not indicate whether there are two firms or 2000. Further, the introduction of a very small firm into an industry characterized by some inequality may substantially alter the value of the coefficient although the structure of the market is not altered in an economically significant way. The Gini measure may thus be too responsive to structural changes that are theoretically trivial for an industry.[21]

This is not to imply that the Gini coefficient is inferior to an index such as the top-four ratio. Rather, the two measure somewhat different aspects of structure. The top-four ratio is especially appropriate for defining fewness—that is, for answering the question of whether a market is dominated by a small group of firms. The Gini coefficient is more useful for making specific statements about disparities in firm size within particular industries.

(4) The Herfindahl Index. The Herfindahl index[22] is a concentration measure that takes account both of the number of firms in an industry and of size inequality among the firms. It is defined as $\Sigma(x_i/X)^2$, where x_i is the size of firm i (in terms of value of shipments, assets, or any other market base) and X is the total size of the industry, the market base held by all firms. In other words, the Herfindahl index is the sum of the squares of the size of each firm in an industry, where firm size is expressed as a percentage of the industry; that is, *the sum of the squares of the market share of each firm.*

---

[21] It should be pointed out that the major application of the Gini coefficient is in the measurement of *income* distributions. Since the number of units is likely to be very large, with no single unit holding a significant portion of total income, the problem of overresponsiveness to "small" units is absent. This problem appears when we attempt to apply the index to industries consisting of varying, but relatively small, populations.

[22] Cited in Gideon Rosenbluth, "Measures of Concentration," in *Business Concentration and Price Policy*, Princeton University Press, Princeton, 1955, pp. 57–100.

The upper limit of the index is 1, attained when one firm has 100 percent of the market. Regardless of the number of firms in the industry, the value of the index approaches 1 whenever the largest firm's share of the market approaches 100 percent. The lower limit of the index is reached when all firms are the same size; however, the limit varies with the number of firms. In a two-firm industry the minimum value of the Herfindahl index is $(.50^2 + .50^2) = .50$. With three firms the minimum is .33, and with 10 it is .10. The lower limit of the Herfindahl index is defined as $1/N$, where N is the number of firms in the industry, and this limit approaches zero as N becomes very large.

The Herfindahl index has two major advantages as a concentration measure. First, it reflects both fewness and inequality. Other things equal, either larger numbers or greater equality decrease the value of the index. Second, the index is insensitive to trivial changes in structure. Obviously no change involving very small firms will have much of an effect on the value of the index.

Despite these virtues, the Herfindahl measure has an important drawback. It combines data on numbers and inequality, but it does not necessarily do so in a way that is either theoretically appropriate or intuitively obvious. For example, in a market of three equal-sized firms, the value of the index is .33, a seemingly low level. It would, of course, be incorrect to infer that such a market is unconcentrated. Consider another case in which a market contains seven firms, one of which has 40 percent of the base and the others hold 10 percent each. The Herfindahl value for such a market is .22, again a seemingly low value for an apparently concentrated structure.

Part of the difficulty is that, because the index combines different kinds of information, its values have no easily interpreted meaning. A given value for a top-four concentration ratio has one reasonably unambiguous meaning: it represents the combined market share of the four largest firms. Similarly, although a particular Gini value may be more difficult to describe intuitively, it does constitute a precise statement about the degree of size inequality among firms. A given value for the Herfindahl index, however, carries no precise implication.

This difficulty is not unique among measures of industry concentration and might not prove too troublesome if the index yielded theoretically consistent values. It could then be utilized to draw meaningful comparisons among industries, even though the interpretation of any specified value might not be obvious. In fact, however, the values the index assigns may be puzzling.

Consider industries 1, 2, and 3 in Table 7.2. In each instance the industry is characterized by a single dominant firm and a large number of very small firms. Although the spread in the values of the Herfindahl index—.81 to .36—appears rather wide, the index does rank these industries correctly: it assigns the higher concentration value according to the apparent degree of dominance of the largest firm. Note, however, that industry 4 has a Herfindahl value considerably higher than industry 3, whereas industry 5 and industry 3 have very similar values. On theoretical grounds it might be argued that industries 4 and 5 are similar to each

Table 7.2

Herfindahl Index Values

Industry	Description of Firm Size Distribution	Approximate Herfindahl Value
1	One firm has 90% of the market; many small firms have negligible market shares	.81
2	One firm has 80% of the market; many small firms have negligible market shares	.64
3	One firm has 60% of the market; many small firms have negligible market shares	.36
4	Two firms have 50% of the market each	.50
5	Three firms have 33.3% of the market each	.33

other because each consists of a small number of equal-sized firms; and that both are dissimilar to industry 3, which is characterized by one dominant firm and a large group of smaller firms. Similarly, industries 1, 2, and 3 are similar in the dominant-firm characteristic, although the degree of dominance varies.

The Herfindahl index assigns rather odd *differences* to the values between the industries. The spreads between 1 and 2, 2 and 3, and 4 and 5 are large, despite the fact that these pairs seem similar; whereas industries 3 and 5, which seem different structurally, have a very small spread. At worst, the index not only reflects puzzling discrepancies in the *distances* among industries, but may actually *rank* them incorrectly. Whether the rankings are incorrect is an arguable point, but it does seem that the index provides less-than-precise comparisons.

Possibly the Herfindahl index would yield more meaningful comparisons—and certainly more consistent rankings—of industries that contain *either* the same number of firms *or* the same degree of inequality. When the industries are not comparable in either respect, however, the index may assign values in a somewhat spurious fashion. This does not mean that the Herfindahl index is inferior to the other measures of concentration, which also may yield misleading comparisons. It does, however, indicate that the index taken alone may not be a wholly reliable measure of market structure.

(5) Summary. None of the concentration measures discussed above provides an ideal index of market structure. The number of indexes that could be constructed is extremely large; these few examples do not represent all possibilities. All measures, however, encounter remarkably similar problems. They may hide information that is relevant or, at times, reflect information that is irrelevant. Even if all pertinent information, and nothing else, is reflected, the information may be combined in ways that are inappropriate or difficult to interpret.

The fundamental problem in formulating measures of concentration lies in the fact that the object of measurement is not entirely clear. A concern with industry behavior requires that the condition of fewness or manyness be defined. But fewness is itself a complex notion that refers not only to the number of firms in a market but to the degree of inequality among them. To be useful a concentration index must reflect both aspects of fewness. That is, it must tell us something about numbers *and* inequality. Precisely how these two kinds of information are to be weighted and combined, however, is far from obvious. Some indexes that reflect both elements may tell us too little about inequality; but a measure that describes inequality in a comprehensive way may preclude sufficient information about numbers. Ideally, we would want an index to measure both factors without in any way diluting the information about either factor in isolation. It is not clear that any of the indexes discussed above accomplish this.

This kind of quagmire is not uncommon in the realm of economic measurement. When we desire a simple and convenient measure of something that is complex, problems are inevitable. There is no question that each of the concentration measures discussed provides useful information, but it should be equally clear that each must be applied with caution. None of the indexes yields more than a clue to the state of competition. But the state of competition is itself so difficult a notion that a mere clue may be as much as any structural measure can be expected to offer.

2. PRODUCT DIFFERENTIATION

A second structural element that is important in defining the state of competition is product differentiation. As noted earlier, differentiation is any distinction that buyers make among the products of various sellers, regardless of whether the distinction is based on "real" physical differences. The purely competitive model assumes a homogeneous product; that is, a product that is not only physically identical throughout the market, but that buyers regard as identical in all relevant ways. Such homogeneity is approached in some areas, but very commonly buyers do make distinctions among closely substitutable products that compete in the same market.

The distinction may originate in a number of ways. Products may actually be physically different. A Ford is not physically identical to a Chevrolet, nor is the 14-cubic-foot refrigerator produced by Westinghouse precisely the same as the 14-cubic-foot refrigerator produced by General Electric. In each case the competing products serve the same function in much the same way. They are close substitutes that clearly deserve to be grouped in the same markets. Yet the differences between them, although perhaps not objectively crucial, are important to the type of competition that is present.

This importance is not reduced even when the origin of product differentiation seems somehow less than genuine. Such products as beers, whiskeys, cigarettes, and detergents are not physically identical in the strict sense. It would seem, however, that the degree of product differentiation in such markets results more from the promotional efforts of sellers than from real product differences. True, a connoisseur can tell the difference between a "good" bourbon and a "cheap" one, but many who cannot tell the two apart may nevertheless insist on the "better" brand.[23] At times even physically identical products can be differentiated through advertising and other means of promotion, as the famous case of aspirin has shown.

To the extent that product differentiation exceeds the level that is justified by real product differences, it can be viewed as a function of ignorance and as an imperfection in the market. It has been suggested that consumer goods are subject to greater differentiation than producer goods precisely because greater ignorance is present in consumer markets. Regardless of the truth of this suggestion, product differentiation in any market may have substantial implications for behavior. As we have seen in Chamberlin's theory of monopolistic competition, the primary effect of differentiation is to yield a degree of pricing control to sellers. No longer must a firm fear that any price increase will cause its sales to disappear; nor is all incentive for price decreases blocked by the fact that the firm can sell all it produces at the prevailing price. In a

[23] A cartoon several years made this point forcefully. A woman ordering a meal in a restaurant says to the waiter: "Now be *sure* you bring me the imported wine because I can't tell the difference."

sense the seller of a differentiated product is a monopolist. He is the sole supplier of his product, although his effective control over price may be circumscribed by relatively close substitutes.

How does product differentiation alter the state of competition? As we have seen, differentiation of products in the presence of all other competitive conditions causes an industry to become less efficient. If entry is free, firms will not earn long-run monopoly profits, but their production will be restricted. Consumer preferences will be exploited, and as a result less will be produced at greater per-unit cost, and higher prices will be charged. Perhaps the most important consequence of product differentiation, however, has not been fully explored by economic theorists. This is the possibility that differentiation of the product may itself become a major battleground of competition. Rather than concentrating on optimal pricing of a defined product, the firm's efforts may be directed toward redefinition of the product, which is no longer a given in the firm's calculations. Because consumers have preferences among differentiated products—rather than selecting randomly among homogeneous goods—it may be more profitable for a seller to experiment with "different" products, than to experiment with different prices. Certainly we are all aware of markets in which there are few signs of price competition, but in which firms compete actively in terms of advertising, promotional campaigns, or superficial product differences.

The scope of this discussion does not permit full development of this line of thought. It should be pointed out, however, that the nature of competition may be altered if firms see as their objective the selection of optimal product characteristics (real or imagined) rather than the selection of optimal prices. At a more basic level, it may be argued that product differentiation implies a less competitive situation than product homogeneity, other factors constant. Each seller in the differentiated market has more pricing power than he would otherwise. Moreover, if the degree of differentiation is high—that is, if consumers have strong preferences among the products sold within the market—potential competition may be discouraged. The would-be competitor may be deterred by the fact that his product is likely to be regarded initially as inferior to established brands. Finally, it is likely that the distribution of the market among existing sellers will be altered by product differences. It has been suggested, for example, that differentiation of products may be a *cause* of market concentration.

Although product differentiation has been cited as an element of market imperfection, this should not be interpreted to mean that heterogeneity is necessarily bad. Differences among products imply, *ceteris paribus*, greater diversity and more choices for consumers. The desire to differentiate has undoubtedly led sellers to develop real and valuable product improvements. Much of the criticism directed against differentiation assumes that distinctions among products are meaningless; whereas advertising and promotion may imply social waste, the term meaningless should not be lightly applied. Product differences cannot be judged important or unimportant on a subjective basis. If the market responds to differentiated products, then the differentiation is in some way meaningful, even though any individual may consider subjectively that the differences are trivial.

The measurement of product differentiation is difficult. Ideally, cross-elasticities of demand might provide a useful description of the degree of product similarity or distinction. More practically, it is often helpful to classify products and markets roughly according to degree of differentiation. Bain has grouped various markets under "very high," "substantial," and "moderate to low" headings[24] by referring to such factors as sales-promotion costs, distinctions in design and quality, and the sensitivity of sellers' market shares to changes in other products. Such classifications can be helpful in formulating expectations about market behavior and in qualifying the inferences that are drawn from other structural information.

3. BARRIERS TO ENTRY

The condition of entry for new firms is a structural factor that carries direct implications for market behavior. If entry is relatively easy, the degree of pricing discretion for existing firms may be limited, even though the firms occupy what appear to be strong positions in the market. For this reason it may prove misleading to look at market concentration without also considering entry barriers.

Various types of barriers to entry may exist in a market. Any factor that serves to place new firms at a disadvantage relative to established firms, may be thought of as a barrier. In this sense it is clear that the absence of barriers—that is, free or easy entry—does not imply that entry is costless to the entrant. Rather the implication is that new entrant does not incur important disadvantages that are absent for established firms.

A common type of entry barrier has already been noted in the discussion of product differentiation. The reputation of established products may constitute a real obstacle to the would-be entrant. Such a firm may calculate that its initial sales potential is limited because of consumer

[24] See Joe S. Bain, *Barriers to New Competition*, Harvard University Press, Cambridge, 1962.

loyalty to established brands. And it may be that the promotional effort required to break into the market with a new product imposes a high cost relative to the (current promotional) costs incurred by existing sellers. The new entrant may not be able to attain much sales volume at existing market prices, and may be forced to cut prices to break in; or the promotional effort required may raise its costs. In either event the result is that the operations of the new firm will be less profitable than the operations of established firms. Although this disadvantage may not be permanent, it reduces the attractiveness of entry.

A second important barrier to entry is what Bain has termed the *absolute cost* advantage of established firms. These firms may possess superior factors of production, or may have access to superior raw materials; they may have agreements with suppliers that assure them of receiving inputs at terms more favorable than any new entrant can obtain; or they may simply have the superior knowledge of production and marketing that goes with experience, with patents, or simply with the collection of trade secrets. However the advantage originates, the end result is the same. An entering firm faces higher per-unit costs than do established firms, and less profitable operations for the new competitor are implied.

A new entrant may face a somewhat different cost disadvantage in an industry characterized by significant economies of scale. Here the problem is that the new firm cannot produce at costs comparable to those of established firms unless its output is very large. If the firm enters the market at a small scale of output, it will be at a disadvantage because it produces inefficiently relative to other firms. Yet even if it is able to enter the market at a high level of output, the addition to industry supply will tend to depress market prices. In either case the existence of important economies of large scale serves to discourage entry.

The variety of barriers to entry is wide, and the discussion could be extended further. The various barriers all carry roughly the same implication, however: a firm contemplating entry will face less profitable prospects than established firms. Accordingly, potential competitors may not enter the market even though established firms earn persistent high profits over some long period of time. In the free-entry case new competitors will enter and compete away such excessive profits in the long run. The ability of a monopolistic industry to earn excess profits thus turns directly on the condition of entry. Bain has pointed out that the condition of entry is likely to affect the pricing decisions of established firms. He has suggested that firms in an industry are constrained by potential entry, and set the most profitable price *that will not induce new firms to come into the market.* This *limit pricing* hypothesis clearly illustrates the sense in which potential competition constrains the power of established firms. If entry is relatively easy, the apparent monopolist may not act in precisely the way we would expect by applying the simple profit maximization model.[25]

The measurement of entry barriers is still a delicate act, and, as Bain's efforts indicate, it may be difficult to go beyond very rough measures. Industries may be classified with respect to entry barriers by referring to estimates of scale economies, product differentiation, and absolute cost advantage. These factors do not lend themselves to precise measurement, and it would be most difficult to define an index of entry ease that will permit fine distinctions to be drawn.

C. Other Indicators of Competition and Monopoly

1. MARKET CONDUCT

Conduct refers to the actual stratagems and policies employed by firms. Price leadership is an example of conduct, as is conspiratorial price fixing or independent pricing. It is obvious that the conduct of firms is the most proximate cause of their performance. Nevertheless, there is disagreement as to whether conduct itself is a meaningful explanation of performance, or even a real clue to the state of a market's competitiveness. It may "cause" performance in much the same sense that stepping on the accelerator causes an automobile to move and turning the steering wheel causes it to turn. If we wish to know *why* someone has followed a particular route at a particular speed, it will be insufficient to examine the behavior of the car's accelerator and steering wheel.

Market conduct is often an unobservable phenomenon. Consider, for example, the common question of whether firms in a market behave independently or conspiratorially. In many instances this question is simply unanswerable. There is no reliable way to tell how independent or interdependent firms' considerations may be, and even the determination of whether something called conspiracy has occurred is ordinarily difficult. Even if we could agree on the significance of market conduct, then, there may be no objective means of measuring it.

In light of these problems it is somewhat surprising that conduct occu-

---

[25] For discussions of the role of entry barriers, see Franco Modigliani, "New Developments on the Oligopoly Front," *Journal of Political Economy*, LXVI, June 1958, pp. 215–32; and Franklin M. Fisher, "New Developments on the Oligopoly Front: Cournot and the Bain-Sylos Analysis," *Journal of Political Economy*, LXVII, August 1959, pp. 410–13.

pies an eminent role in antitrust enforcement. Accurate breakdowns are not readily available, but it appears that the bulk of antitrust resources in recent decades has been employed so as to restrict anticompetitive practices. A partial explanation may lie in the very broad agreement that some forms of conduct are undesirable. An important early motivation of the antitrust laws was to protect individuals against the ruthless and predatory acts of powerful firms and groups. Such protection may have an economic justification, but it is not a purely economic matter.

The government's emphasis on restriction of undesirable conduct indeed may have relatively little to do with economic considerations. This seems plausible when it is realized that antitrust is often viewed as a tool of justice or fairness. The point is not that the conduct restrictions are economically irrational, but rather that noneconomic motivations may explain why so much emphasis has been placed on the enforcement of restrictions whose economic effects may be small. It may well be that the absence of anticompetitive conduct is a good thing economically as well as on other grounds. But it should be clear that good conduct—whatever that may mean—does not alone satisfy the requirements of competition.

2. MARKET PERFORMANCE

The theoretical significance of performance in discussions of competition and monopoly is self-evident. If a market model can be described in structural terms—number and size of firms, condition of entry, degree of product differentiation—so too can it be meaningfully described in terms of results such as prices, outputs, and profits.

Market performance is also of great interest on general economic grounds. Our ultimate concern is with policies that, by encouraging competition, will yield beneficial results. We desire, for example, efficiency in production and responsiveness of the market to consumer desires. These are among the benefits that we expect competition to provide, and it may be argued that the presence of such results is the most sensible definition of competition. In this view competition *is* what competition *does;* and the test of a market's competitiveness is whether it yields results that are themselves "competitive."

This is of course an oversimplification, but it is clear that market performance or results are of fundamental importance. Accordingly, it is appropriate to consider such performance indicators as the following.

1. *Prices and outputs.* Output restriction is a sign of monopolistic elements in the market. Accordingly, if it can be determined that output is held to a sub-competitive level, while prices charged are higher than those of a com-

petitive market (i.e., in excess of marginal cost), an industry might be considered noncompetitive.

2. Profit rates. The existence of abnormally high profits over an extended period may reflect the existence of monopoly elements.

3. Efficiency. In competitive markets production occurs at minimum average unit costs. Deviations would indicate failure to attain a competitive equilibrium.

4. Innovation in products and techniques. Although not considered in the static theories of competition and monopoly, a strong record of innovation could be interpreted as compensation for the existence of monopoly elements.

Economists have been very much interested in patterns of performance, although measurement difficulties have been serious. The problem is not only that the actual patterns may be difficult to measure precisely, but that once measured there may be no way of defining the ideal pattern with which the actual could be compared. It is possible, for example, to examine the actual price-output combinations for various commodities and industry groups; but it is far more difficult to specify what these patterns *would have been* in the ideal competitive situation. Even if it can be determined that performance in an industry deviates from purely competitive performance, the knowledge gained may be of limited usefulness. Purely competitive performance need not be the appropriate yardstick, especially for industries in which large numbers of small firms could not be supported.

Among the foremost objectives of economists concerned with industrial organization are to establish better measures of performance and to learn more about the ways in which performance varies with other characteristics of the market. It may be, however, that performance standards will never be heavily relied on by public policy makers. The obstacle to heavy reliance is the fact that performance itself is not amenable to direct policy control. In the case of market conduct the courts can order undesirable manifestations stopped and can penalize violators. In the case of structure sanctions such as divestiture and dissolution can influence future trends strongly. No similar measures can easily be invoked in dealing with undesirable performance, however.

A court cannot, for example, expect to achieve much by ordering inefficient firms to be more efficient, or poor innovators to increase their innovative activities. Conceivably a court could require that excessive profits be reduced, but such action might violate accepted principles of antitrust. The idea of an antitrust program, as conceived in the United States, implies faith in and dependence on the free market. When markets do not function well the usual approach is to attempt to create an environment in which better operations are likely, whether this implies structural change or simply the curtailment of practices that cause malfunction. To attempt to order the results of free markets is a contradiction in terms. Indeed, such a procedure might imply a kind of public regulation that has thus far been reserved for sectors in which the free-market principle has been found unworkable.

D. Summary

The degree of competition present in any industry is a peculiarly difficult quantity to define and measure. If the strict economic definition of competition were accepted, it would be simple enough to classify virtually all modern markets as noncompetitive or monopolistic, but this would convey little information. It is necessary to know more about the nature and extent of monopolistic elements before meaningful statements can be made.

Measurement of these elements can be approached in various ways, none of which is entirely satisfactory. The economist's approach to this problem has been largely structural. Competition and monopoly in economics are concepts that refer to market power, and the degree to which power is centralized can be inferred—although only in a rough and imperfect way—from structural data. Moreover, the interests of economists lie in the testing of theoretical predictions. The predictions of market theories move conceptually from structure to performance, possibly with an intermediate role for conduct; and although the direction of causation is not always this clear, tentative definitions of markets in terms of their structure is usually consistent with the suggestions of the underlying analysis.

Can we, by specifying structural (and possibly conduct) conditions, make reasonable predictions about the performance of industries? Much of the remainder of this section will discuss the evidence that has been marshaled to date. The importance of the question in a policy context is enormous. The antitrust laws have been used for many years to influence the conduct of business and the structure of markets, but neither structure nor conduct is the ultimate and complete goal of policy. The effects of changes in structure and conduct on performance must be defined, although "good" performance also is not the sole objective of policy. Whatever the goals of antitrust may be—and there is considerable disagreement here—knowledge of structure–conduct–performance relationships is necessary. No policy that affects one or more of these areas can be sensibly pursued without knowledge of the consequences.

8

Some Practical Problems of Measurement

Our discussion has so far ignored some serious problems that arise when actual measurement of market structure and behavior is attempted. Such problems will be of special interest to those who wish to conduct empirical studies. They are of general interest, too because some understanding of the difficulties is necessary to an assessment of the findings presented by others. The practical problems of measurement seem to fall into the following general groups.

1. There may be no obvious way to define the appropriate collection of firms or products to be studied, yet the definition of the collection is likely to affect the findings.
2. Certain important variables within the conceptual framework may not be susceptible to measurement, either because they are inherently immeasurable or simply because data in usable form cannot be compiled.
3. Measures of some variables, although relevant and useful, may introduce inadequacies or biases that alter empirical findings.

A. Problems of Market Definition

Any measurement of market structure, conduct, or performance obviously presupposes that the market is known. The definition of an appropriate market, however, is rarely a simple matter. A market is sometimes defined as a group of *firms* producing identical or closely related products. Such a definition has drawbacks, especially in an economy in which many firms are diversified. In the United States today we find companies that produce both chemicals and spaghetti, farm machinery and rayon, and aircraft and bathroom fixtures. Although diversification, or conglomeration, is not always so dramatic, it is sufficiently widespread that it is often inappropriate to define a market simply as a group of firms. To do so would be to lump together all the unrelated products of companies that happen to produce something in common.

A preferable approach is to define the market in terms of *products*. This brings us to the question of what is meant by a close relationship among products. Goods and services may be closely related in the sense that they are regarded as substitutes by consumers, or they may be close in that the factors and techniques of production used in each are similar; that is, there is substitutability on the producers' side of the market. If products are substitutable for both consumers and producers, we may have no trouble deciding that they belong in the same market classification. In some instances, however, the degree of closeness on the two sides is very different.

A consumer contemplating his leisure hours, for example, might see books, records, or tickets to a baseball game as his relevant choices; but is this the proper set of substitutes on which to base a market definition? To cite another example, men's shoes are a poor substitute for women's shoes from the standpoint of most consumers. Yet all shoes are produced in much the same way, utilizing similar labor, materials, machinery, and distribution systems, and produced by the same firms. Should these products also be grouped in the same market, even though consumer substitutability is weak?

Consumer substitutability would seem to be of prime importance in defining the market, and very misleading conclusions could be drawn on the basis of product groupings that exclude close substitutes or include nonsubstitutes. Yet producer substitutability cannot be totally ignored. The behavior of the market in which some product, A, is produced, will be affected if producers of products, B, C, and D, which are *not* consumer substitutes, could easily produce A as well.

One approach to market definition is to take account of producer substitutability in terms of potential entry, and to define the market primarily according to relationships on the consumer side. That is, markets could be said to consist of consumer substitutes, with producer substitutability considered in its implication for the condition of entry rather than as a dimension of the market boundary. Another possible approach is to define the market so as to include products that qualify *either* as producer *or* consumer substitutes. The trouble with this kind of definition is that we may wind up with "markets" composed largely of commodities that are not close consumer substitutes. Such a problem is illustrated by the Census grouping for "pharmaceutical preparations." It is true that within narrowly defined submarkets there are drugs that are competitive: various pain-killers or tranquilizers, for example. But aspirins are not a substitute for antibiotics, and a vitamin-A tablet is not a substitute for a vitamin-B tablet.

This example raises a more general and very important question for market definition. How broad or narrow should the scope of the market be? Perhaps the difficulty with the pharmaceuticals classification is not that it is based on producer rather than consumer considerations, but rather that the definition of the market is so wide that it encompasses nonsubstitutes. That is, it may make sense to speak of a market for headache remedies or for stomachache remedies, yet be very misleading to combine such markets, among others, into the general pharmaceutical preparations category.

A market definition that is theoretically appropriate must meet two criteria: it must be sufficiently narrow that it excludes all nonsubstitutes; and it must be sufficiently broad to include all substitutes. It turns out that these reasonable criteria can be extremely difficult to satisfy simultaneously, although either criterion alone can be met. Any market grouping may encounter the problem that there exist outside products that are substitutes for some but not all of the products within the group. If such outside products are excluded from the market definition, then the second criterion is violated. Yet if the outside products are included, the first criterion is violated.

In practice it turns out that we often do not know whether the criteria for an appropriate market definition have been met. The question of whether various products are closely substitutable for one another is essentially empirical. In many cases we may be able to make reasonable guesses—for example, a radio is not a close substitute for a head of lettuce —but a priori notions inevitably leave many relationships in doubt. Is tea a good substitute for coffee? Some basic economics textbooks state that it is, yet a truly confident conclusion would require us to find out whether consumers actually make the substitution under varying conditions. Observing these substitutions is not simple, although econometric investigation of relevant behavior offers hope for some answers to such questions.

The problems of market definition are particularly troublesome when we deal with concentration, for the procedures adopted in defining markets may systematically bias the concentration calculations. In general, the narrower the market definition, the higher measured concentration tends to be. The reason is that companies, even though each may pursue diverse activities, are usually specialized to some degree. If, for example, we consider producers of beverages, we would expect to find that some firms specialize in beer, others in soft drinks, and still others in distilled liquors, coffee, and milk. Measurement of a broadly defined "beverage market" probably would disclose a rather low concentration figure—likely much lower than would be found for the beer, soft drink, distilled liquor, coffee, and milk markets individually. Similarly, *within* a market such as distilled liquor, we might find that some firms specialize in Scotch, others in gin. Accordingly, concentration in the still narrower Scotch and gin markets would be higher than in distilled liquors.

The general relationship between the concentration of a broadly defined market and that of its narrower components may be illustrated with the following example. Suppose that a broad market consists of three component (or sub) markets as shown in Table 8.1. Each submarket

Table 8.1

Relation of Concentration in Submarkets to Combined Market

Firm	Units Produced and Sold in Submarket			Units Produced and Sold in Combined Market
	1	2	3	
A	50	40	15	95
B	10	10	10	30
C	10	6	10	26
D	10	5	10	25
E	9	15	15	39
F	8	15	20	43
G	3	9	30	42
Total units	100	100	100	300
Units produced and sold by top-four firms	80	80	80	219
Top-four concentration ratio	80%	80%	80%	73%

contains seven firms (*A* through *G*), and each has a top-four concentration ratio of 80 percent. The top-four ratio for the combined market, however, is only 73 percent. It would be a simple matter to select figures that show a more dramatic difference between measured concentration in the broad and narrow markets. If, for example, a broad market consists of 10 equal-sized submarkets, each of which is fully monopolized by a different company, the top-four concentration ratio for the broad market will be only 40 percent, although concentration is 100 percent in each component. The top-four ratio for the broad market will in fact understate submarket concentration in this fashion in all cases when the four leading firms in each submarket *are not the same firms*.[1]

One way of avoiding the problem of understatement of concentration in the broad market is to take a weighted average of the ratios of the various submarkets. Instead of adding up the submarkets individually it is possible to attribute to the broad market the typical concentration level of its component parts. Thus, for example, if each submarket displays a concentration ratio of 100 percent, the typical concentration level of the broader market is also 100 percent, without reference to the identity of the leading firms in each segment.

Unfortunately, neither the adding-up nor the weighted-average procedure of deriving concentration measures for broad groupings provides an entirely satisfactory method of concentration measurement. If the former approach may understate the concentration levels, so too may the latter approach *overstate* the degree of concentration in a broadly defined market. What is needed is not so much good arithmetic procedures as good theoretical definitions of markets. In the absence of meaningful definitions, no mechanical operation will transfer deficient concentration information into something more useful.

How widespread is the problem of market definition in concentration measurement? It is possible to paint either a fairly optimistic or a fairly pessimistic picture. If we examine the concentration data of the Bureau of the Census—the most readily available source of ratios for a large number of industry and product groupings—it appears that the underlying definitions are in most cases less than ideal. At the same time, however, it is possible to find for many purposes a large number of groupings that seem to represent at least reasonably well-defined markets. Some of the worst problems of concentration measurement can be avoided

---

[1] The problem of understatement is summarized admirably by Professor Fritz Machlup as follows: "If the broad industrial classifications are taken for measurement of concentration, concentration in industries more narrowly defined is hidden, for the chances are greater that firms which control only a negligible proportion of the whole production of the broadly defined industry produce a large proportion of the output of one particular article, which may not directly compete with any other product of the industry. The broader the definition of the industry, the greater the likelihood that the group includes some specialized firms. The concentration index for the broad industry would never reveal this monopoly power." *The Political Economy of Monopoly*, Johns Hopkins Press, Baltimore, 1952, p. 483.

simply by excluding the market groupings that incorporate those problems. It thus may be possible to proceed with empirical examinations by deliberately restricting the sample of markets to those that are well defined.

Census concentration measures nevertheless involve several problems of which it is well to be aware. Every few years the Bureau publishes top-four, top-eight, top-20, and top-50 concentration ratios based on value of shipments for a wide variety of manufacturing groupings.[2] The groups range from the broadest industry classification (two-digit) to seven-digit product classes, as shown in Table 8.2. The data not only cover many manufacturing markets, but treat each in a considerable range of detail.

Table 8.2

Standard Industrial Classification Code	Designation	Name
20	Major industry group	Food and kindred products
201	Industry group	Meat products
2011	Industry[a]	Meat-packing (slaughtering) plants
20111	Product-class	Fresh beef
20111-12	Product	Whole carcass beef

[a] When shipments of products are aggregated into four-digit totals, without regard to the industry classification of the plants making such products, the term used is *product group*.

Source: *Concentration Ratios in Manufacturing Industry, 1963*, Report prepared by the Bureau of the Census for the Subcommittee on Antitrust and Monopoly, Part I, 89th Congress, 2d sess., G.P.O., Washington, 1966.

The Bureau of the Census utilizes two approaches to market classification. Under the *industry approach*, each plant for which data are gathered is assigned to one of the 430 four-digit industry groups listed by the Bureau. A plant is assigned to an industry according to its *primary* product or activity, and its *entire* output is included in that classification, even though some (minor) portion of that output may be of a different kind. Under the *commodity approach*, the output of specific products is assigned to the relevant total product groups without regard to the primary activity—the industry classification—of the plant in which

[2] Ratios based on employment are also published.

the product is produced. The output of a particular plant will be divided among the appropriate commodity or product classifications, even though the plant itself is classified within a single primary industry group.

These classification procedures permit two discrepancies to arise between the industry and commodity categories. On one hand, if all shipments of plants are included in their primary industry category, it is likely that some shipments will be included that do not properly belong to that industry classification. On the other hand, if the shipments of plants are divided up among their appropriate commodity classifications, product output totals will likely include some output that is not primary to the plants in which it originates. These two discrepancies in combination may imply that the four-digit industry as defined by the Bureau of Census—for example, meat-packing plants—may not be comparable with the five-digit product classes underlying it—for example, beef, veal, lamb and mutton, pork, and so on.

The four-digit meat-packing category includes the nonmeat outputs of plants whose primary output is meat; but does not include the meat outputs of plants whose primary output is not meat. Conversely, the five-digit product group excludes the nonmeat output of plants whose primary output is meat, but includes the meat output of plants whose primary output is not meat. This is the essential difference between the industry and product or commodity approach to classification. The Census Bureau provides two measures that enable us to see how important such discrepancies may be.

1. The *coverage ratio* describes the extent to which the primary product of an industry originates in plants classified in that industry. It is simply the ratio,

$$\frac{\text{Shipments of industry } A \text{ that come from plants classified in } A}{\text{Total shipments of industry } A}$$

A ratio of .86 in meat packing for example, indicates that 86 percent of meat-packing output originates with plants classified in the meat-packing industry.

2. The *specialization ratio* (or primary-product specialization ratio) describes the extent to which plants classified in an industry specialize in making the products primary to that industry. It is simply the ratio,

$$\frac{\text{Shipments of industry } A \text{ that come from plants classified in } A}{\text{Total shipments of plants classified in } A}$$

The primary-product specialization ratio of .98 in meat packing indicates that 98 percent of the output of plants classified in the industry actually consists of meat products—or that 2 percent of the output of meat-packing plants consists of something else.

A low specialization ratio indicates that plants classified within an industry are diversified; that is, a good deal of what they produce is outside the product lines that define the industry. An example is paints and allied products, an industry with a specialization ratio of .60; this means that 40 percent of the output of plants in the industry does not consist of anything that could be called paints and allied products. Similarly, a low coverage ratio implies that much of an industry's output is produced in plants whose primary activity lies elsewhere. The .47 ratio for surface active agents, for example, means that most (53 percent) of the output of this industry originates in plants whose primary business is making something other than surface active agents.[3] Used together, the primary-product specialization and coverage ratios yield a reasonably good idea of the degree of correspondence between the industry and product groupings. When the coverage ratio is low there also may be some question about the adequacy of the market definition.

Problems of market definition have been noted in detail because so much empirical work is attempted at this level. If market definitions are deficient, then hypotheses about market behavior may be confirmed or rejected not because a true relationship is established, but rather because the wrong facts have been examined. Many of the definitional problems can be avoided by a judicious selection of markets; but neither empirical investigation nor the interpretation of investigation by others can proceed meaningfully without an understanding of the actual and potential pitfalls.

B. The Immeasurability of Market Conduct

As we have noted, the conduct or actual strategems of firms in a market may have some bearing on ultimate performance. Although many economists would not place primary emphasis on conduct as an explainer or predictor of performance, this element of behavior has been emphasized in antitrust enforcement. It is almost certainly true that conduct directly causes some kinds of performance. For example, a conspiracy among

[3] The low specialization ratio does not necessarily mean that the category is a poorly defined market, since the direct implication is only that the output comes from plants whose primary activity lies elsewhere.

producers to set the price of their product at an agreed-on level causes the price to go to that level. It may be, however, that this conspiratorial conduct is not the most important underlying factor that determines the price. The conspiracy might never have been possible except for structural conditions that made it easy, or even inevitable, for producers to get together. And the prices that have been determined might have come about anyway through tacit reactions, without an agreement that could be termed a conspiracy.

If we wish to make generally reliable statements about firms' conduct, information in two areas is necessary: the goals of firms and the way in which they perceive or measure relevant quantities; and the existence and extent of mutual interdependence, as seen by firms, and their reaction to it. Unless we can say something about what firms are trying to accomplish and how they take account of each other's presence, it will be extremely difficult to interpret their actions. Is a firm that raises its prices trying to earn greater profits or sales revenue? Is it raising price under specific expectations about the reaction of its rivals, or is it simply ignoring them?

Meaningful definition of conduct patterns may not always be possible. Except for the few instances in which a mode of conduct is obvious, the patterns followed by firms seem to defy objective assessment. Indeed, conduct itself is rarely observable. What we usually see is performance, to which we attempt to attach a conduct interpretation. The correct interpretation, however, may depend on what goes on in the minds of business managers—something we are not able to judge with confidence. Does a particular pattern of price response in an industry reflect independence or interdependence? Possibly several firms will charge the same price because they have carefully conspired to do so; and possibly they will charge the same price because they have independently decided to do so. Our observations of the pricing pattern may not enable us to say which of these alternatives is the true one.

Some attempts to measure conduct have yielded interesting results. Recently an effort has been made to relate the incidence of price fixing in industries to their market structures.[4] Further attempts to relate such specifically defined conduct to both structure and performance might prove illuminating, but such efforts cannot avoid the fundamental problems of measuring the relevant conduct. The meaning of price fixing, for example, must almost inevitably be an arbitrary one, perhaps defined as any situation in which the Justice Department brings a charge of price

[4] James M. Clabault and J. F. Burton, Jr., *Sherman Act Indictments, 1955–1965*, Federal Legal Publications, New York, 1966, pp. 128 ff.

fixing under the Sherman Act. Here the measurement problem is resolved by stating, in effect, "Price fixing is whatever the government says it is."

The difficulty of measuring conduct is such that empirical studies of industry structure and behavior usually ignore it, concentrating exclusively on structure and performance aspects. Just how great a loss of knowledge may be implied by this short-circuiting is not obvious. Certainly there are hypotheses concerning market conduct that would be well worth testing, and it is to be hoped that measurement will improve to permit further tests. At the same time, however, it is not clear on a priori grounds that business conduct is necessarily an important independent determinant of either market structure or market performance. Indeed, if the chain of causation runs from structure to conduct to performance—that is, if structural conditions lead to certain modes of conduct, which in turn lead to particular performance patterns—then the loss of knowledge that results from our inability to measure conduct may be minor.[5]

C. Inadequacies in Existing Data

Efforts to test hypotheses are beset by a variety of measurement problems. In some instances the problems are of a very basic nature. It may be, for example, that relevant data are unavailable; or that data are available in deficient forms.

In many cases problems with existing data are specific and mundane, but are nevertheless important. The available data may measure something similar to, but not precisely the same as, the variable we would like to measure. Data may be compiled in forms that are so inconvenient as to be unusable, or compilations across industries or time may not be fully comparable. These kinds of problems can prove extremely troublesome, but at least they possess the virtue in most instances of ready visibility.

Potentially more obscure difficulties often lie within the measurement procedures that have been used to compile basic data, and it is in this area that special care must be exercised. Even if data appear to describe the appropriate variables, significant errors can arise. The compilation of data may be in some way haphazard so that essentially random errors of measurement are introduced. Worse yet, the compilation may intro-

[5] For some arguments and evidence that conduct itself is important, see William L. Baldwin, "The Feedback Effect of Business Conduct on Industry Structure," *Journal of Law and Economics*, XII, April 1969, pp. 123–53.

duce a systematic bias into the measure. It is important to be aware of these problems, for, if they are ignored, wholly misleading and unjustified interpretations of observed facts may follow.

1. SOME OBVIOUS DATA PROBLEMS

Some of the glaring deficiencies in economic data are readily illustrated by referring to measures of market structure and performance. Suppose, for example, that we wish to define the structural characteristics of a number of markets. If the previously noted problems of market definition and concentration measurement can be handled, it probably will be useful to proceed to some description of factors such as degree of product differentiation and ease of entry. Here some new measurement problems arise.

Product differentiation is not easily reduced to a precise index. Not only is there no obvious way of quantifying actual physical differences, but the extent of differentiation is a largely subjective question; it is a matter of how different consumers *think* products are. It is most unlikely that we would ever be able to produce a specific index that assigns meaningful cardinal values to the differentiation of product classes, yet we do have certain relevant information. It is evident that some products are physically more similar than others; the former may well be less differentiated, *ceteris paribus*. Similarly, some products are more heavily advertised, and it is likely (although not inevitable) that these will be relatively more differentiated. If a cardinal index is not possible, it may nevertheless be feasible to attempt a less ambitious index that *ranks* products by degree of differentiation. Even a complete ranking may be impossible if there are many instances in which the proper ordering is unknown. For example, we may be confident that steel bars as a product class are less differentiated than cigarettes, yet we may not be at all sure whether steel bars are more differentiated than aluminum conductor, or whether cigarettes are more differentiated than toothpastes. It may be necessary to rank products broadly by placing them in a small number of categories (steel and aluminum conductor might be categorized as products of low differentiation, cigarettes and toothpastes as products of high differentiation).[6]

The situation with respect to measurement of entry barriers is similar. Some relevant data on the significance of scale economies and absolute cost advantages (and product differentiation as well) may be

[6] Such a procedure was followed by Joe S. Bain in his *Barriers to New Competition*, Harvard University Press, Cambridge, 1955.

obtained, although the compilation is likely to be a cumbersome process. It would be virtually impossible, however, to construct an index of entry ease or difficulty with cardinal properties on the basis of our current information and techniques. Once again the type of broad ranking used by Bain may represent the best possible kind of measure under the circumstances. Such a measure, however, provides far less information than a more precise index, and may restrict the statistical methods that can be applied to the testing of associated hypotheses.

Other obvious kinds of data problems arise in the measurement of firm and market performance. One example was seen in our earlier discussion of Bain's index of monopoly, which requires the calculation of profit rates. Rates of return on sales or some measure of investment[7] are relatively easy to find or derive for many firms and industries. But the rate that is easily derived is not the same profit rate as that to which the Bain index refers—an "economic" profit that takes account of opportunity costs. It may be possible to take the accounting profit rates that are available and make appropriate adjustments; but it is clear that the term profit rate carries more than one meaning. It is also worth noting that because some discretion exists in accounting procedures, even the specific accounting profit rate may not be an identical measure across firms or industries. We may be justified in assuming that the measures are sufficiently close to be treated *as if* they were identical, but it should be recognized that discrepancies are possible and may be troublesome even within an apparently standard measure.

The measurement of inventive and innovative activity has presented difficulties, primarily because there is no observable magnitude that seems to describe precisely the variable in question. Some writers have taken firm and industry *expenditures* on research and development as the best measure. But the expenditure figure describes in effect the effort that is being made to be inventive, whereas our interest may lie more with the end *results* of such effort. Does a highly successful R&D program imply more inventiveness than one that fails? An alternative approach is to measure inventive output by looking at the number of patents taken out by firms and groups of firms. It is obvious, however, that patents are often noncomparable. Some are important and others are trivial; and two comparable developments may result in different numbers of patents assigned. In a sense, both R&D expenditures and number of patents are

---

[7] Investment-based rates of return present some special problems. Not only do methods of valuing investment vary, but the investment figure may be affected significantly by the way in which a company finances itself (debt or equity). For these reasons returns expressed as a percentage of some investment figure may arouse particular skepticism.

relevant to the magnitude investigators would like to describe, but they do not constitute a fully accurate description. Such data may be utilized as the best available, but their shortcomings must be noted carefully and conclusions qualified accordingly.

A host of data problems involves the simple incomparability of many statistics and the unavailability of information. One source of difficulty is the fact that government statistics are often gathered in different ways by different agencies or by the same agency over a period of time. If we wish to study, say, price, production, profit, and concentration data for certain industries, it is possible that we will find the industry definition slightly different for some of the variables. The Bureau of the Census, for example, uses one set of classifications (the SIC), and the Bureau of Labor Statistics uses another. In many instances the differences are small, and industries are easily matched, but this is not always the case. Time-series data gathered by a single agency may also change so that recent information is not entirely comparable with that provided for past years.

In many cases these obvious kinds of data problems are not terribly serious, and it may be sufficient to note that certain possible discrepancies provide qualifications to the conclusions that can be drawn. In other instances, however, it becomes necessary to decide whether existing data —even if they are the best available—are sufficiently accurate and reliable to be useful. No objective rules of thumb exist, and the decisions may become matters of judgment.

2. SOME LESS OBVIOUS DATA PROBLEMS

The variety of nonobvious problems that arise in connection with economic data is very large.[8] Rather than attempting to survey all possible pitfalls, it may be relatively efficient to illustrate such problems by referring to one kind of widely used information: price statistics. Economists concerned with industry structure and behavior have an obvious interest in examining price patterns. Accordingly, much attention is paid to the major price measures published by the Bureau of Labor Statistics: the Consumer Price Index (CPI) and, especially, the Wholesale Price Index (WPI).[9] These indexes provide a detailed picture of price move-

[8] For a general discussion of problems in economic data, see Oskar Morgenstern, *On the Accuracy of Economic Observations*, Princeton University Press, Princeton, second edition, 1963.

[9] The WPI is a more relevant measure for manufacturing industry questions. One reason is that the CPI reflects the combined effect of behavior at various levels of production and marketing, and is therefore a less "pure" measure of what occurs at the manufacturing level.

ments in a large number of product categories (many of which can be matched with SIC product and industry groups).

The availability of such information is of course fortunate for any economist who wishes to compare the pricing patterns of different industries, or to analyze the patterns within an industry over time. But there are also significant drawbacks to the data; certain of these affect the goodness of the indexes *in toto*, and may not be relevant for questions dealing with specific industry patterns.[10] Other shortcomings, however, affect the measures in specific ways.

The most familiar problem associated with price measures concerns changes in the quality of products. When we look at the price of something over a period of time, the changes that we observe are meaningful only if that "something" is constant. If the product itself undergoes changes, then the prices we observe are in effect associated with *different* products. This is clear if it is recognized that the demand for any product can be viewed as a demand for the attributes or characteristics *of that product*. Quality changes yield a different set of attributes and, in some meaningful sense, a different product. Presumably, then, some adjustment in the price measure is required. If product quality improves and its nominal price also increases, the true price increase—if any—will be less than the nominal amount; for although we must pay more money to buy the product, we are buying a better product. Examples of quality increases are legion. Ballpoint pens, when first introduced, were cumbersome, short-lived, and highly unreliable compared with what they are today. The television sets, hi-fi outfits, fishing reels, and typewriters of today simply perform better than the same products of 15 or 20 years ago, and in some cases better than the same products of one year ago. Of course it is also true that some products perform less well today, "They just don't make them the way they used to!" unquestionably has some applicability.

Whatever the direction of quality change, such change must enter a true measure of price. Conceptually, one measure of true price may be defined as: Observed index of price/index of quality change.[11] Thus a

---

[10] For example, it might be that an index such as the CPI is a poor measure of general prices because its weights are somehow unrepresentative of the economy. This problem would not affect the ability of the index to measure price movements in specific industries.

[11] See, e.g., Zvi Griliches, "Hedonic Price Indexes for Automobiles: An Econometric Analysis of Quality Change," Staff Paper 3 in *The Price Statistics of the Federal Government*, A report to the Office of Statistical Standards, Bureau of the Budget, prepared by the Price Statistics Review Committee of the National Bureau of Economic Research, National Bureau of Economic Research, 1961, p. 177.

product whose observed price index is say, 150, but whose quality has "doubled" over the relevant time period, has a true price index of 75. If price and quality both double, true price does not change; and if price falls while quality rises, true price falls by more than the observed change.[12] The Bureau of Labor Statistics is of course aware of quality-change problems, and attempts to make appropriate adjustments when possible. But quality change is immensely difficult to quantify, and for many changes there is no objective method of doing so. Consequently, quality trends may be ignored or inadequately treated, with definite implications for indexes such as the CPI and WPI. To the extent that quality improvement goes unrecorded, the indexes generally overstate price increases and understate decreases. If we observe that prices go up in some industries but not in others, we cannot be sure that true prices have moved in this fashion; perhaps quality has risen in the price-increasing sectors and remained constant in the price-constant sectors.

Very similar problems are raised by the introduction of new products and changes in the specifications of existing products. How, for example, should the introduction of compact cars or filter cigarettes or color television be taken into account? As the Price Statistics Review Committee points out:

The treatment of new products presents a serious problem for any price index. An attempt to introduce all innovations into an index as soon as they appear would clutter the index with the failures that never attain appreciable importance. On the other hand, if new products are introduced only when the old items are completely displaced, the index will become seriously obsolete. . . . [13]

Changes in product specifications are very much like other quality changes. Most automobiles currently have automatic transmissions as a standard part of the product; some cameras have built-in light meters, and some radios have alarm mechanisms and clocks. It would clearly be inaccurate to interpret the increased prices that result from the addition of such new components as true price increases. Once again, however, there may not be an adequate procedure by which to measure such changes.

These problems, troublesome as they are, do not exhaust the funda-

---

[12] There is, however, a question about the adequacy of such indexes under some circumstances. See F. M. Fisher and K. Shell, "Taste and Quality Change in the Price Theory of the True Cost-of-Living Index," in J. N. Wolfe (editor), *Value Capital and Growth: Papers in Honor of Sir John Hicks* (The University Press, Edinburgh, 1968).

[13] *Op. cit.*, p. 37.

mental shortcomings of price measures. Studies by McAllister[14] and Flueck[15] cast serious doubt on whether the WPI represents actual transactions prices. McAllister has shown that the frequency of price change for some commodities in the WPI is closely related to the number of firms that report prices; Flueck has found substantial differences between the behavior of some WPI commodity prices and the prices of the same commodities on government purchase contracts (these differences hold for amplitude as well as frequency of change). Such findings have led the Price Statistics Review Committee to suggest "that the price quotations obtained from manufacturers do not faithfully measure the movements of prices, quite aside from the usual problems of measurement."[16] It is not clear at this point whether the WPI is quoting in many instances transactions prices, list prices, some combination of the two, or something entirely different!

This melancholy listing of deficiencies in price data does not imply that indexes such as the WPI and CPI are of no value. Certainly the measures contain potentially significant inaccuracies, and some possible biases that would render them worthless for certain tasks. There are some kinds of measurement efforts, however, for which these data—although less than ideal—may prove serviceable. Such cases will be discussed later in reference to some actual findings of investigators about the pricing patterns of industries.

The deficiencies of the price measures also ought not to be taken as an indication that all economic data are plagued by inaccuracies of comparable severity. Rather, the lesson to be drawn is one of caution. No index of economic phenomena, no matter how "official," is immune from difficulty. It is necessary to examine closely the ways in which the data in question are gathered, and the possible inaccuracies and biases that could creep in.[17]

---

[14] Harry E. McAllister, "Statistical Factors Affecting the Stability of the Wholesale and Consumers' Price Indexes," Staff Paper 8 in *The Price Statistics of the Federal Government*, pp. 373–418.

[15] John M. Flueck, "A Study in Validity: BLS Wholesale Price Quotations," Staff Paper 9 in *The Price Statistics of the Federal Government*, pp. 419–58.

[16] *Op. cit.*, p. 69.

[17] Perhaps the most infamous example of a failure to consider potential sampling bias occurred in the *Literary Digest* poll during the presidential campaign of 1936. The *Digest* conducted a poll and concluded that Alf Landon would defeat Franklin D. Roosevelt in the November election of that year, a conclusion that was in retrospect not merely wrong but incredible. The error was caused by the *Digest's* procedure of drawing its sample. It took names from the telephone directories, thus excluding from its consideration all persons unable to afford telephones. These persons comprised in 1936 a very large and very pro-Roosevelt group.

9

Some Empirical Clues

The volume of empirical work that has been undertaken in the area of industrial organization is immense, and can in no way be covered here. It will be useful nevertheless to consider a limited number of studies that have provided important clues to the relationships among various characteristics of firms and industries. The studies we shall discuss have involved tests of hypotheses suggested by economic theory and hold some direct implications for public policy.

A. Explanations of Profitability

Economic theory suggests that firms in monopolistic markets may reap persistent excess profits when excess is taken to mean in excess of *normal* profits. A number of persons have attempted to test the hypothesis that monopolistic markets are generally more profitable than nonmonopolistic or competitive markets by: defining some measure of the degree of monopoly for various industries; and comparing this measure with the profit rates of the same industries. A positive correlation, showing that industries with a greater degree of monopoly have higher profit rates, would support the hypothesis.

Pioneering efforts in this area were undertaken almost 20 years ago by Bain. Bain initially examined the relationship between industry concentration—a rough proxy for degree of monopoly—and profit rates for the period 1936–1940, using a sample of 42 industries drawn from the SIC.[1] He distinguished between *highly concentrated oligopolies, less concentrated oligopolies*, and *industries of atomistic structure*, hypothesizing specifically that ". . . the average profit rate of firms in oligopolistic industries of a high concentration will tend to be significantly larger than that of firms in less concentrated oligopolies or in industries of atomistic structure."[2] The reasoning offered in support of this hypothesis is that highly concentrated oligopolies are relatively likely to engage in effective collusion, which drives the industry profit rate towards the pure monopoly level, whereas neither oligopolies of low concentration nor atomistically structured industries will succeed in establishing effective collusion, and consequently will earn lower average profits. Bain did not start with a defined point that would distinguish high from low concentration within the general oligopolistic group, but rather sought to determine whether some such line could be identified on the basis of observed data.

The information on which Bain's major finding was based is presented in Table 9.1.[3] No conclusive indication of a strong linear relationship between concentration and profit rates was established. However, Bain noted "a rather distinct break in average profit-rate showing at the 70 percent concentration line." It seems evident, although it would be necessary to refer to the specific industry observations for confirmation, that the relationship between concentration and average profit rates is not "smooth," and would not be well-approximated by a straight line, that is, a given change in concentration is not associated with consistent changes in profit rates throughout the concentration spectrum. At the same time, however, the 22 industries with eight-firm concentration ratios of 70 percent or higher do appear to have distinctly higher rates than the 20 industries with concentration under 70 percent. Bain found specifically that the 70-and-over group had a mean rate of 12.1, whereas the mean for industries under 70 percent was 6.9; the probability that this difference occurred by chance was determined (under the Fisher z test) to be less than one-tenth of one percent.

The Bain findings are subject to varying interpretation. On one hand, his results establish a distinction in profit performance between two groups of industries at a very high level of statistical significance. On the

[1] Joe S. Bain, "Relation of Profit-Rate to Industry Concentration: American Manufacturing, 1936–1940," *Quarterly Journal of Economics*, **LXV**, August 1951, pp. 293–324. Bain exercised considerable care in selecting a sample of meaningfully defined industries from among all S I C candidates.

[2] *Ibid.*, p. 294.

[3] This is Bain's Table II, *ibid.*, p. 313.

other hand, the relationship that is established does not enable us to formulate very precise predictions about profit performance on the basis of information about concentration. All we know is that industries in the high-concentration category earn higher profits on average than industries in the low-concentration category, and that the difference is most unlikely to be a chance occurrence. We do not know what varying the level of concentration in a particular industry is likely to do to profits in any more specific terms than this.

Table 9.1

Average of Industry Average Profit Rates within Concentration Deciles, 1936–1940, for 42 Selected Industries

Concentration Range (Percent of Value Product Supplied by Eight Firms)	Number of Industries	Average of Industry Average Profit Rates[a]
90–100	8	12.7
80– 89.9	11	10.5
70– 79.9	3	16.3
60– 69.9	5	5.8
50– 59.9	4	5.8
40– 49.9	2	3.8
30– 39.9	5	6.3
20– 29.9	2	10.4
10– 19.9	1	17.0
0– 9.9	1	9.1

[a] Average of net profits after income taxes as percentage of net worth.

Since 1951 several investigators have attempted to develop further explanations of industry profit patterns. It has been found that the introduction of a second explanatory variable—barriers to entry—improves the predictions of profit rates.[4] Predictions also might be improved by

[4] See Joe S. Bain, *Barriers to New Competition*, Harvard University Press, Cambridge, 1955; H. Michael Mann, "Seller Concentration, Barriers to Entry and Rates of Return in Thirty Industries, 1950–1960," *Review of Economics and Statistics*, **48**, August 1966, pp. 296–307; and Peter Asch, "Industry Structure and Performance: Some Empirical Evidence," *Review of Social Economy*, **25**, September 1967, pp. 167–82.

the use of different measures of concentration.[5] The hypothesis of a positive association between profit rates and concentration is now supported by a substantial body of evidence, although statistically significant relationships have not been found at all times.[6]

It is important to realize that the statistical findings of past studies have varied rather widely, and that there is no such thing as a universal, or even a consensus, conclusion as to the precise significance of concentration in explaining profitability. No one has concluded that concentration in any sense completely explains profit performance, and no such conclusion would be supported by economic theory. Even when the condition of entry is also considered, there obviously exist other factors that must be expected to influence profit levels. The degree of risk and behavior of demand are two obviously influential elements that vary from industry to industry. Moreover, a number of writers have suggested that characteristics of the *firm*—such as absolute size—may affect profit levels apart from the influence of industry-wide characteristics.[7]

In addition to the fact that concentration may be only one among several important variables that influence profit rates, there exists a further complicating factor that past efforts at measurement may not have resolved. The only clear expectation that can be drawn from traditional theory is that industries characterized by a degree of monopoly power are relatively likely to earn persistent *excess* profits. An excess profit is one that is greater than normal, that is, greater than is necessary to keep productive factors in their present employment. The normal profit may be defined by the opportunity cost of investment. There is no reason to

---

[5] Average concentration ratios (described in Chapter 8) have been utilized. See Leonard W. Weiss, "Average Concentration Ratios and Industrial Performance," *Journal of Industrial Economics*, 11, July 1963, pp. 237–54; and George J. Stigler, *Capital and Rates of Return in Manufacturing Industries*, Princeton University Press, Princeton, 1963.

[6] Stigler, for example, terms his findings "somewhat ambiguous, but on the whole . . . negative." *Ibid.*, p. 67. Norman R. Collins and Lee E. Preston find support for the hypothesis amidst rather mixed results. *Concentration and Price-Cost Margins in Manufacturing Industries*, University of California Press, Berkeley and Los Angeles, 1968.

[7] Although it has been widely believed that larger firms earn higher rates of profit, the empirical evidence that exists to date is mixed. Some studies have concluded that the effect of size on profitability is minor. See, for example, W. L. Crum, *Corporate Size and Earning Power*, Harvard University Press, Cambridge, 1939; and H. O. Stekler, *Profitability and Size of Firm*, Institute of Business and Economic Research, University of California, Berkeley, 1963. Recently, however, a study by Marshall Hall and Leonard Weiss has concluded that size does exert a significant influence on profitability once other pertinent variables are taken account of: "Firm Size and Profitability," *Review of Economics and Statistics*, XLIX, August 1967, pp. 319–31.

expect that the normal profit level is the same for factors employed in various occupations or industries. But if the normal profit varies among industries, then, by the same token, so does the level at which profit becomes excessive or monopolistic. A 10 percent rate of return may be excessive in some industries but not others; it depends on what return factors in each industry could earn elsewhere (and on the degree of risk as well). The measurement of opportunity cost and normal profit for a large number of industries would at best be a cumbersome and at worst a nearly impossible, task. Most investigators of concentration-profit relationships have taken accounting profits as a rough proxy for pure economic profits, and have proceeded on the assumption that abnormal levels of the former reflect the latter. For this reason there may be some question concerning the accuracy of measured relationships.

Given these qualifications, what is the meaning of the findings on profits and concentration? No categorical answer is possible, but several tentative suggestions may be offered. First, it appears that the theoretical proposition in its broadest form is supported. Under some statistical tests —relatively unrestrictive ones—it frequently is found that highly concentrated industries earn relatively high profits, and the relationship is strengthened, as would be expected, by the inclusion of entry barriers as an explanatory variable. This suggests that industries characterized by high concentration and important barriers to new entry may, on the average, act in ways that misallocate society's resources.

This kind of finding would argue that structurally monopolistic (or oligopolistic) industries may be socially undesirable, and suggests that a public policy designed to retard the growth of concentration and entry barriers may be in order. But there are very significant qualifications to any such conclusion. In the first place the relationship that has been established between concentration levels and profit rates is far from being either precise or completely reliable. The fact that highly concentrated industries earn higher profits in general does not necessarily mean that most or all industries of high concentration earn an excessive profit. It is possible that a public policy designed to reduce or freeze existing concentration levels would have, on the average, the correct effect on profits, if correct is taken to mean a dampening tendency. But a policy that restructures industries has many implications, some of which could well be socially undesirable.

A second, closely related, kind of qualification concerns the economic interpretation of industry performance. The fact that some *statistically* significant associations between concentration and profit rate appear tells us little about the economic significance of such relationships. It may be that the cost to society of having high-profit industries is small. Similarly, it is possible that whatever the costs may be, they are compensated by efficiency and innovation. The difficulty in translating the observed relationship into a policy statement is, then, threefold.

1. The relationship between concentration and profit rates may not be sufficiently strong or reliable to permit confident policy manipulations.
2. The social disutility or cost of high-profit industries is not known.
3. Profit rates comprise only one element of industry performance, and may be outweighed by other performance patterns associated with concentration.

These difficulties state only the obvious. Any variable such as the profit rate is, at best, a single clue to the nature and quality of industry operations. It would be unrealistic to expect that one clue could provide the basis for a public policy dealing with industrial structures. Indeed, there is no reason to think that an economically appropriate public policy can rest on simple rules of thumb. It would be surprising to find that consistent opposition to concentration (or consistent encouragement of it) would maximize economic welfare. This does not mean that past studies of profitability have failed to say anything useful for policy purposes. The evidence that has been marshaled does identify certain industrial structures that may be relatively likely to misallocate resources. To the extent that such misallocation is relevant to public policy, empirical evidence lends some support to concern about growth in concentration and barriers to entry.

B. Explanations of Pricing: The Administered-Price Controversy

In the most rudimentary analysis of competition and monopoly it is concluded that the latter extracts a relatively high price from consumers. This might suggest that we should expect the prices of commodities sold in monopolistic markets to be generally higher than those sold in more competitive circumstances. (By the same token, we should expect a smaller volume of sales in the monopolistic areas.) Such a hypothesis, however, may be empirically intractable because of the incomparability of different products. We know that an automobile costs more than a raincoat, yet it would be absurd to attribute the difference in price largely to the fact that raincoats are produced in a relatively competitive environment. In fact the comparison between automobile and raincoat prices tells us nothing about the effect of monopoly power on price. What we would want ideally is (a) some estimate of what the price of raincoats *would be* if sold under monopolistic conditions, and (b) a similar estimate of what automobile prices would be under competitive conditions. Although such estimates might be attempted, the difficulty and magnitude of the task for even a single product would be formidable. For this reason efforts to define empirically the effect of monopoly power on prices and quantities sold have been very limited.[8]

If efforts to measure the effect of monopoly power on the *height* of prices are unpromising, however, considerable attention has been devoted to the possible effects on patterns of price *change* through time. The more prominent hypotheses that have been suggested are associated with what has come to be known as the *administered-price controversy*, and represent an unusual episode in the study of industrial organization.

Anyone who has been exposed to an introductory course in economics is aware that market prices are expected to respond to changes in supply or cost conditions and to changes in demand. In practice, however, it appears that many prices in the American economy tend to be inflexible or sticky, changing—if at all—only at infrequent intervals. Price inflexibility may be detrimental to the economy. It means in effect that the market mechanism is failing to take account of changes in the cost of resources and consumer preferences, or that it is doing so only after significant time lags. Inflexible prices received special attention during and after the Great Depression of the 1930's, for had prices generally fallen faster and farther, it is at least possible that much of the severe and self-feeding unemployment of the period could have been avoided. Any tendency for prices to be sticky implied a lower quantity of goods demanded (than would have been demanded at lower prices), less output, and fewer jobs.[9]

A study by Means in 1939 examined the behavior of industrial prices during the depression period 1929–1932.[10] Means, however, did not treat

[8] The price effect of monopoly power is indirectly treated in studies of profit rates, since the rates themselves reflect the deviation of price from average cost. For reasons noted in the earlier discussion of the Bain and Lerner monopoly indexes, however, profit measures are probably less meaningful than estimates of the deviation of price from *marginal* cost.

[9] Flexible (downward) prices, however, might have been associated with flexible wage levels. Had lower prices been accompanied by lower wages, the result could have been to depress aggregate demand. For this reason the desirability of flexible prices is questionable at the macroeconomic level.

[10] Gardiner C. Means, *The Structure of the American Economy*, Part I, National Resources Committee, Washington, 1939.

price inflexibility during this period as either a general or a random problem. Rather, he suggested that the phenomenon of inflexibility was associated with particular industry characteristics, and was confined largely to what have come to be known as administered-price industries. The meaning of an administered price has not been made fully clear (and has not been used in the same way) throughout the entire controversy; Means originally defined it as

. . . a price which is set by administrative action and held constant for a period of time. We have an administered price when a company maintains a posted price at which it will make sales or simply has its own price at which customers may purchase or not as they wish.[11]

Such a definition appears to encompass all prices except those negotiated for every individual transaction (e.g., the retail sale of most automobiles) or set in auction-type markets such as the stock exchanges. In contrast to this extremely broad definition, however, administered-price industries often are widely identified as those in which control over price by firms is substantial.

Means himself found a positive relationship between industry concentration and percentage increase in price for the 1929–1932 period, based on an examination of 37 selected manufacturing industries. This finding suggested that the more highly concentrated industries resisted pressures for price decreases during the depression or, conversely, that the lower an industry's concentration level the larger its price decrease (i.e., the lower its rate of increase). If accepted, this conclusion would tie the price inflexibility problem primarily to highly concentrated industries.

The Means finding stimulated an extensive debate over depression price behavior. Thorp and Crowder concluded in an independent study that no measurable relationship between concentration and amplitude of price change existed during 1929–1933.[12] Neal found that industry price changes were closely correlated with changes in cost, stating,

. . . amplitude of price decline in depression is for the most part explained (in the statistical sense) by amplitude of direct cost decline, a matter over which particular industries have little if any discretion. This evidence completely controverts Mean's contention so far as manufacturing industry is concerned.[13]

[11] "Industrial Prices and Their Relative Inflexibility," Senate Document 13, Washington, D.C., January 17, 1935.

[12] Willard E. Thorp and Walter F. Crowder, *The Structure of Industry*, Temporary National Economic Committee, Washington, 1941.

[13] Alfred C. Neal, *Industrial Concentration and Price Inflexibility*, American Council on Public Affairs, 1942, p. 124.

Thus the evidence on depression price patterns was mixed and in conflict. Means found a rough relationship between concentration and the failure of prices to decline; Thorp and Crowder saw no relationship; and Neal concluded that price declines could be explained adequately without reference to concentration. A number of criticisms of the three studies, based largely on methodology and reliability of data, have been made,[14] but it does not appear that the issue has been resolved.

The late 1950's saw what Stigler termed "the second life" of the administered-price theory,[15] this time in a somewhat different form. The newer version of the administered-price hypothesis sought to explain not the failure of prices to decline during depression, but rather the tendency of prices to rise during a period (the middle 1950's) of apparent stability in aggregate demand. Means presented evidence before the Senate Antitrust and Monopoly Subcommittee,[16] showing that administered-price industries, which he had found to be price insensitive during depression, were now, in a sense, too price *sensitive*. If Mean's evidence was correct—and whether correct or not it was scanty—administered price industries were again to blame for a formidable but different economic problem: inflation.

More detailed studies of administrative or oligopolistic inflation, as it was sometimes called, were forthcoming in the 1960's. DePodwin and Selden examined a large number of Census industry and product classes for the period 1953–1959, and reached the following conclusions:

1. The relationship between price change and concentration for 322 five-digit SIC product classes is extremely low . . . the best one can do is to explain 9 percent of the price variation by referring to economic concentration.

2. When the data on five-digit product classes are combined and analyzed by major industry groups, only one group yields a significant coefficient of correlation, and more than half of the groups yield negative coefficients.

3. On a four-digit industry class basis the best that one can do is to explain 10 percent of price variation in terms of economic concentration.[17]

---

[14] See, for example: John M. Blair, "Means, Thorp and Neal on Price Inflexibility," *Review of Economics and Statistics*, **38**, November 1956, pp. 427–35; Jules Backman, "Economic Concentration and Price Inflexibility," *Review of Economics and Statistics*, **40**, November 1958, pp. 399–404; and John M. Blair, "Rejoinder," *Review of Economics and Statistics*, **40**, November 1958, pp. 405–6.

[15] George J. Stigler, "Administered Prices and Oligopolistic Inflation," *Journal of Business*, **35**, January 1962, pp. 1–13.

[16] *Hearings Before the Subcommittee on Antitrust and Monopoly of the Committee of the Judiciary*, United States Senate, 1958, Parts I, IX and X.

[17] Horace J. DePodwin and Richard T. Selden, "Business Pricing Policies and Inflation," *Journal of Political Economy*, **LXXI**, April 1963, pp. 116–27; quotation on p. 124.

The DePodwin-Selden study encompassed linear and curvilinear regressions of a specially constructed price index for product classes, both weighted and unweighted, on various measures of concentration. The results of the statistical analysis uniformly supported the hypothesis that there was no significant relationship between concentration and price change during 1953–1959, and the authors concluded by saying: ". . . we suggest that it is time to put the administrative inflation hypothesis to rest."

In 1966, however, Weiss presented new evidence that lends some credence to the administered-price inflation arguments.[18] Using the DePodwin-Selden price and concentration data, Weiss constructed measures of cost and demand change for 81 four-digit industries. He found that once these other significant explanatory variables were introduced the coefficients for concentration also became significant in explaining price changes. Weiss' explanation of this finding is highly instructive for any approach to empirical hypothesis testing. It was clear, he noted, that simple correlations between concentration and price change were unimpressive. This had been convincingly demonstrated by the DePodwin-Selden study. But such results, Weiss argued, were to be expected, for concentration is at most a secondary determinant of price movements. Once the primary determinants—cost and demand change—were taken account of in his regression equations, the existing relationship between concentration and price change became visible. This relationship—which appears to be significant—had been previously swamped and thus hidden by the effects of cost and demand change in the simple analysis.

The administered-price controversy has proceeded on both the empirical and theoretical levels. Economists such as Stigler have argued strongly that the empirical demonstrations of distinctive behavior in administered-price industries have been based on faulty data and methodology. The Wholesale Price Index, as we have noted, is subject to a variety of errors, some of which may introduce bias into examinations of price behavior. This would be especially damaging if, as Stigler has argued, the bias tends to work in favor of the hypotheses proposed by Means. If, for example, the WPI systematically understates price declines and overstates increases in administered-price industries, many findings would have to be fully discounted. Means and Blair, on the other hand, have argued that some of the shortcomings of the WPI are irrelevant for questions of price *change*, although they may render the index useless for comparing the *height* of prices at a point in time.

---

[18] Leonard W. Weiss, "Business Pricing Policies and Inflation Reconsidered," *Journal of Political Economy*, LXXIV, April 1966, pp. 177–87.

A further methodological objection raised by Stigler concerns Means' classification of administered-price industries. It is not fully clear, even now, what an administered-price industry is. Means' categorization seems to have something to do with market power, but he has also utilized infrequency of price change as a measure of administrativeness. Here it appears that the WPI may do a poor job of measuring frequencies, and this method of assigning industries to the administrative category is therefore questionable.

It is pertinent even now to ask whether anything that could be called an administered-price phenomenon has been convincingly demonstrated. A different, but equally important, question is whether the notion of administered pricing has theoretical content. As we have seen, it is expected that monopolistic industries will charge higher prices than competitive industries in comparable circumstances. But there is no expectation in the orthodox body of economic analysis that patterns of price *change* will consistently differ among industries. Even if we could unambiguously identify administered-price industries as those possessing some specified degree of monopoly power, there is no obvious reason to expect that their prices would, for example, rise more during the middle 1950's than the prices of other industries.

The way in which the prices of monopolistic and competitive firms change over time will depend on the ways in which their cost and demand functions may change. Should costs and demand increase in an industry, price increases will presumably be forthcoming. There is no obvious reason to expect, however, that prices charged in concentrated or monopolistic industries will generally rise more (or fall less) than other prices. Moreover, the kind of argument presented by Means is not fully convincing. He has stated in effect that the inflation of 1955–1957 occurred simply because large firms raised their prices; and that the prices were raised because the firms had the power to do so. This begs the obvious question: why, during the period in question, were firms in administered-price industries *motivated* to raise prices more than other firms? The fact that they had the power to do so is hardly an explanation.

Several explanations of administered-price or oligopolistic inflation have been advanced by those who accept the existence of the phenomenon. One possibility that has had some currency among economists is that the kinds of industry that fit most administered-price descriptions are peculiarly vulnerable to increases in labor cost. Such vulnerability may be traced to a specific form of the countervailing-power hypothesis: powerful firms breed powerful opposing trade unions, which then formulate and press relatively heavy wage demands. The labor component of the large firms' cost structure rises by more than the average and, *ceteris paribus*, larger over-all cost increases and price increases will be evidenced by such companies and by their industry groups.

The vulnerability of administered-price firms and industries to labor union demands may be argued without reference to the empirically questionable countervailing-power hypotheses. If these industries earn higher-than-average profits—and we have seen some evidence that they may—then union wage demands and bargaining positions are likely to be enhanced. Moreover, the companies, as possessors of substantial pricing power, may regard a wage hike as a cost that is readily transferable to consumers by means of price increases.[19] The granting of union demands may therefore not be viewed as an especially costly action. On the contrary, it may even be taken by some companies under close antitrust scrutiny as an excuse for *profitable* upward revisions in price.

A second possible explanation of an oligopolistic inflation has been offered by Galbraith, who argues that oligopolists typically make imperfect price adjustments in periods of rising demand.[20] Specifically, Galbraith contends that, as demand rises, oligopoly prices rise by less than an appropriate amount. After a period of demand increase oligopolists find themselves charging suboptimal prices, and confront what Galbraith calls the unliquidated monopoly gain. The 1955–1957 price increases can be interpreted in Galbraith's terms as an effort to liquidate this gain—that is, to move from suboptimal to optimal (profit-maximizing) prices several years after a period of rising demand. This argument is an ingenious one; however, its policy implications may be disappointing to many who accept the administrative-inflation hypotheses. If the price movements of the middle 1950's were in fact an attempt by oligopoly firms to compensate for earlier imperfect adjustments, neither these firms nor the industries they comprise can be held responsible for inflation. Under the Galbraith line of reasoning, such price increases are economically justified by demand conditions; and the firms that impose them are not saddling the economy with a somehow illegitimate inflation. One could argue to the contrary that such firms actually behaved with considerable pricing *restraint* during the earlier period of demand expansion.

A third interesting explanation of administered-price inflation, formulated by Adams and Lanzillotti, suggests that firms with considerable market power set prices in a way that differs basically from conventional

---

[19] Such a consideration makes good sense, for at the very least a powerful firm will be able to pass on cost increases in the form of higher prices more quickly than a firm that can only react to a market-determined price.

[20] John Kenneth Galbraith, "Market Structure and Stabilization Policy," *Review of Economics and Statistics*, **39**, May 1957, pp. 124–33.

profit-maximizing behavior.[21] According to Adams and Lanzillotti, powerful firms are likely to act as *target-return pricers*, seeking a defined long-run return on investment, whereas less powerful concerns behave more in conformity with the usual maximization calculus. Such a dichotomy carries several implications for price patterns. One that is especially pertinent for the 1950's is that target-return pricers will respond positively in the short run to increases in overhead costs, whereas profit-maximizing pricers will not. It has been shown by Schultze that the period 1955–1957 was characterized by rapid increases in fixed overhead.[22] Thus although the Adams-Lanzillotti hypothesis has not been proved, it is consistent with any observed tendency for the prices of powerful firms and concentrated industries to rise at higher-than-average rates.

The most remarkable fact about the administered-price controversy is that it continues. Three decades of sporadic data gathering and debate have failed to establish the presence of the phenomenon or to rationalize the possibility of its presence in satisfactory theoretical terms. At the very least it must be concluded that administered pricing is not a readily demonstrable event. The evidence that administered-price industries—meaning those that are oligopolistic or monopolistic or highly concentrated—pursue pricing patterns inimical to the interests of the American economy, is scanty. A harsher judgment might be that the debate itself has been ludicrous, centering around a possibly nonexistent occurrence. In the words of Adelman, it may be that: " 'Administered prices' is a catchy phrase which promises everything, explains nothing, and thereby gets in the way of our learning something."[23]

C. Explanations of Inventive Activity

As noted earlier, a number of arguments have been made that inventive and innovative activity flourish in large firms and highly concentrated

[21] Walter Adams and Robert F. Lanzillotti, "The Reality of Administered Prices," *Administered Prices: A Compendium on Public Policy*, Subcommittee on Antitrust and Monopoly, G.P.O., Washington, 1963.

[22] Charles L. Schultze, "Recent Inflation in the United States," Study Paper No. 1 in *Employment, Growth and Price Levels*, Joint Economic Committee, 86th Congress, 1st Session, G.P.O., Washington, 1959.

[23] M. A. Adelman, "A Commentary on 'Administered Prices,'" *Administered Prices: A Compendium on Public Policy*, Subcommittee on Antitrust and Monopoly, G.P.O., Washington, 1963, p. 22.

industries. Among these arguments, most often associated with Schumpeter, are the following:

1. Significant inventions in a world of complex technology require a substantial outlay of resources, which only large companies can provide.
2. The riskiness of inventive effort is such that only large firms, with the ability to sustain losses or to pursue so many inventive efforts that risk is effectively pooled, can undertake major programs.
3. The primary motivation for inventive activity is the profits that may ultimately accrue to new innovations; for this motivation to be sufficient, firms must occupy a strong enough market position to assure that the fruits of inventive activity will be exploited.

The first two arguments imply that firms must be large in an absolute sense in order to become active inventors, whereas the last implies that firms must be relatively large in their markets—that is, that the markets must be relatively concentrated. There are also plausible arguments that reach different conclusions, however. It may be that firm size and industry concentration simply have little or no effect on inventive activity; and it is even conceivable that monopolistic structures will hinder the development of new products and techniques or, perhaps more likely, retard the *introduction* of inventions to the marketplace. Whatever the relative attractiveness of the various arguments, it is clear that the relationship of inventiveness to firm size and market structure cannot be decided deductively. The question is essentially empirical.

Attempts to measure the behavior of inventive activity have been hampered both by difficulty in defining precisely what the meaning of inventive activity may be, and by some scarcity of data. One of the early contributions to the empirical literature by Villard, was based simply on the information that,

The percentage of companies undertaking research increases steadily with the size of the firm: 8 percent of those with fewer than 100 employees, 22 percent of those with fewer than 500, 42 percent of those with fewer than 1,000, 60 percent of those with fewer than 5,000, and 94 percent of those with more than 5,000 employees were reported [by a National Science Foundation Survey for 1953–1954] as conducting research and development.[24]

This information, in addition to Villard's intuitive sympathy with the Schumpeterian position, led him to conclude that large, oligopolistic firms engage in relatively more research effort than their smaller counterparts in competitively structured industry.

[24] Henry H. Villard, "Competition, Oligopoly and Research," *Journal of Political Economy*, **LXVI**, December 1958, pp. 483–97. Quotation on p. 486.

The evidence presented by Villard is so fragmentary that it cannot be considered persuasive. However, the kind of information presented raises questions about the meaning and appropriate measurement of inventive activity. Clearly the proportion of firms engaged in research is a very crude measure of the amount of inventive activity carried on. In an article critical of Villard, Schmookler showed that, within the group of firms conducting research, the amount of *expenditures* on such programs was proportionately about the same for small as for large companies.[25] A later study by Worley indicated that although larger companies hire *more* research and development personnel than do smaller firms, their staffs do not in general consist of *proportionately more* R&D employees than the staffs of smaller companies.[26] A study by Hamberg utilized a similar measure of R&D intensity, and concluded that ". . . there is no solid evidence in support of the 'Schumpeterian' hypothesis."[27]

The measures of inventive activity utilized by these authors all reflect in some way the inventive *effort* or *input* of firms. Although the measures suggest something about R&D patterns, it is possible that similar efforts on the part of different companies will yield widely varying degrees of achievement. A study by Mansfield has attempted to approximate a more direct measure of inventiveness by examining the relationships between actual innovations and firm size and market structure in three industries (iron and steel, petroleum refining, and bituminous coal).[28] Mansfield's findings do not support any simplified hypothesis about inventive activity. In petroleum and coal, for example, the largest firms accounted for "a disproportionately large share of the innovations," but this was not the case in steel, where their contribution was disproportionately small.

Further evidence on inventiveness has been presented by Scherer,[29] who took *patents* as a measure of inventive activity. This measure contains shortcomings: different firms or industries may, for example, have different propensities to patent a given quantity of invention. Scherer's findings failed almost uniformly to support the hypothesis that large, semimonopolistic firms are more inventive than other companies. He concluded that the major determinant of inventive output is technical op-

[25] Jacob Schmookler, "Bigness, Fewness and Research," *Journal of Political Economy*, LXVII, December 1959, pp. 628–35.

[26] James S. Worley, "Industrial Research and the New Competition," *Journal of Political Economy*, 69, April 1961, pp. 183–86.

[27] D. Hamberg, "Size of Firm, Oligopoly and Research: The Evidence," *Canadian Journal of Economics and Political Science*, 30, February 1964, pp. 62–75.

[28] Edwin Mansfield, "Size of Firm, Market Structure, and Innovation," *Journal of Political Economy*, LXXI, December 1963, pp. 556–76.

[29] Frederic M. Scherer, "Firm Size, Market Structure, Opportunity, and the Output of Patented Inventions," *American Economic Review*, 55, December 1965, pp. 1097–1125.

portunity. Inventive output was found to increase with firm sales, "but generally at a less than a proportional rate." And no systematic relationship to market power or a number of other factors was discovered. In a later study[30] Scherer found somewhat more ambiguous results in testing for relationships between market concentration and employment of research scientists and engineers.

It is difficult to draw clear conclusions about firm size, market structure, and inventive activity on the basis of the studies cited. But a number of tentative suggestions can be made. First, it must be noted that evidence in support of the Schumpeterian hypothesis is very meager. It simply does not appear that increasing the size of firms or the concentration of markets yields generally disproportionate gains in inventive or innovative activity. At the same time, the negative findings of past studies require considerable qualification. Not only are the available data imperfect, but there are at least some hints that the true relationships between activity, size, and structure may be considerably more complex than has been thought. It may be, for example, that additional size does stimulate inventiveness within some (relatively low) size range, that is, the larger firms within a group of relatively small firms may be more active. Possibly, then, higher concentration could be an important stimulus to inventive activity in some industries but not others. There may exist threshold levels such that any firm (industry) becomes more inventive up to a specified size (concentration level), but does not continue to increase its inventive activity beyond this point. The threshold may vary widely among industries.

It must be concluded that little has been resolved. The simplest and strongest form of the Schumpeterian contention does not seem to be empirically defensible. Maximization of firm size and degree of monopoly apparently will not maximize inventive and innovative activity; but this finding does not necessarily imply that no relationship exists between firm size and market structure, on one hand, and inventiveness on the other.

D. Some Tentative Clues

The empirical evidence noted above relates largely to suggestions about the effects of industry structure on performance. Other hypotheses imply

[30] "Market Structure and the Employment of Scientists and Engineers," *American Economic Review*, **67**, June 1967, pp. 524–30.

different chains of causation. Performance may affect structure, or one kind of performance may determine another; conduct may affect structure or performance, or vice versa. In general, less is known about the relationships that do not appear to involve direct causality of structure on performance, but brief mention should be made of some fragmentary evidence.

1. CHANGES IN CONCENTRATION

Because it appears that concentration exerts some influence on firm and industry behavior, it would be of interest to know what factors seem to produce change in industry concentration levels.[31] The presence or absence of economies of scale may strongly influence the *level* of concentration in any industry. Thus changes in concentration may be traced to changes in technology that alter the efficiency of large-scale operations. If technology can be taken as given for relatively short time periods (and there are of course industries in which such an assumption is *not* warranted), it may be possible to associate concentration change within the periods with other variables.

Concentration change can result from a change in the number or size distribution of firms, and the problem could accordingly be treated as one of explaining the phenomenon of firm growth. If, for example, large firms tend to grow relatively faster than small firms, increases in measured concentration are likely; should small firms grow relatively fast, the expectation is reversed. Although the determinants of firm growth are not fully understood, there does exist some evidence that growth is independent of initial size. If this is the case, explanations of concentration change must be couched in other terms.

An obvious possibility is that concentration increases are caused by events such as mergers involving a leading firm or firms in an industry. This sort of causality is of limited interest, however, for it says little more than that increases in concentration follow events that increase concentration. The more pertinent question is why mergers that raise the concentration level occur in some industries but not others.

Although it seems that the causes of changing concentration may be neither simple nor readily measurable, an apparently significant factor has been identified in a study by Shepherd.[32] Shepherd found a consistent

---

[31] This question is distinct from the more general issue of what actually has happened to concentration on a national level in recent decades.

[32] William C. Shepherd, "Trends of Concentration in American Manufacturing Industries, 1947–1958," *Review of Economics and Statistics,* **XLVI,** May 1964, pp. 200–12.

negative association between *industry growth* and concentration change for 1947–1958, and also found a positive association between concentration change and *net entry*—the change in the number of firms in each industry for the same period. Because both concentration change and net entry are affected by industry growth, the implication of the latter relationship is unclear; but the influence of the growth variable is of interest. Apparently, leading firms tend to lose some degree of dominance in rapidly expanding industries, but lose relatively little in contracting ones.[33] This suggests that high concentration may be a more permanent condition of stagnant or declining industries than it is of expanding industries. If so, the concern of public policy with concentration perhaps ought to be modified with respect to the latter group.[34]

2. MARKET STRUCTURE AND BUSINESS CONDUCT

The measurement difficulties associated with business conduct make it almost impossible to tell whether various modes of behavior are associated with performance in a systematic way. By the same token, little is known about relationships between market structure and conduct. It seems likely that conduct patterns are strongly influenced by the structural characteristics of markets. The kinds of decision that a business firm makes must depend in part on the firm's market position vis-a-vis rivals. At the same time, however, it may be that conduct influences structure.[35]

To define conduct in such a way that it can be measured—expressed in some quantitative terms—is a primary but difficult task. At least one interesting effort has been made, however. Clabault and Burton present data, as shown in Table 9.2, that relate the incidence of Sherman Act penalties to industry concentration.[36] Penalties under the Sherman Act

[33] George J. Stigler has suggested that it may pay large firms to set high prices and sacrifice market shares in rapidly growing industries. *The Theory of Price*, Macmillan, revised edition, New York, 1952.

[34] Interestingly, it has also been suggested that highly concentrated industries grew more rapidly during the 1946–1955 period (S. Hymer and P. Pashigian, "Turnover of Firms as a Measure of Market Behavior," *Review of Economics and Statistics*, XLIV, February 1962, pp. 82–87). If this were the case, it might be expected that highly concentrated industries would show concentration declines, yet Shepherd's findings do not indicate that this occurred during 1947–1958.

[35] Causality might thus run in either direction, and no empirical test can make a distinction of this sort.

[36] James M. Clabault and John F. Burton, *Sherman Act Indictments 1955–1965: A Legal and Economic Analysis*, Federal Legal Publications, New York, 1966. Table 9.2 is taken from Clabault and Burton's Table 3, p. 130.

are largely those assessed on conviction for price fixing and other kinds of conspiratorial conduct, and thus constitute a rough index of collusive conduct *as defined by Federal antitrust agencies and the courts.*

Table 9.2

Distribution of Manufacturing Industries by Concentration Ratios

Concentra-tion Ratio, Top 4 Firms	(1) All Industries		(2) Industries with Criminal Penalties		(3) Industries with Criminal Penalties Weighted by Cases	
	Number	Percentage	Number	Percentage	Number	Percentage
80–100	14	3.6%	2	3.1%	2	1.6%
70– 79	15	3.9	2	3.1	5	3.9
60– 69	30	7.8	1	1.6	1	0.8
50– 59	31	8.0	3	4.7	13	10.2
40– 49	47	12.2	5	7.8	8	6.3
30– 39	59	15.3	14	21.9	26	20.5
20– 29	88	22.8	19	29.7	39	30.7
0– 19	102	26.4	18	18.1	33	26.0
TOTAL	386	100%	64	100%	127	100%

Column 1 shows the distribution of all industries by concentration groups. If Sherman Act violations are essentially random with respect to concentration, that is, if the propensity of an industry to violate has nothing to do with concentration level, then the distribution of violations, both unweighted, as in Column 2, and weighted as in 3, should be about the same as the distribution of industries. It appears, however, that the distributions are different. Column 3 shows that only 6.3 percent of the industries in which penalties were imposed, had concentration 60 percent or above; yet 15.3 percent of all industries fall within this concentration range. In other words, there seems to be a disproportionately low incidence of violations among industries of very high concentration. This fact may be interpreted in various ways. One possibility is that these industries are so close-knit that the kind of formal, overt conspiracy most often punished by the Sherman Act is unnecessary. When the concentration level is extremely high, collusive modes of conduct may be sufficiently subtle and informal to escape prosecution. A second possibility is that highly concentrated industries may tend to be under relatively close antitrust scrutiny, which in itself deters firms from entering into clearly illegal actions.

Aside from the Clabault-Burton study there has been little systematic effort to measure relationships involving business conduct. Isolated efforts occur whenever a private party attempts to show that he has been harmed by some illegal act such as price fixing. In damage suits the party claiming damages may attempt to show the extent to which price fixing raised the prices he was charged. This constitutes measurement of the effects of conduct; however, the results have been less than encouraging. The estimates of a conspiracy's impact on prices vary over a broad range, and are based on widely divergent approaches. The choice among them, in fact, often seems arbitrary. Once again the problem seems to be that the definition of conduct itself is vague and unsatisfactory. We have difficulty ascertaining the effects of a pricing conspiracy because we really do not know how firms would have behaved in the absence of conspiracy with all other factors constant.

To the extent that conduct remains a phenomenon not susceptible to measurement, empirical examination of its implications is foreclosed. It may be possible to assess the effects of conduct in limited ways, but unless the conduct is itself meaningfully defined there seems little reason to expect that significant relationships will be discovered.

3. ADVERTISING AND COMPETITION

Advertising has received considerable attention in recent years both from antitrust officials and economists. The treatment of advertising in traditional economic theory is limited, and may even involve implicit conflict. On one hand, advertising provides information and may thus serve one requirement of competition; on the other hand, much advertising is designed to differentiate products and, to the extent that it succeeds, positions of market power are enhanced. Donald F. Turner, until recently Assistant Attorney General in charge of the Antitrust Division, has stated that heavy advertising promotes industry concentration and may thus harm competition.[37]

Telser has presented evidence that seems to show that competition and advertising are compatible.[38] Telser performed several tests, one of which defined the relation between advertising intensity (ratio of advertis-

[37] "Advertising and Competition," address delivered before the Briefing Conference on Federal Controls of Advertising and Promotion, June 1966 (mimeographed).

[38] Lester G. Telser, "Advertising and Competition," *Journal of Political Economy*, LXXII, December 1964, pp. 537–62.

ing expenditure to sales) and concentration. The correlation, although positive, was not significant, and, based partly on this finding, he concludes that there is "little empirical support for an inverse association between advertising and competition. . . ." There are, however, a number of reasons for treating Telser's finding and conclusions with caution. It may be that advertising influences the level of industry concentration,[39] but it seems unlikely that any simple test of such an association will show strong results. Even if advertising has an effect on concentration it is probably overshadowed by other factors, most notably economies of scale and optimum firm size and the absence or presence of efficient predators or monopolists in the market. These factors are of course difficult to measure, but the meaningful question remains: what is the effect of advertising on concentration, abstracting from other determinants of concentration?

It is not clear that Telser's procedure tests the kind of relationship that observers such as Turner have suggested. Advertising intensity may change concentration over time. It is not widely believed that advertising expenditures constitute a major determinant of industrial organization generally. Yet it would be difficult to argue a priori that advertising has no effect whatever on industry structure and performance. Recent evidence presented by Comanor and Wilson[40] has shown that advertising plays a role in the profit rates of industries, along with industry concentration, technical barriers to entry, and growth of demand. Some advocates of federal controls suggest that the primary effect of advertising is a heightening of industry barriers to entry, a suggestion that is consistent with an effect on profitability. Once again it appears that the role of the variable in question may be different in some industries than in others. Consequently, the general relationship of advertising to industry structure and performance may prove difficult to define.

4. FIRM SIZE AND EFFICIENCY

One of the most important questions in industrial organization is whether large firm size—and, *ceteris paribus*, higher concentration—imply effi-

---

[39] The direction of causality is not completely clear, however. Industry structure, as approximated by measures of concentration, may also exert considerable impact on advertising.

[40] William S. Comanor and Thomas A. Wilson, "Advertising, Market Structure and Performance," *Review of Economics and Statistics*, **XLIX**, November 1967, pp. 423–40. See also P. Asch and M. Marcus, "Returns to Scale on Advertising," *Antitrust Bulletin*, **XV**, Spring 1970, pp. 33–41.

ciency in production and distribution. This is simply the other side of the question of whether existing firm size and concentration can be justified on efficiency grounds.

As we have suggested, the empirical evidence bearing on this issue is fragmentary. The most promising development is econometric investigation of returns to scale. It is possible to estimate the production function for different industries and to draw some conclusions about size-efficiency relationships. To date, however, detailed information has not been developed for most areas.

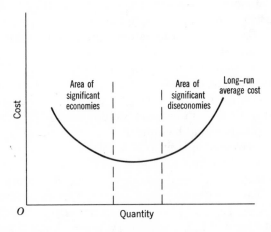

Figure 9.1

The relevant question may be seen in terms of the long-run average cost curve portrayed in Figure 9.1. It is normally assumed in economic analysis that the curve is U-shaped, as drawn. The declining portion reflects positive economies of scale; the bottom or flat portion indicates an essentially neutral range (costs do not respond much to changes in scale); and the rising segment shows the level of production at which diseconomies of scale set in. Economic theory does not provide us with any inkling as to where—at what production level—a firm's cost curve may bottom out or turn up. Yet this is in a sense the most immediate efficiency question.

Does the present size distribution of American firms reflect economies of scale? Again the evidence is scattered and incomplete. Undoubtedly some part of the very wide disparity in firm size is based in economies of scale. This is simply to state that some degree of firm bigness (and industry concentration) is economically justified. At the same time, a number of investigators suggest that, beyond some minimum critical point, size variations are largely random and do not reflect significant economies or diseconomies of scale.[41] Categorical statements are not yet possible. It should be noted, however, that present evidence does not strongly argue that firm size and industry concentration levels are even approximately optimal.

[41] See H. A. Simon and C. P. Bonini, "The Size Distribution of Business Firms," *American Economic Review*, **68**, September 1958, pp. 6–12.

10

Empirical Evidence and Policy: Some Cases and Conclusions

To this point we have considered some general empirical problems and evidence on firm and industry behavior. It may now be helpful to examine a few specific industries in somewhat more detail. In addition to conveying a better feel for observed behavior, such examination may illustrate the inherent limitations of more general empirical relationships. The characteristics of industries vary widely, and attempts to base policy on "average" or "typical" structure-conduct-performance relationships may prove futile. Indeed, as our specific examples should indicate, the application of *any* simple and consistent rules of thumb may not be a promising approach to public policy.

A. Competitively Structured Markets: Agriculture and Textiles

We have noted at several earlier points that the requirements of perfect competition—a very large number of small firms, product homogeneity, and free entry and exit—are rarely found in real markets. Agriculture and textiles, however, are two important markets that possess most of the competitive properties.

1. AGRICULTURE

Our agricultural markets are structurally about as close to the competitive model as we are likely to come. The number of firms (in this case *farms*) is large: there are, for example, over one million producers of hogs and cotton. Farm products are truly homogeneous; there may be differences in wheat, for example, but within any category there exist no distinctions in the wheat of various farmers. In addition, entry into agricultural markets is easy. The capital requirement is low, there are no product-differentiation barriers, and, although larger farms may be somewhat more efficient than smaller ones, it is possible to attain efficiency at a very small size relative to the market.

Despite the fact that agriculture is so close to the competitive ideal, it has been plagued by serious and persistent problems. Farm prices and incomes are subject to severe fluctuation. Farm income, moreover, tends to be extremely low, and poverty, a condition usually associated with the cities, abounds in rural areas. Average farm income may be no more than two-thirds of the national average, even after adjusting for such factors as consumption of goods produced, imputed rentals, and appreciation of property. The existence of these difficulties has stimulated extensive government intervention in the agricultural markets, perhaps a surprising development in a competitive setting.

In order to understand the reasons behind agricultural problems, we must consider the nature and behavior of market supply and demand. It appears that the demand for most farm products is inelastic, as would be expected. There simply are no substitutes for food generally, and there are often few close substitutes for particular foods. Estimates of the elasticity of demand for all foods have fallen in the .2 to .5 range;[1] although elasticity estimates for some food products such as fruits[2] exceed unity, demands for many specific products tend to be low.

The elasticity of supply in agricultural markets also tends to be very low in the short run at least. The average and marginal cost curves of farmers appear to be conventionally shaped, as shown in Figure 10.1. Because of substantial fixed costs such as taxes, rents, and property

---

[1] See Karl A. Fox, *The Analysis of Demand for Farm Products*, U.S. Department of Agriculture, Technical Bulletin No. 1081, September 1953; M. A. Girshick and T. Haavelmo, "Statistical Analysis of the Demand for Food," *Econometrica*, **15**, April 1947; and James Tobin, "A Statistical Demand Function for Food in the U.S.A.," *Journal of the Royal Statistical Society*, Series A, Part II, 1950.

[2] See Fox, *op. cit.* The demand elasticity for all fruit is estimated to be 1.1 and is as high as 1.5 for peaches.

depreciation, the average unit cost curve declines at first (as fixed costs are spread over larger numbers of units). With certain productive factors fixed in the short run, however, it becomes increasingly expensive to expand output beyond some point. Marginal costs rise rapidly, and the average cost curve turns up as well. An *MC* curve as in Figure 10.1 indicates that marginal costs rise sharply with increases in output beyond some level; accordingly, the response of quantity supplied to price increases will be quite low.

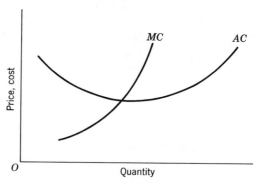

Figure 10.1

The inelasticity of market supply and demand curves provides one clue to the instability of farm prices. Rapid shifts in supply or demand will tend to produce major changes in price. If, for example, bad weather reduces the supply of wheat one year, the supply curve of wheat shifts to the left; but, given the inelastic demand for wheat, any leftward supply shift results in a relatively large price increase.

Price instability in agriculture cannot be explained fully by inelastic supply and demand conditions, however. Another cause of instability has to do with the time lags in the supply-adjustment process. A farmer who finds that he has miscalculated his market by producing either more or less than he would have liked at the prevailing price usually cannot make an immediate adjustment; he must wait until the next production period, perhaps a half year later. The price instability that results from such a lag is illustrated by the familiar *cobweb theorem* shown in Figure 10.2. Suppose initially that farmers anticipate a price of P for their product; perhaps this is the price at which the product could have been sold previously. Acting appropriately, the farmers produce quantity Q in the next production period. In the next selling period, however, they discover that quantity Q can only be sold at a lower price such as P'. If the farmers now expect P' to prevail in the future, they will restrict output to Q'; but when Q' is placed on the market it brings price P; farmers now go back to producing quantity Q; and so forth. The result will be an oscillation of prices between P and P'.[3]

Of course demand and supply curves are not likely to stand perfectly still over extended periods, and we thus may have difficulty observing such oscillations; some economists however, believe that the existence of

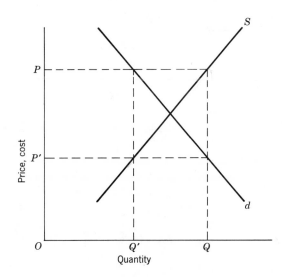

Figure 10.2

such cobwebs is supported by empirical evidence. The point, however, is not that prices are expected to behave in strict conformity with a cobweb diagram. It is rather that miscalculation of future prices by farmers is a real problem; and that such miscalculation will contribute to price fluctuations. When this difficulty is considered in addition to the fact that farm supply may shift unexpectedly with weather conditions, the reasons for unstable prices should be abundantly clear.

The fact that farm prices tend to fluctuate does not tell us why farmers' incomes tend to be low. This phenomenon can be explained by the behavior of supply and demand over time: generally, supply has

[3] The oscillation could become greater or smaller over a series of periods, depending on shapes of the supply and demand functions.

expanded rapidly while demand has expanded at a much slower rate. The tendency has thus been for prices and revenues (given inelastic demands) to fall. Why has this occurred? The expansion of supply seems to be attributable to two factors. First, technological improvements have made it possible to produce more with a given set of inputs (e.g., more corn can be grown on an acre of land). The second factor, perhaps even more important, is the increased price of labor vis-a-vis capital. It simply has become cheaper to employ more capital in relation to labor, and the resulting shift in factor proportions has been productive.

As supply has expanded, however, demand has risen only slowly. When population increases the demand for food increases as well. This stimulus to demand, however, has been relatively small in comparison with the growth of supply. As per capita income rises there is also some tendency for expenditures on food to rise; but the demand for food appears not to be highly elastic with respect to income. Moreover, increased food expenditures may not affect farmers very much. Consumers may demand more services with their foods—for example, frozen, prepared, and convenient items—without demanding greater amounts of the products of farms.

Although it is easy to see why farm incomes are low at any point in time, an important question remains: why is it that long-run market adjustments have failed to alleviate the problem? We have seen earlier that in a competitive industry profits beneath the normal level will cause firms to exit until the normal return is restored for the remaining firms; indeed, a similar process is expected to occur in any industry that produces unsatisfactory rates of return. Why, then, has the low-income problem in agriculture not been solved by exit of farmers from the agricultural markets? There has been a substantial exodus of farm workers in recent decades, but it seems to have been insufficient.

One commonly cited reason for insufficient exit is the fact that farmers are reluctant to switch occupations. A change to nonfarm employment involves a new way of life and is thus unlike a change in many other jobs. This may be; however, if exit is impeded by the fact that people do not want to leave, it might be argued that we have underestimated the real value of farm incomes. Perhaps a farmer earns only $3000 per year in readily measurable terms; but his enjoyment of his way of life may be regarded as a kind of psychic income that also ought to be valued in monetary terms. A precise valuation of psychic income may be impossible, but if it is substantial farmers are in some meaningful sense better off than we generally believe.

A further obstacle to exit is the structural problem of those who do not know how to do other kinds of work. The alternative earnings of many agricultural workers—and thus the alternative cost of remaining on the farm—may be extremely low. Perhaps many agricultural workers *do* earn their normal profit.

The response of government to farm problems has been vigorous but not entirely effective. Federal prices supports have been commonly utilized. The government agrees to buy up (in effect) any surplus products at specified prices. This policy resulted in a serious surplus problem in the late 1940's, after which support levels were reduced somewhat. The determination of support levels has long plagued the price program. Prices have been tied to notions of *parity* or fairness in the vague sense of equality. For many years government supports were specified in terms of the base parity period 1910–1914, in order to assure farmers of prices that would yield them some percentage of the purchasing power yielded by the same products during the base. The support system was later revised so that a moving average of more recent years was used as the base.

In addition to price supports, the government has made use of crop restriction programs. Restrictions of supply create higher prices and, given inelastic demands, tend to raise revenue levels as well. Since 1961 strict crop restrictions have been coupled with price supports. Payments to farmers depend on adherence to the crop controls; thus the system creates the proper incentives to restrict supply.

Government controls so far have proved to be partially effective in combating the problems of instability and low income. The guaranteed price floors take some of the guesswork out of farmers' future price calculations; they are thus unlikely to suffer severe price and revenue declines. The price-support and crop-restriction programs, however, have been less effective in easing low-income difficulties. There is some relationship between farm size and efficiency, so that large farms tend to need government assistance least and small farms most. The program, however, aids farmers in precisely the opposite way; it is the large farm that qualifies for the greatest amount of assistance, whereas smaller farms may benefit only by small amounts. In light of this perverse quality of farm support programs some observers have suggested that a guaranteed annual income for farmers might be a more appropriate type of aid program.

Within the context of this book, perhaps the most interesting fact about agriculture is the existence of serious economic problems. Obviously a competitive market does not necessarily operate free from difficulty, despite the fact that we are used to terming it the ideal form of industrial organization. The problems of agriculture are not difficult to understand and are consistent with theoretical expectations. Competitive firms are expected to earn normal profits, and if exit is impeded in the presence of increasing supply, extremely low profits will result.

2. TEXTILE MANUFACTURING

The textile manufacturing industries do not present as clear an example of pure competition as does agriculture, but are nevertheless similar in some respects to the competitive model. The industries are characterized by low concentration; products tend to be standardized, although they are not always completely homogeneous; and entry is relatively easy.

The textile manufacturing process encompasses several distinct steps. Raw fibers such as cotton, synthetics, and wool are first spun to form yarns or threads. The yarns and threads are then woven or knit into fabrics, which are in turn treated or finished by processes such as bleaching, dyeing, and shaping. The finished cloth enters the fabrication stage, at which final products such as clothing, sheeting, and industrial fabrics are produced. Typically, the term textile industry refers to any and all of these productive stages. Concentration levels for the major textiles industries are shown in Table 10.1. It is evident that, although production is not highly concentrated in the hands of a few firms, the industries are not strictly atomistic. The trend of concentration, moreover, has been upward in most areas.

The technology of the textile industries generally involves the application of labor to relatively simple machines. Although there have been some significant technical improvements in machinery recently, the production process has not changed basically, and the industries remain highly labor intensive. The relatively low capital requirements of the industry, combined with product standardization, especially at the earlier stages of production, imply easy entry for new firms.

By similar token, most costs for a textile firm are variable; there is little in the way of fixed overhead, and the primary costs are raw materials, energy, and labor. Marginal costs for textile producers are relatively constant during any plant shift, perhaps rising slightly as plant production expands to two and three eight-hour shifts per day. Obviously productive capacity in the short run will reach its limit at the amount that can be produced when a plant is utilized 24 hours a day. At this point the marginal cost curve becomes perfectly inelastic (vertical).

In the long run, scale of plant is variable and firms' cost curves are accordingly different. Efficient operations can be attained at relatively small plant size; as Weiss said, "mills that employ only a few hundred people are large enough to use the most advanced methods of production at each stage in the textile process."[4] In addition, small *firm* size does not

[4] Leonard W. Weiss, *Economics and American Industry*, Wiley, New York, 1961, p. 133.

Table 10.1

Percentage of Value of Shipments Accounted for by Largest Firms

Product	Year	Top Four Firms	Top Eight Firms
Weaving mills, cotton	1963	30	46
	1958	25	40
	1954	18	29
Weaving mills, synthetics	1963	39	48
	1958	34	44
	1954	30	39
	1947	31	39
Knit outerwear mills	1963	11	16
	1958	7	10
	1954	6	10
	1947	8	13
Men's and boys' suits and coats	1963	14	23
	1958	11	19
	1954	11	18
	1947	9	15
Women's suits, coats, and skirts	1963	8	11
	1958	3	5
	1954	3	6
Dresses	1963	6	9

Source: Concentration Ratios in Manufacturing Industry 1963, Report prepared by the Bureau of the Census for the Subcommittee on Antitrust and Monopoly of the Committee on the Judiciary (Senate), 89th Cong., 2nd Sess., 1966.

seem to be an especially imposing disadvantage. The data in Table 10.2 on rates of return indicate that relatively small companies can do well, although it is interesting to note that Burlington Industries—by far the largest firm—showed the highest profit rate in three of four recent years.

Public policy in textiles has long centered on tariffs against competitive goods from abroad. Although tariff levels are now lower than they were a

Table 10.2

Rates of Return in the Knit Apparel & Woven & Knit Fabrics
(Except Floor Covering) Markets, 1960, 1961, 1964, 1965

Company	1960		1961		1964		1965	
	Assets (in thousands)	Rate of return[a]	Assets (in thousands)	Rate of return[a]	Assets (in thousands)	Rate of return[a]	Assets (in thousands)	Rate of return[a]
Burlington Industries, Inc.	$606	10.7	$614	6.8	$756	12.7	$909	15.3
J. P. Stevens & Co., Inc.	358	6.7	370	4.5	469	6.8	511	10.6
Dan River Mills, Inc.	168	7.8	174	5.3	185	7.7	249	11.5
West Point-Pepperell, Inc.[b]	97	10.9	105	6.7	112	9.5	191	12.2
Cannon Mills Co.	163	9.5	170	8.2	172	7.9	191	7.6
Cone Mills Corp.	164	3.2	166	2.3	172	7.9	190	7.6
M. Lowenstein & Sons, Inc.	195	6.1	189	1.8	185	4.0	188	6.3
Beaunit Mills, Inc.	101	4.3	102	6.5	117	8.4	166	10.1
Kendall Co.	81	9.2	90	8.6	100	10.6	110	11.6

[a] Net income after taxes as a percentage of stockholders' investment.
[b] Formerly West Point Mfg. Co.

Source: *Report of the Federal Trade Commission on Rates of Return for Identical Companies in Selected Manufacturing Industries, 1940, 1947–61; and 1956–65.*

few decades ago,[5] importation of foreign fabrics is still limited by this most questionable device. In recent years antitrust authorities have shown increased interest in the textile industries. Numerous mergers—horizontal, vertical, and conglomerate—have caused the Federal Trade Commission to call textiles "one of the most merger-prone of American industries."[6] The Commission announced in 1968 a specific merger policy with respect to the industry,[7] designed to discourage further acquisitions by the leading six firms.

The question of what constitutes an appropriate antitrust policy toward textiles is not easily answered. The Federal Trade Commission is concerned that the industry seems to be moving away from its traditional competitive structure. Such a trend may be troublesome, especially when there is no obvious economies-of-scale justification for it. On the other hand, textile performance as an atomistic industry has not been obviously superior. If structural change were to carry with it the possibility of more rapid technological advance, larger firms and higher concentration might be a reasonable price to pay.

B. Oligopolistic Markets: Cigarettes and Steel

1. STEEL

The steel industry presents a classic picture of oligopoly. The four largest producers (United States Steel, Bethlehem, Republic, and Armco) account for something over 50 percent of national ingot capacity; and the eight largest have close to 75 percent. The leading companies tend to be vertically integrated and to produce highly standardized products that are sold primarily to large buyers such as the automobile manufacturers. Entry into the industry is difficult and infrequent because of high initial capital requirements and the concentrated control of basic ore sources.

The behavior of the steel industry has long been a topic of vigorous debate in the United States. The pricing patterns of steel firms often appear collusive in the broad sense. During the early part of the century many products were priced under various basing-point systems. These

---

[5] The Reciprocal Trade Agreements Act, passed in 1934, resulted in some tariff reductions; the impact on textiles, although substantial, has left average tariffs at a fairly high level.

[6] News Release, Federal Trade Commission, August 18, 1969.

[7] *Enforecment Policy with Respect to Mergers in the Textile Mill Products Industry*, Federal Trade Commission, November 22, 1968.

pricing schemes, which will be discussed in more detail below, had the effect that identical prices were charged by all manufacturers to customers in any given geographic location. When basing-point pricing was declared illegal by the courts, partly because of its collusive implications, the industry retreated to a type of price leadership. In recent years different firms have assumed the role of price leader. The result by all measurable indices has been that active price rivalry, an occasional phenomenon 30 or 40 years ago, has largely disappeared.

The steel industry, among others, is frequently blamed for inflationary pressures in the national economy. It is true that the prices of many steel products have risen very substantially during the past 20 years, more than doubling in some cases. Unfortunately, however, the discussion that has raged over this phenomenon has often proved less than illuminating. The producers have blamed labor unions for the price increases, citing rapidly rising earnings of steelworkers. Some critics of the industry, however, claim that hourly wage rates have been partially offset by improved productivity, and that labor *costs* per unit of output have risen more slowly than prices.

The task of sorting out such arguments is a difficult one. It may be noted that, whatever price increases have accomplished, they have not resulted in an abnormal level of profits for the steel industry. After-tax rates of return for the major companies have averaged less than 10 percent during the past decade. Interestingly, the largest companies have not earned consistently higher returns. United States Steel, which is more than twice the size of the next-largest producer, has frequently experienced profit levels below the industry average; conversely, both National and Inland, the fifth and sixth companies, have enjoyed profits well above the average in many recent years.

One possible explanation of profit-rate differentials may lie in the fact that relatively small companies have been active innovators. Armco, National, and Republic, for example, are associated with some of the most important technological changes of the century. This observation raises the question of what a socially desirable firm size in the steel industry may be. It has long been maintained that large plants are necessary for efficient operations in the industry. Whereas this is undoubtedly true, it is questionable whether existing levels of firm size and industry concentration can be fully justified by economies of scale. Recent estimates indicate that an integrated steel mill requires annual average capacity of 3.8 million tons in order to attain minimum average production costs. Since national steel capacity exceeds 150 million tons, the contention that current concentration is mandated by underlying economic forces should perhaps be viewed with some skepticism.

The structure and performance of the steel industry raise some peculiar public policy issues. Some observers argue that more direct public control of the industry is in order, citing "undesirable" patterns in pricing, innovation, and growth. The industry is in some respects similar to a public utility, but would this type of intervention improve its performance? Public regulation would not act to dissolve exorbitant profits, for they do not exist. Further, it is questionable whether public controls would effectively stimulate invention and innovation. To the contrary, we might conclude, based on past records, that encouragement of more "independent" firms of a size smaller than United States Steel could lead to improved technological advancement.

It may be puzzling that a tightly knit oligopoly behaving in a collusive fashion has been unable to reap abnormal profit levels. Several reasons may be pertinent. First, as we have noted, monopoly power is no guarantee of high profits; consumers must still be willing to purchase appropriate quantities at prices in excess of average costs. Despite this, it might be expected that in the long run the industry would adjust to create more profitable levels of activity. That this has not occurred may be in part because of *in*efficiencies of large size; and in part because of an unstable (fluctuating) demand that requires that the industry build in excess productive capacity much in the manner of an electric power company. Finally, segments of the industry may have made serious miscalculations about the nature of demand conditions. Typically it has been assumed that the demand for steel is highly inelastic; accordingly, steel producers have often undertaken substantial price increases without serious concern that quantities demanded would be adversely affected. To the extent that substitute materials and foreign steel have become increasingly close substitutes for domestic steel, however, this sanguine view of the world may already have proved to be costly.

What ought public policy to do about the steel industry? The primary difficulty with this question is that there is no objective way to assess the "goodness" of industry performance. Those who are satisfied would likely recommend no additional public action; those who are distressed might argue that more firms of medium size could induce greater competition and innovation.

2. CIGARETTES

Like steel, the domestic cigarette industry is highly concentrated. Under some measures concentration has fallen slightly in recent years, but the top four firms still account for close to 80 percent of industry sales. The reasons for high concentration, however, appear to be much different than they are in steel. Cigarette manufacturing does not require large production facilities for efficient operations. At the same time, however, costs of production do not turn up rapidly and firms are thus encouraged to grow.

product differentiation

The existence of large companies reflects in part the nature of industry competition. There are some physical differences among cigarette brands, yet the product is essentially standardized. In economic terms, however, cigarettes are differentiated. Companies spend large sums on advertising and promotion, and it is these efforts that constitute the major area of competition for the industry. It may be that economies of scale in advertising—both real and pecuniary—account for the existing size structure of firms.

Cigarette industry demand appears to be inelastic with respect to price. Given rivals' prices constant, however, it is likely that the demand curve faced by any individual firm would be highly elastic.[8] This might suggest that price cutting would be an attractive policy for firms, yet industry-wide prices have shown substantial uniformity for some years. The obvious explanation for this pattern is the companies' fear of active price competition and price warfare. Despite product differentiation through advertising, the demands for various cigarette brands are probably highly cross-elastic. Price cutters would initially be so successful in attracting sales away from rivals that the rivals would have little choice but to retaliate; and at that point the war would be on. Given the circumstances, it seems clear that the companies have opted to avoid price competition, competing rather for shares of the market by means of promotional expenditures.

In this case it appears that the conduct patterns of firms have influenced market structure. Promotional expenditure and product differentiation have become important barriers to new entry. A potential entrant could begin producing cigarettes efficiently with a relatively small capital outlay; but breaking into the market effectively would require substantial advertising costs in order to overcome the existing brand loyalties of consumers. The profits of the cigarette producers have tended to be somewhat above the average for all manufacturing concerns,[9] yet new entrants have not come in to compete away this reward. It

---

[8] It is interesting to note that under a monopoly measure of the Rothschild type the cigarette manufacturers would be seen to have little monopoly power. Whereas one may disagree with such an assessment, it is clear that the top-four concentration ratio as a description of monopoly requires substantial qualification.

[9] In recent years diversification of the leading manufacturers has made it more difficult to observe the profits of the cigarette industry in isolation.

seems plausible that such a failure is explained by the obstacles to entry.[10]

For purposes of public policy analysis, the cigarette industry may not fit conveniently into our market categories. It is true that the industry is structurally oligopolistic, and the nature of the product market is such that price competition would not be expected to flourish. Yet there are reasons why an attempt to introduce a more competitive environment might not be an appropriate policy. There is little reason to expect that even a complete metamorphosis in the structure of the industry could alter the nature of competition. The market power of the manufacturers seems to reside in their advertising capacity rather than the size of their physical plants; and merely to create more firms (say, by splitting up the present market leaders) would not change the distribution of power significantly. Further, it is difficult to see how a less concentrated cigarette industry would alter a situation in which competition by means of advertising is clearly safer, and thus preferable to, active price rivalry.

Many observers contend that the cigarette industry is socially wasteful. Large sums are spent with the sole purpose of attracting consumers to one or another brand. The industry has frequently—but not always— appeared to reap a monopoly reward. Yet these socially costly elements cannot readily be mitigated by the usual policies of promoting competition. Treatment of the cigarette industry will likely require some innovative approaches to public policy.

C. A Word on Pure Monopoly and Monopolistic Competition

Our discussion has so far neglected two market forms analyzed in earlier chapters: pure monopoly and monopolistic competition. The pure monopolist is defined as the sole seller of a product for which no close substitutes exist. This definition is so demanding that it is difficult to find current examples in the American economy. Utilities companies often enjoy pure local monopoly, but their performance is publically regulated and thus may tell us little about the behavior of an unrestricted monopolist. Occasionally some firms (e.g., I.B.M., Procter & Gamble, Alcoa) attain a degree of market dominance that carries them close to pure monopoly, but not quite all the way. More frequently, we see genuine

---

[10] Alternatively, we might argue that because entry is risky for new firms the profit rates of established companies do not accurately reflect the expectations of potential competitors.

but short-lived monopolies: the producer of a patented invention or an unpatented innovation that has not yet been copied by rivals. These examples are very limited, and must be heavily qualified by actual or potential substitutability from other products.

The obvious present-day example of monopolistically competitive markets is to be found in the various areas of retailing: food, drugs, liquors, and so on. Here we see many sellers of substitutable goods, differentiated by location and other factors that cause consumers to prefer some stores over others. General trends in retailing seem to indicate some tendency for concentration to rise. This change, associated with the growth of large, nationwide chains, has not yet made retailing trades highly concentrated; but in some areas it has moved sufficiently to cause a question as to whether the large-group aspect crucial to monopolistic competition still survives.

Indeed, one of the major problems in attempting to discuss retailing is definition of the market. Retailers typically deal in a variety of products, and even the specialty store may carry more than 100 distinct items. What, then, is the retailer's "product?" It is in effect a basket of commodities, the composition and weights of which may vary considerably from store to store. The geographic market also presents definitional problems. In an urban area, for example, what is the proper boundary? Is New York City a pertinent market for retail foods? Is Manhattan? Or is it perhaps a particular neighborhood, or even a part of a neighborhood? Difficulties such as these make quick generalizations about retail market behavior all but impossible.

In very general terms the behavior of retailing seems to bear out theoretical expectations. The intensity of price competition is attested to by high mortality rates among firms. Relatively easy entry in many areas is reflected in low rates of return (a noteworthy exception is liquor stores; here entry is effectively blocked by governmental restriction).

D. Theory, Evidence, and Policy

Empirical evidence bearing on industrial organization and behavior serves two distinct and important purposes. First, it tells us something about the validity and usefulness of the theoretical framework from which hypotheses are drawn. Second, it provides some indication of the consequences of policies that deal with organization and behavior.

As we have seen, empirical measurement is beset by a wide range of conceptual and practical problems. Theoretical suggestions are often difficult to translate into testable hypotheses. Data deficiencies are common, and even hypotheses that are in principle testable may prove difficult to examine. For these reasons alone, the interpretation of empirical evidence is frequently difficult. In light of these problems, mild optimism may be justified when we consider the relationship of existing evidence to the theoretical apparatus. In the words of Clabault and Burton,

If one were to be generous about the justifiable conclusions which can be drawn from the empirical studies made of the American economy . . . it could be argued that there is a relationship between structure and performance, and this relationship seems to be *roughly* what the neoclassical economist expected: i.e., the more firms in an industry the better.[11]

Other observers might be somewhat less positive in judging the implications of past empirical studies, but it would seem at the very least that some support for and little outright contradiction of a variety of theoretical suggestions has been found.

Of more direct concern to us, however, are the policy implications of evidence, and here the picture is far from clear. Empirical relationships are imprecise. Moreover, since the thrust of policy is influenced by various goals, it could not be anticipated that even unambiguous empirical evidence on the consequences of alternative policy would always be decisive. That is, we cannot expect to move even from a clear statement of the economic implications of policy directly to a statement of what policy is or ought to be. The weight of empirical evidence, however, will be meaningful so long as policy is *in some degree* responsive to purely economic considerations.

What, then, does existing empirical evidence contribute to policy formulation? As we have noted, simple rules of thumb have not been forthcoming, and may be inherently impossible. The differences between even such structurally similar industries as steel and cigarettes are so important that *no* common policy would suffice. It may be that more-or-less automatic rules will apply in the future; but this will require insight into what are certainly more complex relationships than have been isolated empirically thus far.

If we have failed to derive policy rules, however, empirical evidence has at least indicated some variables that are of policy concern. We could not, for example, base a broad program regarding concentration or firm

---

[11] James M. Clabault and John F. Burton, *Sherman Act Indictments, 1945–1965*, Federal Legal Publications, New York, 1966, p. 127.

size on existing evidence; but we do have reasons to think that these factors may carry broadly predictable implications for performance.

If a policy maker were to ask what attitudes toward concentration and firm size are appropriate on purely economic grounds, the answer would necessarily be qualified. The only certainty is that generalization is at this point impossible. At first glance it may seem that the burden of empirical evidence is itself so mixed and conflicting that it is not of much use. Yet within the context of a policy that must consider multiple objectives this is not inevitably so. Confident generalizations might be more useful and easier to work with, but even the knowledge that generalizations cannot be made is worth having. Suppose, for example, that antitrust policy administrators begin with a social and political presumption against high market concentration. On the basis of evidence gathered so far, it can at least be stated that observations of economic consequences do not lead us generally in the opposite direction; that is, there is no clear indication that highly concentrated areas display consistently superior economic performance.

The kind of information that empirical investigation has adduced cannot be readily applied in specific situations. Undoubtedly lower levels of concentration would be beneficial in some industries and detrimental to others, but this does not tell us whether antitrust action to deconcentrate any particular industry would be good or bad.

The argument for proceeding in many antitrust areas on a case-by-case approach is strong. But, as empirical investigations proceed, we accumulate more than a bank of information. New approaches to measurement will be tried out and refined. Different techniques for measuring "immeasurable" magnitudes will appear. The end result may never be a complete set of rules of thumb under which the agencies and courts can make automatic disposition of all questions bearing on competition, but the relevant bits and pieces multiply, and as they do, the possibilities for economically rational judgment are enlarged.

PART III

Antitrust Policy

This section deals with the nature and economic interpretation of antitrust policy. As we have seen, neither economic theory nor the existing body of empirical evidence provides clear prescriptions for public policy. There are general theoretical arguments in favor of competition, but these are often inapplicable to specific situations. Similarly, it is observed that different kinds of industries may behave differently, but again it proves difficult to draw specific implications for particular industries under particular conditions. Any economic interpretation or evaluation of antitrust, then, cannot compare actual policy with some rigid and well-defined ideal.

To point out that economics has not provided antitrust with comprehensive guideposts is *not* to imply that it has provided nothing at all. Indeed, the clues to policy contained in the theory and evidence discussed above are both abundant and important. If we do not have a theoretical road map for policy, we at least have a large number of road signs and signals. Economic theory and evidence are most useful in predicting—albeit imprecisely and with limited confidence—the consequences of alternative policies. If the government were to consider, for example, a major effort to lower market concentration in the manufacturing sector, it would be possible to suggest some possible results of such a policy move. Even if the contemplated policy were much

223

narrower—say, an effort to lower concentration in steel production—there is an analytical framework within which possible effects can be evaluated. Objective analysis stops short, however, of defining the "rightness" or "wrongness" of any policy. This kind of judgment depends on the *goals* of policy, an element beyond the scope of economic theory or empirical measurement.

In general, antitrust goals are little different from the broader economic and political objectives of society. Antitrust seeks to promote economic progress and efficiency and to protect individual liberty and freedom of choice. Such objectives are hardly unique. What is special to antitrust is the more proximate objective of maintaining competitive markets. This is the lower-order goal that is a means toward the ultimate ends. Although it is easy to list ultimate aims on which some general consensus exists, the problem of defining antitrust objectives is not so simple, for a meaningful definition must be more than a listing. It must include, at the least, some *ordering* or ranking of objectives, and ideally it should provide some even more specific notion of the relative importance accorded to each.

It may be helpful to resurrect an earlier example in somewhat greater detail. Suppose it is specified that technical efficiency and competitiveness are the sole goals of antitrust policy. By itself this listing does not tell us very much about what policy ought to do. It is likely that one group of policy moves will increase efficiency, and another will increase competition. Both elements cannot be maximized simultaneously, for with a given level of resources some of the moves that are undertaken to enhance one objective necessarily limit our ability to make moves that would increase the other. All that is specified so far, however, is that we are interested in both objectives. Without knowing whether we should be *equally* interested in efficiency and competition, or *more* interested in one, there is no clear indication of the appropriate mixture of policy moves.[1]

Let us now make our example much more specific. Suppose that we are concerned with the (hypothetical) widget manufacturing industry, in which technical efficiency and competitiveness are known to conflict. We know, in other words, that large firms, which imply high concentration, will enjoy lower unit costs but also will restrict output and impose

---

[1] For simplicity, competition may be thought of here in terms of the degree of atomism in market structures—i.e., something akin to the absence of concentration posited in the competitive model.

a welfare loss on the community; conversely, we know that low concentration, which implies a welfare gain, will result in higher costs of production. The conflict is obvious: we can raise efficiency only by accepting noncompetitive conditions that imply a monopoly loss; and we can increase competitiveness only by accepting lower technical efficiency. What levels of competitiveness and efficiency ought we to seek?

This problem can be portrayed in terms of indifference curve analysis as in Figure A.[2] Curve TT is something akin to a transformation function. It tells us the unit production costs associated with any con-

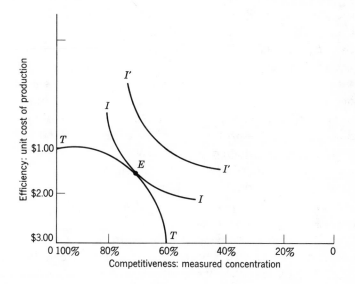

Figure A

centration level within a relevant range, and indicates that higher concentration implies lower costs. Indifference curves II and $I'I'$ represent the efficiency-concentration combinations among which the community is indifferent. The higher curve $I'I'$ is presumably preferred, but we are limited implicitly by this technology and resource constraints embodied in TT. The convex shape of the indifference curves reflects the

[2] The figure assumes that "competitiveness" can be measured by concentration. In light of earlier discussions, it should be clear that this assumption is made solely for illustrative convenience.

assumption of diminishing marginal rates of substitution; that is, the more we have "of one commodity", the less valuable it is in substitution for the other. For reasons that are familiar, a point of tangency, such as E, between TT and II represents an equilibrium or optimal position.[3]

Presentation of the problem in these terms does not enable us to solve the policy issue. Indeed, the issue here may be atypical, because in other industries it may be that greater efficiency and more competitiveness are compatible (TT would in such cases be positively sloped through some range). Given our assumptions about the widget industry, however, the presentation does allow us to define the problem more clearly. The slope of TT is in a sense the ratio of the marginal costs of efficiency and competitiveness, each cost expressed in terms of the other characteristic or commodity. The slope tells us how much competitiveness must be sacrificed in order to gain an additional unit of cost saving, and vice versa. This information is essentially economic. Given ideal measurement, this slope—the real trade-offs between efficiency and competitiveness—could be defined; and it is precisely this kind of information that economics strives to provide. The slope of the indifference curves reflects the preferences of the community. It tells us, at any given efficiency-competition point, how much of one commodity the community is willing to sacrifice in order to obtain one more unit of the other. This kind of information would be included in an ideal statement of policy goals and priorities, but it is not the kind of information that economic theory and measurement provide.

It goes almost without saying that the state of our definition of antitrust goals, as well as of our economic facts, is far from ideal. In fact it is not clear that more than the most general and vague kinds of criteria have been established. The example of efficiency and competition is a prime case in point. A system in which power is highly concentrated limits competition in the traditional sense, and such a limitation implies social and political as well as economic costs. At the same time, it is possible, although not inevitable, that the economic efficiency we desire is tied in part to large producing units that in turn imply some concentration of power. There is thus a possible direct conflict of goals. Efficiency and competitiveness may compete not only in the sense that they bid for the common resources of public policy programs, but also

[3] Any point on TT other than E would imply that the community has not attained the highest—that is, most desirable—indifference curve that its expenditure of resources makes possible.

in the sense that a high level of one may be incompatible with a high level of the other.

This is not the only possible conflict in policy objectives, and it may not even be the most common one. Perhaps our desire for progressiveness (invention and innovation) will lead to patterns of income distribution that are thought to be less than ideal; or it may be that by placing a high value on individual freedom we shall incur the waste of some resources. The pursuit of any particular objective may well imply costs in addition to the obvious direct costs of supporting a public policy program.

The need for clear and well-established priorities is manifest, yet there is little indication that consistent priorities exist in antitrust enforcement. At the same time, the real trade-offs, or technical marginal rates of substitution, between objectives are not fully known. That is, we often cannot say just how much of one goal we would have to give up to attain a specified level of another. We do not, in other words, know how much our objectives cost. This being the case, even a well-defined system of priorities might not lead to more rational policies.

Many descriptions of antitrust objectives retreat into discussions of more immediate goals such as the preservation of "competition" and the prevention of "anticompetitive" practices. These more proximate goals are of course both real and important, but to discuss objectives in these terms is not to mitigate the problem of confused priorities. Competition, as we have seen, is an ambiguous term, and it is likely that a person who sees efficiency as the ultimate objective of policy will give it a different interpretation than will one who stresses economic freedom.

It is difficult to avoid a degree of pessimism in discussing the goals of antitrust policy. This is not because policy makers are bent on pursuing the wrong goals, but rather because the assignment of priorities and reconciliation of conflicts are extremely difficult problems. The degree of justified pessimism should not be overstated, however. We do know something about the aims of antitrust, and there are at least some implicit priorities to be drawn from its history. The problem of defining objectives in a meaningful way—and consequently specifying the questions that economics may be able to answer—remains an important one.

11

The Language of the Antitrust Laws

The stated policy of the United States government is to maintain a competitive economy. Many deviations from this policy can be observed, but there is a large sector of the economy within which the principle is generally pursued. This is the segment that is thought to be amenable to competition; that is, areas in which market-type solutions are feasible.

Legal challenges to monopolistic or anticompetitive practices began, even in the United States, long before the adoption of federal antitrust laws. Certain kinds of contracts and agreements have long been unenforceable because of their anticompetitive and socially undesirable nature. The immediate precedent for the legal framework of United States is found in the body of English common law. During the nineteenth century extensive private litigation in the United States drew on and expanded earlier notions of restraint of trade. Various sorts of market-rigging agreements such as price fixing, output limitation, and territorial division were viewed by the courts with disfavor.

As antimonopoly sentiment increased in the period following the Civil War, there was some legal recourse open to injured parties. The support of competition in American courts, however, faced obvious limitations, most notably the absence of *public* action. Litigation was confined largely to instances in which persons acting in their private capacity could demonstrate direct harm from agreements of a restraining nature. The first public reaction to this situation was the adoption of state antitrust laws in the 1870's and 1880's. These laws, however, were notable primarily for the fact that they were rarely enforced. This impotency, exemplified by the formation and behavior of large trusts, alarmed the American public and paved the way for federal intervention. Intervention, when it came, did relatively little to expand the existing law of monopoly. Rather, its significance lay in the fact that restraints of trade were now to be opposed by federal action.

A. The Sherman Act

The Sherman Act,[1] passed in 1890, carried the following important provisions:

Section 1: Every contract, combination in the form of trust or otherwise, or conspiracy, in restraint of trade or commerce among the several states, or with foreign nations, is hereby declared to be illegal.

Section 2: Every person who shall monopolize, or attempt to monopolize, or combine or conspire with any other person or persons to monopolize any part of the trade or commerce . . . shall be guilty of a misdemeanor. . . .

The Act reflected the language of the common law, yet it is interesting to note precisely how vague these provisions are. There is no definition of either "restraint of trade or commerce," or of "monopolization" (although the terms did carry meaning within the common law). Section 2 is the broader provision, applying to individuals as well as to combining or conspiring groups of individuals.

B. The Clayton Act

It did not take long for some disillusionment with the Sherman Act to appear. Various kinds of monopolistic abuse were known to go unchallenged under the law, and the result was the adoption of the Clayton Act[2] in 1914. The Clayton Act prohibits or limits a number of specific practices:

[1] 26 Stat. 209 (1890).
[2] 38 Stat. 730 (1914).

Section 2: Makes it illegal "to discriminate in price between different purchasers," but does allow for price differences when the differential reflects "only due allowance for differences in the cost of selling or transportation. . . ."

Section 3: Forbids sellers to lease or sell "on the condition, agreement or understanding that the lessee or purchaser thereof shall not use or deal in the goods . . . of a competitor or competitors of the lessor or seller. . . ."

Section 7: Prohibits corporations from holding the stock of another company or of two competing companies "where the effect . . . may be to substantially lessen competition. . . ."

Section 8: Prohibits interlocking directorates for corporations larger than $1 million.

The first three Clayton Act prohibitions are limited to cases in which the result of the practice in question may be "to substantially lessen competition or tend to create a monopoly in any line of commerce." The Act further provides, in Section 4, that any individual "who shall be injured in his business or property by reason of anything forbidden in the antitrust laws" may sue to recover "threefold the damages by him sustained. . . ."

C. The Federal Trade Commission Act

Section 5 of the Federal Trade Commission Act[3] states: ". . . unfair methods of competition in commerce are hereby declared unlawful." The remainder of the Act is largely devoted to establishing the Federal Trade Commission.

Passed at about the same time, the Federal Trade Commission and Clayton Acts aimed at a variety of abusive practices. Once again, little new substantive matter was added by these laws. The Clayton Act did, however, clarify somewhat the legal status of specific practices, and provided the government with a potentially important preventive measure.

D. The Robinson-Patman Act

The Robinson-Patman Act[4] amends Section 2 of the original Clayton Act. The original provision was designed primarily to prevent large manu-

[3] 38 Stat. 717 (1914).
[4] 49 Stat. 1526 (1936).

facturers from driving out smaller competitors by means of selective, discriminatory price cuts. Prior to Robinson-Patman, however, many complaints were heard from small wholesale and retail sellers whose existence was threatened by large chain organizations. The mass distributors were underselling the smaller independents by obtaining preferential prices from suppliers. Various devices were employed. The chains, for example, often received "broker's commissions" in the form of a price discount on sales in which no broker was employed; similarly they received "allowances" for services rendered (e.g., promotion of the supplier's commodities) or received services without charge. The Robinson-Patman Act is aimed directly at such discriminatory practices:

Section 2(a): Restates and broadens somewhat the language of original Section 2.

Section 2(b): Provides that a seller charged with price discrimination may defend his actions on the ground that they were made in good faith to meet an equally low price of a competitor, or the services or facilities furnished by a competitor.

Section 2(c): Prohibits the discriminatory brokerage commissions.

Section 2(d): Prohibits allowances for services rendered "unless such payment or consideration is available on proportionally equal terms to all other customers. . . ."

Section 2(e): Forbids sellers from performing services for customers, unless such services are available to all on "proportionally equal terms."

Section 2(f): Forbids any person from knowingly inducing or receiving a discriminatory price.

The Robinson-Patman amendments thus provide extensive and specific coverage of discriminatory pricing practices.

E. The Wheeler-Lea Act

The Wheeler-Lea Act[5] of 1938 amends Section 5 of the Federal Trade Commission Act to read, "Unfair methods of competition in commerce, and unfair or deceptive acts or practices in commerce, are hereby declared unlawful." The addition of the phrase "and unfair or deceptive acts or practices in commerce," was stimulated by an earlier court decision[6] that indicated that the Commission could not curb "unfair methods" unless harm to *competitors* was demonstrated.

---

[5] 52 Stat. 111 (1938); 15 U.S.C. Sec. 41.
[6] *F.T.C. v. Raladam Co.*, 283 U.S. 643 (1931).

F. The Miller-Tydings Act

The Miller-Tydings Act[7] of 1937 amends Section 1 of the Sherman Act to exempt from antitrust prosecution certain resale price maintenance contracts and agreements. The amendment states in part:

Provided: That nothing herein contained shall render illegal, contracts or agreements prescribing minimum prices for the resale of a commodity which bears, or the label or container of which bears, the trademark, brand, or name of the producer or distributor of such commodity and which is in free and open competition with commodities of the same general class produced or distributed by others. . . .

The Act thus states that such "fair trade" agreements cannot be prosecuted as restraints of trade or commerce under Section 1.

G. The McGuire Act

The McGuire Act[8] of 1952 amends Section 5 of the Federal Trade Commission Act to allow enforcement of nonsigners' clauses in resale price maintenance agreements. A nonsigners' clause binds all sellers within a state to follow a manufacturer's resale price specification once *one seller* in that state signs a contract and the others are notified.

The impact of resale price maintenance legislation has been widespread. As of 1967, only eight states had failed to enact or had repealed fair trade enabling statutes. In about half the states with fair trade laws, however, nonsigners' clauses had been invalidated by the courts, and in at least four cases the laws in general were found to violate state constitutions.

H. The Celler-Kefauver Act

Section 7 of the Clayton Act prohibited corporate stock acquisitions when the effect might be a substantial lessening of competition. In 1950 the

---

[7] 50 Stat. 693 (1937); 15 U.S.C. Sec. 1.
[8] 66 Stat. 632 (1952); 15 U.S.C. Sec. 45.

Celler-Kefauver Act[9] amended Section 7 to include asset acquisitions. It provides that:

. . . no corporation engaged in commerce shall acquire, directly or indirectly, the whole or any part of the stock or other share capital . . . [or] the whole or any part of the assets of another corporation engaged also in commerce, where in any line of commerce in any section of the country, the effect of acquisition may be substantially to lessen competition, or to tend to create a monopoly.

Few corporate acquisitions had been challenged under original Section 7, and the amendment, by closing a loophole of Gargantuan proportions, marked the beginning of a new era in public policy toward corporation mergers.

I. Summary

The statutes described above comprise the principal antitrust laws of the United States. As we have noted, the term antitrust is today a misnomer. It would be more accurate to speak of public competition or even anti-monopoly laws and policies. In general, the Clayton and Federal Trade Commission Acts cover anticompetitive practices that, if left untouched, might lead to monopoly. The Sherman Act also deals with practices involved in attempts to monopolize, but this law stands as the principal means of treating the *fait accompli* of established monopoly positions. The fair trade statutes—Miller-Tydings and McGuire—provide for one of the most significant and controversial exemptions from the competition-encouraging provisions of antitrust.

Although the antitrust laws are relatively brief and are worded, for the most part, in straightforward fashion, associated litigation has been both voluminous and complex. The simple wording of the laws is a bit misleading, for numerous words and phrases—for example, restraint of trade, monopolization, and unfair methods—are capable of innumerable interpretations. The task of interpretation falls largely to the courts, and for this reason our attention will be focused on court decisions. What the courts say about the meaning of various terms, however, is not the entire sum and substance of antitrust. Public policy is also deeply influenced by the behavior of federal agencies charged with enforcement of the laws—most notably the Federal Trade Commission and the Department of Justice. Of course the kinds of legal action taken by the agencies depend

[9] 64 Stat. 1125 (1950); 15 U.S.C. Sec. 18.

partly on what the courts have previously said, but the process works in both directions. That is, the thrust of public policy is determined by court interpretation of the law, but is also affected by the kinds of situations that the agencies bring before the courts. A timid approach by executive agencies can effectively limit the impact of even the boldest judicial outlook.

Even within the decisions of the courts, interpretation of the law is not the only important aspect of antitrust. A separate question is the relief or remedy imposed on the finding of a violation of law. There are many instances in which sweeping interpretations by the courts are significantly modified by a relatively weak remedial policy. To look only at the language of interpretation in such instances could thus grossly overstate the real result of antitrust policy.

12

Antitrust Treatment
of Monopoly

It is somewhat misleading to classify antitrust policies according to
subject. Specific cases and episodes often fail to fit any single category
precisely, but rather overlap several. The process of categorizing may
therefore convey the impression of a much neater and more orderly antitrust record than in fact exists. In the instance of monopoly, however, the
classification is at least relatively distinct.

As we have noted, the economic meaning of monopoly may be viewed
in either broad or narrow fashion. Any firm with some control over the
terms at which it supplies the market possesses a degree of *monopoly
power*. In this sense monopoly may refer to virtually any market situation
that differs from the purely competitive. Clearly, however, not every
firm with a degree of monopoly power is likely to be called a monopolist.
Indeed, any situation short of the purely monopolistic may also be said to
reflect a degree of competition. The legal meaning of monopoly in antitrust has been closer to the narrow than to the broad economic definition;
although it has not been confined to pure monopoly, the legal category
encompasses only firms that are dominant in a market—that is, firms
possessing a very high degree of monopoly power.

The treatment of dominant firms generally falls within Section 2 of the
Sherman Act, although other statutes—most notably Section 1—often are
involved as well. The issue in Section 2 cases is twofold: first, has monopoly
in the legal sense been achieved; second, if it has been achieved, is the firm
in question guilty of monopolizing within the meaning of the law?

In the years immediately following passage of the Sherman Act, the status of monopoly was, at best, confused. Few cases were initiated by the government, and of those that were, at least one resulted in a stunning defeat. A legal attack on the sugar trust was dismissed by the Supreme Court on the grounds that, although monopoly had been shown to exist, interstate commerce had not been affected.[1] It appeared that the Court did not regard manufacturing activity as commerce, an interpretation that came as a shock to supporters of the Sherman Act. In the later 1890's, however, the Act was effectively applied to a number of rate and price-fixing agreements.

A. A Review of Relevant Cases

1. THE STANDARD OIL CASE OF 1911

The strength of the Sherman Act was still in question when, in 1906, the government charged the Standard Oil Company of New Jersey with violations of Sections 1 and 2.[2] Standard Oil was a huge and dominant company that controlled almost 90 percent of the nation's refining capacity. During the latter half of the nineteenth century the company had expanded by driving competitors out of business and in many cases absorbing them. Standard had obtained preferential treatment from the railroads, thus placing considerable pressure on smaller rivals. In addition, there was evidence of predatory price cutting and other practices that enabled the company to sweep local areas clean of competitors. Standard was convicted of Sherman Act violations in a district court and the company appealed to the Supreme Court.

The Standard Oil Company presented the Court with a classic example of aggressive monopoly. Indeed, there was no disagreement either about the company's power or the means by which that power had been attained. What was at issue was the legal status of a clear factual situation. The government argued for a literal interpretation of the Sherman Act. Section 1 states that *"Every* contract, combination . . . or conspiracy, in restraint of trade,"[3] is illegal, and the government's position was that a strict application of this language was appropriate. There was

---

[1] *United States* v. *E. C. Knight,* 156 U.S. 1 (1895).
[2] *Standard Oil Co. of New Jersey* v. *United States,* 221 U.S. 1 (1911).
[3] Italics added.

little question that the company had imposed restraints, and, under the government's line of reasoning, establishment of this fact would be sufficient for conviction.

Chief Justice White, speaking for the Court, rejected this strict interpretation. It is not merely the fact of a contract, combination or conspiracy in restraint of trade that is at issue, he stated, but also the *nature* of the restraint. The job of the courts thus goes beyond fact-finding, and must encompass judgments about the "nature and character" of restraints. Said the Court, "If the criterion [for judging the legality of a restraint] is the direct or indirect effect of the acts involved, then of course the rule of reason becomes the guide . . . ."[4] The courts were, then, to apply a *rule of reason* to restraints of trade. The government's contention that all restraints are illegal without reference to their character was denied. Rather, the Sherman Act would be construed to prohibit only unreasonable restraints. Chief Justice White did not spell out the conditions under which a restraint is reasonable or unreasonable, but he did cite intent as an important factor. It would thus be necessary to draw inferences about the intentions of individuals and companies accused of violations.

Having asserted the rule of reason, the Chief Justice could find "no cause to doubt the correctness" of the lower court's conviction of Standard Oil. The company's power and control of the market were such as to create "a prima facie presumption of intent and purpose to maintain dominancy . . . not as a result of normal methods of industrial development, but by means of combination. . . ." Moreover, the Supreme Court found, the behavior of the company made evident "the intent to drive others from the field and to exclude them from their right to trade . . ." The remedy ordered was dissolution of the combination. When dealing with a *fait accompli*, said the Court, it is not sufficient to curtail the practices that have created the situation.

The *Standard Oil* decision was important in two respects. It firmly established the Sherman Act as a means of dealing with monopolistic combinations; and it made equally clear that the application of the Act would be limited to *unreasonable* combinations. The rule of reason the Court enunciated marked an apparent break with precedent. In an earlier case[5] Justice Peckham had specifically rejected a contention by the defense that railroad rate-fixing agreements could be justified by their reasonableness. Peckham argued that the Sherman Act should be taken literally, and that the courts ought not to read into law "an exception that is not placed there by the law-making branch of the government." To accept a

---

[4] *Standard Oil Co. of New Jersey* v. *United States, op. cit.*, p. 66.
[5] *United States* v. *Trans-Missouri Freight Assn.*, 166 U.S. 290 (1896).

rule of reason, he predicted, would open the floodgates to future litigation in which defendants would plead the reasonableness of their illegal schemes.

Despite the unquestioned importance of the Standard Oil case, the decision is in some ways vague. The strength of the Sherman Act was amply exploited by the Court, not merely in finding a large company guilty of violations, but in following this finding with a remedy designed to reduce the company's power and restructure the market. What the decision might mean for future cases, however, was not clear. The Court had held that an unreasonable restraint of trade had occurred, but virtually nothing was said about the line that divides reasonableness from unreasonableness. The significance of the decision, then, is not that it spelled out a rule of reason against which future acts could be judged—for it really failed to do so—but rather that it placed on future courts the burden of formulating such a rule.

The reasoning implicit in *Standard Oil* is, in economic terms, somewhat obscure. Obviously the Court was not concerned primarily with economic definitions of monopoly. Standard Oil had violated the Sherman Act not because it possessed monopoly power, but rather because it had acted with obvious intent in acquiring and maintaining such power. Indeed, the Court stated:

It is remarkable that nowhere at common law can there be found a prohibition against the creation of monopoly by an individual. This would seem to manifest . . . a profound conception as to the inevitable operation of economic forces . . . That is to say, as it was deemed that monopoly in the concrete could only arise from an act of sovereign power, and, such sovereign power being restrained, prohibitions as to individuals were directed not against the creation of monopoly, but were only applied to such acts . . . which might result if unrestrained, in some of the consequences of monopoly. . . .[6]

This statement represents a viewpoint that still has wide acceptance today. Monopoly is regarded as a condition that cannot arise in what might be called the natural course of events. It can be created, in the absence of sovereign acts of power, only by deliberate actions on the part of individuals. Accordingly, in this view, the antitrust laws need not take aim at the *fact* of monopoly. It is sufficient instead for the laws to prohibit those *actions* that are necessary to the establishment of a monopoly position.

This argument raises basic questions. Although various anticompetitive practices may be important in creating or enhancing monopoly

[6] *Standard Oil, op. cit.,* p. 55. It should be noted that the word sovereign means simply *governmental.*

power, it is not at all clear that monopoly can arise only through a particular set of practices. Certainly economists are aware that partial monopolies do arise "naturally," as the result of such factors as significant economies of scale. The tendency is in fact so strong in some industries that public regulation is substituted for the "natural" alternative of monopoly.

The Standard Oil decision leaves open many important questions about antitrust treatment of monopoly. It is evident, however, that in this case violation had to do with the power *plus the intent* of the company as it was inferred from actual methods of business behavior. This point was reiterated by Chief Justice White in a companion case, *United States* v. *American Tobacco Co.*[7] Wrongful purpose or intent in addition to market power is necessary, he stated, to demonstrate a violation of the Sherman Act. In this case the actions of American Tobacco—most notably ruthless price competition—were interpreted not as the ordinary behavior of a company exercising its right to contract trade, but as that of a company intending to drive out competitors and monopolize trade. Once again, it was not the company's actual domination of the tobacco market but the means by which domination was achieved that was decisive.

2. THE UNITED STATES STEEL CASE OF 1920

The United States Steel Company was created in 1901 as a combination of 12 concerns that had originally consisted of about 180 separate entities. United States Steel, a holding company that controlled the 12 producing units, was a dominant force, with roughly 50 percent of the basic steel market at the time of its formation. Although its position had weakened a bit, the company still controlled about 41 percent of the market when it was charged by the government with illegal restraint of trade and the exercise of monopoly.[8]

The four-man District Court that first heard the case dismissed the charges against U.S. Steel, but divided on the reasons for dismissal.[9] One opinion, written by Judge Buffington with the concurrence of Judge McPherson, argued that the company was not formed with the intent or purpose of monopolization. Rather, the opinion stated, the size and dominance of the company were a response to natural economic forces, notably economies of large scale operation. The second opinion, written

[7] 211 U.S. 106 (1911).
[8] *United States* v. *United States Steel Corp.*, 251 U.S. 417 (1920).
[9] 223 F. 55 (1915).

by Judge Wooley with Judge Hunt concurring, held that the steel combination was not economically justified, and had been undertaken with intent to monopolize. But although the company was large, Judge Wooley argued, its organizers had underestimated the task of monopolization. The testimony heard did "not show that the corporation in and of itself ever possessed or exerted sufficient power when acting alone to control prices. . . ." In other words, the company represented an attempt to monopolize that had failed.

Both District Court opinions agreed that U.S. Steel had never succeeded in monopolizing the steel industry. Indeed, the judges concluded that evidence of pricing agreements between the company and its rivals demonstrated this failure. Had U.S. Steel monopolized, they reasoned, the need for such agreements would not have arisen.

The Supreme Court opinion, written by Justice McKenna, concurred with the Wooley-Hunt position. U.S. Steel, said the Court, failed to achieve a monopoly and was thus forced to enter agreements with competitors. In one of the most quoted phrases in antitrust law, Justice McKenna stated: ". . . the law does not make mere size an offense, or the existence of unexerted power an offense . . . It, we repeat, requires overt acts."[10] Here, then, was a carrying forward of the rule of reason. It is size or power *plus* overt acts that constitute a violation of law, and in the case of United States Steel the overt acts observed were considered benign. The company had resorted to none of the "brutalities" practiced by Standard Oil or American Tobacco. There had been no evidence of systematic action to harm or exclude competitors. Indeed, the company's actions were interpreted as a sign of weakness. As Singer has pointed out,[11] previous price-fixing agreements in the steel industry may have done damage to competition, but competitors were left unharmed.

Justice Day dissented from the majority opinion, arguing that although the law does not make mere size an offense, the size of United States Steel had been illegally obtained. In his view the formation and early practices of the company violated the Sherman Act. The company, he argued, was guilty of *attempting* to monopolize, regardless of the success of its venture.

The United States Steel decision added a second dimension to the rule of reason. If companies such as Standard Oil and American Tobacco were guilty of unreasonable restraints of trade, United States Steel presumably stood as an example of reasonable restraint. The company had, in the view of the majority, failed to monopolize; further, its actions

[10] *U.S.* v. *U.S. Steel, op. cit.*, p. 451.
[11] Eugene M. Singer, *Antitrust Policy*, Prentice-Hall, Englewood Cliffs, N.J., 1968, pp. 40–41.

during the early part of the century were not sufficiently repugnant to permit a conclusion of guilt.

Although the Court decision is clearly worded, there is considerable ambiguity about its treatment of the company's intent. Justice McKenna seemed to concede the likelihood of illegal intent in the formation and growth of U.S. Steel. Size alone was not sufficient to violate the Sherman Act; it appeared that intent alone was equally insufficient. This dichotomy, however, was not symmetrical. Justice McKenna was apparently influenced by the absence of ruthless or brutal behavior on the part of United States Steel. Presumably, brutal behavior without success might have been enough to sustain a finding of guilt. Thus it may not be accurate to say that intent without power is inadequate. Rather, the Court's decision may imply that intent *as evidenced by brutality* is itself a violation of the Sherman Act; whereas intent as evidenced by less harmful methods is a violation only if accompanied by success in the form of great power.

It is rather futile to speculate about what may have been in the minds of the judges. However, it does seem that the government may have committed a major blunder in its presentation of the case. United States Steel's monopoly position was assumed as an obvious fact in the government's argument. When this "fact" was rejected by the Court, the government's position was undermined, for it had not sought to emphasize the *attempt* to monopolize. As in earlier cases, the Court's implicit definition of monopoly bore little resemblance to the economic concept. Apparently United States Steel would not have been considered to have successfully monopolized unless its dominance had approached that of a pure monopolist.

3. THE ALCOA CASE OF 1945

The Supreme Court decision in *United States Steel* marked the beginning of a closed season on prosecution of dominant firms. It was not until 1937 that the government again mounted a major attack, this time against the Aluminum Company of America.[12]

The history of Alcoa's dominance in the production of virgin or primary aluminum is traced to the beginning of the twentieth century. Until 1909 the company had a legal-patent monopoly on feasible methods of aluminum production. During the period 1909–1912 it had entered into illegal cartel agreements with foreign manufacturers to limit imports of aluminum; however, it had been ordered to abandon such arrangements and had apparently done so. As of 1937, however, Alcoa was still the sole

[12] *United States* v. *Aluminum Co. of America*, 148 F. 2d 416 (2nd Cir., 1945).

domestic producer of virgin ingot. The government charged that this position constituted a violation of Section 2 of the Sherman Act, and asked that the company be dissolved.

Charges against Alcoa were dismissed by the District Court in 1942,[13] and the government appealed. Judge Learned Hand of the Court of Appeals[14] defined two pertinent legal questions: first, whether Alcoa's monopoly of virgin ingot production, which was known to exist in the early 1900's, had in fact persisted in subsequent years; second, whether such a monopoly, if it were found to persist, violated Section 2. The first question in Judge Hand's view rested on the proper definition of the market and of Alcoa's relevant production. There were at least three distinct ways of calculating the company's position:

1. If the market were defined to include secondary (scrap) as well as primary ingot, and if Alcoa's relevant production were defined to exclude ingot that it produced and fabricated—that is, did not supply to the open market —the company's share of the market was about 33 percent. This was the figure on which District Court Judge Caffey relied in finding that the company had not monopolized trade in aluminum.

2. If the market were defined to include secondary and primary aluminum, but Alcoa's total production (including ingot not placed on the market) were taken as its relevant output, the company's share was about 64 percent.

3. If the market were defined to include primary but to exclude secondary aluminum, and Alcoa's total production were taken, the market share would be about 90 percent. (The remaining 10 percent is accounted for by foreign imports.)

These alternatives posed a problem, for in the Judge's view 33 percent of a market would not constitute monopoly, 64 percent might, and 90 percent definitely would.

Judge Hand concluded that the 90 percent figure was appropriate. Virgin ingot produced and fabricated by the company, he argued, affected the ingot market even though Alcoa did not sell it to other fabricators. Further, although secondary ingot does compete with primary, the Judge noted that the majority of the secondary was salvaged from the primary, which Alcoa had produced in the first place. Alcoa therefore had indirect control over secondary ingot production. Judge Hand concluded that: "The competition of 'secondary' must therefore be disregarded, as soon

[13] 44 F. Supp. 97 (1942).

[14] The case was sent to the Court of Appeals because the Supreme Court could not provide a quorum of Justices qualified to hear it.

as we consider the position of 'Alcoa' over a period of years; it was as much within 'Alcoa's' control as was the production of the 'virgin' from which it had been derived."[15] Having excluded secondary aluminum from the market and included Alcoa's production for own use in its output total, the company's relevant market share of 90 percent followed as above.

This conclusion is difficult to defend in light of our earlier discussion of market definitions. Judge Hand was correct in counting Alcoa's production for own use as part of its total output; the fact that this primary aluminum was not offered to other firms does not remove its influence on the market. But the exclusion of secondary aluminum from the relevant market is more dubious. Secondary and primary aluminum were admittedly substitutes, and this is the essential meaning of a market grouping. To define the market as if secondary did not matter was to construct an artificial product grouping. The definition, moreover, is in no way strengthened by the fact that most secondary aluminum was recovered from primary that Alcoa happened to produce. Had the primary been produced by the ABC company instead, the competitive role of secondary in the aluminum market would have been precisely the same. It thus seems that Alcoa's market share should have been defined as 64 percent.

Nevertheless, once the 90 percent market share was defined, the pertinent question was whether "this is a monopoly within the meaning of Section 2." The District Court had found that Alcoa's profits during its lifetime had been less than spectacular, on the order of 10 percent on invested capital. Judge Hand, however, refused to accept this figure as evidence that Alcoa had not exerted monopoly control. Noting that the company's over-all profit figure might not reflect accurately its profit on ingot, the Judge went on to state:

But the whole issue is irrelevant anyway, for it is no excuse for "monopolizing" a market that the monopoly has not been used to extract from the consumer more than a "fair" profit. The Act has wider purposes. Indeed, even though we disregarded all but economic considerations, it would by no means follow that such concentration of producing power is to be desired, when it has not been used extortionately. Many people believe that possession of unchallenged economic power deadens initiative, discourages thrift and depresses energy; that immunity from competition is a narcotic and rivalry is a stimulant, to industrial progress; that the spur of constant stress is necessary to counteract an inevitable disposition to let well enough alone. Congress did not condone "good trusts" and condemn "bad" ones; it forbad all. Moreover, in so doing it was not necessarily actuated by economic motives alone. It is possible, because of its indirect social or moral effect, to prefer a system of small producers. . . .[16]

[15] *United States* v. *Aluminum Co. of America, op. cit.*, p. 425.
[16] *Ibid.*, p. 427.

Further, Judge Hand asserted, the distinction between the existence and exercise of monopoly power is "purely formal." A monopolist must sell at some price, and the only price at which it can sell "is a price which it itself fixed."

By arguing in this fashion Judge Hand was effectively stating that there are reasons for opposing monopoly *power*, as distinct from the *methods* the monopolist happens to employ. Nevertheless, he stopped short of concluding that Alcoa's power could by itself, violate the law:

It does not follow because "Alcoa" had . . . a monopoly, that it "monopolized" the ingot market; it may not have achieved monopoly; monopoly *may have been thrust upon it* . . . .

. . . from the very outset the courts have at least kept in reserve the possibility that the origin of a monopoly may be critical in determining its legality . . . This notion has usually been expressed by saying that size does not determine guilt; that there must be some "exclusion" of competitors; that the growth must be something else than "natural" or "normal"; that there must be a "wrongful intent," or some other specific intent; or that some "unduly" coercive means must be used. . . .[17]

Was the origin of Alcoa's monopoly such as to place it beyond the reach of the Sherman Act? Again in Judge Hand's words:

It would completely misconstrue "Alcoa's" position in 1940 to hold that it was the passive beneficiary of a monopoly, following upon an involuntary elimination of competitors by automatically operative economic forces . . . continued and undisturbed control did not fall undesigned into "Alcoa's" lap; obviously it could not have done so. It could only have resulted, as it did result, from a persistent determination to maintain the control with which it found itself vested in 1912. . . . It insists that it never excluded competitors; but we can think of no more effective exclusion than progressively to embrace each new opportunity as it opened, and to face every newcomer with new capacity already geared into a great organization. . . . Only in case we interpret "exclusion" as limited to maneuvers not honestly industrial, but actuated solely by a desire to prevent competition, can such a course as Alcoa's . . . be deemed not "exclusionary." So to limit it would in our judgment emasculate the Act; would permit just such consolidations as it was designed to prevent.[18]

Alcoa's defense consisted in large part of evidence demonstrating the absence of any intent to monopolize. But, said Judge Hand, "We disregard any question of 'intent.'" It was not necessary, he held, to find that the company had pursued practices that were in themselves unlawful. Rather, it was sufficient to find that the company acted to retain its control over the market, "however innocently it otherwise proceeded."

17 *Ibid.*, p. 429; italics added.
18 *Ibid.*, p. 430.

The extent to which the Alcoa decision broke new ground in the law of monopoly should be apparent. Given a company of Alcoa's dominance, said Judge Hand, it is not necessary to show brutal, ruthless, or otherwise unpalatable behavior to bring it within the prohibitions of the Sherman Act. There is a strong presumption, perhaps on noneconomic as well as on economic grounds, against concentration of power. Under the *Alcoa* doctrine, such power is not alone tantamount to a violation of the Act. But it is only necessary to show in addition that the company's actions were instrumental to the achievement or maintenance of that power. In other words, so long as a company in a monopoly position has worked to achieve and retain that position it violates Section 2.

Despite the strong opinion of Judge Hand, unique circumstances in the aluminum industry prevented the adoption of the government's proposed dissolution scheme. The government had built aluminum-producing facilities for wartime use and had been directed to dispose of these properties at the end of the war to maximize "free" independent private enterprise. Since Alcoa's market position after the disposal was not predictable, Judge Hand adopted a wait-and-see approach. The company was prohibited from resuming certain restrictive practices cited in testimony, but the government's dissolution proposal was neither accepted nor specifically rejected. Any action with respect to dissolution, said the Judge, would be a matter for the District Court if the disposal of government facilities failed to reestablish competition after the war.

The disposal program did effect changes in the structure of the aluminum industry; Reynolds Metals and Kaiser Aluminum arose as significant competitors. Indeed, by 1948 Alcoa's share of aluminum reduction capacity was 50 percent, with Reynolds holding 30 percent and Kaiser 20 percent. In 1947 Alcoa requested a District Court to find that competitive conditions prevailed in aluminum and that its position as a monopolist had therefore ceased. The government contested this petition and asked that Alcoa be required to divest itself of some plants in order to enhance competition.

In 1950 the court ruled that although Alcoa retained the power to exclude competitors, a further diminution in the company's market position would likely harm competition.[19] Judge Knox contended that competition in aluminum depended on the existence of the three major producers, each of which possessed substantial market power. To weaken one of the companies, in his view, could have destroyed the competitive balance. This is an interesting position in that something akin to countervailing powers—rather than concentration of market shares—is posited as the critical competitive element.

[19] F. Supp. 333 (1950).

4. THE UNITED SHOE MACHINERY CASE OF 1953

In 1918 the United Shoe Machinery Corporation had been acquitted of monopolization charges arising from its acquisition of about 50 shoe machinery producers.[20] The original power of the company was based in patents, but in subsequent years United Shoe had maintained dominance in the shoe machinery field. The company was again charged with monopolizing in violation of Section 2 of the Sherman Act in a case decided by Judge Charles Wyzanski.[21]

Judge Wyzanski noted that the market position of United Shoe, which supplied 75 percent to 85 percent of the market, had been built up largely through patented inventions before and after 1918. United Shoe held 3915 patents, 95 percent of which were "attributable to the ideas of its own employees." Although Judge Wyzanski termed the shoe manufacturing industry itself "highly competitive," and although the major processes for shoe manufacturing could be carried on without the use of United Shoe machines, the dominant position of the company was undeniable. This dominance may have derived from the company's own research and development efforts; however, the Judge found that United Shoe's provisions for leasing machines to manufacturers also enhanced its position. Three leasing requirements were central:

1. . . . United's leasing system . . . deters a shoe manufacturer from disposing of a United machine and acquiring a competitors' machine . . . The lessee is now held closely to United by the combined effect of . . . the requirement that if he has work available he must use the machine to full capacity, and by the return charge which can . . . be reduced to insignificance if he keeps this and other United machines to the end of the periods for which he leased them.

2. . . . when a lessee desires to replace a United machine, United gives him more favorable terms if the replacement is by another United machine than if it is by a competitive machine.

3. United's policy of offering to repair, without separate charges, its leased machines, has had the effect that there are no independent service organizations to repair complicated machines. In turn, this has had the effect that the manufacturer of a complicated machine must either offer repair service with his machine, or must face the obstacle of marketing his machine to customers who know that repair service will be difficult to provide. . . .[22]

[20] *United States* v. *United Shoe Machinery Co. of New Jersey*, 247 U.S. 32 (1918).
[21] *United Shoe Machinery Corp.* v. *United States*, 110 F. Supp. 295 (1953).
[22] *Ibid.*, p. 340.

These provisions, Judge Wyzanski stated, served to create barriers to entry into the shoe machinery industry and to limit competition.

Did United Shoe Machinery thus violate Section 2 of the Sherman Act? Judge Wyzanski noted that the question could be approached in three distinctive ways. One approach, antedating *Alcoa*, would hold that monopolizing in violation of Section 2 requires an unreasonable restraint of trade in violation of Section 1. A more recent approach, adopted by Justice Douglas in *United States* v. *Griffith*,[23] argues that a company monopolizes if it has the power to exclude competition, and exercises or has the purpose to exercise it. Finally, the *Alcoa* doctrine suggests that anyone enjoying an overwhelming share of the market monopolizes "whenever he does business"; but the doctrine is tempered by Judge Hand's statement that the defendant may not violate Section 2 if existing monopoly power results solely from superior skill.

Judge Wyzanski concluded that the facts of the case made it unnecessary to choose between the Douglas and Hand approaches. Rather, he stated, the evidence shows that:

1. United's strength is so overwhelming as to constitute control of the market.
2. This strength "excludes some potential, and limits some actual, competition. . . ."
3. "This strength is not attributable solely to defendant's ability, economies of scale, research, natural advantages, and adaptation to inevitable economic laws. . . ."[24]

United Shoe's control of the market was thus not *purely* the result of its own superiority. This was, said the Judge, an

. . . intermediate case where the causes of an enterprise's success were neither common law restraints of trade, nor the skill with which the business was conducted, but rather some practice which without being predatory, abusive, or coercive was in economic effect exclusionary.[25]

Although United Shoe was "free from any taint of . . . wrongdoing," its monopoly position depended in part on company policies that had limited competition. These policies, neither immoral nor illegitimate in themselves, were nevertheless one instrument by which United Shoe gained a monopoly.

Finally, Judge Wyzanski disposed of the question of intent, stating:

. . . Defendant intended to engage in the leasing practices and pricing policies which maintained its market power. That is all the intent which the law requires

---

[23] 344 U.S. 100 (1948).
[24] *United Shoe Machinery Corp.* v. *United States, op. cit.*, p. 343.
[25] *Ibid.*, p. 341.

when both the complaint and the judgment rest on a charge of "monopolizing," not merely "attempting to monopolize." Defendant having willed the means, has willed the end.[26]

United Shoe was thus found to have violated Section 2, despite an exemplary record of performance. The company had contributed greatly to the technology of shoe production, and had engaged in no acts that could be termed predatory or immoral. Yet in the course of doing business, Judge Wyzanski found, United Shoe had deliberately pursued policies that restricted competition and contributed to monopoly power.

Having found against the company, Judge Wyzanski rejected the government's proposed dissolution scheme, which would have split United Shoe into three separate manufacturing companies. All machine manufacturing was centered in one plant, and, said the Judge, "It takes no Solomon to see that this organism cannot be cut into three equal and viable parts. . . ." Minor divestitures were ordered, but the remedy centered on the leasing practices. The restrictive provisions were ordered purged: the term of the lease was shortened, full-capacity clauses were eliminated, discriminatory commutative charges were removed, and the company was required to charge separately for repair services. Finally, the remedy required that any machine the company offered to lease must also be offered for sale. In this way, it was hoped, a secondhand market would ultimately arise to offer "a type of substitute competition. . . ."

The precise implications of Judge Wyzanski's decision have been actively debated. It appears that certain practices that do not alone violate the law may amount to a violation in conjunction with overwhelming market power. Practices such as United Shoe's leasing provisions presumably would be acceptable so long as they were not part of a monopolist's history. Within the context of monopoly, however, such practices indicated that the defendant's power was not inevitable, natural, or resulting solely from superior skills.

The *United Shoe* decision seems further to establish the limited role of intent in cases of monopolization. A company that is accused of *attempting* to monopolize must be shown to have intended to do so—a demonstration that can be inferred from predatory or otherwise anticompetitive acts. But a company accused of *monopolizing* need not have intended to do so in quite the same sense. Under *United Shoe* it is sufficient to demonstrate that monopolizing resulted in part from exclusionary practices that were deliberate but that would not alone have constituted an attempt to monopolize. The general thrust of Judge Wyzanski's opinion places it largely in the tradition of *Alcoa*. A finding of monopolization necessitated some

[26] *Ibid.*, p. 346.

attention to practices, but the power of the company within its markets was the controlling factor. At the very least, the company's great power meant that its practices would have to conform to an exceedingly rigid standard in order to escape a finding of monopolization.

5. THE duPONT "CELLOPHANE" CASE OF 1956

The duPont cellophane case[27] is notable for its treatment of the market definition problem. E. I. duPont de Nemours was for many years the major producer of cellophane sold in this country. Cellophane was developed by a Swiss chemist, Jacques Brandenberger, in the early 1900's. His patents were assigned to a French company, La Cellophane Societe Anonyme, in 1917; and this company in turn granted duPont exclusive rights to make and sell cellophane in North and Central America under its patented processes. The virtually complete monopoly in cellophane that duPont enjoyed was disturbed in 1925 when two La Cellophane employees left to help establish a company whose American subsidiary produced cellophane. The market share held by duPont after this time remained fairly stable at about 75 percent.

In 1947 the government charged duPont with monopolizing, attempting to monopolize, and conspiracy to monopolize commerce in cellophane and cellulosic caps, in violation of Section 2 of the Sherman Act. The company won its case in the lower court when it was held that the relevant market was not cellophane but "flexible wrapping materials," a much broader product group of which duPont's market share was only about 20 percent. The government's appeal to the Supreme Court was confined to an attack on the lower court conclusion that duPont had not monopolized trade in cellophane.

The opposing arguments were clear-cut. DuPont, not denying that cellophane was a separate product, nevertheless contended that it was under severe competitive pressure from substitute flexible wrapping materials such as waxed paper, glassine, and aluminum foil. Because of this pressure, the company argued, it lacked the power to exclude competitors that would have violated Section 2. The government's argument was that the other wrapping materials did not offer sufficient competition to qualify duPont's control of the cellophane market; that is, that cellophane itself was the relevant market, although it was subject to competitive pressures from outside products.

The decision of the Court hinged on this question, for under the first

[27] *United States* v. *E. I. duPont de Nemours & Co.*, 351 U.S. 377 (1956).

market definition duPont very likely had monopolized, whereas under the second it had not. As Justice Reed stated for the Court,

Every manufacturer is the sole producer of the particular commodity it makes but its control . . . of the relevant market depends upon the availability of alternative commodities for buyers. . . .[28]

If cellophane is the "market" that duPont is found to dominate, it may be assumed it does have monopoly power over that "market." Monopoly power is the power to control or exclude competition. It seems apparent that duPont's power to set the price of cellophane has only been limited by the competition afforded by other flexible materials. . . . The trial court consequently had to determine whether competition from the other wrappings prevented duPont from possessing monopoly power in violation of Section 2.[29]

The definition of the relevant market, according to the Court, depends on "how different from one another are the offered commodities in character or use, how far buyers will go to substitute one commodity for another."[30] The pertinent question was, then, specific: how are differences in or similarities among products to be measured? The Court rejected the government's contention that products must be "substantially fungible" and must sell "at substantially the same price," to be considered part of the same market. Rather, the Court stated, ". . . where there are market alternatives . . . illegal monopoly does not exist merely because the product said to be monopolized differs from others. If it were not so, only physically identical products would be a part of the market."[31] What was needed, according to the Court, "is an appraisal of the 'cross-elasticity' of demand in the trade. . . ." If a price change in one product substantially affects the sales of another, both products presumably may be classified in the same market.

Having noted the relevance of cross-elasticities, however, the Court did not pursue actual measures. Rather, it pointed out that cellophane, despite distinctive property combinations that gave it market advantages, "has to meet competition from other materials in every one of its uses. . . ." The government did not challenge statistics showing that cellophane provided less than 7 percent of bakery products wrappings, 25 percent for candy, 32 percent for snacks, 35 percent for meats and poultry,

---

[28] *Ibid.*, p. 380.

[29] *Ibid.*, pp. 391–92. The Court noted that the sources of duPont's power were not at issue because the government's appeal was limited to the monopolization charge. Had charges of attempting and conspiring to monopolize been relevant, the Court would have had to consider the means by which duPont's market position had been attained.

[30] *Ibid.*, p. 393.

[31] *Ibid.*, p. 394.

47 percent for fresh produce, and 34 percent for frozen foods. These data indicated that cellophane shared its markets with other materials, and were interpreted by the Court as evidence of competitiveness among wrappings. Further, the Court said, ". . . a very considerable degree of functional interchangeability exists between these products . . . except as to permeability to gases, cellophane has no qualities that are not possessed by a number of other materials. . . ."[32] The lower court had found that customers for wrapping materials were sensitive to changes in prices and qualities, and took this as indicative of significant cross-elasticities. In this finding the Supreme Court concurred. The government had argued that very large price differences between cellophane and other materials indicated the separateness of their markets. To this the Court responded that packaging materials were a small portion of the total cost of packaged goods, hence that large price differentials were not necessarily a significant consideration for customers.

Justice Reed concluded that the relevant market was broad. DuPont had done nothing to exclude competitors, he said, and the company's "liberal" profits (15.9 percent net after taxes), did not demonstrate the existence of monopoly, in the absence of evidence that other prosperous industries had not earned similar returns. Justice Reed stated in summary:

. . . The "market" which one must study to determine when a producer has monopoly power will vary with the part of commerce under consideration. The tests are constant. That market is composed of products that have reasonable interchangeability for the purpose for which they are produced—price, use and qualities considered. While the application of the tests remains uncertain, it seems to us that duPont should not be found to monopolize cellophane when that product has the competition and interchangeability with other wrappings that this record shows.[33]

Chief Justice Warren, joined by Justices Black and Douglas, issued a sharp dissenting opinion. The dissent contends that cellophane itself is the relevant market, and that the majority's lumping together of cellophane with highly differentiated wrapping materials serves to "emasculate Section 2 of the Sherman Act." The Chief Justice argued that cross-elasticity of demand between cellophane and other materials was not high, as the majority had claimed:

. . . during the period 1933–1946 the prices for glassine and waxed paper actually increased in the face of a further 21 % decline in the price of cellophane. If "shifts of business" due to "price sensitivity" had been substantial, glassine and waxed

[32] *Ibid.*, p. 399.
[33] *Ibid.*, p. 404.

paper producers who wanted to stay in business would have been compelled by market forces to meet duPont's price challenge just as Sylvania [a domestic cellophane producer] was.[34]

The markets for cellophane and other wrapping materials were, in the minority view, quite distinct. The company's power, said Chief Justice Warren, was evident. Moreover, he stated, the majority's findings of fact did nothing to demonstrate the absence of power—rather, they demonstrated that the power was used in a benevolent and enlightened fashion. DuPont was indeed a "good monopolist" in this view, but a monopolist nonetheless.

Was the majority's market definition correct? The issue posed is the how-close-is-close-enough question; whether other flexible wrapping materials were sufficiently close substitutes to be grouped with cellophane. The Court's answer was based on the subjective notion of *reasonable interchangeability.* Whether a more objective standard based on cross-elasticities of demand would have supported this view is questionable.

The cellophane decision has provoked considerable controversy among economists. To some it appeared that the Supreme Court's attention to market performance, ". . . rapidly declining prices, expanding production, intense competition stimulated by creative research, the development of new products . . . ," heralded a new era. Henceforth the courts might be expected to look at implications for future market activity in deciding questions of monopolization. To some other economists duPont appeared a deliberate and cunning, if progressive, monopolist of a product that was distinct from substitutes.[35] Whatever the view, there was broad agreement that the Court had been influenced by the company's brilliant record of research and innovation.

B. Monopoly in Economics and Law

The distinction between legal and economic conceptions of monopoly was discussed in a classic article by Mason more than 30 years ago.[36] Mason pointed out that monopoly in economics is a tool of analysis. It refers to a market situation whose essence is the existence of control or power. The

---

[34] *Ibid.*, p. 417.

[35] See George W. Stocking and Willard F. Mueller, "The Cellophane Case and the New Competition," *American Economic Review*, **XLV**, March 1955, pp. 29–63.

[36] E. S. Mason, "Monopoly in Law and Economics," *Yale Law Journal*, **47**, November 1937, pp. 34–49.

law, however, uses monopoly as a "standard of evaluation," where the relevant question is whether control or power is mobilized to *restrict* competition. Similarly, the economic antithesis of monopoly is competition, a market situation of powerlessness for all participants. But the legal antithesis of monopoly is, in Mason's words:

> . . . the freedom of any individual or firm to engage in legitimate economic activity . . . not restrained by the state, by agreements among competitors, or by predatory practices of a rival. But free competition thus understood is quite compatible with the presence of monopoly elements in the *economic* sense of the word monopoly.[37]

Both approaches are demonstrated in the cases discussed above. In *Standard Oil* and *United States Steel* control of the market alone was not sufficient to conclude that the Sherman Act had been violated. What was needed was control *plus* an intent to monopolize, as demonstrated by overt acts. In *Alcoa* Judge Hand's statements that the law condemns *all* trusts rather than just *bad* ones, and that a monopolist cannot act without exercising his power, indicate a turning toward the economic concept of monopoly. Emphasis on market control was heightened vis-a-vis emphasis on what was done with that control. But even the *Alcoa* decision does not conform fully to the economic definition. Control is emphasized, but it is still deemed necessary to determine what actions have been used to acquire and maintain it. Similarly, in *United Shoe* it was the company's exclusionary *practices* that made its imposing market power vulnerable to the law.

There is no simple or clearly indicated choice between economic and legal meanings of monopoly. The former, if strictly accepted, implies that policy should be used in order to limit power; the latter implies that power itself is not the problem, and that policy should limit only the abuse of power. Neither implication is a happy one. Few economists would argue that the antitrust laws should be used to curtail all efficient and progressive organizations whose superiority has generated market dominance. On the other hand, few economists would agree that the problem of monopoly disappears if the monopolist is "well behaved." Monopolistic control implies certain economic effects regardless of whether the monopolist is in some sense benevolent.

Presumably the appropriate standard lies somewhere between. But where? The efforts of Judges Hand and Wyzanski, eloquent as they are, do not provide an obvious answer. Economic investigation, as Mason noted, has made an essentially negative contribution to the discussion of monop-

[37] *Ibid.*

oly policy. It has cast doubt on and to a degree discredited the legal attitude that market control is unimportant unless abused. It is generally agreed that abuses ought to be curbed, but economics has not provided a workable criterion for curbing power itself. We need to know in what circumstances the costs of power exceed its benefits to the community. But neither the measurement of costs and benefits nor the weight that society would wish to assign to each is known with accuracy.

C. Monopoly and the Law Today

To define the current legal status of monopoly we must ask how much the doctrines of *Alcoa* and *United Shoe* have altered the old rule of reason. It appears that the alteration has been a very substantial one, although the degree of dominance necessary for an inference of monopoly power remains fuzzy. For Judge Wyzanski a market share in excess of 75 percent was sufficient. For Judge Hand 90 percent was sufficient, and 64 percent would have made for a troublesome decision. The cellophane case, however, illustrates a distinct problem. A market share cannot be calculated without a relevant market, and the definition of market boundaries may be so unclear that *any* definition that is accepted appears arbitrary.

Alcoa and *United Shoe* established that a firm that has been shown to possess monopoly power may be guilty of monopolizing even though its power is not based in illegal practices. The company need not have been ruthless or predatory, and need not have demonstrated specific intent to exclude competitors or to monopolize. The practical implication of this doctrine is that a company possessing monopoly power has a far more difficult time in trying to show that it has not monopolized, within the meaning of Section 2, than it would have had before 1945.

It may be tempting to interpret the conclusions of *Alcoa* and *United Shoe* too strongly, however, and some words of caution are in order. Whatever these decisions may have done, they clearly did *not* make possession of monopoly power, however defined, a per se violation of law. The old rule of reason has been altered, but not eliminated. Reasonable restraints on trade are still possible, although reasonable does not mean precisely what it may have meant in 1911 or 1920.

We might be inclined to argue that this is a quibble; companies found to have monopoly power will—especially under the *Alcoa* approach—have great difficulty escaping a charge of monopolization. Why, in other words, should it matter that escape is technically possible if it is practically so difficult as it appears? One answer, noted by Mrs. Keyes,[38] lies in the implication for appropriate remedies. If monopoly power itself is defined as a violation of law, the clearly indicated remedy is some disintegration of that power. But so long as a violation is tied to the company's past practices, a sufficient remedy might well be confined to termination of the offending practices. As Mrs. Keyes states with respect to *United Shoe:*

. . . a fully adequate remedy for the violation could be found without any direct attack upon the Corporation's share in the shoe machinery market. Where the crime of monopolizing requires, in addition to market control, exclusionary practices for its completion, it cán always be extirpated by the simple termination of these practices; and the real operational significance of the law against monopolizing is to provide a basis for a distinct and stricter code of business conduct to be applied to enterprises that exercise market control.[39]

Judge Wyzanski's remedy in *United Shoe* supports this interpretation. The defendant's overwhelming market power was left intact; instead of being dissolved, the company was forbidden to pursue certain practices that were not clearly crucial to its achievement and maintenance of monopoly power. Viewed in this way, the *United Shoe* decision loses part of its apparent strength. Paradoxically, *United Shoe* may have made it easier to prosecute monopoly, but harder to do anything about it.[40]

The government's victories in *Alcoa* and *United Shoe* have not paved the way for further significant antimonopoly cases. An important reason is, of course, that few companies have quite the degree of dominance that seems necessary to demonstrate monopoly power under law. It is also possible that the difficulty of formulating and winning acceptance for an appropriate remedy has discouraged litigation. Traditionally the courts have been reluctant to break up a going concern. It often appears that no logical form of divestiture or dissolution is possible; large companies are extremely complex organizations, and the problem of formulating a dissolution scheme has often been compared with unscrambling scrambled eggs. The Courts have at times taken Judge Wyzanski's view that specific dissolution proposals suggested are unrealistic. The government frequently appears to concentrate its efforts on winning the case, and fails to come in with a plausible dissolution scheme. The results may be legal victories devoid of economic meaning.

[38] Lucile Sheppard Keyes, "The Shoe Machinery Case and the Problem of the Good Trust," *Quarterly Journal of Economics,* **68**, May 1954, pp. 287–304.

[39] *Ibid.,* pp. 290–91.

[40] The circumstances surrounding the aluminum industry in 1945 were so special that the absence of a strong remedy in *Alcoa* cannot be given general importance. That is, the nature of the remedy was not really tied to the logic of the decision, and thus did nothing to illuminate the implications of that decision.

It seems likely that resistance to dissolution is related also to concern about consequences for market efficiency. Even if a logical scheme were proposed, its effects on efficiency might not be known with certainty. The smallest probability of affecting markets adversely may be a strong deterrent to dissolution, and it cannot be denied that the breaking up of companies is a course of action with which we have little experience.

Finally, a powerful argument against dissolution has been stated in terms of equity.[41] Any company, no matter how excessive its power and no matter how undesirable its influence, carries the vested interests of many individuals. To break up the monopoly is also to tamper with, and perhaps harm, the future of those associated with it. Although systems of compensation to such individuals may be possible, the argument that dissolution hurts innocent investors is not easily dismissed by the courts.

The current status of monopoly under Section 2 of the Sherman Act is a potpourri. A company will not likely be found to have achieved monopoly unless it has gained overwhelming dominance of a defined market. Once monopoly is found, it may be difficult for a court to avoid the conclusion that Section 2 has been violated; such a conclusion seems to follow under the doctrine of *Alcoa* and *United Shoe* unless the company in question can demonstrate that monopoly was not achieved by its own deliberate actions. Yet even the finding of a violation may result in no more than a curtailment of these deliberate actions.

This treatment of monopoly contains two economic weaknesses. First, the approach to remedies may be inconsistent with the problem posed by a monopolist. Any remedy that merely curtails modes of behavior makes little sense unless that behavior is shown to have been instrumental in the attainment of the monopoly position. If it is peripheral, curtailment will have no more than peripheral effects.

The second weakness is in the definition of monopoly itself. The courts have found monopoly when single-firm dominance of a market exists. The economic problem of monopoly, however, may arise long before one firm attains 75 percent, or even 64 percent, market control. Indeed, resource misallocation is a problem in oligopolistically structured markets that lack a dominant firm. This is not to suggest that a broad effort to break up the existing structures of such markets is necessarily desirable. Clearly, however, the courts' view of the "monopoly problem" is a narrow one, confined to the few situations that resemble pure monopoly most closely.

[41] See, e.g., Donald Dewey, "Romance and Realism in Antitrust Policy," *Journal of Political Economy*, LXIII, April 1955, pp. 93–102.

13

Antitrust Treatment of Restraint of Trade and Conspiracy to Monopolize

The Sherman Act has been utilized extensively to deal with certain kinds of anticompetitive practices such as conspiracy to fix prices, restrict output, or divide markets among competitors. Such acts have been interpreted both as conspiracies in restraint of trade, in violation of Section 1, and as conspiracies to monopolize, in violation of Section 2. Unlike the Section 2 infringements discussed in Chapter 12, market-rigging conspiracies raise no question of whether companies succeed or fail to achieve positions of monopoly power. The focus traditionally is on the action itself as distinct from the market power of participating firms.

Conspiratorial behavior, which often takes the form of price-fixing agreements, falls within the collusive oligopoly pattern discussed in Chapter 3. Mutually dependent firms may attempt rationally to avoid the consequences of unlimited price competition, and an obvious method is to agree on coordinated pricing policies. Any such tendency raises two basic policy questions. First, should conspiratorial behavoir be condemned in general, or should it be treated on a case-by-case basis according to some rule of reason? Second, how is conspiratorial behavior to be defined, that is, at what point does taking account of mutual interdependence by firms become a violation of law?

The courts have provided a relatively clear answer to the first question. The second, however—which goes to the fundamental meaning of conspiracy—continues to plague antitrust; and the disposition of cases in the courts has raised questions about economic rationality in this area of policy enforcement.

A. A Review of Relevant Cases

1. OUTRIGHT PRICE-FIXING AND MARKET-RIGGING: DEVELOPMENT OF THE PER SE DOCTRINE

The legal status of "obvious" conspiratorial conduct is well established by several Supreme Court decisions on relatively open agreements among competitors to fix prices or divide markets. There has been little disagreement about the facts surrounding the cases, and the existence of conspiratorial behavior is usually not in doubt. Rather, the issue has been whether extenuating evidence of any kind can justify such agreements.

(a) The Addyston Pipe and Steel Case (1899)

One of the earliest conspiracy cases pursued after enactment of the Sherman Act involved a series of agreements among six leading producers of iron pipe. The companies had divided the market into regional monopolies and had instituted a system of fixed prices for each territory. These facts were not contested. Rather, the companies made two separate contentions in their defense:

1. That the purpose of the agreements was the avoidance of ruinous price competition in the industry, a condition attested to by a high mortality rate among firms.

2. That the prices at which cast iron pipe was sold in each region or "pay territory," were reasonable.

Judge Taft in the Circuit Court of Appeals found the defense unconvincing.[1] He noted that the effect of the agreements had indeed been to deprive the public of the salutory forces of competition. Prices had been set high enough so that buyers received little advantage from the proximity of nearby manufacturers, yet low enough to discourage competition

[1] 85 F. 271 (6th Cir. 1898).

from more distant producers. Specifically it appeared that prices in non-Eastern areas were fixed at levels slighlty below East Coast prices plus transportation cost. Judge Taft noted that the restraint of trade did not cover the entire country and did not amount to complete monopoly; but this, he said, could not remove the agreement from the coverage of the "rule against monopolies."

Judge Taft did not regard the prices fixed as reasonable. He went on to say, however, that the issue of reasonableness was not an important one, and under common law precedent was not a question left open to the courts. The Circuit Court decision was upheld by the Supreme Court in 1899,[2] with the statement that "the facts . . . show conclusively that the effect of the combination was to enhance prices beyond a sum which was reasonable. . . ."

The Addyston case is the precursor of an unqualified, or per se, prohibition on conspiracy to rig markets. The Supreme Court did not state such a doctrine explicitly, but its approval of Judge Taft's decision and language pointed to it.

(b) The Trenton Potteries Case (1927)

The first unequivocal statement of a per se doctrine with respect to price fixing was enunciated in a case that reached the Supreme Court in 1927.[3] Twenty individuals and 23 corporate manufacturers of vitreous china belonged to an association that had fixed prices for the sale of sanitary pottery, and had limited sales to so-called legitimate jobbers. Defendants, who held 82 percent of the market, had been convicted in a District Court trial, but had won a reversal in a Circuit Court of Appeals. The reversal was based on the grounds that the trial judge had incorrectly instructed the jury that it could return a verdict of guilty without considering the reasonableness of prices fixed by the conspiracy.

The issue presented to the Supreme Court did not concern the facts of the case or any question as to whether a finding of guilt was supportable. Rather, the issue was the propriety of the judge's instructions. Justice Stone, speaking for the Court, stated simply that:

The aim and result of every price-fixing agreement, if effective, is the elimination of one form of competition. . . . The reasonable price fixed today may through economic and business changes become the unreasonable price of tomorrow. Once established, it may be maintained unchanged because of the absence of competition secured by the agreement for a price reasonable when fixed. Agreements which create such potential power may well be held to be in themselves

---

[2] *Addyston Pipe and Steel Co.* v. *U.S.*, 175 U.S. 211 (1899).
[3] *U.S.* v. *Trenton Potteries Co.*, 273 U.S. 392 (1927).

unreasonable or unlawful restraints, without the necessity of minute inquiry whether a particular price is reasonable or unreasonable. . . .[4]

Under this doctrine the establishment of the existence of a price-fixing agreement ends the responsibility of the prosecution. There is no need to show that the prices fixed are in any way unreasonable or damaging, and, by similar token, there can be no showing that the fixed prices are in any way justifiable.

The Supreme Court thus held that the trial judge had correctly charged the jury. There was no need for the reasonableness of fixed prices to be considered, and apparently any such consideration would have been out of order. This is the basic statement of the per se approach: the action is *in itself* illegal. The circumstances surrounding the action and the consequences flowing from it are irrelevant.

(c) The Appalachian Coals Case (1933)

The condition of the bituminous coal industry in the United States was one of continual depression during the early part of this century. Excess capacity was chronic, the use of substitute fuels was growing, bankruptcy was common, and aggregate net income for the industry was at times actually negative. Faced with such conditions, which were clearly not to be remedied by natural economic forces, coal producers had sought government assistance in reorganizing the market. When such aid was not forthcoming, 137 companies joined together to form Appalachian Coals, Inc. This company, which was owned jointly by participants in accordance with their shares of total production, was to act as exclusive selling agent for the 137, and was to seek more effective marketing systems and obtain the best prices possible. The 137 producers accounted for about 12 percent of national coal production in 1929, but held almost 75 percent of the output in the Appalachian region. Thus, although the combination hardly comprised a monopoly, its size was not trivial. One purpose of the combination was manifestly the elimination of price competition among the 137 producers.

The combination was challenged by the government, which won its case in the District Court in 1932.[5] Judge Parker, writing for the three-man court, adhered closely to the principles set forth in *Trenton Potteries*. The combination, he stated, was designed to eliminate competition, and could not be interpreted as a "bona fide corporate organization resulting from normal growth and development." The decision was appealed to the Supreme Court, and final disposition made in 1933.[6]

[4] *Ibid.*, p. 397.
[5] *U.S.* v. *Appalachian Coals, Inc.*, 1 F. Supp. 339 (W. D. Va., 1932).
[6] *Appalachian Coals, Inc.* v. *U.S.*, 288 U.S. 344 (1933).

The Court was obviously responsive to the "deplorable" economic conditions of the coal industry and to the obvious need for reform and reorganization. Citing the Sherman Act's "essential standard of reasonableness," Chief Justice Hughes stated:

. . . a close and objective scrutiny of particular conditions and purposes is necessary in each case. Realities must dominate the judgment. The mere fact that the parties to an agreement eliminate competition among themselves is not enough to condemn it. . . .[7]

The conditions surrounding the case were evident; the Court found the defendants' purposes to be equally clear. The agreement was intended, according to the producers, to foster "a better and more orderly" marketing system, and not to restrict output. The Court majority saw no reason to question this statement of motivation, but held that the issue of legality ultimately rested on the likely effects of the agreement rather than the intentions of its participants.

The plan had not yet gone into effect, and its implications therefore had to be predicted. Here the Court placed emphasis on the competitive conditions of the industry. The cooperating firms were relatively small in the national market even when their production was pooled. Although the producers held most of the Appalachian area coal production, much of this coal was sold in other parts of the country. Chief Justice Hughes found it impossible to predict that the plan would enable the coal producers to fix prices. Moreover, he noted, a merger of the producing companies, involving actual integration of facilities, would have been regarded as natural and acceptable under the law. The device of a common selling agency, while not quite the same, could not thus be judged abnormal.

The *Appalachian Coals* decision was obviously a departure from the per se doctrine of *Trenton Potteries*. Chief Justice Hughes' conclusion that the coal producers' agreement was reasonable in light of industry conditions and the intent of the companies is persuasive. But under the per se approach reasonableness simply could not have been considered.

(d) The Socony-Vacuum Case (1940)

The Supreme Court decision in *Appalachian Coals* left the legal status of price fixing in considerable doubt. This doubt was resolved in a case that reached the Court in 1940,[8] involving price rigging in the oil refining industry.

---

[7] *Ibid.*, p. 360.
[8] *U.S.* v. *Socony-Vacuum Oil Company*, 310 U.S. 150 (1940).

The refining industry was substantially depressed during the 1930's, and independent producers were experiencing particularly difficult times. Oil refiners sold gasoline to jobbers, who in turn resold to retail service stations. During this period, in which prices were depressed, several major oil refiners, including Socony-Vacuum, embarked on coordinated programs of gasoline purchasing from the independents. Purchases made were of "distress gasoline," for which the independents had no regular outlets. Buying in coordination, under an informal gentlemen's agreement, the major refiners managed to maintain and even drive up the spot market price of gasoline. The spot price determined directly the price at which gasoline was sold to jobbers in tank-car lots. This price in turn influenced the price of gasoline to retail service stations, and ultimately, the price paid at retail by consumers. Each of the major refiners was fully integrated, from wells to retail stations. By manipulating the relatively thin spot market the conspirators managed to support prices throughout the various distribution stages of the industry. In effect, they kept price above the level that competitive conditions in the industry would otherwise have dictated.

The major refiners argued that their buying programs were designed to maintain order in a weak and deteriorating market. The initial problem of depressed demand had been aggravated by an increased supply of gasoline when new oil fields were discovered, and the companies argued that their actions served to stabilize the market and keep the bottom from falling out. This defense, in some ways similar to that accepted in *Appalachian Coals*, was rejected by the Supreme Court. Justice Douglas held that the buying programs of the companies constituted a combination designed to raise prices, and stated:

The elimination of so-called competitive evils is no legal justification. . . . If the so-called competitive abuses were to be appraised here, the reasonableness of prices would necessarily become an issue in every price-fixing case. In that event the Sherman Act would soon be emasculated; its philosophy would be supplanted by one which is wholly alien to a system of free competition. . . .[9]

Further, Justice Douglas said:

The Sherman Act places all such schemes beyond the pale and protects . . . our economy against any degree of interference. Congress . . . has not permitted the age-old cry of ruinous competition and competitive evils to be a defense to price-fixing conspiracies. It has no more allowed real or fancied competitive abuses as a legal justification for such schemes than it has the good intentions of the members of the combination. . . .[10]

[9] *Ibid.*, pp. 220–21.
[10] *Ibid.*, p. 221.

The *Socony-Vacuum* decision thus returned price fixing to the status of a per se offense. Justice Douglas made some effort to distinguish the circumstances from those surrounding *Appalachian Coals*. It seems clear, however, that the *Appalachian* decision was a temporary aberration in the development of price-fixing law, consistent with neither *Trenton Potteries* nor with *Socony-Vacuum* and a series of more recent cases affirming the per se doctrine.[11]

2. TRADE ASSOCIATION CASES

Despite the fact that price-fixing and similar agreements are clearly established to be per se violations of the Sherman Act, difficulty often is encountered in defining the circumstances under which such agreements can be said to exist. One of the borderline areas concerns trade-association activities. Typically these associations are formed to pursue legitimate activities such as the dissemination of information among producers and sellers. The question that has arisen under the Sherman Act concerns the point at which such activities may invite, or actually amount to, market rigging. The courts have thus been faced with the difficult task of assessing practices that serve a legal and beneficial purpose, but that may simultaneously facilitate illegal patterns of conduct.

(a) The American Column and Lumber Case (1921)

The first major trade-association case to reach the Supreme Court involved an association of 400 hardwood manufacturers.[12] Of the 400 members of the American Hardwood Manufacturers' Association, 365 participated in what was known as the "Open Competition Plan." Under the provisions of the Plan, each participant supplied extensive information on his business activities, including daily reports on prices and shipments, documented by actual invoices; monthly production and stock reports; and price lists. According to the Plan, any member failing to report such information could not *receive* the reports of the Association, which summarized and condensed the data supplied by all members.

Justice Clarke for the Supreme Court held that:

This elaborate plan for the interchange of reports does not simply supply to each member . . . the data for judging the market on the basis of supply and demand and current prices. It goes much farther. It not only furnishes such information

[11] Among the decisions affirming the per se doctrine are: *U.S.* v. *Frankfort Distilleries*, 324 U.S. 293 (1945); *Schine Chain Theatres, Inc.* v. *U.S.*, 334 U.S. 110 (1948); and *Kiefer-Stewart Co.* v. *Joesph E. Seagram and Sons*, 340 U.S. 211 (1951).

[12] *American Column and Lumber Co. et al.* v. *U.S.*, 257 U.S. 377 (1921).

. . . but also significant suggestions as to both future prices and production. . . .
It is plain that the only element lacking in this scheme to make it a familiar type
of the competitive suppressing organization is a definite agreement as to production and prices. But this is supplied: By the disposition of men "to follow their
most intelligent competitors," especially when powerful. . . .[13]

The Plan was thus interpreted as something that went beyond a simple
interchange of market information. Referring to pricing suggestions of
the Association and the actual course of price changes in the industry,
the Court found that the Plan amounted to a subtle kind of conspiracy,
designed to "procure 'harmonious' individual action."

The decision was important in two respects. First, it made clear that
an illegal scheme could not be legalized by tying it to the legitimate
function of providing information to sellers. Second, the showing of
illegality did not necessitate proof of a formal or tangible overt agreement.
The Court was willing to infer such agreement from the provisions of the
Plan, in conjunction with evidence showing the forcefulness with which
price and production "suggestions" of the Association were presented.[14]

(b) The Maple Flooring Manufacturers' Association Case (1925)

A different decision was reached by the Supreme Court in a case involving
the 22-member Maple Flooring Manufacturers' Association.[15] Members
had supplied information on prices, costs, and stocks, which the Association circulated. However, there was evidence that after the *American
Linseed* decision prices were not discussed at Association meetings. Moreover, pricing patterns among member firms did not give the appearance
of conspiracy. Prices were as a rule nonuniform, and in many instances
the prices charged by members were lower than those of nonmember
firms in the industry.

The Supreme Court held that a distribution of commercial information
does not in itself impose a restraint on competition. The convictions obtained in the earlier trade-association cases, said the Court, turned not
on the distribution of information but rather on the Court's ability to
infer "that concerted action had resulted or would necessarily result."
The distinction depended also on the role of the trade association apart
from gathering and circulating information. The Maple Flooring group
had put together market data similar to that gathered by the associations
in *American Column and Lumber* and *American Linseed*, but, unlike the
first two, this Association had made no suggestions or recommendations

[13] *Ibid.*, pp. 398–99.
[14] A similar case was similarly decided by the Court in *U.S.* v. *American Linseed
Oil Co.*, 262 U.S. 371 (1923).
[15] *Maple Flooring Manufacturers' Association* v. *U.S.*, 268 U.S. 563 (1925).

concerning future price and production policies of members. Moreover, the Association had freely publicized the information it gathered, in contrast to the earlier groups, which had withheld information from interested buyers.

There is some question as to whether the *Maple Flooring* decision was based on real distinctions between circumstances surrounding the case and those surrounding the earlier cases. If the differences were artificial, then the Supreme Court had shifted toward a more lenient view of trade-association activities.

(c) The Sugar Institute Case (1936)

The Sugar Institute was a trade association of 15 firms that controlled 70 to 80 percent of the production of domestic refined sugar.[16] The industry had been characterized by chronic excess capacity since the end of World War I, a condition that led some producers to give secret price concessions in an effort to expand sales. The purpose of the Institute was to end these concessions, which were regarded by members as "vicious and discriminatory."

Under the workings of the Institute, members entered into an agreement whereby they announced in advance prices to be charged, and adhered to those prices. There was no provision for agreement on price announcements; that is, each member could presumably determine his announced price independently. But once announced, the price was to be honored until altered by a subsequent announcement. The agreement was apparently effective in ending the secret price concessions and in raising profit margins for the industry.

The Supreme Court, referring to "the essential standard of reasonableness" embodied in the Sherman Act, stated that concerted action to curb competitive abuses does not always violate the law. Rather, Chief Justice Hughes said the issue is whether coordinated policies go so far as to amount to an unreasonable restraint of trade. In the present case, the Chief Justice held that the gathering and distribution of information by the Sugar Institute was not inherently offensive, but that the requirement of *adherence* to price announcements was an unreasonable restraint on competition; the requirement curtailed "deviations in price which fair and open competition might require or justify." This finding by the Court was not independent of conditions in the sugar refining market. The defendant companies comprised a dominant group, and, since the products were physically standardized, price was seen as the critical variable of market competition. The relief granted by the Court prohibited the Institute from pursuing its plan insofar as adherence requirements were

---

[16] *Sugar Institute* v. *U.S.*, 297 U.S. 553 (1936).

concerned; however, the Court modified a lower court decree that would have forbidden the sugar refiners from pursuing *any* program involving "the sale, marketing, shipment, transportation, storage, distribution or delivery of refined sugar."

In its effect the Supreme Court decision seemed consistent with earlier cases. The trade association was barred only from going beyond the information-gathering and -dissemination processes. But the rule-of-reason orientation of the decision served, along with *Appalachian Coals*, to create uncertainty about the legal status of price-fixing agreements.

(d) The Tag Manufacturers Institute Case (1949)

The Tag Manufacturers Institute, whose members accounted for 95 percent of tag products sales, gathered from participating firms list prices for each component of various products: strings, wires, eyelets, and so on. Since the actual products were largely custom made, prices were generally quoted on a component basis.

The Federal Trade Commission filed suit against the Institute under Section 5 of the F.T.C. Act, charging unfair methods of competition.[17] The Commission cited the Institute's system of fines to be levied against firms that did not comply with its procedures. The Circuit Court, however, absolved the Institute of any violation of law, citing two decisive factors: first, the system of fines was for failure to *report* list prices; there was no requirement of *adherence* to announced lists. Second, the Institute had freely publicized the data it gathered, making no effort to withhold information from customers of its members. Further, the Court pointed out, real transaction prices could easily deviate from list by means of concessions. The treatment of the case was thus broadly consistent with *Sugar Institute*. Concerted action pursued through the device of a trade association was to be judged on its reasonableness; and such action would likely be found reasonable as long as information was made available to all who might want it and as long as no agreement to adhere to announced prices could be inferred.

3. IMPLIED CONSPIRACY AND CONSCIOUS PARALLELISM: THE FIRST PHASE

Although the status of conspiratorial conduct under the Sherman Act is well established, the question of what constitutes a conspiracy remains troublesome. As is clear in a number of cases cited above, the courts have

---

[17] *Tag Manufacturers Institute et al.* v. *Federal Trade Commission*, 174 F. 2d 452 (1st Cir., 1949).

not required direct proof of overt conspiracy in order to find that defendants conspired in violation of the law. In neither *Trenton Potteries* nor *Socony-Vacuum*, for example, was there evidence of an actual agreement among competitors. Rather, the Supreme Court has been willing to draw an implication of agreement from the surrounding circumstances. The pertinent question becomes: what are the circumstances? That is, how far will the courts go, or how far ought they to go, to find that a conspiracy is implied by facts in the absence of direct evidence?

(a) The Eastern States Retail Lumber Dealers' Association Case (1914)

The origins of the implied-conspiracy doctrine are usually traced to this early trade-association case.[18] The facts were simple. The Association circulated lists of wholesale lumber dealers who were known to be selling at retail as well. After circulation of the Association lists, members generally stopped buying from the companies that had been named. This was a type of group boycott, a concerted effort on the part of lumber retailers to punish those wholesalers who were bypassing them in the market.

As clear as the behavior of Association members seemed, however, there had been no known agreement to boycott firms named on the lists. The lists were simply circulated, and it could be argued that each retailer made an independent decision, after seeing the lists, to cease dealing with the companies that appeared. The Supreme Court, however, saw the facts as sufficient to find an unlawful agreement, noting that "conspiracies are seldom capable of proof by direct testimony, and may be inferred. . . ." A conspiracy, in other words, could be found to exist by inference from the behavior of participants.

(b) The Interstate Circuit Case (1939)

The implied-conspiracy doctrine, which received at least tacit support in the trade association cases, was clearly reaffirmed by the Supreme Court in a case involving movie distribution.[19] The manager of Interstate Circuit, Inc., a major chain of movie theaters in Texas, sent identical letters to each of eight movie distributors. The letters demanded that the distributors not release their first-run films to any theater charging admission of less than $0.25; and that such films not be released for showing on double bills. If these demands were not met, Interstate Circuit would no longer place the distributors' films in their first-run movie theaters. Each distributor compiled with these demands, and as a result the admissions prices in many movie houses underwent drastic increases.

The situation that existed represents a classic case of what has come to

---

[18] *Eastern States Retail Lumber Dealers' Association* v. *U.S.*, 234 U.S. 600 (1914).

[19] *Interstate Circuit, Inc.* v. *U.S.*, 306 U.S. 208 (1939).

be known as *conscious parallelism*. Each movie distributor acted in identical fashion, placing the same restrictions on first-run films. Moreover, every letter sent to distributors by the manager of Interstate Circuit named all distributors as addressees; that is, each distributor knew that all the others were receiving identical letters, and might accede to the demands. Yet, although each distributor pursued the same course of action in the knowledge that others might well do the same, there was no evidence of direct agreement among them.

The Supreme Court held that the absence of direct evidence did not preclude the finding of an unlawful agreement. Actual testimony that an agreement exists is the exception rather than the rule in such cases. The question, said the Court, is whether circumstances point to the likely existence of conspiracy. In this regard Justice Stone stated:

> It taxes credulity to believe that the several distributors would . . . have accepted and put into operation with substantial unanimity such far reaching changes in their business methods without some understanding that all were to join, and we reject as beyond the range of probability that it was the result of mere chance. . . .[20]

> Acceptance by competitors, without previous agreement, of an invitation to participate in a plan, the necessary consequence of which . . . is restraint of interstate commerce, is sufficient to establish an unlawful conspiracy under the Sherman Act. . . .[21]

Two significant points were thus made. First, the test of an agreement need not involve direct evidence of its existence. Rather, the issue turns on the actions of competitors. In the present case the Court could not reconcile the actions of the eight distributors with an assumption of independence. The second point is even farther-reaching. Even if there is *no* agreement in the sense of an overt joint decision, competitors can act so as to imply unlawful conspiracy under the Sherman Act. Under the doctrine of *Interstate Circuit*, it appeared that proof of conspiracy was divorced from questions of overt or formal agreement; the issue had become one of judging the market behavior of competing firms. If such behavior seemed consistent only with a mutual understanding of some kind, the Sherman Act was breached without any need to demonstrate the mechanics involved.

(c) The American Tobacco Case (1946)

The American Tobacco Case of 1946[22] raised again the question of when conspiracy can be inferred in the absence of a demonstration of actual

---

[20] *Ibid.*, p. 223.
[21] *Ibid.*, p. 227.
[22] *American Tobacco Co.* v. *U.S.*, 328 U.S. 781 (1946).

agreement. Three major tobacco products manufacturers—American, Liggett & Myers, and R. J. Reynolds—and several company officials had been charged with multiple violations of the Sherman Act: conspiracy in restraint of trade; monopolization; attempt to monopolize; and conspiracy to monopolize. Defendants were convicted on all counts (the third and fourth being merged for purposes of imposing penalties) in a District Court trial.

The trial court's findings against the companies were based on extensive evidence of market behavior that the Supreme Court reviewed. The three defendants, known as the Big Three of the tobacco industry, had accounted for 91 percent of cigarette sales in 1930, but their joint share had fallen to 68 percent in 1939. The main factor in this drop was the introduction of economy-brand cigarettes, which sold for about 10 cents per pack as compared with the 14 to 16 cent price of the regular brands. Although the Big Three continued to dominate regular-brand sales, they had no share of the growing economy-brand portion of the market. The actions of the major companies that comprised the alleged violations of law were undertaken in response to this threat from economy-brand producers. Among these actions, the following were considered by the courts:

1. The Big Three had entered the market for low-grade tobacco and bid up prices (this tobacco was the type used in economy, but not in regular, brands of cigarettes). It was never known what the major companies did with the cheap tobacco they purchased, but the effect of the purchases was to raise the cost of materials to the economy producers.

2. Although the Big Three all bought and used the same kinds of tobacco in their regular brands, they seemed to avoid direct competition in purchasing; that is, they rarely, if ever, bid against each other for the same tobacco.

3. Price differentials among the regular brands were the rule in the industry up to the approximate time when the threat of economy brands was recognized; but there had been no price differentials since that time.

4. In 1931, during the Great Depression, Reynolds had raised the price of Camels, and the other major companies followed suit. This price increase was in retrospect the error that opened the way for the economy brands. By 1933 the economy brands held more than 20 percent of the market, and at this point the majors, led by American, introduced a series of price cuts. During 1933 both Lucky Strike and Camels were sold at a loss; but when the threat of the economy brands appeared to subside the Big Three again raised prices. The pattern of pricing thus appeared closely coordinated to drive out the smaller competitors.

A question placed before the Court by defendants was whether actual exclusion of competitors is necessary to demonstrate monopolization under Section 2. The Supreme Court agreed with the lower court that it is not. Rather, it stated, the crime of monopolizing requires only that defendants be shown to have combined or conspired to acquire or maintain the *power* to exclude—provided also that such power is actually attained and that intent to use it can be inferred.

The pertinent question, then, was whether the tobacco manufacturers had in fact conspired to acquire or maintain a dominant market position— that is, sufficient power to enable the exclusion. Based on detailed evidence relating to the points noted above, the Court concluded that conspiracy in violation of the Sherman Act had occurred. Justice Burton said:

> It is not the form of the combination or the particular means used but the result to be achieved that the statute condemns. . . . No formal agreement is necessary to constitute an unlawful conspiracy. Often crimes are a matter of inference deduced from the acts of the person accused and done in pursuance of a criminal purpose. Where the conspiracy is proved, as here, from the evidence of the action taken in concert by the parties to it, it is all the more convincing proof of an intent to exercise the power of exclusion acquired through that conspiracy. The essential combination or conspiracy in violation of the Sherman Act may be found in a course of dealing or other circumstances as well as in an exchange of words. . . . Where the circumstances are such as to warrant a jury in finding that the conspirators had a unity of purpose or a common design and understanding, or a meeting of minds in an unlawful arrangement, the conclusion that a conspiracy is established is justified. Neither proof of exertion of the power to exclude nor proof of actual exclusion of existing or potential competitors is essential to sustain a charge of monopolization under the Sherman Act. . . .[23]

Once again, then, conspiracy was found without direct evidence of overt agreement. If the actions of competitors reflect conspiracy, it is not necessary to show that an exchange of words also took place.

The *American Tobacco* decision was widely hailed as a new departure in antitrust law. An illegal conspiracy had been found on the basis of evidence showing only that the companies had acted in parallel ways. Their prices had moved together. They had entered markets and made purchases that, in combination, could only have helped their cause and hurt their competitors. And they had avoided any hard competition with each other in the purchase of tobacco. To some, the Big Three had done no more and no less than rational oligopolists normally attempt to do. Yet, if this were the case, the courts had in effect condemned ordinary oligopoly. As Nicholls put it, ". . . the courts have at last brought

[23] *Ibid.*, pp. 809–10.

oligopolistic industries within reach of successful prosecution under the antitrust laws."[24]

Although this conclusion appears in retrospect to have been premature, the courts had unquestionably reaffirmed the conscious-parallelism doctrine. Conspiracy could be inferred from action rather than words, and a long history of coordinated policies by three competitors could violate the law. Even among those who saw the case as a landmark, however, one point rankled. No meaningful remedial action was taken with respect to the cigarette industry. Each defendant was fined for criminal violations, but conditions in the industry remained unchanged.

(d) The Paramount Case (1948)

The conscious-parallelism doctrine was applied again in a case involving five major integrated movie companies.[25] The companies demonstrated a long history of parallel behavior in various aspects of their businesses: they specified the same minimum admission prices in licenses granted to exhibitors of their copyrighted films; the clearances—time periods separating the first run of a film from subsequent runs—were substantially the same; and in dealing with exhibitors, identical terms frequently were imposed by the five.

The Supreme Court decision in the *Paramount* case ratified the earlier doctrine of *Interstate Circuit* and *American Tobacco*. Justice Douglas stated, "It is not necessary to find an express agreement in order to find a conspiracy. It is enough that a concert of action is contemplated and that the defendants conformed to the arrangement."[26] The conclusion that conspiracy may be inferred from parallel practices was the same as that in *American Tobacco*, but the remedial action was more significant. In addition to prohibiting specific trade practices, the Court ordered a review of the theater holdings of the major producer-distributors. By 1952 all major companies had agreed to consent decrees requiring divestiture of their theater interests. It is widely agreed that the divorce of exhibition from distribution and production created a more vigorous competitive environment, and some observers consider the *Paramount* remedy one of the most successful in recent antitrust experience.

(e) The Cement Institute Case (1948)

The *Cement Institute* case[27] involved the operation of a multiple basing-point system, and raised a number of issues distinct from that of con-

---

[24] William H. Nicholls, "The Tobacco Case of 1946," *American Economic Review*, **39**, May 1949, pp. 284–96.

[25] *United States* v. *Paramount Pictures, Inc.*, 334 U.S. 131 (1948).

[26] *Ibid.*, p. 142.

[27] *Federal Trade Commission* v. *Cement Institute*, 333 U.S. 683 (1948).

spiracy under the Sherman Act. Under the system the delivered price quoted to buyers was determined by the base price, or price at point of origin, plus freight charges from the relevant basing point rather than from the seller's location. The Federal Trade Commission had brought suit also under the F.T.C. Act—for unfair methods of competition—and under the Clayton Act—for price discrimination. The Sherman Act issue was whether adherence to the basing-point system by sellers amounted to conspiracy in the absence of any demonstrable overt agreement to do so. The Court's finding on this point was in keeping with earlier decisions. It ruled that the Commission was justified in finding an implied agreement, in light of evidence that members of the Institute had acted so as to maintain the multiple-point pricing system.

(f) The Griffith Case (1948)

The *Griffith* case[28] appears to represent an extension of the conscious-parallelism doctrine. Four affiliated corporations that were commonly owned operated theaters in the Southwest and bargained with movie distributors through common agents. The theater operators obtained similar exclusive privileges from distributors, which prevented competitors from obtaining first- and second-run films. The defendants were acquitted in District Court of conspiracy, restraint of trade, monopolization, and attempting to monopolize.

The Supreme Court, however, reversed this verdict without reference to the effect of the practices in question on competitors or competition. The Court stated simply that the companies and the members of the family that owned them had obtained monopolistic advantages that violated the Sherman Act, even without a showing of specific intent to monopolize. This decision made it appear that conscious parallelism of action might itself violate the law.

(g) The Rigid Steel Conduit Case (1948)

Such an impression was reinforced in the *Rigid Steel Conduit* case, also decided in 1948.[29] Here a Circuit Court held that general use of a basing-point pricing system constitutes circumstantial evidence of conspiracy. Said the Court,

. . . each conduit seller knows that each of the other sellers is using the basing point formula; each knows that by using it he will be able to quote identical delivered prices and thus present a condition of matched prices under which purchasers are isolated and deprived of choice. . . .[30]

[28] *U.S.* v. *Griffith*, 334 U.S. 100 (1948).
[29] *Triangle Conduit and Cable Co.* v. *Federal Trade Commission*, 168 F. 2d 175 (7th Cir. 1948).
[30] *Ibid.*

4. IMPLIED CONSPIRACY: RECENT DEVELOPMENTS

By the end of 1948 any highly detailed parallelism of action among competing firms was suspect. The courts had not gone so far as to say that uniform pricing by companies that are aware of the uniformity is itself illegal; but uniformity had been the key to a demonstration of illegal conspiracy in numerous cases. In retrospect, however, it appears that whatever the courts may have meant, 1948 was the high-water mark of the conscious-parallelism doctrine. Beginning in 1949, the trend of judicial opinion seemed to turn in a different direction.

(a) The Pevely Dairy Case (1949)

The *Pevely Dairy* case[31] raised in a graphic way the question of whether consciously parallel action by competitors violates the law. Two St. Louis dairies, which accounted for almost two-thirds of relevant market sales, behaved identically in many aspects of their businesses. The companies charged identical prices, and when one changed its price the other followed within 48 hours. Moreover, the companies' frequency of delivery was the same, and the cooling equipment they provided to retailers was identical. In short, there was no deviation in pricing, products, or services; the parallelism between the two was virtually complete.

The trial court found, on the basis of parallel behavior, a conspiracy in violation of the Sherman Act. This decision, however, was reversed in Circuit Court.[32] This Court held that the behavior of the companies, although it might have implied conspiracy, was also compatible with innocent, nonconspiratorial, action. Because criminal charges were involved, the doubt was resolved in favor of the defendants. The Court's position was that the observed behavior of the companies could have resulted from a conspiracy, but also could have resulted from independent decisions. The two dairies offered a standardized—physically identical, if not "homogeneous"—product. Both firms paid the same (government-controlled) prices for fluid milk, and paid identical wages (they bargained with the same labor union). In view of the Court,

. . . milk . . . was a standardized product. Its cost items being substantially identical for both appellants, uniformity in price would result from economic forces. . . . We are clear that mere uniformity of prices in the sale of a standardized commodity is not in itself evidence of a violation of the Sherman Act.[33]

[31] *Pevely Dairy Co.* v. *U.S.*, 178 F. 2d 363 (8th Cir. 1949).
[32] The decision of the Circuit Court became final when the Supreme Court refused certiorari, 339 U.S. 942.
[33] *Pevely Dairy Co.* v. *U.S.*, *op. cit.*, pp. 368–69.

This decision represented a step back from the strict conscious parallelism doctrine. It raised clearly the argument that in certain market circumstances, competitors can "independently" arrive at identical policies. Such a possibility was not explicitly denied by the courts in earlier decisions, nevertheless *Pevely* does appear to represent something of a break with earlier doctrine.

(b) The Milgram-Loew's Case (1951)

The *Milgram-Loew's* case[34] was instigated by an independent drive-in-theater operator. Eight major film distributors refused to supply the drive-in with first-run films, even though the operator offered to pay more than the prevailing market price for such films. The operator charged that distributors had conspired to boycott him. In response, the distributors argued that their actions, although identical, had not been conspiratorial. Rather, they maintained, their classifications of theaters were based on independent business judgment, and their refusal to place first-run films in the drive-in was based on such factors as the seasonal nature of the drive-in business, the threat of bad weather, and the relatively narrow audience to which such theaters appeal.

The trial court held that the denial of films by the eight distributors demonstrated a conspiracy in violation of the Sherman Act. This decision was upheld by the Circuit Court of Appeals, which noted the rarity of direct evidence in conspiracy cases. Said the Court,

. . . There is no dispute over the proposition that circumstantial evidence will sustain a finding of conspiracy. . . . Uniform participation by competitors in a particular system of doing business, where each is aware of the others' activities, the effect of which is restraint of interstate commerce, is sufficient to establish an unlawful conspiracy. . . .[35]

Conscious parallelism, then, played a role in establishing conspiracy; but this role, the Circuit Court continued, is limited: "This does not mean, however, that in every case mere consciously parallel business practices are sufficient evidence in themselves, from which a court may infer concerted action.[36] *Milgram-Loew's* seems to reassert conscious parallelism; however, the qualification of the Circuit Court is a significant one. Parallel behavior may help to establish conspiracy in some cases, yet it may be insufficient in others. This kind of judicial outlook suggests that clear rules for establishing the existence of conspiracy may be impossible. It is

[34] *Milgram* v. *Loew's, Inc.*, 192 F. 2d 579 (3rd Cir. 1951), certiorari denied 343 U.S. 929.
[35] *Ibid.*, pp. 583–84.
[36] *Ibid.*, p. 583.

at least conceivable that in marginal cases the courts will simply have to get the feel of the situation, rather than rely on well-established guides to illegality.

(c) The C-O Two Case (1952)

In the *C-O Two* case[37] four manufacturers of fire extinguishers were accused of conspiracy. The companies charged uniform prices for extinguishers of identical size and design. They had uniform licensing agreements with distributors and a history of identical bids submitted to public agencies. In their defense the companies claimed that, as in *Pevely*, parallelism is natural when products are standardized. This defense was rejected by the Circuit Court, which cited the "artificial standardization" of the product, the detailed parallelism in all aspects of the businesses, and the companies' history of coordination. The Court refused to believe that this record could be explained except by conspiracy. The companies' actions, it stated, are "inconsistent with any other reasonable hypothesis."

(d) The Theater Enterprises Case (1954)

In Theater Enterprises[38] a suburban Baltimore theater, located in a shopping center, was unable to obtain first-run films from distributors and sued for treble damages. The distributors limited these films to eight downtown theaters, three of which were owned by them. The arguments of the theater operator and the distributors were substantially similar to those in *Milgram-Loew's*. Here, however, the Supreme Court found in favor of the distributors, holding that their behavior was consistent with independent business judgment.

The distributors had indeed acted uniformly, restricting first-run status to the downtown houses. The Court, however, found that such uniformity did not amount to a conspiracy. Justice Clark, speaking for the Court, stated,

To be sure, business behavior is admissible circumstantial evidence from which the fact finder may infer agreement. . . . But this Court has never held that proof of parallel business behavior conclusively established agreement or, phrased differently, that such behavior itself constitutes a Sherman Act offense. Circumstantial evidence of consciously parallel behavior may have made heavy inroads into the traditional judicial attitude toward conspiracy, but 'conscious parallelism' has not yet read conspiracy out of the Sherman Act entirely. . . .[39]

[37] *C-O Two Fire Equipment Co.* v. *United States*, 197 F. 2d 489 (9th Cir. 1952), certiorari denied, 344 U.S. 892.

[38] *Theater Enterprises, Inc.* v. *Paramount Film Distributing Corp.* et al., 346 U.S. 537 (1954).

[39] *Ibid.*, pp. 540–41.

Although the language of the Court seems clear, the precise status of parallelism after *Theater Enterprises* remains somewhat ambiguous. "Mere" parallel behavior is not sufficient for a showing of conspiracy, yet it may constitute part of such a demonstration. The pertinent question in conspiracy cases is apparently whether parallel business behavior could have been the product of independent decisions. If an independence hypothesis does not tax the credulity of the court, a conclusion of innocence may be reached.

(e) The Eli Lilly Case (1959)

During the 1950's, six drug manufacturers had contracted with the National Foundation for Infantile Paralysis to produce Salk polio vaccine. After expiration of the agreement, the companies submitted competing bids to government agencies for new orders of vaccine. The prices quoted on these bids were uniform, and similar changes in price were undertaken by various companies within weeks of each other. The district court dismissed charges against the companies on the grounds that their behavior could have been the result of independent action; that is, their behavior was consistent with a hypothesis of innocence.[40]

This decision serves to emphasize the difficulties that the federal, state, and local government frequently encounter in their role as purchasers. The purpose of competitive sealed bidding is to force potential suppliers to quote their best price. If bidding is truly competitive a supplier can quote a high price only at the risk of losing business. In many instances, however, government agencies receive identical bids. In 1965, for example, agencies reported that more than $58 million in advertised procurement was affected by identical bidding; the existence of such uniformity often must raise the suspicion of conspiracy. One economist, Mund, has argued that conspiracy is the *only* plausible explanation of identical bidding under some circumstances.[41] Yet, as the *Lilly* decision indicates, it is difficult to show that such bids imply a violation of law. So long as the product is standardized, bidding companies face similar costs, or there is some "traditional" pricing system in the industry, the hypothesis of innocence may well be accepted.

(f) The Container Case (1969)

In its latest decision on price fixing the Supreme Court seemed to move in the direction of a stricter conscious-parallelism doctrine.[42] Eighteen manu-

---

[40] *U.S.* v. *Eli Lilly & Co.*, Crim. No. 173-58, D.N.J. (1959).

[41] Vernon A. Mund, "Identical Bid Prices," *Journal of Political Economy*, LXVIII, April 1960, pp. 150–59.

[42] *United States* v. *Container Corp. of America*, 393 U.S. 333 (1969).

facturers of corrugated boxes violated Section 1 by supplying each other with the prices they charged to specific customers. The exchanges of price information were found by the Court to fall within the per se prohibitions on price fixing. Future developments will tell whether the *Container* decision has marked another important turn in the law of conspiracy.

5. REFUSALS TO DEAL

We have already seen one case, *Eastern States Retail Lumber Dealers*, in which the proximate objective of an agreement was not to fix price but rather to boycott certain sellers. Although individual firms have a right to refuse to deal with other firms, concerted boycotts by groups of firms have long been regarded as per se violations of Section 1 of the Sherman Act.

The beginnings of a per se doctrine may be traced to *Montague & Co.* v. *Lowry*,[43] a 1904 case. The defendants were an association of wholesale dealers in tiles, mantels, and grates in the San Francisco area and manufacturers of these products located in other states who sold to dealer members. The bylaws of the association provided that no dealer member should purchase from any manufacturer not also a member and also provided that sales at less than list price not be made to any nonmember. The penalty for violation of these laws was expulsion from the association. The Supreme Court held that the association "constituted or amounted to an agreement or combination in restraint of trade"; and termed defendants' contention that the amount of commerce involved was negligible, "not very material."

Later rulings have followed a similar approach. In *Paramount Famous Lasky Corp.* v. *United States*,[44] a group of motion picture distributors and producers had adopted standard contracts with exhibitors. The contracts provided that any disputes go to arbitration, but also stated that the failure of an exhibitor to agree to arbitration, or to abide by an arbitrated award, would result in common punitive action by the group. The Supreme Court held that despite the usefulness of arbitration in the industry, the agreement suppressed competition and was illegal. The Sherman Act, said the Court, cannot "be evaded by good motives."

In *Fashion Originators' Guild of America, Inc.* v. *Federal Trade Commission*,[45] a 1941 case, the Guild (an association of textile manufacturers and designers) had entered into an agreement with an association of

[43] 193 U.S. 38 (1904).
[44] 282 U.S. 30 (1930).
[45] 312 U.S. 457 (1941).

garment manufacturers. Under the agreement, the garment makers would not deal in the textiles of "pirate" manufacturers that were copied from designs of Guild members. The argument of the Guild was that the agreement was "reasonable and necessary to protect the manufacturer, laborer, retailer and consumer against the devastating evils growing from the pirating of original designs. . . ." The Court held that the Federal Trade Commission had been correct in refusing to hear much of the evidence on reasonableness. The purpose and object of the agreement, said the Court, were such as to bring it within the prohibitions of the Sherman Act, as well as the Clayton and F.T.C. Acts. Indeed, the Court stated, ". . . the reasonableness of the methods pursued by the combination to accomplish its unlawful object is no more material than would be the reasonableness of the prices fixed by unlawful combination."[46] The per se status of refusal to deal has been repeatedly reaffirmed. In *Klor's, Inc.* v. *Broadway-Hale Stores, Inc.*[47] the Supreme Court held that Broadway-Hale's use of its monopolistic buying power to induce major appliance companies not to deal with Klor's violated the Sherman Act. Said the Court, "Group boycotts, or concerted refusals by traders to deal with other traders have long been held to be in the forbidden category. They have not been saved by allegations that they were reasonable. . . ."[48] The legal status of refusals to deal thus seems clear. Such arrangements violate the Sherman Act uniformly. Moreover, there has been little difficulty—in comparison with price fixing—in establishing the existence of concerted boycotts. Such agreements are, by their nature, much more difficult to effect on a tacit and informal basis.

B. The Current Legal Status of Conspiracy

As we have seen, certain kinds of restraint and conspiracy are considered illegal per se under the Sherman Act. The apparent simplicity of the per se doctrine, however, is misleading.[49] It condemns market-rigging agreements without defining them. As a result the courts are faced with a rather

---

[46] *Ibid.*, p. 468.

[47] 359 U.S. 207 (1959).

[48] *Ibid.*, p. 212.

[49] In the recent *Pfizer (tetracycline)* case, high profits and "unreasonable" prices were admissable evidence for reaching a judgment about the presence of a conspiracy. The very meaning of the *per se* doctrine here seems questionable. See *Chas. Pfizer & Co.* v. *F.T.C.* 401 F. 2d 574 (6th Cir., 1968); certiorari denied 394 U.S. 920 (1969).

strange dilemma. Certain areas of behavior are clearly proscribed by legal precedent; at the same time, however, the existence of the offensive behavior can be extremely difficult to establish. Consequently, the courts are required to consider not so much the fate of conspiracy as the meaning of the term.

The reaction of the courts to this task has not been surprising. Cases of obvious conspiracy are dealt with most uniformly. When there is direct evidence of agreement conviction is virtually certain. At the other extreme, mere similarity of behavior on the part of competitors is unlikely to result in legal action, much less conviction for violation of the Sherman Act, unless accompanied by other incriminating evidence. Price leadership, for example, is a mode of parallelism that has not been brought within the Act's coverage.

In general, the more elaborate a conspiracy is, the greater is the likelihood of legal sanctions. This is simply because complex and detailed agreements will often require conspirators to communicate. When evidence of overt communication can be produced in court, the outcome of a trial is no longer in doubt; but such direct information is seldom obtained.

A crucial question is how far the courts are willing to go to infer conspiracy from circumstantial evidence. In other words, what do the courts do in the absence of direct proof that accused firms overtly agreed to terms? This question can be answered only tentatively, for recent decisions are ambiguous. *Theater Enterprises* indicated that parallel business behavior does not "itself" violate the Sherman Act; yet the *Container* case seems to imply that parallelism is evidence from which conspiracy might be inferred.

In some cases involving conscious parallelism, the courts have stated that a judgment must be made about the possible independence of firms' actions. If the parallel behavior is such that it could have resulted from independent decisions, then it is legally acceptable; if, on the other hand, it could only have resulted from conspiracy, it violates the law. The difficulty with this superficially plausible standard is its vagueness. Although it may be simple enough to categorize extreme cases, there often is no obvious distinction between innocent and guilty parallelism.

If it is difficult to say precisely what the courts' standards of conspiracy *are*, it is somewhat easier to note what they are *not*. Certainly the last 20 years of litigation do not bear out the post-*American Tobacco* notion that rational oligopoly is somehow illegal. The courts have not moved to condemn "normal" oligopolistic behavior, and have given no indication that concerted action by firms will be generally presumed to violate the law. At the same time, it would be incorrect to conclude that conscious parallelism no longer plays a role in conspiracy cases. Identical behavior by firms may be legally significant in conjunction with other factors. Phillips suggests, for example, that parallelism in a context that is somehow "unreasonable" will be condemned more quickly than similar parallelism without undesirable implications.[50] And it may be that when uniformity of action is complete and highly detailed, it will likely be found inconsistent with a hypothesis of independent action.

The language of conspiracy cases is at times extremely vague. It is evident, however, that the judicial definition of conspiracy is now a rather narrow one, and is certainly narrow in comparison with the definitions implicit in decisions through 1948. Although the courts have continued to note that direct evidence of overt agreement is rare, they are less hospitable to indirect inferences than they once were. Much tacit conspiracy—the type of collusive behavior that proceeds without overt agreement—seems today to be beyond the reach of the Sherman Act.

C. The Economic Meaning of the Conspiracy Doctrines

Having reviewed the legal status of conspiracy, it is now pertinent to ask whether this area of public competition policy has been developed in an economically rational way.

1. DEFINITIONS OF CONSPIRACY

As we have seen, the courts have tried to distinguish between independent and interdependent (conspiratorial) behavior. Phillips points out, however, that such a distinction may be more semantic than real.[51] In certain markets the actions of any firm affect the conditions facing other firms. A new decision with respect to price or output by a firm A will change the feasible price-quantity combinations for firms $B, C, \ldots, N$. Similarly, what any other firm, $B, C, \ldots, N$, does, must "react back" on its rivals. This is the meaning of interdependence. Firms may attempt to deal with such interdependence in various ways. But what the courts have failed to realize is that "independent" action is an impossibility in these circumstances. Even if firms should choose to "ignore" interdependence, perhaps in the manner of Cournot duopolists, it simply will not go away!

[50] Almarin Phillips, *Market Structure, Organization and Performance*, Harvard University Press, Cambridge, 1962, especially pp. 62 ff.

[51] *Ibid.*, pp. 72–73.

Consider the automobile manufacturing industry. The prices at which the Ford Motor Company can sell various quantities of new cars depends in part on the price and output policies of General Motors and Chrysler, and to a somewhat lesser extent on the policies of American Motors and foreign manufacturers. The Ford company has a variety of policy options, but it does not have the option of behaving as if its rivals did not exist. No matter how "independent" the company would like to be, no matter how "independent" its decision makers may feel, Ford simply cannot do the things that it might be able to do if General Motors and Chrysler were to disappear. Both its demand and its cost conditions are affected by the actions of its rivals. The results the company can attain are necessarily dependent on others, and in this sense it can only act in an interdependent way.

Clearly, then, it makes little sense for the courts to search for truly independent behavior in markets whose structures imply interdependence. But what are the implications of the courts' apparent determination to undertake such a search? The immediate result is semantic confusion. Beyond this, however, it is evident that judges are making distinctions of some kind, even if the distinctions are not actually between independence and interdependence in firms' behavior.

What is being distinguished seems rather to be the degree of *explicitness* or *formality* in coordinated behavior. The courts have not required direct proof of overt agreement, and convictions have been obtained without transcripts of conversations or reports of meetings among competitors. But it does appear that an important element in conspiracy cases is the presence or absence of a presumption that such overt communication has occurred. The trade-association cases, for example, did not yield conclusive evidence of what could be called formal or explicit agreement to fix prices and output levels; but an important factor in these cases was the kind of communication that the associations facilitated. Similarly, the *American Tobacco* case evidenced no open agreement among the Big Three; but their actions were so finely dovetailed that the presumption of overt communication was strong. In contrast, the *Pevely Dairy* case showed a history of complete and precise parallelism. Here, however, it was possible to believe that the two companies had attained their existing state of coordination without explicit communication and agreement.

This distinction cannot be offered as a full interpretation of recent judicial actions. Other factors, for example, the effectiveness of concerted behavior and the damage suffered by competitors or customers, may enter in. It does appear, however, that the courts are proceeding from a rather narrow definition of agreement. An agreement seems to be found when there is strong reason to believe that companies must have overtly agreed to formulate concerted policies. When concerted policies can be interpreted as the result of purely tacit understandings—when overt communication is not necessary—illegal agreement is much less likely to be found by the courts. In applying this kind of standard the courts are not distinguishing meaningfully between independent and collusive behavior. What oligopolistic firms do is never done independently, and might be regarded as a mixture of dependence and independence. Perhaps the mixture varies, but the degree of overtness in communication among rivals tells us little about the degree of interdependence in business behavior.

To the extent that the courts search for evidence of classic overt conspiracy, there must be considerable skepticism about the economic value of policy in this area. It is true, as we have seen in Chapter 3, that a collusive oligopoly may yield significantly different market results than an oligopoly in which firms compete actively. But there is nothing to indicate that *formal* or *overt* conspiracy is in general necessary to effective collusion. Explicit communication may of course be necessary in some cases. As Kaysen has pointed out,[52] the larger the number of firms and the greater the degree of uncertainty and ignorance in a market, the less likely it is that collusive results can be effected without overt dealings among competitors. Once the situation is sufficiently complicated that firms cannot naturally follow a coordinated course, communication is required.[53] In many of the conspiracy cases discussed above, however, the number of firms involved is relatively small, and here there may be no need for explicit agreement. As Kaysen states:

The significance of . . . recognition of mutual dependence . . . is that, given a common goal of action . . . no machinery of reporting or enforcement is needed to secure adherence to the goal by the rivals. Each seller, knowing the common goal, realizes that he can gain nothing by actions not in conformity with it.[54]

Consider an example in which a small group of firms sells closely substitutable products. Each firm may be aware that a price cut will cause the other firms also to reduce their prices, and will thus prove to be unprofitable. Indeed, price cuts could lead to price warfare, a contingency that all firms are likely anxious to avoid. Cognizance of the situation may well prevent any company from cutting its price. As market conditions change the need for price adjustments will become apparent. Some firm or firms may over time assume the role of leading their rivals in such

[52] Carl Kaysen, "Collusion Under the Sherman Act," *Quarterly Journal of Economics*, **65**, May 1951, pp. 263–70.

[53] As noted in Chapter 9, this may account for the Clabault-Burton finding of a higher incidence of Sherman Act indictments in industries of lower concentration.

[54] *Op. cit.*, p. 267.

adjustments, but as adjustments occur each rival will continue to recognize the desirability of staying in line. Price competition may disappear in this fashion, even though there is no actual communication among the rivals. In fact, it is possible that purely informal price leadership will establish the same market results that overt communication would have produced.

This possibility points out the artificiality of the legal standards currently applied to conspiracy. If overt communication occurs the Sherman Act has certainly been violated; without such communication the behavior of firms is more likely to be considered legal. Yet there is no necessary *economic* distinction between the two cases. The judgment of the law turns here on the purely mechanical aspects of what is in both instances collusive action. Of course there are many potential complications for firms that attempt to pursue coordinated policies, and it can be argued cogently that prohibitions on formal collusion at least make it more difficult for participants to achieve their desired ends.

If the prohibitions imposed by antitrust serve to make effective conspiracy more difficult, it may be said that the policy has some beneficial effects. The courts, however, have apparently failed to recognize that oligopolistic industries may imply economically desirable or undesirable performance that has little if anything to do with narrowly defined agreement or conspiracy. Indeed, if conspiratorial oligopoly is a problem worthy of public policy concern, that concern must extend far beyond the relatively few instances in which conspiracy involves actual conversations among business rivals.

2. TREATMENT OF CONSPIRACY

American courts have long accepted the proposition that conspiracy is a bad thing. Firms acting in concert presumably do so in order to raise prices and profits—in short, to act more as a monopolist would. About the only positive benefit of conspiracy that can be cited is the order it may impose on a market. In the absence of some type of coordination competition among firms could at times become chaotic and some markets might become unstable. It is impossible to say what the social cost of such instability would be, but it is conceivable that society would suffer from such consequences as a high rate of business failures. In condemning conspiracy as a per se offense the courts have ignored any possible benefits that might be associated with such behavior.

Few economists have argued strongly against the per se doctrine as it applies to conspiracy and restraint of trade.[55] At the same time, how-

---

[55] A notable exception is Phillips, *op. cit.*

ever, there is little apparent enthusiasm for the public policy that has evolved under this doctrine. Part of the difficulty with defending the policy on an economic basis goes back to the definitions of conspiracy employed by the courts. Most economists would probably agree that collusion is undesirable; yet it is far from obvious that the kinds of collusive behavior proscribed by the courts are worse than the kinds of collusive behavior that tend to be accepted as nonconspiratorial or independent. Formal price fixing, for example, may be "bad" in some objective sense; but if the alternative is *informal* price fixing, then prosecution of the formal variety may not yield great benefits. When one notes that the antitrust agencies devote a very extensive portion of their limited resources to fighting conspiracy, the lack of enthusiasm for the program on purely economic grounds is understandable. Even if limitations on overt conspiracy do some economic good—and they may well do so—the value of a major expenditure in this area is at best unknown.

A second, very closely related objection to public policy on conspiracy has to do with the nature of the remedies imposed. The usual penalty for a criminal conviction is a fine, limited legally to $50,000 per defendant per violation.[56] This kind of punishment probably has only limited effectiveness in deterring companies from future violations. Moreover, to the extent that it is effective, it probably operates in a highly discriminatory fashion. A $50,000 penalty is a negligible burden to large firms, but may be significant to companies that are small. Beyond the statutory fines, companies convicted of conspiracy may be vulnerable to private treble-damage actions, which are usually undertaken by customers who were presumably forced to pay artificially high prices while a conspiracy was in effect. The sums that can be recovered in such suits are potentially much larger, and may serve as a more effective deterrent.

The remedy problem, however, goes beyond the question of how much punishment can be heaped on companies that have conspired to rig market transactions. The very notion that there is such a thing as a punitive "remedy" hinges again on the proposition that conspiracy is a kind of conduct. Since the law defines it as such, the punitive procedure is consistent: a conspirator is someone who behaves badly; therefore, to induce better behavior, the bad behavior is punished. The broader economic notion of collusion, however, suggests that punishment will not solve anything. Generally collusive behavior cannot meaningfully be described as a pure conduct phenomenon. It is not something so simple and precise

---

[56] In the early 1960's several executives of large electrical equipment manufacturers were sent to prison after convictions for conspiracy. The use of prison terms has been rare, however, and it is not obvious that even such severe treatment constitutes a satisfactory remedy.

as a series of meetings. Rather, it is taking into account the mutual interdependence implied by the *structural* conditions of the market.

Viewed in these terms, it is clear that punishment cannot remedy a collusive situation. It does not matter how great the punishment may be; there is simply no way that a court can order firms to act independently in a market whose structural conditions imply interdependence. So long as conspiracy is seen as a simple matter of conduct, firms have the options of conspiring or not conspiring; and punitive measures may be an appropriate way of inducing them to select the "right" option. When collusive behavior is viewed, however, as something that is inherent in the structure of certain markets, the futility of punishment as a remedy is evident. To be sure, punishment may have some effect on conduct. It may force firms into different *modes* of collusive action. It may well stimulate firms to devise more subtle and sophisticated, and generally less direct, forms of conspiracy. The one thing it cannot bring about, however, is truly independent behavior.

14

Antitrust Treatment
of Mergers

Corporate merger has long been a common method by which firms grow. A company that desires growth can expand internally by building new plant and taking on additional personnel, but acquisition of a going concern is often seen to have important advantages. The acquired company has established facilities and distribution outlets. Perhaps even more important, it has established good will. When one company takes over another it acquires not only its physical assets but its intangible assets as well. It is in effect purchasing a market position that it otherwise would have to fight to obtain as a new entrant. It is hardly surprising, then, that many firms seeking growth prefer the merger route to internal expansion.

Although mergers may appeal to corporations, however, they are often a matter of concern from the standpoint of public competition policy. Acquisitions frequently change the structure of markets. If the acquiring and acquired firms are in the same market, merger eliminates a competitor and enhances the power of the surviving company; if they are in a supplier-customer relationship, merger may yield to the (now-integrated) survivor certain competitive advantages over its rivals; even if the merging companies operate in unrelated markets, the acquiring firm may obtain a greater degree of power, in some sense, than it had before. Since power that is centralized in one or a few firms may carry undesirable economic implications, it is clear that the merging of two independent companies is at least of potential concern.

A. Background: The Merger Phenomenon

The record of corporate mergers in the United States is an interesting one because of its uneven character. There apparently have been at least two and perhaps three great "merger waves" in our history.[1] The first covered the approximate period 1898–1903. As Nelson's figures, reproduced in Table 14.1, indicate, something over 2800 mergers in mining and manufacturing took place during these five years, and merger activity did not sharply abate until after 1906. Moreover, the amount of assets that changed hands was, in comparison with the size of the economy at the turn of the century, impressive. The magnitude of the merger movement was in fact so great that, although some students of history associate its conclusion with the rise of strong antitrust enforcement, others have noted that it may have come to an end simply because few salable companies remained. The second merger wave occurred roughly during 1925–1930, as shown in Table 14.1; the third wave, according to Mueller, "has been underway since the closing years of World War II."[2] Although data on mergers are incomplete (primarily because relatively small acquisitions may escape notice), the existence of these periods of abnormal activity seems well established. Precisely why the waves occurred when they did or ended when they did is less certain.[3]

The history of public policy toward mergers demonstrates great change and innovation since the beginning of the century. At the time of the first merger wave, the Sherman Act was the only relevant antitrust statute in existence. Its effectiveness in dealing with the movement was less than overwhelming. Although it might have been possible to charge some companies with monopolizing or attempting to monopolize trade by virtue of

[1] See Ralph L. Nelson, *Merger Movements in American Industry*, Princeton University Press, Princeton, for the National Bureau of Economic Research, 1959; George W. Stocking, "Comment on Mergers," in *Business Concentration and Price Policy*, Princeton University Press, Princeton, for the National Bureau of Economic Research, 1955, pp. 191–212; and Willard F. Mueller, Testimony reprinted in *Economic Concentration*, Hearings Before the Senate Subcommittee on Antitrust and Monopoly, 89th Cong., 1st Sess., part 2, pp. 501–37.

[2] Mueller, *op. cit.*, p. 502.

[3] There has been some speculation that merger waves follow major innovations—for example, the development of the railroad, telephone, radio, and television—but the causal relationship is not well established. The most recent movement is, according to latest estimates, continuing. The Federal Trade Commission has reported that merger activity in mining and manufacturing underwent "the sharpest increase in modern industrial history" during 1967, when 1496 mergers were recorded.

Table 14.1

Mergers and Acquisitions in Manufacturing and Mining[a]

Nelson Series, 1895–1920

Year	Annual Total	Year	Annual Total
1895	43	1908	50
1896	26	1909	49
1897	69	1910	142
1898	303	1911	103
1899	1208	1912	82
1900	340	1913	85
1901	423	1914	39
1902	379	1915	71
1903	142	1916	117
1904	79	1917	195
1905	226	1918	71
1906	128	1919	171
1907	87	1920	206

Source: Ralph L. Nelson, *Merger Movements in American Industry, 1895–1956*, Princeton University Press, Princeton; 1959, p. 37.

Thorp Series, 1919–1939

Year	Annual Total	Year	Annual Total
1919	438	1930	799
1920	760	1931	464
1921	487	1932	203
1922	309	1933	120
1923	311	1934	101
1924	368	1935	130
1925	554	1936	126
1926	856	1937	124
1927	870	1938	110
1928	1058	1939	87
1929	1245		

Source: Willard L. Thorp and Walter Crowder, *The Structure of American Industry*, Temporary National Economic Committee Monograph 27, 1941, pp. 231–34.

Table 14.1 (Cont.)

FTC Series, 1940–1964

Year	Annual Total	Year	Annual Total
1940	140	1953	295
1941	111	1954	387
1942	118	1955	683
1943	213	1956	673
1944	324	1957	585
1945	333	1958	589
1946	419	1959	835
1947	404	1960	844
1948	223	1961	954
1949	126	1962	853
1950	219	1963	861
1951	235	1964	854
1952	288		

[a] Reprinted as Appendix to Testimony of Willard F. Mueller in *Economic Concentration,* Hearings Before the Subcommittee on Antitrust and Monopoly of the Committee on the Judiciary (Senate), 89th Cong., 1st Sess., part 2, G.O.P., Washington, 1965, p. 847.

their acquisitions, such an approach was never really attempted. As we saw in Chapter 12, the prosecution of major trusts such as Standard Oil and American Tobacco was based largely on their "ruthless" practices. It is true that the market power of the companies was considered, and that merger was one means by which market power had been attained; but the Act was not construed as a weapon to be used against mergers as such.

The antimerger provision in the Clayton Act of 1914 was stimulated by the earlier merger movement. The original Section 7 prohibited a corporation from acquiring the stock of another corporation when the effect might be "to substantially lessen competition"; and the language of the law seemed to limit this prohibition to situations in which competition between the acquiring and acquired concerns would be affected. Because stock acquisition was the usual merger mechanism at the time, and because mergers between competitors were common, the provision was an apparently meaningful one. As early as 1927, however, the Federal Trade

Commission began to recommend legislative extensions. Section 7 as it stood could not prevent corporations from making direct acquisitions of assets, and this form of merger circumvented the law with some frequency. The F.T.C. suggested—and for years continued to suggest—revision of the law to include asset acquisition.

Although these suggestions were not followed quickly, Congress believed by 1950 that a serious gap existed in public merger policy. An important stimulus to this belief was provided by the *Columbia Steel* case of 1948.[4] The United States Steel Corporation had contracted to buy the assets of the Consolidated Steel Corporation, the largest independent steel fabricator on the West Coast. As an asset acquisition, the merger was immune under Section 7, but the government brought suit under Sections 1 and 2 of the Sherman Act, charging restraint of trade and attempted monopolization. The merger was viewed by the Supreme Court in a vertical context. United States Steel, the nation's largest producer of basic rolled steel, was purchasing a fabricator of finished steel products. The government argued that the merger would exclude producers of rolled steel—United States Steel's competitors—from supplying Consolidated with the materials it used in fabrication. This type of argument refers to *vertical foreclosure:* the merger of a customer and a supplier forecloses other suppliers (or customers) from the portion of the market that the customer (or suppliers) controls.

The Supreme Court held that such a merger could not be construed as an unreasonable restraint of trade. Further, since the merged company would not hold "unreasonable" market control, and since there was no evident intent to monopolize, the merger did not violate the Sherman Act prohibition on monopolization. Justice Reed stated that vertical integration raises questions of policy that are not to be decided by the courts: "It is not for courts to determine the course of the Nation's economic development. . . . If businesses are to be forbidden from entering into different stages of production that order must come from Congress, not the courts."[5] The issue was thus clearly defined. The *Columbia Steel* decision indicated that antitrust could provide no meaningful check on corporate mergers. If the nation's leading steel producer could legally acquire an important fabricator, then few significant mergers could be prohibited by existing law. Moreover, as Justice Reed made plain, a change in policy could come only from Congress. Congressional reaction to the decision was prompt. A number of Committees examined existing merger policy and found it wanting. In 1950 the Celler-Kefauver amendment to Section 7 of the Clayton Act became law. The new Section 7 extended its pro-

[4] *U.S.* v. *Columbia Steel Co. et al.,* 334 U.S. 495 (1948).
[5] *Ibid.,* p. 526.

hibitions to asset as well as stock acquisitions, and was directed at any merger whose effect "in any line of commerce in any section of the country . . . may be substantially to lessen competition or to tend to create a monopoly."

The meaning of a "substantial" lessening of competition had yet to be defined by the courts, but it was immediately obvious that the potential importance of the new law was tremendous. It would no longer be necessary to prove, in the case of asset acquisition, monopolization or an attempt to monopolize under the Sherman Act; and the intention of Congress clearly was to provide a more stringent legal obstacle. The amendment was noteworthy in that it provided for the first significant *preventive* antitrust policy. In the words of a Senate report, "The intent here . . . is to cope with monopolistic tendencies *in their incipiency and before they have attained such effects as would justify a Sherman Act proceeding.*"[6] Typically, antitrust policy moved against monopolistic conditions only after such conditions had become established facts of life. It was now conceivable that in the merger area the chronology would be reversed.

The questions to be brought before the courts were both important and difficult. What meaning was to be ascribed to a "line of commerce" or "section of the country"? When would a merger be likely to lessen competition, and what standards of probability and substantiality were to be applied? The language of amended Section 7 was sweeping, and its translation into workable and effective policy would require nothing less than a definition of both competition and markets.

In recent years these formidable tasks have been complicated further by the disproportionate growth of conglomerate mergers. As shown in Table 14.2, conglomerates now dominate the American merger phenomenon. This probably reflects in part the effects of public merger policy itself. Section 7 was employed with vigor against horizontal and (to a somewhat lesser extent) vertical mergers during the 1950's; and is at precisely this time that the growth of conglomerates is most dramatic.

The conglomerate merger complicates policy in part simply because it is a new phenomenon. Such mergers have of course existed for many years, but their quantitative significance is a recent development. The courts during the 1950's developed some rather well-defined rules with respect to the competitive effects of horizontal and vertical mergers, and these could not be applied directly in conglomerate cases.

The conglomerate merger is in addition more difficult to treat conceptually. Both vertical and horizontal mergers carry some implications for market structure; and it is possible to draw some inferences about competitive impact. The conglomerate merger, however, involves firms in

[6] *Senate Report* 1775, 81st Cong., 1st Sess. (1950). Italics added.

Table 14.2

Percentage Distribution of Mergers by Type and Period, 1926–1968

	1926–1930	1940–1947	1951–1955	1956–1960	1961–1965	1966–1968
Horizontal type	75.9	62.0	39.2	30.1	22.5	8.6
Vertical	4.8	17.0	12.2	14.9	17.5	9.8
Conglomerate type	19.3	21.0	48.6	55.0	60.0	81.6
Total	100.0	100.0	100.0	100.0	100.0	100.0

Source: Staff Report of the Federal Trade Commission, *Economic Report on Corporate Mergers,* Hearings on Economic Concentration, Subcommittee on Antitrust and Monopoly, U.S. Senate, 91st Cong., 1st Sess., Washington, 1969, Adapted from Table 1–6, p. 63.

different markets. It is thus extremely difficult to formulate judgments about competitive effects. Moreover, the conglomerate firm does not occupy a clear position in economic theory. Expectations about its behavior are speculative, and the ability to suggest appropriate public policies is therefore limited.

B. A Review of Relevant Cases

1. THE duPONT-GENERAL MOTORS CASE (1957)[7]

During the period 1917–1919, E. I. duPont de Nemours and Company had acquired a 23 percent stock interest in the General Motors Corporation. DuPont was a major supplier of automotive finishes and fabrics, and General Motors, the nation's leading automobile producer, was a major user of these products. Further, the record showed that "duPont supplies the largest part of General Motors' requirements. . . ."

The substantive question before the Court was whether duPont's position as a major stockholder and supplier lessened competition substantially by foreclosing other suppliers from a portion of the market; that is, did duPont's insulated possession of the General Motors business

[7] *U.S. v. E. I. duPont de Nemours and Company et al.,* 353 U.S. 586 (1957).

in finishes and fabrics violate Section 7? First, however, it was necessary for the Court to contend with two peculiar legal circumstances:

1. The government had attacked the stock acquisition some 30 years after its consummation, an unusual procedure.

2. Although the case reached the Supreme Court after passage of the amendment to Section 7, charges had been brought originally in 1949 under the old law.

The first issue caused the Court little difficulty. It was true, said Justice Brennan, that earlier Section 7 cases had been filed "at or near the time of acquisition," but there was nothing in these cases that ". . . holds, or even suggests, that the Government is foreclosed from bringing the action at any time when the threat of the prohibited effects is evident." The question, in other words, was not when the merger took place, but rather when the possibility of a substantial lessening of competition arose.

The second issue, although disposed of quickly by the Court, presented greater difficulty. Legal action had been brought against duPont and General Motors under the old Section 7, which specifically proscribed mergers that might substantially lessen competition "between the corporation whose stock is . . . acquired and the corporation making the acquisition." DuPont and General Motors argued that because they did not compete with each other, they were not covered by the prohibition; that is, if the stock acquisition lessened competition, it did not do so by diminishing rivalry *between* the acquired and acquiring firms. This argument was rejected by the Court on the grounds that the intention of the original Section 7 was broader than its qualifying phrase would indicate. Said Justice Brennan,

. . . Section 7 . . . plainly is framed to reach not only the corporate acquisition of the stock of a competing corporation, where the effect may be substantially to lessen competition between them, but also the corporate acquisition of stock of any corporation, competitor or not, where the effect may be either (1) to restrain commerce in any section or community, or (2) tend to create a monopoly of any line of commerce.[8]

On the basis of this interpretation, Justice Brennan held that:

. . . any acquisition by one corporation of all or any part of the stock of another corporation, competitor or not, is within the reach of the section whenever the

---

[8] *Ibid.*, pp. 590–91. The first paragraph of original Section 7 reads: "That no corporation engaged in commerce shall acquire, directly or indirectly, the whole or any part of the stock . . . of another corporation engaged also in commerce where the effect of such acquisition may be to substantially lessen competition between [the two] . . . or to restrain such commerce in any section or community or tend to create a monopoly of any line of commerce."

reasonable likelihood appears that the acquisition will result in a restraint of commerce or in the creation of a monopoly of any line of commerce.[9]

DuPont and General Motors contended that their relationship was based on objective business judgments and did not restrain commerce. General Motors' purchases of duPont products depended, said the companies, on the quality and price of those products—that is, on the same considerations that governed all purchases. The Court, however, refused to accept the suggestion that duPont's strong position as a supplier of General Motors was based simply on the excellence of its performance. The Court did note that in later years competitors had obtained a larger proportion of the General Motors business, but went on to say:

The fact that sticks out . . . is that the bulk of duPont's production has always supplied the largest part of the requirements of the one customer in the automobile industry connected to duPont by a stock interest. The inference is overwhelming that duPont's commanding position was promoted by its stock interest and was not gained solely on competitive merit.[10]

The Court concluded:

The statutory policy of fostering free competition is obviously furthered when no supplier has an advantage over his competitors from an acquisition of his customer's stock likely to have the effects condemned by the statute. . . . The conclusion upon this record is inescapable that such likelihood was proved as to this acquisition. . . .[11]

This decision, reached under the old Section 7, seemed consistent with the *new* law, perhaps more than with the old. The Court had found that substantial vertical foreclosure violated Section 7. DuPont's access to the General Motors' business by virtue of its stockholder relationship, rather than on pure merit, had in some way hampered competition.

2. THE BETHLEHEM-YOUNGSTOWN CASE (1958)

The proposed merger of the Bethlehem Steel Corporation and the Youngstown Sheet and Tube Company has been termed the first "big case" under amended Section 7.[12] Steel is a key industry in the American economy. In part because its products are the inputs for many other manufacturing industries, steel price and output behavior carries serious implications for

[9] *Ibid.*, p. 592.
[10] *Ibid.*, p. 605.
[11] *Ibid.*, p. 607.
[12] *U.S.* v. *Bethlehem Steel Corp.*, 168 F. Supp. 576 (S.D.N.Y., 1958).

many sectors. The industry has long been characterized by high concentration and the existence of a dominant firm, United States Steel; and the merger at issue involved the second and sixth leading producers. As if this were not enough to focus attention on the case, it was the first new Section 7 prosecution to reach final determination in the courts. Previously the Federal Trade Commission had ruled on specific acquisitions,[13] and a number of suits had been settled by mutual consent,[14] but *Bethlehem* would provide the first possibility for important legal precedent in the future treatment of mergers.

The facts of the acquisition were clear. Bethlehem, the number two steel producer, accounted for 15.4 percent of national ingot capacity; and Youngstown, the sixth largest firm, held 4.7 percent. Since United States Steel had almost 30 percent of the market, the merger would not have created a new market leader, but would have strengthened the second largest company. Indeed, the companies argued that the primary effect of the acquisition would be to establish a firm better able to compete with United States Steel. The merger, they contended, would actually increase competition in the industry. The government's contention was the reverse. The merger would increase market concentration, however measured. For example, the four largest firms accounted for 58.3 percent of the market before merger, but would have held 63 percent afterward. Moreover, the strengthening of the number two producer was, as Singer has put it, double-edged.[15] A combined Bethlehem-Youngstown might be better able to compete with United States Steel, but such a firm would also become more powerful vis-a-vis smaller competitors (Bethlehem was already much larger than the third largest producer, Republic Steel, which held 8.3 percent of the market).

Not the least of the District Court's problems in reaching a decision was the finding of a relevant geographic market. Section 7 requires a showing that competition may be lessened substantially in a "line of commerce"[16] and a "section of the country." With respect to section of the country, the defendants argued that their businesses were carried on primarily in separate regions, Bethlehem in the eastern and western portions of the

[13] *Pillsbury Co.* v. *Federal Trade Commission, 50 F.T.C. 1110* (1954); this case ultimately was appealed and decided in Circuit Court: 354 F. 2d 952 (5th Cir., 1965).

[14] At least five challenged acquisitions were settled by mutual consent of the government and defendants before the time of the Bethlehem decision. The consent agreements generally provided for full or partial divestiture of acquired facilities and/or some limitation on future acquisitions.

[15] Eugene M. Singer, *Antitrust Economics*, Prentice-Hall, Englewood Cliffs, N.J., 1968, p. 131.

[16] The lines of commerce, or *product* markets, in the *Bethlehem* case were defined by the Judge as (a) the iron and steel industry, (b) hot rolled sheets, (c) cold rolled sheets, (d) hot rolled bars, and (e) buttweld pipe.

nation, and Youngstown in the center. Judge Weinfeld, finding that both actual and potential steel shipments of the companies did overlap geographically, held that there were multiple relevant markets: the United States; the northeastern quadrant of the United States; Michigan, Ohio, Pennsylvania, and New York; Michigan and Ohio; and Michigan.[17]

In concluding that the merger would violate Section 7, the Judge stressed several points:

1. The merger would increase market concentration and would widen the gap between the two largest firms and remaining competitors.

2. An addition to concentration in an already concentrated market such as steel may be especially damaging, and approval of the immediate merger might open the door to further concentration-increasing mergers, each "justified" by the fact that the merging companies would be better able to compete with larger rivals.

3. To allow a merger merely because the emergent company would not be the largest in the industry would violate the purpose of amended Section 7.

4. The merger would eliminate a significant competitor in an industry whose history indicated that replacement by a new entrant was most unlikely.

The most important aspect of the *Bethlehem* decision is, in retrospect, the emphasis placed on market shares and concentration. The merger was horizontal—the companies were, primarily, competitors at the same production stage—and the immediate question concerned the meaning of a lessening of competition in such circumstances. Although Judge Weinfeld did not say so explicitly, his underlying notion of lessened competition seems closely tied to measurable increases in the centralization of market power: an increased market share for the emergent firm, an increase in the concentration level of the industry, and a reduction in the number of competitors. These structural indicia have continued to play a prominent role in the evaluation of competitive consequences of horizontal mergers.

3. THE BROWN SHOE CASE (1962)

The *Brown Shoe* decision[18] was the first expression of Supreme Court opinion on mergers under amended Section 7. At issue was the acquisition

---

[17] It is interesting to consider whether such definitions might be mutually inconsistent. That is, it may be that if any one of the above definitions is correct, then the others logically ought to be considered incorrect. Such a suggestion has been made by M. A. Adelman, "The Antimerger Act, 1950–1960," *American Economic Review*, **51**, May 1961, pp. 236–44.

[18] *Brown Shoe Co., Inc.* v. *United States*, 370 U.S. 294 (1962).

by Brown, the nation's fourth largest shoe manufacturer and a retail chain as well, of the G. R. Kinney Company, the largest "family-style" retail shoe chain in the country and the twelfth largest shoe producer. The merger thus presented both vertical and horizontal considerations: Brown as a manufacturer was acquiring Kinney as a retailer, and was thus integrating forward into the distribution of shoes; but Brown was also a retailer and acquisition of Kinney would add to Brown's existing market share at retail.

Although both aspects were considered, the Supreme Court based its decision largely on vertical grounds. The relevant product markets were defined as men's, women's, and children's shoes, and the relevant geographic area with respect to vertical impact was the nation as a whole. The companies had argued that the product lines should be more narrowly drawn according to differences in grade of material, quality of workmanship, price, and end use; but the Court rejected such distinctions as unrealistic.

Chief Justice Warren, writing for the Court, stressed the legislative history of Section 7. Congress' dominant motivation in revising the law, he stated, was to arrest "a rising tide of economic concentration in the American economy." The intention was to stop mergers at a time when this trend "was still in its incipiency." The history and language of the law, according to the Chief Justice, indicated Congressional determination to have a strong merger policy, one that would place important legal obstacles in the way of further concentration increases. Thus, although Section 7 did not spell out specific tests for determining either relevant markets or diminutions of competition, its mandate was strong.

With this general outlook the Court turned to the question of vertical effects on competition. Chief Justice Warren held that a lessening of competition in a vertical merger arises "primarily from a foreclosure." The question is: does the acquisition of a customer by a supplier (or vice versa) foreclose other suppliers (customers) from a portion of the market? Although noting that such foreclosure is the main index of lessened competition, the Court stopped short of saying that any substantial foreclosure would automatically render a merger illegal. The size of the market share foreclosed, said the Chief Justice, is "seldom determinative"; it is necessary to look further into the historical and economic background of affected markets.

In the immediate case the Court noted that the shoe industry was atomistic in structure. Brown's share of the national manufacturing market was on the order of 5 to 6 percent, while Kinney's retail sales accounted for less than 2 percent of the national market. Thus, although the merger involved leading firms in the shoe industry, it would not have produced a company whose size would overwhelm the market. Nevertheless, the Court noted, "In this industry, no merger between a manufacturer and an independent retailer could involve a larger potential market foreclosure."[19] Both past history and the testimony of Brown Shoe's president indicated that Brown would indeed force its shoes into Kinney stores by virtue of ownership—that is, the potential for foreclosure would be exploited. Further, said the Chief Justice, a trend toward vertical integration in the industry was already apparent, and made it increasingly difficult for nonintegrated shoe manufacturers to place their shoes in retail outlets. The Court did not quarrel with Brown Shoe's contention that the industry was highly competitive, but held that "remaining vigor" in competition cannot immunize a merger if "the trend in the industry is towards oligopoly. . . ."

The Court's position on the vertical aspect was, then, clear. Congress had revised Section 7 to preserve competition and prevent the formation of oligopolies or industries of high concentration. Given this purpose, and considering the circumstances of the industry, the merger was suspect. The Court concluded:

. . . the trend towards vertical integration in the shoe industry, when combined with Brown's avowed policy of forcing its own shoes upon its retail subsidiaries, may foreclose competition from a substantial share of the markets . . . without producing any countervailing competitive, economic or social advantages.[20]

Although the merger thus violated Section 7 on vertical grounds, the Court considered horizontal effects as well. Here the product markets were the same, but in addition to the nation as a whole, the relevant geographic markets were defined as cities with populations of over 10,000 in which Brown and Kinney both operated retail stores. At the national level, the merger would have yielded a firm with about 5 percent of the market; however, in specific cities the combined share would have been higher, ranging up to 24.8 percent in Dodge City, Kansas. The Court was aware that a 5 percent national share did not constitute impressive evidence of market power, but stated:

In an industry as fragmented as shoe retailing, the control of substantial shares of trade in a city may have important effects on competition. If a merger achieving 5% control were now approved, we might be required to approve future merger efforts by Brown's competitors seeking similar market shares. The oligopoly Congress sought to avoid would then be furthered. . . .[21]

[19] *Ibid.*, pp. 331–32.
[20] *Ibid.*, p. 334.
[21] *Ibid.*, pp. 343–44.

Given the atomism of the market, the Court argued, the emergent Brown-Kinney retail chain would be in a strong position even though its national market share were low. Citing testimony that strong national chains "can insulate selected outlets from the vagaries of competition," Chief Justice Warren concluded:

The retail outlets of integrated companies, by eliminating wholesalers and by increasing the volume of purchases from the manufacturing division of the enterprise, can market their own brands at prices below those of competing independent retailers. Of course, some of the results of large integrated or chain operations are beneficial to consumers. . . . But we cannot fail to recognize Congress' desire to promote competition through the protection of viable, small, locally owned businesses. Congress appreciated that occasional higher costs and prices might result from the maintenance of fragmented industries and markets. It resolved these competing considerations in favor of decentralization. We must give effect to that decision.[22]

Although the *Brown Shoe* decision makes several important points, none seems to reach farther than this last paragraph. The Supreme Court was searching for standards under which a lessening of competition could be inferred. In examining the horizontal side of the merger the Court found that a tendency toward centralized or concentrated power was the key; but here it appeared to be making a further statement. A merger that created a firm with a 5 percent share of an atomistic market was found likely to diminish competition *without examination of other economic consequences* such as possible changes in costs and prices. Apparently the Court was proposing a strict structural standard with regard to horizontal acquisitions. The *competitive* effect of a merger would be judged purely in terms of its effect on the *structure* of relevant markets; and if it were found to be anticompetitive on this basis not even an expectation of improved market performance could save it from the Section 7 prohibition. This strict view was undoubtedly influenced strongly by the Court's reading of Congressional intent.

4. THE PHILADELPHIA NATIONAL BANK CASE (1963)

The Philadelphia National Bank merger case[23] presented the Supreme Court with an array of legal and economic questions. The merging banks,

---

[22] *Ibid.*, p. 344.
[23] *United States* v. *Philadelphia National Bank*, 374 U.S. 321 (1963).

Philadelphia National and Girard Trust Corn Exchange, were the second and third largest of 42 commercial banks in the Philadelphia area. The merger would have produced the largest bank in the area, with control of 36 percent of total bank assets, 36 percent of deposits, and 34 percent of net loans. This would have made the emergent company substantially larger than First Pennsylvania Bank, which had been the largest single concern with about 23 percent of the market, and it would have raised the four-firm concentration level in the area to about 78 percent.

Viewed in these terms, the effect of the merger was dramatic in raising the concentration of the market. But before the Court could consider this impact, two separate issues required disposition: the vulnerability of bank mergers to Section 7 prosecution; and the definition of the relevant geographic market. It is safe to say that before the *Philadelphia National Bank* decision, few individuals in the Justice Department, the Federal Trade Commission, the judiciary, or the banking industry believed that bank mergers were subject to prosecution under Section 7.[24] In fact, the merger was attacked by the government primarily as a violation of Section 1 of the Sherman Act; the argument with respect to Section 7 appears to be an afterthought. The reason for this confusion is the status of banking as a regulated industry. The Bank Merger Act of 1960 expressly directed the bank regulatory agencies (the Federal Reserve Board of Governors, the Federal Deposit Insurance Corporation, and the Comptroller of the Currency) to consider competitive factors before approving mergers; and it was the defendants' argument that this law effectively removed bank mergers from the scope of the federal antitrust laws.

This contention was denied by the Supreme Court. Justice Brennan for the majority noted that immunity from the antitrust laws is not lightly implied. And, he went on, there was nothing in either the legislative history of the Section 7 amendments or in the Bank Merger Act itself that conferred express immunity on the banking industry. Presumably Congress had the power to confer such immunity, but except in the most extreme circumstances the Court would not infer it indirectly. Thorough regulation of an industry by federal agencies might remove the industry from the realm of antitrust prosecution, but, said Justice Brennan:

The fact that the banking agencies maintain a close surveillance of the industry with a view toward preventing unsound practices that might impair liquidity or lead to insolvency does not make federal banking regulation all-pervasive. . . .[25]

[24] See, for example, Jesse W. Markham, "Mergers and the New Section 7," in Almarin Phillips (editor), *Perspectives on Antitrust Policy*, Princeton University Press, Princeton, 1965, p. 178.

[25] *United States* v. *Philadelphia National Bank, op. cit.*, p. 352.

Having established the absence of antitrust immunity for the banking industry, the Court was to decide the proposed merger under Section 7. The relevant line of commerce was held to be commercial banking. More troublesome was the determination of the relevant geographic market. The position of the companies, which had been accepted by the District Court, was that the relevant area was a broad one.[26] The emergent bank, it was argued, would compete for business among large customers with banks in New York and throughout the Northeastern United States. But, said the Court:

The proper question to be asked in this case is not where the parties to the merger do business or even where they compete, but where, within the area of competitive overlap, the effect of the merger on competition will be direct and immediate.[27]

The Court went on to note that large customers may do a large portion of their banking business outside their home community, whereas small customers are confined by convenience to the immediate neighborhood, and intermediate sized customers "deal with banks within an area intermediate to these two extremes." What, then, is *the* relevant geographic area? Said the Court:

. . . that . . . the relevant geographical market is a function of each separate customer's economic scale means simply that a workable compromise must be found: some fair intermediate delineation which avoids the indefensible extremes of drawing the market either so expansively as to make the effect of the merger upon competition seem insignificant, because only the very largest bank customers are taken into account in defining the market, or so narrowly as to place appellees in different markets, because only the smallest customers are considered. We think that the four-county Philadelphia metropolitan area . . . which would seem roughly to delineate the area in which bank customers that are neither very large nor very small find it practical to do their banking business, is a more appropriate "section of the country" in which to appraise the instant merger than any larger or smaller or different area.[28]

The determination of the metropolitan area as a relevant market was, then, the compromise that permitted the Court to decide on the basis of the market share and concentration data noted above. Here the Court's position was clear. Section 7 reflected intense Congressional concern with

---

[26] It is very common for defendants to argue for a broad market in merger cases, since, as we have seen, this is likely to reduce the impact of the merger on measured changes in concentration.

[27] *U.S.* v. *Philadelphia National Bank, op. cit.,* p. 357.

[28] *Ibid.,* p. 361.

rising industrial concentration. This concern according to the Court,

. . . warrants dispensing, in certain cases, with elaborate proof of market structure, market behavior, or probable anticompetitive effects. Specifically, we think that a merger which produces a firm controlling an undue percentage share of the relevant market, and results in a significant increase in the concentration of firms in that market, is so inherently likely to lessen competition substantially that it must be enjoined in the absence of evidence clearly showing that the merger is not likely to have such anticompetitive effects.[29]

The Court refused to specify what constitutes "an undue percentage share" of the market. The immediate merger, however, would produce a firm with over 30 percent; and, said Justice Brennan, "we are clear that 30% presents that [competitive] threat."

The merger was thus enjoined, somewhat in the manner of *Brown Shoe*, on the basis of Congressional concern with rising concentration. The position taken by the Court was one of apparently unqualified hostility to such increases. Justice Brennan noted in conclusion that a merger that lessens competition "is not saved because on some ultimate reckoning of social or economic debits and credits, it may be deemed beneficial."

Despite the strength and clarity of the *Philadelphia National Bank* decision, a potentially troublesome inconsistency must be noted. The Court held that Section 7 is designed to bar anticompetitive mergers even when such mergers may have social and economic benefits. In Justice Brennan's words, "some price might have to be paid" for denying certain mergers that threaten competition. The Court claimed that its standard of judgment was faithful to economic theory, which holds that "competition is likely to be greatest when there are many sellers, none of which has any significant market share." Restating the Court's position: protection of competition requires the encouragement of atomistic or unconcentrated market structures, and this requirement holds even when the result may be the denial of benefits to consumers.

The economic inconsistency of this position should be obvious. It is true that competition in a strict sense is associated with powerlessness, or atomistic structure. But the economic rationale for competition is not atomism itself; it is rather the *economic results* that atomism implies. If competitively structured (atomistic) markets do *not* imply desirable economic results, then the economic rationale for such markets breaks down. The Court's position, however, seems to be that atomistic structures are desirable even when it is conceded that they may cause a deterioration in performance. Such a position may be defensible, but not on the grounds of traditional economic arguments for competition.

[29] *Ibid.*, p. 363.

5. THE ALCOA-ROME CASE (1964)

The acquisition of the Rome Cable Corporation by the Aluminum Company of America presented somewhat different issues from those raised by either Brown-Kinney or PNB-Girard.[30] Alcoa, the nation's leading aluminum producer, was also the leader in production of aluminum conductor, a type of line used to transmit electric power from generating plants. Rome was one of the 10 largest producers of copper conductor wire and cable, and was a "substantial" producer of aluminum conductor as well. Aluminum conductor and copper conductor were competitive in use, but in recent years aluminum had captured most of the conductor market.

The District Court, in finding that the merger did not violate Section 7, held that insulated aluminum conductor and insulated copper conductor fall within the same market grouping. The Supreme Court, however, found that aluminum conductor—both insulated and noninsulated—was a submarket and a separate line of commerce. Although it received some competition from copper, the Court regarded it as sufficiently distinct in quality and price to be treated alone. Both aluminum conductor and insulated aluminum conductor, a narrower product group, were defined as the relevant markets. In aluminum conductor Alcoa's share of the market was 27.8 percent; Rome accounted for 1.3 percent; and the nine largest producers jointly held 95.7 percent.

The Supreme Court held that Alcoa's acquisition of Rome violated Section 7. Any acquisition of a significant competitior by one of the dominant firms in a highly concentrated industry, said Justice Douglas, may lessen competition substantially. It was true, he noted, that Rome's share of the market seemed small (even in the narrower insulated aluminum conductor market it held only 4.7 percent). But here two points were relevant: Alcoa already controlled an "undue" percentage share of the market; and Rome was a significant competitive factor within a highly concentrated market. Only a dozen companies had accounted for as much as 1 percent of the market in the last five years, and Rome, which was known as an efficient and aggressive firm, posed the threat of effective future competition to market leaders.

The *Alcoa-Rome* decision in one sense comes full circle from *Brown Shoe*. In *Brown Shoe* the Court had expressed particular concern about merger in a fragmented market, arguing that it would be a step on the road to oligopoly. Here, however, the Court expressed equal concern about a small merger in an already concentrated market, stating: ". . . the

[30] *United States* v. *Aluminum Co. of America*, 377 U.S. 271 (1964).

more advanced the oligopoly, the more objectionable each step becomes." Clearly, the evolving position on horizontal acquisitions was a stringent one. Read together, *Brown Shoe, Philadelphia National Bank,* and *Alcoa-Rome,* indicate that mergers between leading firms in the same market may inevitably violate Section 7.

6. THE CONTINENTAL CAN CASE (1964)

The issues presented to the Supreme Court under the new Section 7 in the cases discussed above were handled in relatively straightforward fashion. Vertically, the Court looked to market foreclosure as a test of lessened competition; horizontally, problems of market definition were ever present, but once settled, the Court relied on measures of concentration and market shares. The acquisition of Hazel-Atlas by the Continental Can Company,[31] however, posed a somewhat different problem, for the merger did not quite fit either the vertical or horizontal category. Continental was the nation's second largest manufacturer of metal containers, accounting for 33 percent of the market (the American Can Company had 38 percent, making the metal container industry something akin to a duopoly). Hazel-Atlas was the third largest producer of glass containers, with a 9.6 percent market share.

The difficulty in treating this merger arose from the fact that although metal and glass containers serve some similar uses, they are not really "the same" product. Even when they competed directly—for example, in beer, soft drinks, and baby foods—customers might not readily switch back and forth in response to price or quality changes. In many areas, moreover, the characteristics of the two types of container were sufficiently distinct to preclude competition.

The Supreme Court recognized the nature of the relationship, conceding that "interchangeability of use" between metal and glass containers is not so great as that normally found in intraindustry mergers. Nevertheless, the Court contended, the *interindustry* competition between the two was sufficiently great to justify definition of a combined glass *and* metal container market as a separate line of commerce. Having established the combined market as relevant, the Court proceeded to consider the usual kinds of structural measure. Continental's share of the combined market was 21.9 percent, making it the second largest producer; Hazel-Atlas accounted for 3.1 percent, and the six largest manufacturers held a joint share of over 70 percent.

The Supreme Court held that the merger would violate Section 7. The

[31] *United States* v. *Continental Can Co.,* 378 U.S. 441 (1964).

combined market share of Continental and Hazel-Atlas, about 25 percent, approached the presumptively anticompetitive 30 percent figure cited in *Philadelphia National Bank*. The merger "reduced from five to four" the number of significant competitors that might have challenged the position of the dominant firm. The Court also stated that a diversified (metal-and-glass) manufacturer would hold an advantage over single-line rivals that could not be permitted when the diversified firm was already dominant. Moreover, said the Court, the merger could trigger further mergers by firms seeking the same advantages.

The statements cited to this point are very much in line with the earlier condemnations of horizontal acquisitions. The Court, however, did not rest its entire conclusion on these conventional statements, perhaps because it recognized the somewhat artificial nature of the relevant market it had defined. Said Justice White:

Market shares are the primary indicia of market power, but a judgment under Section 7 is not to be made by any single qualitative or quantitative test.

Where a merger is of such a size as to be inherently suspect, elaborate proof of market structure, market behavior and probable anticompetitive effects may be dispensed with in view of Section 7's design to prevent undue concentration.[32]

Further, said the Court, Section 7 deals with "probable and imminent" competition, as well as with that competition existing at the moment. Glass and metal containers were becoming increasingly competitive in certain areas. Indeed, the nature of competition between the two was long run. In this light the merger would reduce potential *future* competition between Continental and Hazel-Atlas, even though the two companies might not compete much with each other at present.

The Supreme Court had, then, defined a relevant container market, but had stopped short of tying its decision exclusively to projected changes in the concentration of that market. For the first time, the notion of "future" and "potential" competition was introduced, and although the Court does not concede it explicitly, this turn toward a different concept was probably dictated by the novel circumstances of the merger and by the arguable nature of the relevant market as defined.

7. THE EL PASO NATURAL GAS CASE (1964)

The El Paso Natural Gas Company's acquisition of Pacific Northwest Gas[33] marked the first horizontal merger case in which market shares and concentration were not relevant to the final decision. At the time of the

[32] *Ibid.*, p. 458.
[33] *United States* v. *El Paso Natural Gas Co.*, 376 U.S. 651 (1964).

merger El Paso was one of the largest gas pipeline companies in the country. El Paso had assets of almost $1 billion and was the sole out-of-state supplier to what the government called the "vast and still expanding California market." Pacific Northwest, with assets of $250 million, was termed "the only other important pipeline company west of the Rocky Mountains."

The Supreme Court defined California as the relevant section of the country, and the production, transportation, and sale of natural gas as the relevant line of commerce. These definitions made for a rather unusual structural situation. El Paso was an important supplier of natural gas in the California market; but Pacific Northwest, although attempting to make inroads, had no outlet to California and had not sold natural gas there. The merger thus had *no immediately visible effect* on the structure of the relevant market area as defined. Had the Supreme Court adhered strictly to its earlier tests of lessened competition, it might have had to conclude that no competitive impact was discernible, for Pacific Northwest had a zero share of production and sales in the relevant market. Whatever the implications of the merger might be, it would not immediately alter El Paso's existing market share or market concentration.

The Court, however, refused to be bound by its own past tests. Justice Douglas took careful note of Pacific Northwest as a competitive factor in the California market. The company had made efforts to sell natural gas in California, and despite its failure, was a "substantial factor" in the market. In one instance Pacific had negotiated and reached tentative agreement to supply Southern California Edison, a major user of natural gas in California. Edison ultimately terminated the agreement and came to terms with El Paso; but on the basis of its bargaining with Pacific the company was able to obtain price discounts from El Paso. Thus the Court concluded that even Pacific Northwest's unsuccessful efforts could exert a "powerful influence on El Paso." Said Justice Douglas:

Unsuccessful bidders are no less competitors than the successful one. The presence of two or more suppliers gives buyers a choice. Pacific Northwest was . . . one of two major interstate pipelines serving the trans-Rocky Mountain States . . . It was so strong and militant that it was viewed with concern, and coveted, by El Paso. If El Paso can absorb Pacific Northwest without violating Section 7 of the Clayton Act, that section has no meaning in the natural gas field.[34]

8. THE LEXINGTON BANK CASE (1964)

Evidence that certain mergers might be challenged successfully under the more difficult standards of the Sherman Act was supplied by the Lexing-

[34] *Ibid.*, pp. 661–62.

ton Bank merger case.[35] The government had not argued that the merger of the first and fourth (of six) banks in Fayette County, Kentucky, would violate Section 7 because at the time the case was initiated—before *Philadelphia National Bank*—it did not believe that the Section applied to bank mergers.

The acquiring company, First National Bank and Trust Company of Lexington, accounted for about 40 percent of county bank assets, loans, and deposits, and was more than twice the size of the second largest bank; Security Trust Company, the acquired bank, accounted for about 13 percent of the market, and held more than 50 percent of the total value of trust assets in the county. The Supreme Court found it "clear that significant competition will be eliminated" by the merger. Justice Douglas noted that the merged bank would be larger than all other remaining banks combined (its market share would be greater than 50 percent). The Comptroller of the Currency had approved the merger after being advised by the Attorney General, the Federal Deposit Insurance Corporation, and the Board of Governors of the Federal Reserve that it would adversely affect competition in commercial banking in Fayette County. Three of the four other banks that would have remained after the merger had stated that the merger would seriously affect their ability to compete.

The Court concluded that the elimination of significant competition between First National and Security Trust "constitutes an unreasonable restraint of trade in violation of Section 1 of the Sherman Act." As in *Philadelphia National Bank*, the Court indicated that mergers between two large competitors would be found illegal without reliance on precise structural rules of thumb. Quoting from the *Columbia Steel* decision, Justice Douglas stated:

We do not undertake to prescribe any set of percentage figures by which to measure the reasonableness of a corporation's enlargement of its activities by the purchase of the assets of a competitor. The relative effect of percentage command of a market varies with the setting in which that factor is placed.[36]

9. THE PENN-OLIN CASE (1964)

The Penn-Olin case[37] did not, strictly speaking, involve corporate merger or acquisition. It was rather a "joint venture" in which the Pennsalt

[35] *United States* v. *First National Bank and Trust Company of Lexington*, 376 U.S. 665 (1964).

[36] *Ibid.*, p. 672; quotation at *Columbia Steel, op. cit.*, pp. 527–28.

[37] *United States* v. *Penn-Olin Chemical Co.*, 378 U.S. 158 (1964).

Chemical Corporation and the Olin Mathieson Chemical Corporation jointly formed a new company, the Penn-Olin Chemical Corporation. The purpose of the new company was to produce and sell sodium chlorate (an industrial chemical used primarily by the pulp and paper industry) in the southeastern United States. There was no argument among the parties concerning the relevant line of commerce (sodium chlorate) or section of the country (southeastern United States). Rather the issues were whether Section 7 applies to joint ventures; and if so, whether this joint venture violates either Section 7 or Section 1 of the Sherman Act.

The Supreme Court held that Section 7 does apply to joint ventures, although the language of the provision does not specifically extend to such situations. The test, said Justice Clark, is "the effect of the acquisition." Citing the Court's earlier language in *Philadelphia National Bank*, Justice Clark stated that to place joint ventures beyond the scope of Section 7 "would be illogical and disrespectful of the plain Congressional purpose in amending" the law. Such ventures could threaten competition in much the same way as formal merger, and were not to be treated differently.

An assessment of the competitive consequences of this "merger," however, was not directly made by the Court. Rather it confined its decision to the legitimacy of tests applied by the lower court, which found that the venture did not violate Section 7. The District Court had noted that both Pennsalt and Olin possessed the resources to enter the southeastern market separately, and that the forecasts of the companies themselves indicated that plants could be operated profitably. However, the District Court stated, these considerations were significant only insofar as they shed light on the probability that each company would enter individually. This Court held that the relevant test of the venture, in terms of its impact on competition, depended on the likelihood that *both* Pennsalt and Olin would move into the southeastern section as active rivals. Since the Court found it "impossible to conclude that as a matter of reasonable probability *both* . . . would have plants in the southeast if Penn-Olin had not been created," it concluded that no violation of Section 7 was implied.

The Supreme Court held that the basis of the District Court decision was incorrect. The probability of substantially lessened competition, said Justice Clark, could not be judged solely according to the likelihood of separate entry by both companies. One might have entered "while the other continued to ponder," and,

There still remained for consideration the fact that Penn-Olin eliminated the potential competition of the corporation that might have remained at the edge of the market, continually threatening to enter. Just as a merger eliminates actual competition, this joint venture may well foreclose any prospect of competition between Olin and Pennsalt, in the relevant sodium chlorate market. The difference of course is that the merger's foreclosure is present while the joint venture's is prospective.[38]

The point made in this passage is important in the development of merger law. The notion of potential competition that the Court utilized in both *Continental Can* and *El Paso* seemed to refer to actual future competition between merging companies; that is, competition was expected to occur, and the merger would in each case have foreclosed it. Here, however, Justice Clark was going farther in asserting that the mere presence of a potential competitor—even one who may *never actually enter* the market—carries significant competitive implications.

In discussing the problem of proof of lessened competition the Court seemed clearly to indicate its hostility to the Penn-Olin joint venture. The industry was a rapidly expanding one, and "each company had compelling reasons for entering the southeast market." Under the circumstances, the probability of diminished competition seemed high. The Supreme Court, however, confined its decision to an order that the case be reconsidered in light of the above-mentioned guidelines. The case was to be retried in light of the competitive effect of entry by one firm while the other remained a potential entrant. Somewhat ironically, in view of the Court's expression of opinion, the Penn-Olin venture was again found by the lower court not to violate Section 7. On a second appeal the Supreme Court *upheld* this decision by a tie (4 to 4) vote.[39]

10. THE VON'S GROCERY CASE (1966)

The acquisition by Von's Grocery Company of Shopping Bag Food Stores, a competing grocery chain in Los Angeles, demonstrated again the Supreme Court's stringency toward horizontal mergers.[40] The companies operated in the same line of commerce and section of the country. The merger gave the combined firm only 7.5 percent of the market; however, Justice Black, for the majority, laid heavy emphasis on the trend toward merger and concentration in the relevant market. From 1950 to 1963 the number of owners operating a single grocery store in the Los Angeles retail market decreased from 5365 to 3590; similarly, the number of food chains with two or more grocery stores had increased during 1953–1962 from 95 to 150, and these trends were explained partially by merger and acquisition. The combined Von's-Shopping Bag chain had 66 retail stores, making it the second largest in the market.

[38] *Ibid.*, pp. 173–74.
[39] *United States* v. *Penn-Olin*, 389 U.S. 308 (1967).
[40] *United States* v. *Von's Grocery Co. et al.*, 384 U.S. 270 (1966).

Viewed against this background, said Justice Black, the merger clearly violates Section 7. The combination of two significant and growing competitors in a market characterized by trends toward merger and concentration could not be permitted in view of the basic purpose of Section 7: ". . . to prevent economic concentration in the American economy by keeping a large number of small competitors in business."[41] Although it had been present in earlier decisions, nowhere was the Court's concern with small business expressed as directly as in *Von's Grocery*. The Sherman Act, it noted, "failed to protect the smaller businessman from elimination through the monopolistic pressures of large combinations which used mergers to grow ever more powerful." The stated purpose of the Clayton Act, and of amended Section 7 in particular, was to foster *competition*. As the Supreme Court interpreted this purpose in horizontal merger cases, it was a mandate to encourage markets composed of *small competitors*.

An interesting dissent from the majority opinion was lodged by Justice Stewart, joined by Justice Harlan. Justice Stewart pointed out that although the Court majority had spoken in terms of *concentration* of the market, it had cited only evidence bearing on the *number of firms* and mergers. Had the majority looked further, he argued, it would have seen considerable evidence that concentration was declining even as the number of independent competitors declined as well. The evidence was in fact mixed. For example, between 1952 and 1958 the combined shares of the three, four, and five largest firms in the market decreased while the share of the top 20 firms increased. But the point of the dissent is a real one. The majority opinion relied heavily on the contention that the relevant market was undergoing increases in concentration, yet the information it cited did not directly support this contention. This does not render illegitimate many of the arguments made by the Court. If, for example, the proper purpose of Section 7 is to protect small businessmen, then it is indeed appropriate to take a harsh position on a horizontal merger between significant competitors. It seems clear, however, that the Court's own tests of anticompetitive impact were relying progressively less on actual market data. Something approaching a per se prohibition on horizontal acquisition could be inferred from the language of the *Von's Grocery* decision.

11. THE PABST-BLATZ CASE (1966)

In 1958 the Pabst Brewing Company, the nation's tenth largest brewer, acquired the Blatz Brewing Company, the eighteenth largest brewer.[42]

---

[41] *Ibid.*, p. 275.
[42] *United States* v. *Pabst Brewing Co. et al.*, 384 U.S. 547 (1966).

The government brought suit in 1959, charging that the merger might lessen competition in the production and sale of beer in "the United States and in various sections thereof, including the State of Wisconsin and the three-state area encompassing Wisconsin, Illinois and Michigan . . . ." The District Court dismissed the government's case on the grounds that a relevant geographic market had not been established. Specifically, the court held that neither Wisconsin nor the three-state area had been shown to be "a relevant geographic market within which the probable effect of the acquisition . . . should be tested"; whereas for the nation as a whole (which the court considered a relevant market), a probability of lessened competition had not been demonstrated.

The Supreme Court reversed this decision on the grounds that the merger increased Pabst's share and the concentration level of the beer industry. Pabst became the fifth largest national brewer by virtue of the merger; and there had been "a very marked thirty year decline in the number of brewers" and a sharp rise in nationwide concentration throughout the industry. Said Justice Black, "We hold that a trend toward concentration in an industry, whatever its causes, is a highly relevant factor in deciding how substantial the anticompetitive effect of a merger may be."[43]

The *Pabst* decision is clearly consistent with earlier cases, and closely parallels *Von's Grocery* in certain respects. At least as interesting as the actual result, however, is the Court's treatment of geographic market definition. Justice Black held that the District Court had erred in thinking "it was essential for the Government to show a 'relevant geographic market' in the same way the corpus delecti must be proved to establish a crime." The law, according to Justice Black, requires no such precise showing. Rather,

The language of this section requires merely that the Government prove the merger has a substantial anticompetitive effect somewhere in the United States— "in *any* section" of the United States. This phrase does not call for the delineation of a "section of the country" by metes and bounds as a surveyor would lay off a plot of ground. The Government may introduce evidence which shows that as a result of a merger competition may be substantially lessened throughout the country, or on the other hand . . . only in one or more sections of the country. In either event a violation of Section 7 would be proved. Certainly the failure of the Government to prove by an army of expert witnesses what constitutes a relevant "economic" or "geographic" market is not an adequate ground on which to dismiss a Section 7 case.[44]

[43] *Ibid.*, pp. 552–3.
[44] *Ibid.*, p. 549.

Taken literally, this statement is unclear. The Court appears to contend that although the government must demonstrate a probability of lessened competition, it need not prove a precise relevant market. Yet the kinds of evidence that the Court accepts as indicative of lessened competition necessarily presuppose a precisely defined market! It is impossible to count numbers of firms, market shares, and concentration levels without drawing such data from a defined market grouping.

What the Court may actually be saying is something a bit different than its language conveys: in order to show a lessening of competition the government must have a clearly defined market, both in terms of product lines and geography; but the market definitions it employs *need not be closely defended on logical or theoretical grounds.* If, in other words, *any* market definition exists under which evidence of reduced competition can be shown, it does not matter whether that market definition is theoretically "good" in economic terms. The government's use of Wisconsin is a case in point. Here it was clearly shown that the Pabst-Blatz merger would increase concentration, and that the number of brewers had been dropping significantly. Apparently the Court's position[45] is that this showing proves a Section 7 violation whether or not Wisconsin is a meaningful economic market.

This conclusion encounters an understandably adverse reaction among many economists, and lawyers as well. Neither the legislative history nor the economic meaning of Section 7 indicates that poor market definitions are appropriate. At the same time, however, the Court is attempting to deal with an immensely difficult situation. Market definitions, as we have seen repeatedly, present complex problems; indeed, it is often difficult to avoid use of a somewhat arbitrary definition. The Supreme Court itself is not well equipped to deal with these problems. It appears to be saying in *Pabst* that it will not be placed in the position of having to approve a merger that seems to lessen competition substantially merely because the science of defining markets has not been well developed by others. The Court has thus opted for an extremely strict position, one that appears to reduce the government's burden of proof in Section 7 cases.

12. THE PROCTER & GAMBLE-CLOROX CASE (1967)

The merger cases that had come before the Supreme Court before 1967 were, for the most part, horizontal. *Brown Shoe* was a partial exception,

---

[45] Although there were no dissenting opinions, four of the nine justices appear to disassociate themselves from the majority position on the government's burden of proof with respect to the relevant market.

and was decided on both horizontal and vertical grounds. *Continental Can* was not truly horizontal, for the merging companies produced different products; but the products were sufficiently close in use for the Court to place an essentially horizontal context on its considerations.

There was no way, however, that Procter & Gamble's acquisition of the Clorox Chemical Company could be treated as horizontal.[46] Procter was "a large, diversified manufacturer of low-price, high-turnover household products sold through grocery, drug and department stores." Its primary activity was the production of soaps and detergents, and it accounted for more than 54 percent of detergent sales. Clorox was the leading producer of household liquid bleach with 48.8 percent of the market; its largest competitor, Purex, accounted for only 15.7 percent. The soap and detergent products of Procter were not competitive with liquid bleach. In fact, the relationship, if any, was *complementary:* liquid bleach was used in conjunction with detergent products, and a greater demand for detergents, other things equal, would imply a greater demand for bleach. The relationship between the companies thus was not horizontal, but neither was it vertical, for Procter and Clorox were not in a supplier-customer relationship.

A merger that is neither horizontal nor vertical is usually termed *conglomerate,* and this is the broad category into which Procter-Clorox fell. Neither the Federal Trade Commission nor the Supreme Court called the merger conglomerate, preferring to reserve the term for those rare instances in which the products of the acquiring and acquired firm bear no economic relationship to each other. Procter's acquisition of Clorox was termed by the F.T.C. a *product-extension merger,* since their products were related.[47] Procter, the Commission said, had not diversified in the sense of expanding into an "unfamiliar market," but had instead entered an "adjoining" one.

Whatever the terminology, such mergers present the antitrust agencies and the courts with a peculiar problem in proving anticompetitive consequences. Since the acquiring and acquired firms are in different markets, the merger can have no immediately predictable impact on the structure of the market for the products of either firm. In a horizontal merger initial structural effects are readily visible; it is necessary only to add up the market shares of the merging firms. Similarly, it is fairly easy to define the immediate degree of foreclosure of suppliers or customers that may result from vertical acquisitions. In the case of conglomerate mergers, however, there is no convenient guide. Procter's acquisition of Clorox

[46] *Federal Trade Commission* v. *Procter & Gamble Co.,* 386 U.S. 568 (1967).

[47] Bleach and detergents, in addition to showing some complementarity, utilize the same retail distribution system.

would initially have no affect on the market shares within either the soap and detergent or the liquid bleach markets.[48]

Because the Supreme Court had relied so heavily on structural tests to demonstrate competitive consequences in earlier cases, the issue posed by Procter-Clorox was an important one. What are the appropriate tests of such an acquisition? Does the absence of changes in market shares imply that *no* competitive consequences will be found? Or, alternatively, if such a merger is found to threaten competition, does this imply that the market-share criterion is inappropriate or superfluous?

The Procter-Clorox merger was subject initially to hearings and disposition by the Federal Trade Commission.[49] The F.T.C. opinion, written by Commissioner Elman, noted that conglomerate mergers do not occupy a special legal category. They are subject to Section 7 despite the fact that the first 17 years of enforcement under the amended statute had largely ignored them. Congress and the courts had placed heavy emphasis on market concentration; but, said the Commission, "the concept of competition which underlies Section 7 has no simple or obvious meaning." The concept need not be *limited* to concentration, the Commission implied, and could logically extend to a second vital dimension of market structure: the condition of entry.

The effect of the immediate merger on the condition of entry was found by Commissioner Elman to be potentially great. Procter was a huge company and the nation's largest advertiser. It could obtain quantity discounts in advertising. Further, the Commission argued, there is a variety of increasing returns to advertising. A company of Procter's size could purchase sponsorship of television programs rather than being confined to less effective spot commercials; and, because of its diversification, could advertise several products on one program, thus reducing their per-product cost.

The Commission saw other important advantages to a company of Procter's size and resources in the liquid bleach market. It would have great bargaining power with retailers (primarily supermarkets) in an area in which shelf space and store displays are thought to have important effects on sales. Its tremendous financial depth would enable it to mount special promotional campaigns against new products of competitors, and to focus its promotional efforts in specific sections of the country. Further, the company would be so large vis-a-vis rival bleach producers that it might undertake predatory pricing policies if it so desired.

---

[48] It may be recalled that the El Paso-Pacific Northwest merger presented a similar situation. The two companies had not sold in the same geographic market; thus the merger had no effect on market shares or concentration.

[49] *In the Matter of Procter & Gamble Co.*, Docket No. 6901 (1962).

The thrust of these points was that the immediate impact of the Procter-Clorox merger was to discourage entry of new firms into the liquid bleach market. Procter's imposing size—apart from its behavior after consummation of the merger—would scare potential competitors away, and might also prevent existing rivals from competing too actively, lest they antagonize the dominant firm. It was primarily on this basis that the Commission concluded that the Procter-Clorox merger violated Section 7.

In considering the merger the Supreme Court was responsive to virtually all arguments employed by the F.T.C. Justice Douglas, for the majority, reiterated earlier statements that Section 7 is intended to arrest monopolistic elements "in their incipiency," and that the Section deals with the probability, not the certainty, of lessened competition. The substitution of the giant Procter for the already dominant Clorox, said Justice Douglas, could have several effects:

1. It "may substantially reduce the competitive structure of the industry by raising entry barriers and by dissuading smaller firms from aggressively competing."
2. It "eliminates the potential competition of the acquiring firm." Procter was not only large, but was a growing and diversifying concern, which was regarded by both the Commission and the Court as a prime candidate for entry into the liquid bleach industry. The merger thus foreclosed the possibility that Procter would enter *as a competitor of* Clorox.

As in *Brown Shoe* and *Philadelphia National Bank*, the Court reiterated its position on the positive benefits that might accrue to mergers: "Possible economies cannot be used as a defense to illegality. Congress was aware that some mergers which lessen competition may also result in economies but it struck the balance in favor of protecting competition."[50] The Court concluded that the Procter-Clorox merger offered a threat to competition in the liquid bleach industry that could not be compensated by the fact that efficiencies might also accrue to the merged company. The decision demonstrates once again that, although mechanical tests of concentration and market share may be utilized in horizontal cases, the Court will not be bound to such tests in considering competitive impact. The Court thus adopts an asymmetrical (but not necessarily illogical) position: increases in concentration are usually sufficient to demonstrate that a merger may substantially lessen competition; but the *absence* of such increases is not sufficient to demonstrate that a merger will not likely harm competition.

[50] *Fed. Trade Comm.* v. *Procter & Gamble Co., op. cit.*, p. 580.

C. The Current Legal Status of Mergers

It is clear that antitrust policy under the new Section 7 has had far-reaching effects. The acquisitions that have been held illegal by the courts and Federal Trade Commission represent only the top of the iceberg.[51] Many more have been settled by consent, without full hearing or trial; and it is impossible to estimate how many prospective mergers have been abandoned because of the implicit threat of antitrust prosecution.

The legal lines that have been drawn are formidable. Horizontal mergers in which one or both firms are market leaders clearly violate Section 7 under current interpretation; and vertical mergers that involve significant foreclosure are similarly condemned. The "hard" policy on such traditional types of merger seems partially responsible for recent trends toward conglomerates; and whereas Procter-Clorox may herald more stringent treatment of conglomerate merger in the future, the criteria by which such acquisitions will be judged are not yet clear.

The Supreme Court has adopted a stringent position on corporate mergers. The Court stresses structural criteria of competition,[52] especially concentration and market shares; and, in a more general way, the *number of alternatives* the market provides to sellers and consumers alike. At times this position has become so rigid that the Court has been accused of applying purely mechanical standards. If any criticism of the Court seems persuasive it is that in early merger cases—and in some later ones—it seems to expound the simplistic notion that an assessment of competition demands nothing more than a counting of the number of firms and their market shares. The Court, however, has demonstrated its ability to free itself from rigid structural doctrines. In *El Paso* and *Penn-Olin* the previous arithmetic tests were discarded; and the *Procter & Gamble* decision contained imaginative discussions of possible competitive implications. The Court's approach to mergers has remained essentially structural, but it is evident that, when necessary, it will depart from the more confining manifestations of this approach.

[51] Even the top of the iceberg is of impressive dimensions. Willard F. Mueller has estimated that blocked acquisitions and subsequent divestitures under the new Section 7 have a value "well in excess of $3 billion." See his *The Celler-Kefauver Act: Sixteen Years of Enforcement*, A Staff Report to the Antitrust Subcommittee of the House Committee on the Judiciary, 90th Cong., 1st Sess. (G.P.O., Washington, 1967), p. 33, footnote 3.

[52] See Peter Asch, "Public Merger Policy and the Meaning of 'Competition,'" *Quarterly Review of Economics and Business*, 6, Winter 1966, pp. 53–64.

In considering the harshness of Supreme Court merger policy it must be recognized that the cases it has received are hardly typical of corporate acquisitions generally. The Court rules on mergers that are ordinarily big in terms of both the absolute size of the merging companies and their market position. The cases that come before the Court result from a complex interaction between the Court and the antitrust enforcement agencies. The Court is influenced by the kinds of cases the Department of Justice and Federal Trade Commission pursue; and the types of cases pursued by these agencies are influenced by what the Court has previously said about mergers. Whatever the precise nature of this process, the Supreme Court considers only special subcategories of corporate acquisitions.

This is not to minimize the strength of the prevailing judicial attitudes. The Supreme Court is indeed "hard" on the kinds of acquisitions that it has had to consider. Nowhere is this more evident than in its repeated refusal to consider the likely effects of mergers on the future behavior of firms and industries. If a merger fails those tests that have become accepted as indicators of lessened competition, it cannot be redeemed by other, positive, benefits, even if these are potentially important. Such an approach reflects not only the philosophy of the present Supreme Court, but the need for relatively simple legal decision rules. Whereas economists are inclined to argue that many factors ought to be considered in merger cases, such a luxury might tie up the judicial processes in an unimaginable way. The courts' search for workable rules conflicts with the need for thorough economic investigation, and has led some observers to propose that separate judicial bodies be established for the disposition of antitrust matters.

The recent attitude of the Supreme Court on mergers is of course subject to change. But whatever route the Court may follow, the antitrust enforcement agencies bear a heavy burden of responsibility in shaping future policies. It is the Federal Trade Commission and the Antitrust Division of the Department of Justice that initiate the cases that ultimately reach the courts. Both these agencies operate under the significant constraint of limited resources, and must be selective in the cases they pursue. During the last few years the government has had a relatively easy time winning legal victories in merger cases. The social purpose of the agencies, however, is not to win victories but rather to obtain action on situations that could, if left untouched, damage competition. Ideally, of course, there is no distinction between these goals. In fact, however, they need not coincide. Some legal victories are trivial in economic terms, and some important situations may be neglected if the prospects of victory are higher in other areas. The courts can decide only on those situations that they have brought before them, and even the boldest judicial outlook may be thwarted by a timid approach in the executive agencies.

D. The Economics of Merger Policy

The courts and, to a lesser extent, the Federal Trade Commission have been criticized for their interpretations of Section 7.[53] Although critics vary widely in their points of view, many charge that, in one way or another, "bad economics" is being applied to the legal disposition of corporate mergers.

As the cases above have demonstrated, the legal view of competition under Section 7 is largely structural. That is, in attempting to estimate the effects mergers have on competition, dimensions of market structure are taken to be the primary clues. A structural approach conforms generally to the basic precepts of economic analysis. Whatever we may mean by "competition," it is something that is strongly influenced by such factors as the number and size of firms in a market and the condition of entry for new firms. These elements influence the ways in which firms and industries behave. Criticisms of merger policy, then, do not often propose that market structure be ignored; this would make little economic sense. Rather, the objections that have been lodged tend to cluster around two slightly different propositions:

1. That the *wrong* structural approach is being utilized, and ought to be replaced by different structural standards.

2. That the structural approach is misguided because it dominates the consideration of mergers to the exclusion of all other information bearing on competitive effects.

The first proposition has some appeal to those who believe that the courts are in general either too hard or too easy on mergers. At one extreme, a test of "quantitative substantiality" might be suggested under which any merger involving a "substantial" volume of commerce is automatically considered illegal. At the other extreme, it might be proposed that only mergers that involve a very high market share for the

[53] See, for example: M. A. Adelman, *op. cit.;* Robert H. Bork and Ward S. Bowman, Jr., "The Crisis in Antitrust," *Fortune,* **68**, December 1963, pp. 138–40; and Donald Dewey, "Mergers and Cartels: Some Reservations About Policy," *American Economic Review,* **51**, May 1961, pp. 255–62.

emergent firm be struck down. In between, compromises may be possible. Stigler, for example, has suggested that a legal presumption be made against mergers that yield the combined firm a market share of 20 percent or more; and a presumption be made in favor of mergers that result in a share of not more than 5 to 10 percent.[54] Between these limits more extensive economic investigation is deemed desirable.

All proposals for new structural standards, however, encounter a common problem. The more general the proposal, the less useful it is likely to be. To tell the courts, for example, that automatic rules should be applied in extreme cases, whereas further analysis is in order for intermediate cases, provides relatively little guidance. This is especially true if the preponderance of cases falls within the intermediate range. On the other hand, structural standards that are so specific as to be broadly applicable would result in the same rigidity for which the Court has been criticized. To tell the courts that they ought to approve all mergers that result in less than an X percent market share, while condemning mergers that result in X percent or more, would be highly objectionable. In the first place there is no obvious basis for selecting the number X—should it be 5 percent? 15 percent? 40 percent? Secondly, and more importantly, no single "appropriate" number exists because the meaning of any given number varies with other conditions in the industry. A merger between two firms, each of which has 5 percent of the market, is simply not the same event in the steel industry as it is in the book-manufacturing industry.

It is true that sensible structural rules would have to go further than providing a single market-share number. But the more general problem is the arbitrary nature of *any* rules. There is simply nothing in economic analysis or in the available body of empirical information that offers clear structural prescriptions for merger policy. This is precisely the problem that plagues policy makers. The implication to be drawn is not that policy decisions ought to be avoided, but that it is necessary to grope further for appropriate standards. It is most unlikely that we will ever develop wholly automatic structural criteria. The ways in which a merger may affect competition are too complex to be reduced in this fashion. Moreover, some kinds of mergers—most notably conglomerates—cannot be easily assessed in quantitative structural terms. Thus, no matter how sophisticated we might become in measuring the impacts of structural change, important areas of merger activity would remain untouched.

The second kind of objection that is frequently lodged against current merger policy has to do with the tendency of the courts to rely solely on

[54] George J. Stigler, "Mergers and Preventive Antitrust Policy," *University of Pennsylvania Law Review*, **104**, November 1955, pp. 178–84.

structural information while ignoring other factors that could provide some clue to competitive effects. This tendency is clearly revealed in *Brown Shoe, Philadelphia National Bank,* and *Procter & Gamble.* The Supreme Court states categorically that mergers that lessen competition cannot be redeemed legally by the fact that they might, on balance, benefit society. But since the Court infers a lessening of competition from structural indicators, the doctrine amounts to one of structural exclusivity. The ways in which the Court relies on structure need not imply rigidity; but the reliance, even if flexible, is nevertheless so complete that potentially important kinds of information are precluded from its considerations.

The exclusively structural approach to mergers raises very basic questions, not only about the meaning of competition that the Court holds, but about the entire purpose of merger policy and perhaps public competition policy in general. The notion of competition to which the Supreme Court subscribes is highly specific: it is, in effect, akin to the economist's definition of pure competition. Competition is seen as a market setting in which there is a large number of small firms and entry is relatively easy. Virtually any movement toward fewer firms or growth in market shares is thus interpreted as a lessening of competition.

How valid an approach is this in economic terms? Certainly it is a very narrow view that at times seems literally to equate competition with concentration, albeit in an inverse way. Such an equation, crude as it is, might not be a poor working definition if it were qualified by other types of information. As Adelman has stated:

. . . competition, or monopoly, is not a brute physical fact but rather a hypothesis confirmed by the available evidence. A high level of concentration, plus price behavior very different from competitive expectations, etc., indicates, let us say, chances of 9 to 1 of effective market control.[55]

The task of the courts under Section 7 is not to determine how much competition exists in a market, but what the direction of change will be when merger occurs. Nevertheless, Adelman's point is pertinent. The notion of competition is complex, if not actually elusive, and it is not amenable to extremely simplified measurement. The courts are in need of simple rules, but their pursuit of simplicity has unquestionably led to an overly restrictive definition of competition and competitive change.

Although economists may wish to quarrel with the ways in which judges define economic terms, this is not the primary issue. The significant question with regard to mergers is rather one of results: what kind of policy have legal definitions of competition yielded? To describe merger

[55] *Op cit.,* p. 237.

policy more precisely it may be helpful to review briefly the kinds of change that growth in firm size may imply. As we have seen earlier, increases in market concentration presumably occur because they are profitable. This profitability in turn may reflect genuine economies of scale, the ability to produce more efficiently in a larger operation; or it may reflect pecuniary economies that allow the larger firm to operate more cheaply, but not more efficiently in a technical sense. At the same time, larger firm size may be profitable for reasons related to the demand rather than to the cost or supply side. The larger firm has greater market power and is thus better able to exploit consumers' demand for its products.

From society's point of view, growth that is related purely to market power is undesirable. Firm growth that is related to genuine economies, however, may be socially desirable because it permits the production of more goods at any given level of resource employment. Growth for reasons of pecuniary economies might be considered undesirable as a rule since it implies more market power, but the question is empirically complicated by the possibility that pecuniary economies may in part reflect true economies. Merger is a method by which firms grow. Whether any particular merger is socially desirable depends on whether the positive benefits of increased efficiency outweigh the negative effects of increased market power. Diagrammatically, the trade-off between efficiency and power is shown in Figure 14.1. Suppose that before merger firms produce at point A (quantity Q^0, price P^0); and that after merger, market power is enhanced so that production shifts to point C (quantity Q', price P'). The welfare loss attributable to this increment in market power is represented by triangle ABC, the difference in society's position before and after merger. But suppose also that the merger introduces efficiencies into the production process, causing the average cost curve to shift down from AC^0 to AC'. Rectangle P^0EFB represents the efficiency gain of the merger—the difference between the cost of producing quantity Q' before and after merger. The question is whether the efficiency gain of a merger is greater or less than the market power loss.

Williamson, who has stated the problem in these terms, finds some surprising results using simple numerical examples.[56] It appears generally that even a relatively small drop in average costs produces an efficiency gain that can be offset only by a much larger relative rise in price. Even if the elasticity of demand is as high as 2, for example, a cost decrease of 1 percent produces gains that can be wiped out only if price rises by 10 percent; or, stated in reverse fashion, a merger that enables firms to raise

---

[56] Oliver E. Williamson, "Economies as an Antitrust Defense: The Welfare Trade-offs," *American Economic Review*, **58**, March 1968, pp. 18–36.

price by 10 percent will not prove to be bad on balance if average costs fall by only 1 percent. If demand elasticity were 1, costs would only have to fall by 0.5 percent to compensate a 10 percent price rise.

It is obvious that the evaluation of mergers by the courts has ignored this kind of calculation. Not only are efficiency gains disregarded as a possible defense for merging, but the Supreme Court has at times hinted

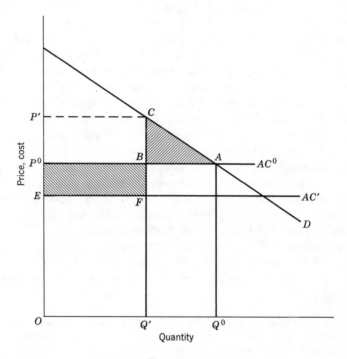

Figure 14.1

that efficiencies may *condemn* a merger because competitive advantages are created for the combined firm! On what basis can this attitude be defended? Williamson hints at one possibility when he states, "Indeed there is no way in which the tradeoff [between efficiency and market power] . . . can be avoided. To disallow tradeoffs altogether merely reflects a particularly severe a priori judgment as to net benefits."[57] In other words, one might disallow trade-offs, as the Court has done, by arguing that the net benefits of merger are inevitably negative—that the

[57] *Ibid.*, pp. 22–23.

market power loss always exceeds the efficiency gain. Interestingly enough, however, the Supreme Court has made no such argument. To the contrary, it has readily admitted that some "anticompetitive" mergers could carry substantial benefits, but it has held that these benefits, if they exist, *are not relevant* to the legality of mergers. The Court has rejected the suggestion that it ought to weigh efficiency gains against competitive losses; rather, its position has been simply that any merger involving substantial competitive losses is illegal.

At this point it may seem that the economic justification of our legal approach to mergers is rather precarious. Nevertheless, there exists some rationale for what the courts and agencies have been doing. Williamson himself notes some potentially significant qualifications to the suggestion that "good" mergers are probable. The most important is perhaps the observation that if economies of scale exist in an industry, they may be exploited by means other than merger. If bigness implies efficiency, then it is likely that firms will ultimately grow big, whether by internal expansion or by merger. The efficiency gain of the merger is thus not a "pure" one, but is instead associated with the fact that the efficiencies may be attained somewhat *sooner* through merger than they would otherwise.

Put differently, a legal prohibition on efficiency-creating mergers is not the same thing as a legal prohibition on increased efficiency. It can be argued in fact that internal expansion is a preferable method of firm growth because it is subject continually to market-type tests; that is, an expanding firm cannot continue to expand unless market rewards are forthcoming. Growth by merger, however, presents a different situation. As Heflebower has said,

. . . a merger does not necessarily (or often in fact) involve a significant market test. In part this is because the merger may change the location and elasticity of the acquired firm's (imagined) revenue curve, and therefore it is not tested in an unchanged market. Aside from that, if the acquired firm is sizable, its purchase is a once-over expansion of the acquiring firm rather than a step by step expansion subject to repetitive reexamination of costs and revenues.[58]

A firm that expands internally can do so only by outcompeting others in the market. Expansion through merger involves simply the purchase of an already established market position.

Perhaps the most plausible defense of recent merger policy is stated by Heflebower in terms of the economic ignorance surrounding corporate acquisition. According to Heflebower, no one is in a good position to predict the competitive effects of merger. Economic theory is "inconclusive"

[58] Richard B. Heflebower, "Corporate Mergers: Policy and Economic Analysis," *Quarterly Journal of Economics, 77,* November 1963, pp. 556–57.

and empirical evidence is "paltry," yet the courts are required to decide whether mergers may lessen competition. In Heflebower's view the policies pursued by the Supreme Court may be interpreted as a strategy designed to make the least damaging kinds of mistakes. The Court has taken a hard position on mergers and, given its ignorance of future economic effects, it may well have prohibited some mergers that would not have harmed competition. Heflebower's argument is that this kind of error may be preferable to the mistakes that would be made by pursuing a too-easy merger policy—permitting some mergers that would reduce competition. Once mergers are permitted under an easy policy the die is cast; but a hard policy is always reversible. If the easy policy is pursued and found to be wrong, little can be done. The merged companies are a fact of life, and the courts are most reluctant to break up going concerns. But if a hard policy is pursued and found to be wrong, the remedy is simple; make the policy easier. Mergers that are prohibited today can be allowed tomorrow if we find that they are desirable.

An assessment of merger policy is not an easy task, and it is not the purpose of this discussion to grade the courts or the antitrust agencies on their performance. It is clear that Section 7 as amended has become a tremendously important antitrust tool. Large and medium-sized horizontal mergers appear to be all but illegal; large vertical acquisitions run a very substantial legal risk; and large conglomerates also appear vulnerable, although definitive standards are not yet visible. Even relatively small mergers may violate Section 7 if the history of the companies and trends in the industry are undesirable. The main criticism of public merger policy is that it has become an indiscriminate weapon against corporate bigness, used to strike down large combinations without considering the possibility that large size may be economically justified. The Supreme Court's implicit answer to this criticism is that it is not concerned with economic justifications—nor with any benefit-versus-cost approach—but rather is concerned with competition, defined in a particular structural fashion. Here the economist may argue that the Court's definition of competition is inadequate, but the Court's (again implicit) response is: that is what Congress intended.

We are once again at the impasse mentioned at several earlier points. Objective economic analysis cannot tell us what a correct policy with respect to mergers may be. Such a definition depends also on noneconomic value judgments. The task of the economist here is to inform the policymaker of his options.

15

Price Discrimination

Price discrimination is a practice that is probably familiar even to those who are unaware of the term. For example, most people are aware that physicians often charge different fees for the same service, depending on patients' ability to pay. Lawyers may make similar adjustments for clients, and in certain instances fees for a client vary with the outcome of the litigation. Housewives will frequently find that the per-unit price of foods varies with the quantity purchased; soup may sell for 25 cents a can or two cans for 49 cents. Even the telephone company may charge different prices per unit: a long distance caller may be charged more for the first three minutes than for the second three; thus a caller who speaks for six minutes pays a lower price per minute than a caller who speaks for three.

Each of these instances *may* constitute price discrimination. As economists use the term, however, discrimination refers not simply to the practice of charging different customers different prices for the same commodity or service; rather it refers to the imposition of *varying cost-price differentials* on different customers. A seller may be said to discriminate in price whenever the relationship between his costs and the price he charges varies among his customers—that is, when sales to some customers yield a higher net revenue or profit than sales to others. The examples cited above constitute price discrimination only if the different prices charged for the same good or service do not reflect corresponding differences in the cost of production or distribution. If the cost of providing telephone service is the same, per minute, for six-minute calls as for three-minute calls, then the telephone company is discriminating against the three-minute caller. If, however, the cost of the longer call is less per minute—and this is certainly possible—the lower charge for the second three minutes may only reflect this cost difference.

Section 2(a) of the Robinson-Patman Act, amending Section 2 of the original Clayton Act, makes it illegal

. . . to discriminate in price between different purchasers of commodities of like grade and quality . . . where the effect of such discrimination may be substantially to lessen competition or tend to create a monopoly in any line of commerce.

Section 2(a) also provides that

. . . nothing herein contained shall prevent differentials which make only due allowance for differences in the cost of manufacture, sale, or delivery resulting from the differing methods or quantities in which such commodities are . . . sold or delivered.

In other words, a seller accused of discrimination can justify his activities if he proves that price variations reflect different costs in selling to different customers.

The legal definition of price discrimination differs from the economic. By referring only to *price* differences, rather than to differences in the *price-cost relationship*, the law takes a relatively narrow view. Under the Robinson-Patman Act a seller can discriminate only by charging different prices for the same (or substantially similar) goods. In economic terms, however, the seller may discriminate also by charging *the same price* to all customers when *different costs* are incurred in selling to some. So long as the price-cost differential is not the same among all customers, price discrimination in the economic sense exists. Accordingly, the Robinson-Patman Act may be said to focus on a particular subset of all price discrimination, that in which prices vary but costs do not.

A seller charged with price discrimination has two possible "absolute" defenses. The first is simply to show that his price differences made "only due allowance" for cost differences. The second, sometimes called the good faith defense, is provided by Section 2(b) of the Robinson-Patman Act, which states:

. . . nothing herein contained shall prevent a seller from rebutting the prima facie case . . . by showing that his lower price or the furnishing of services or facilities to any purchaser . . . was made in good faith to meet the equally low price of a competitor . . .

A seller may thus argue that price differentials, although not cost justified, were designed purely to meet competition. Both the cost-differential and good-faith defenses are absolute in the sense that, if proved, the seller's activities do not abridge the Act. If neither of these defenses can be established, the pertinent question concerns the effect of the seller's discriminatory activities: specifically, were they such as to substantially lessen competition or tend to create a monopoly?

At this point, it may be useful to consider two questions suggested by the existence and treatment of price discrimination: Why and under what conditions would firms be expected to discriminate? Why ought we to have legal sanctions against discrimination? The first question may be answered in a reasonably unambiguous way. Any firm with some degree of power over the price it charges[1] may find discrimination profitable if its product is sold in separable markets containing demand curves of differing elasticity at a monopoly price. Consider the somewhat whimsical example of a company that sells air conditioners in both Miami and Siberia. Such a company would probably not wish to charge the same price for the same air conditioner in the two locations, since the desirability of air conditioners (or consumer tastes), as well as a host of other economic variables, would likely imply distinct demand curves. It is, in other words, likely that the price that maximizes profits in Miami is not the same as the optimum price in Siberia.[2] Moreover, the wide geographic separation of the markets insures that a two-price system is workable. Residents of Siberia (or speculators) could not very easily purchase air conditioners at a low price and resell them at higher prices in Miami. If such a practice were possible, price differentials in the two locations could not persist.

The potential for profitable price discrimination does not necessarily require such a dramatic separation of markets. Any time a seller offers his commodities at a specified price he is likely selling to some customers who would have been willing to pay more. Accordingly, such a seller would benefit if he could find some way of extracting the higher price from those with the greater willingness to pay. Such a practice—which is again discriminatory unless it happens that it costs more to sell to those who pay more—may be feasible if the seller can discover which customers have the greater willingness and if the product offered cannot readily be resold. If the product is in fact a service—say an appendectomy or a telephone

---

[1] In purely competitive markets price occurs at marginal cost and, in the long run, is forced to the level of average cost. Thus, with the exception of special cases, it would be impossible for a seller to impose two prices for the same product.

[2] The way in which a discriminating seller determines his two (or more) optimal prices is not immediately obvious. The relevant analysis is to be found in virtually all intermediate price theory texts. See, for example: Richard A. Bilas, *Microeconomic Theory: A Graphical Analysis* (McGraw-Hill, New York, 1967), pp. 195 ff.; and Alfred W. Stonier and Douglas C. Hague, *A Textbook of Economic Theory* (Longmans Green, London, 1958), pp. 172–81.

call—it obviously cannot be resold. Cans of soup, on the other hand, might be, but so long as the price discounts on higher quantities are readily available to all it is unlikely that this will occur.

If price discrimination can be profitable, it may not yet be obvious why such a practice is undesirable and ought to be subject to legal restrictions. Indeed, price discrimination is not inevitably undesirable from society's point of view.[3] The law, however, takes aim only at those discriminatory practices that may substantially lessen competition. Such cases often involve buyers with sufficient market power to extract price concessions from sellers. As noted in Chapter 11, pressure for enactment of a strong price-discrimination law came from relatively small wholesalers and retailers who complained that larger rivals were obtaining preferential treatment from suppliers. It is precisely this kind of situation at which the Robinson-Patman Act is directed. If a large firm can purchase supplies at more favorable terms than its smaller rivals, it holds a competitive advantage. Indeed, one of the more troublesome aspects of discrimination is that favored companies may be able to establish prices that are profitable for them but unprofitable for smaller firms that must pay more for inputs. Such a contingency is what the Robinson-Patman Act was designed to prevent.

A. Delivered Pricing System

Sellers and buyers in a line of commerce are often geographically dispersed. When this is the case costs of transporting the product may be relatively important, for distances between buyers and sellers may vary widely. Sellers in this situation must choose among pricing procedures with respect to customers at different locations. The initial decision is whether to quote price at the point of origin (seller's location)—often termed the *f.o.b.* (free on board) *price*—or at the point of destination (customer's location)—a *delivered price*.

Perhaps the most obvious possibility is that every seller will quote prices f.o.b. and have each customer pay the cost of transportation. Assuming similar or identical products, each seller will have an advantage with nearby customers, who pay little freight, but may be strongly disadvantaged with respect to distant customers. Conceivably, each seller

[3] See Joan Robinson, *The Economics of Imperfect Competition*, Macmillan, London, 1938, p. 206; and Lucile Sheppard Keyes, "Price Discrimination in Law and Economics," *Southern Economic Journal*, **27**, April 1961, pp. 320–28.

will have a sheltered market and a market that he cannot penetrate.[4] Whether such a pricing system proves to be workable is a complex problem that depends on the geographic distribution of the market, among other factors. It is possible that certain sellers will find that they sell too little under such conditions; they may thus attempt to penetrate more distant segments of the market by absorbing part or all of the freight charges for customers so located.

A second possibility is that sellers may quote *the same delivered price* to all customers. Such a price would include an average freight charge—a charge for transportation of goods that, if imposed uniformly on all customers, would cover total transportation costs. Such a pricing system implies that nearby customers will pay more than the actual cost of transporting to them; this extra charge is known as *phantom freight*. Distant customers pay less than the actual cost of transportation; they are the beneficiaries of *freight absorption* by the seller. Clearly, this delivered pricing system is economically discriminatory. The seller, in charging a uniform delivered price, has failed to take account of cost differences among customers; he discriminates against nearby customers who must pay for transportation they do not require, in favor of distant customers who do not pay the full cost of transporting to them. In effect, the close customer subsidizes the faraway customer.

Under a variation of this delivered pricing system a seller will establish geographic zones and charge a uniform delivered price within each zone. Here the price charged in any zone presumably includes the average cost of transporting to customers in that zone. Once again, the seller undertakes freight absorption for customers within a zone who are relatively far away and charges phantom freight to customers within the zone who are relatively near.

A wide variety of delivered pricing systems has appeared at various times in American industry. Primary policy attention has been given to *basing-point systems*, a category of delivered pricing in which selling firms act in a generally concerted way. The usual effect of such systems—and perhaps the primary purpose—is to modify or eliminate the delivered price differentials that might occur were each seller to pursue an independent pricing policy. As Machlup points out:

The basing-point technique of pricing makes it possible for any number of sellers, no matter where they are located and without any communication with each other, to quote identical delivered prices for any quantity of the product in standardized qualities and specifications, going to any of the 60,000 or more possible destinations in the United States.[5]

[4] See the discussion of the Hotelling duopoly model in Chapter 3.
[5] Fritz Machlup, *The Basing-Point System*, Blakiston, Philadelphia, 1949, p. 7.

1. THE SINGLE BASING-POINT SYSTEM

Under a single basing-point system, every seller uses *the same point of origin* in calculating the freight charge to be added to his base, or f.o.b., price. If the base prices are the same, every seller's price at any given destination will be identical, although the price will vary among destinations.

Consider, for example, the old Pittsburgh-plus system once utilized by steel producers. Under this system Pittsburgh was the single basing point; every steel producer in calculating his delivered price to a customer acted as if he were shipping steel *from Pittsburgh* to the customer's location, regardless of where the shipment actually originated. The system is illustrated in Figure 15.1 and Tables 15.1*a* and *b*. Every producer has a

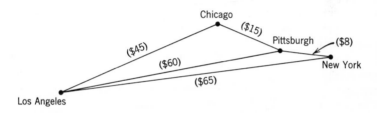

Figure 15.1

Numbers in parentheses indicate actual unit cost of transportation between cities.

uniform base price, specified arbitrarily as $100 per unit;[6] costs of shipping a unit between various cities are specified, also arbitrarily for purposes of illustration. Table 15.1*a* illustrates the workings of the pricing scheme in sales to a Pittsburgh customer—that is, to a customer located at the basing point. Here the uniform freight charge dictated by the system is zero since the customer is located at the basing point. All shippers—whether in Pittsburgh, Chicago, New York, Los Angeles, or elsewhere—charge nothing for transportation to the Pittsburgh customer. Thus all charge a delivered price of $100. In this situation every seller not located in Pittsburgh must absorb freight—that is, must charge the Pittsburgh customer less than the actual cost of shipping the goods.

In Table 15.1*b* sales to a Los Angeles customer are considered. Again, every seller determines his delivered price to this customer by adding to the base price the cost of shipping *from Pittsburgh* to the customer. Every seller charges the Los Angeles customer $160; the base price of $100 plus

[6] It is interesting to contemplate how a uniform base price is established. Basing-point cases before the courts are often concerned with this aspect of the system.

Table 15.1

A Pittsburgh-Plus System: Basing-Point Pricing
with Pittsburgh as the Single Basing Point

(a) *Sales to a Pittsburgh Customer*

	Location of Producer			
	Pittsburgh	Chicago	New York	Los Angeles
Base price	$100	100	100	100
Freight cost from Pittsburgh to customer	0	0	0	0
Delivered price quoted by producer	100	100	100	100
Actual freight cost from producer to customer	0	10	8	30
Phantom freight				
Freight absorption		10	8	60
Discrimination	No	Yes	Yes	Yes

(b) *Sales to a Los Angeles Customer*

	Location of Producer			
	Pittsburgh	Chicago	New York	Los Angeles
Base price	$100	100	100	100
Freight cost from Pittsburgh to customer	60	60	60	60
Delivered price quoted by producer	160	160	160	160
Actual freight cost from producer to customer	60	45	65	0
Phantom freight		15		60
Freight absorption			5	
Discrimination	No	Yes	Yes	Yes

the shipping cost from Pittsburgh of $60. Shippers who are farther away from the customer than Pittsburgh is from the customer will absorb freight; the New York producer, for example, incurs shipping costs of $65 but charges only the $60 that it would cost to ship from Pittsburgh to Los Angeles. Shippers who are closer to the customer than Pittsburgh is to the customer will charge phantom freight; the Chicago producer charges $60 although his actual freight cost is $45; and the Los Angeles producer, whose actual shipping cost is zero, also charges $60.

Producers located at the basing point never discriminate, since the freight they charge to customers is calculated from the point at which they are located. Their delivered price to varying locations differs by precisely the difference in their actual freight to those locations—in other words, the price variation makes "only due allowance" for cost differentials. Sellers not located at the basing point, however, invariably discriminate, since their price differentials do not reflect actual differences in their shipping costs. Whenever a non-basing-point producer makes a sale he either charges phantom freight (if the customer is closer to him than to the basing point) or absorbs freight (if the customer is farther from him than from the basing point).[7]

2. MULTIPLE BASING-POINT SYSTEMS

A number of systems may arise in which two or more basing points are used. Generally the controlling basing point will be the one that is closer to the customer. Suppose that in the example of Figure 15.1 both Pittsburgh and Chicago were used as basing points. Chicago would be the relevant point for sales to Chicago and Los Angeles, as well as all other locations closer to Chicago than to Pittsburgh; Pittsburgh would be the controlling point for sales to Pittsburgh and New York, as well as any other location closer to Pittsburgh than to Chicago.

In the extreme case of a multiple basing-point system *every* production location is a basing point governing sales to the closest customers. The delivered price to any customer is therefore the base price charged by all producers plus freight from the closest producer; all sellers meet the delivered price offer of the one closest to the customer.[8] Such a system is

[7] The non-basing-point producer does not discriminate when he sells to a customer who happens to be the same distance from both him and the basing point. Conceivably the location of producers and customers might be such that the system is largely non-discriminatory, but this is highly unlikely.

[8] The charging of identical base (f.o.b.) prices by all producers is an assumption that does not always apply in such systems. If producers do not charge the same base price, analysis of the system may be more complicated.

termed a *plenary* basing-point system, and is sometimes referred to as *systematic freight equalization*. The plenary system is distinct from other basing-point arrangements. Because every production point is also a basing point, no seller is ever in the position of charging phantom freight.

The plenary system might be viewed as one in which each seller simply meets his competition. The seller charges true freight to any customer within his zone—to those who are closer to him than to any other seller. Outside the zone, the seller meets the best price that any customer can obtain. It thus can be argued that the plenary system results in a good faith meeting of competition by all, and ought not to be illegal under Robinson-Patman.

3. A REVIEW OF RELEVANT CASES

Basing-point systems have been attacked in three distinct ways under the antitrust laws. They have been prosecuted under the Sherman Act as unreasonable restraints of trade or attempts to monopolize; here the government's contention is likely to be that the establishment and maintenance of the system reflects a conspiracy among participating producers. Basing points have also been attacked as violations of Section 5 of the Federal Trade Commission Act; the common argument is that pricing is unfair to customers who happen to be located near some producers but a greater distance from the nearest basing point. Finally, and of primary interest to the immediate discussion, basing-point pricing has been prosecuted under the Robinson-Patman Act as price discrimination.

(a) The Corn Products Refining Case (1945)

The *Corn Products Refining* case[9] represents the first Supreme Court decision on the status of basing-point systems under the Robinson-Patman Act. Earlier, in both the *Maple Flooring*[10] and *Cement Manufacturers*[11] cases, the Court had considered the legality of behavior involving basing-point systems; but in neither case was price discrimination an issue.

The immediate case concerned a manufacturer of glucose—a candy ingredient—and its subsidiary. Although located in Kansas City, the companies used Chicago as a basing point, charging glucose buyers a base price plus transportation from Chicago to each buyer's location. The Federal Trade Commission found that this pricing system resulted in

---

[9] *Corn Products Refining Co.* v. *Federal Trade Commission*, 324 U.S. 726 (1945).

[10] *Maple Flooring Manufacturers Association* v. *United States*, 268 U.S. 563 (1925).

[11] *Cement Manufacturers Protective Association* v. *United States*, 268 U.S. 588 (1925).

systematic price discrimination. The appeal of the F.T.C. decision to the Supreme Court raised two issues: first, did the basing-point system constitute price discrimination; and second, if it did, was the effect of the system damaging to competition?

On the first point the companies argued that their practices were not discriminatory under the Robinson-Patman Act. The Act, they contended, was aimed only at discrimination between buyers at the same delivery points, and covered only discrimination in price itself. Since the basing-point system did not discriminate among buyers at the same location, and since the discrimination that existed involved different conditions of sale rather than different prices,[12] the companies argued that their pricing policies did not fall within Section 2(a). These arguments were rejected by the Court. Chief Justice Stone found no basis in law for distinguishing between discrimination at a single location and discrimination among different locations. Further, the Court held, any sales practice that results in effective price discrimination falls within the Robinson-Patman provisions, even though price itself may not be the manipulated variable.

The question remained whether the effect of the system on competition was such as to make it illegal under Section 2(a). On this issue the Court noted that the law

. . . does not require a finding that the discriminations in price have in fact had an adverse effect on competition. The statute is designed to reach such discriminations "in their incipiency," before the harm to competition is effected. It is enough that they "may" have the prescribed effect.[13]

It was thus not necessary to demonstrate that the basing-point system had actually damaged competition; it would suffice to show that the system might, with some unspecified probability, be expected to have such an effect. Here the Court noted that,

Since petitioners' basing point system results in a Chicago delivered price which is always lower than any other, including that at Kansas City, a natural effect of the system is the creation of a favored price zone for the purchasers of glucose in Chicago and vicinity. . . . Since the cost of glucose, a principal ingredient of low-priced candy, is less at Chicago, candy manufacturers there are in a better position to compete for business. . . .[14]

---

[12] This contention is the result of hair splitting. The argument was, in effect, "We charged all customers the same price but provided some with more extensive shipping services."

[13] *Corn Products Refining Co.* v. *U.S.*, *op. cit.*, p. 738.

[14] *Ibid.*

The competitive advantage conferred on Chicago-area producers of candy was found to support a conclusion of illegality. The advantage was significant enough in the eyes of the Court to justify the Commission's inference of a reasonable probability that competition might be lessened substantially.

(b) The Staley Case (1945)

The *Staley* case[15] concerned another facet of the basing-point system employed in *Corn Products Refining*. The A. E. Staley Company and its sales subsidiary utilized the Chicago-plus basing-point system in selling glucose, although the glucose itself was produced in Decatur, Illinois. The defendant companies mounted a good faith defense, arguing that their adoption of a discriminatory pricing system was made purely to meet the equally low prices of competitors.

The facts presented to the Court indicated that in 1920, when Staley entered the glucose manufacturing business, a Chicago-plus pricing system was already established. The Company thus went along, "by first quoting the same prices as were quoted by competitors and then making whatever reduction in price . . . was necessary to obtain business."[16] This, then, was the companies' good faith defense: they had entered the market at a time when existing firms were already pursuing a system of uniform prices at any delivery point; in order to sell, the companies had to adopt the same prices as their competitors, which in this instance meant the adoption of a discriminatory pricing system.

The Supreme Court rejected this defense. If the companies' argument were sound, said Chief Justice Stone, it would mean that any firm could legitimately adopt discriminatory pricing practices so long as the practices had first been employed by others. The good faith provision, he said, "places emphasis on individual competitive situations, rather than upon a general system of competition." Thus, although a company might argue the need to match competitors' prices on particular occasions, it could not justify adoption of competitors' pricing systems. Beyond this, said the Court, the Robinson-Patman Act permits only the matching of a competitors' *lower* price or additional services. In the case at issue the Staley company had adopted a system under which it charged phantom freight to customers who were farther from Chicago then from Decatur; it had, in these instances, *raised* its price to conform to the system.

The *Staley* and *Corn Products* decisions together strike a hard blow against geographic price discrimination of the basing-point variety. If such a system results in major cost advantages for buyers near the point,

---

[15] *Federal Trade Commission v. A. E. Staley Mfg. Co.*, 324 U.S. 746 (1945).
[16] *Ibid.*, p. 751.

it is not only discriminatory but is also likely to lessen competition substantially within the meaning of the law. Further, there appears to be no way in which a company adopting a discriminatory pricing system can maintain successfully that it has done so in good faith.

(c) The Cement Institute Case (1948)

The Cement Institute, consisting of 74 companies and 21 associated individuals, employed a multiple basing-point system in the sale of cement. The practice was attacked as a violation of both Section 5 of the Federal Trade Commission Act and the Robinson-Patman Act. The Supreme Court found that the system was a concerted effort to suppress competition, and was thus illegal under Section 5.[17]

With respect to price discrimination, the circumstances were somewhat distinct from *Corn Products* and *Staley*. The Supreme Court again found that the system employed violated the Robinson-Patman Act, but its treatment is noteworthy in one respect. In concluding that a multiple basing-point system was discriminatory the Court relied on F.T.C. findings that the companies had made different net returns on sales to different customers. By concentrating on the differences in returns rather than simple price differences, the Court seemed to take a view of price discrimination that was closer to an economic definition than the language of the Robinson-Patman Act might suggest.

One point accepted by the Circuit Court in the *Cement Institute* case— and argued by defendants in the *Rigid Steel Conduit* case[18]—was a distinction between favorable and unfavorable price discrimination. The Circuit Court had held that freight absorption works to the benefit of the customer, and was in the particular circumstances justifiable as a good faith meeting of competition. Similarly, the *Rigid Steel Conduit* defendants argued that an F.T.C. order that prohibited freight absorption had limited their right to meet competition by matching the lower price of a competitor.

In both cases the distinction was rejected on appeal. Freight absorption and the charging of phantom freight are, it is true, different from the viewpoint of the affected customer. The essence of price discrimination, however, is that customers are treated *differently*. This condition is present regardless of whether only freight absorption, only phantom freight, or both, exist in a pricing system. If phantom freight is charged to some, those who are charged are treated less favorably than those who are not. But if freight is absorbed for some, those for whom it is *not* absorbed are similarly treated in a worse fashion than those for whom it is.

---

[17] *Federal Trade Commission* v. *Cement Institute*, 333 U.S. 683 (1948).

[18] *Triangle Conduit and Cable Co.* v. *Federal Trade Commission*, 168 F 2d 175 (1948).

B. Other Forms of Price Discrimination

The kind of geographic price discrimination implied by most basing-point systems was not the primary target of framers of the Robinson-Patman Act. Rather, the Act was aimed at major buyers who could gain competitive advantages by extracting concessions from their suppliers. Discrimination in such cases is based on the size and market power of the customer rather than on his location.

1. DISCRIMINATION IN FAVOR OF THE LARGE BUYERS: A REVIEW OF RELEVANT CASES

(a) The Morton Salt Case (1948)

The Morton Salt Company[19] was a major salt producer that sold to both wholesalers (or jobbers) and to large retailers, including major chains. The company offered the following price schedule for its high-grade salt:

Less-than-carload purchase	$1.60 per case
Carload purchase	1.50 per case
5,000-case purchase in any 12 consecutive months	1.40 per case
50,000-case purchase in any 12 consecutive months	1.35 per case

This schedule represents a combination of quantity discounts and volume discounts, the latter referring to discounts given for cumulative quantities purchased over time. Such a discount system favors larger buyers, and only five companies—major retail food chains—had ever bought enough salt to obtain the minimum ($1.35) price.

The first question confronting the Supreme Court was whether such a volume or quantity discount schedule is discriminatory within the meaning of Section 2(a). The company argued that because its discounts were "available to all on equal terms," they were not discriminatory. The Supreme Court disagreed, stating that the discounts were available to all only in a theoretical sense. In practical terms, large customers received larger discounts, and smaller independents sometimes bought salt from Morton in quantities that did not qualify them for any discount. It was precisely this kind of advantage for large buyers that the Robinson-Patman Act sought to prevent, said the Court.

---

[19] *Federal Trade Commission* v. *Morton Salt Co.*, 334 U.S. 37 (1948).

Having found the discount system to be discriminatory, the Court considered the question of whether it had also had the proscribed effect on competition. The company maintained that no harm to competition had been demonstrated by the Federal Trade Commission, and argued specifically that the salt it sold in low volume was an insignificant portion of its customers' business. Morton claimed in other words that its discriminations in price were not important; salt was, after all, only one of many items its retail grocery buyers carried. This contention was rejected by the Court, which stated:

There are many articles in a grocery store that, considered separately, are comparatively small . . . Congress intended to protect a merchant from competitive injury attributable to discriminatory prices on any or all goods . . . whether the particular good constitutes a major or minor portion of its stock. Since a grocery store consists of many comparatively small articles, there is no way to protect a grocer . . . except by applying the prohibitions of the Act to each individual article. . . .[20]

The Court noted further that the Robinson-Patman Act was specifically "concerned with protecting small businesses which were unable to buy in quantities, such as the merchants here who purchased in less-than-carload lots. . . ."[21] The nature of the discounts and the purpose of the law thus justified the conclusion that competition might have been injured, said the Court. This injury to competition was tied directly to the injury done to the position of small competitors who were forced to pay higher prices for salt.

A question remained as to whether the discounts might yet be justified on a cost basis. If it were more economical for the company to sell in large lots, the price discrepancies might make "only due allowance" for cost differences. Here again the company argued that the F.T.C. had failed to demonstrate illegality. But, said the Court, the burden of proof was on the company to show that its price differences were justified; it was not up to the Commission to show that they were not. Although it was reasonable to believe that larger sales could be made more cheaply, the Court said, the company would have to demonstrate that its price differentials *precisely* reflected cost differentials in order to escape the sanctions of the Act. This the company had not done, and, in the absence of such proof, evidence that *some* cost differences might exist did not satisfy the requirements of the cost justification.

[20] *Ibid.*, p. 49.
[21] *Ibid.*

The Supreme Court found the price schedule to be in violation of Section 2(a) and restored a sweeping F.T.C. order against future discounts. The order, which had been limited by the Circuit Court of Appeals, went beyond a prohibition on the precise discount schedule used by the company. This was necessary according to the Supreme Court, for, "Had the order done no more than that, respondent could have continued substantially the same unlawful practices despite the order by simply altering the percentages applied. . . ."[22]

The *Morton Salt* decision indicates that the existence of "substantial" price differentials among customers may well be sufficient to establish a violation of law. Such differentials, the Court reasoned, harm the position of companies that buy at higher prices, and thus harm competition. Any extensive inquiry into the actual competitive mechanism was apparently considered unnecessary. The decision also makes it clear that a cost justification of discriminatory prices will be extremely difficult to prove. It would be necessary to show not merely that lower prices to certain customers correspond to lower selling costs, but that the price differentials are *precisely* matched by cost differentials. Such evidence is often difficult to derive. A company may be aware that large-volume customers cost less per unit to service. But precisely how much less—especially when the company distributes many products or when part of its gain is seen to be "better" planning and timing of deliveries—may be impossible to estimate.

(b) The First Standard Oil Case (1951)

The first *Standard Oil* case[23] raised the issue of the good faith defense under the Robinson-Patman Act. Standard had been selling gasoline to large jobbers at $1\frac{1}{2}$ cents less per gallon than it sold to retail service stations, and was ordered to cease this practice by the Federal Trade Commission. In appealing the Commission's order the company argued that its lower prices had been offered in good faith to meet the equally low prices of competitors.

The Commission had found that Standard's price discounts to jobbers damaged competition. Two of the jobbers to whom it sold had lowered retail prices in their own service stations and had also lowered their wholesale price to other retail stations. This result, according to the Commission, had disadvantaged those retail service stations that could not purchase gasoline at the lower price. Standard argued that its lower prices had been granted under competitive pressure in order to retain the jobbers as customers—had the discounts not been granted, the jobbers would have gone

[22] *Ibid.*, pp. 52–53.
[23] *Standard Oil Co.* v. *Federal Trade Commission*, 340 U.S. 231 (1951).

elsewhere. But the Commission held in effect that this defense was irrelevant, stating:

. . . even though the lower prices in question may have been made . . . in good faith to meet the lower prices of competitors, this does not constitute a defense in the face of affirmative proof that the effect of the discrimination was to injure, destroy and prevent competition. . . .[24]

The Commission had thus asserted that good faith is not an absolute defense to a charge of price discrimination.

It was on this point that the Supreme Court took exception to the Commission's findings. Said the Court:

. . . there has been widespread understanding that, under the Robinson-Patman Act, it is a complete defense . . . for the seller to show that its price differential has been made in good faith to meet a lawful and equally low price of a competitor. . . . We see no reason to depart now from that interpretation.[25]

The Court noted that the wording of the Robinson-Patman Act was identical with respect to both the cost justification and good faith defenses. There was, said the Court, no basis for treating the two differently, as the Commission had done. The Court refrained from deciding on the merits of the case, that is, it did not judge the validity of Standard's good faith argument. Rather, it held that the company's argument should be considered, and ordered the case remanded to the F.T.C. for rehearing.

(c) The Second Standard Oil Case (1958)

On rehearing, the Federal Trade Commission again ruled that Standard's discounts to jobbers violated the Robinson-Patman Act.[26] The Commission considered the good faith defense, but held that although Standard's price discounts had in fact been made to meet the equally low prices of competitors, they were not made in good faith. This conclusion, which the Supreme Court termed "not altogether clear," had been overruled by an appeals court.

The Supreme Court upheld the appeals court on narrow grounds. The case, said the Court, turned on a factual issue. The appeals court had made a fair assessment of the record; thus there was no basis for overturning its decision. The Court did go on to note briefly that Ned's—the only jobber to have its price discount instituted after passage of the Robinson-Patman Act—had indeed pressured Standard with information about "more attractive price offers. . . ." Ned's had given Standard ultimatums,

[24] Cited in *ibid.*, p. 239 (41 F.T.C. 263, 281–82).
[25] *Ibid.*, pp. 246–47.
[26] *Federal Trade Commission* v. *Standard Oil Co.*, 355 U.S. 396 (1958).

after which it had received price discounts. It was on this kind of information, said the Court, that the Court of Appeals had legitimately found the discounts to be a response to specific competitive situations.

The Court's decision, on a five-to-four vote, was sharply criticized in a dissenting opinion by Justice Douglas. Standard's definition of a jobber, said Justice Douglas, was entirely arbitrary; a jobber was simply a big customer, so the discount system was discriminatory. A discriminatory system, he went on, cannot be protected under Section 2(b) simply because it succeeds in holding customers against competitive offers.

The effect of the second *Standard Oil* decision was to reaffirm the status of good faith as an absolute defense to a charge of price discrimination. If a seller discriminates within the meaning of Section 2(a) in good faith to meet the equally low price of a competitor, he is protected even if the effect of his discrimination had been to harm competition.

(d) The Sun Oil Case (1963)

The issue raised in *Sun Oil*[27] is whether a seller can discriminate in price to meet the lower price of a *buyer's* competitor; that is, can the seller lower price to one customer in order to enable that customer to meet *his* competition?

Sunoco had sold gasoline–at a discount to McLean, an independent service station dealer in Jacksonville, Florida, for precisely this purpose. The Federal Trade Commission found that this discrimination in price damaged other Sunoco service stations and thus violated Section 2(a). The company argued that McLean was simply a "conduit" of Sunoco, and that the price cut was thus a good faith meeting of competition. The Supreme Court held that the good faith defense cannot be extended to include the meeting of competition by the discriminating seller's customers.

The Court might well have decided differently had Sunoco *owned* McLean. (Courts are not in the habit of policing the terms at which companies sell "to themselves.") It is interesting to consider whether the distinction between treatment of an owned subsidiary and an independent agent is justified by any meaningful difference in the economic functions served by each.

2. "COMPETITIVE" DISCRIMINATION

There are a variety of practices that, although not so consistent and highly structured as basing-point systems or discount schedules, may result in

[27] *Sun Oil Co.* v. *Federal Trade Commission*, 371 U.S. 505 (1963).

price discrimination. Suppose, for example, that a retailer offers a special price on some item "this Monday only." It might be said that the seller has discriminated against buyers who do not shop on Monday. Similarly, a seller may price his product differently in one city or region than in another. Although no one is discriminated against within each area, it could be argued that discrimination between areas exists.

The attitudes of the courts on such issues have not been fully or consistently developed, but such discriminations pose a dilemma. The company that prices differently in one area than it does in another may not only be acting rationally but may in some sense be acting "more competitively" than it would if forced into uniform pricing patterns. Possibly a firm will be willing to cut prices in some areas but not in others; or at some times but not others. Such a firm may be competing by cutting its price, yet under the constructions placed by the courts, it may also be discriminating illegally.[28]

Indeed, by prohibiting price discrimination Congress and the courts may well have made prices more rigid generally. Concessions to individuals are an important means by which prices are eroded, and to the extent that concessions are prohibited, prices may not be cut. This possibility poses a potentially strong economic argument against the Robinson-Patman Act.

The question of what constitutes a proper public policy toward price discrimination, when discrimination is part of the competitive process, is a difficult one. The record of legal precedent is still scanty and inconsistent, but there is some indication that the courts demand policies that will tend to hurt no one, even if such policies imply the stifling of competition. At times, as Adelman points out,[29] the courts may even *require* price discrimination. This will occur whenever the large, low-cost buyer is required to pay the same price as other buyers because any differentials are regarded as discriminatory.

C. The Legal and Economic Status of Price Discrimination

Price discrimination encompasses such a wide variety of business practices that it is difficult to summarize its legal or economic status precisely.

---

[28] See *United States* v. *The New York. Great A. & P. Tea Company*, 67 F. Supp. 626 (E.D. Ill., 1946).

[29] Morris A. Adelman, *The A & P Case—A Study in Applied Economic Theory*, Harvard University Press, Cambridge, 1949.

The attitude of the courts has not been fully consistent. Price differentials that occur under a basing-point system or that result from policies favoring large, high-volume customers are likely to violate the Robinson-Patman Act. Yet, because of the difficulty of proving a cost justification, this illegality may either prevent *or* require price discrimination. If costs are similar for all sales, then similar prices are nondiscriminatory. If costs differ, nondiscrimination requires prices to differ as well; but if the cost differences are not amenable to precise proof, a company that reflects such differences in price leaves itself open to prosecution.

The consistency of the courts in their treatment of price discrimination, is not an issue of primary economic significance. As we have noted earlier, discrimination itself is not necessarily undesirable, and a treatment that seems inconsistent could be economically appropriate. The more basic question concerns the judicial attitudes toward competition itself, as reflected in price-discrimination cases. What is it that the courts are trying to accomplish in their treatment of discriminatory practices?

The Robinson-Patman Act prohibits discrimination only when the effect may be substantially to lessen competition. Yet it seems fair to observe that the courts have made little inquiry into the competitive implications of price discrimination or nondiscriminatory price differences. In place of inquiry and analysis the courts have substituted an assumption: if differentials in price give some competitors an advantage over others, harm to competition is implied. In other words, a price difference that hurts one or more *competitors* is interpreted as hurting *competition*.[30] This is the fundamental premise of basing-point decisions such as *Corn Products Refining* and *Staley*, in which the disadvantage incurred by customers distant from the basing point was presumed to harm competition; and of decisions such as *Morton Salt*, in which competition was assumed to be lessened by the higher charge to smaller buyers.

It is interesting to note that this view of competition is in close accord with the position taken by the courts in merger cases. In both situations hardship to competitors is equated with damage to competition. The economic difficulty with such an outlook should be quite obvious. Competition as a process is inevitably hard on competitors. Its rationale is precisely that it drives competitors to their best efforts and penalizes those who do not perform well. Certainly the economist's defense of a private market system would be unimpressive if inefficient firms within the system were to be protected. The *raison d'etre* of the system is its efficiency, and the maintenance of inefficient competitors in order to protect competition is a contradiction in terms.

---

[30] See Adelman, *ibid.*

To be sure, the courts have not deliberately set out to promote inefficiency. The emphasis placed on protection of competitors, however, is such as to raise questions about the priorities that are operative. Such questions are broader than the treatment of price discrimination, and extend into virtually all areas of antitrust enforcement. Presumably we do not want competitors to be hurt without economic justification. But the difficult policy question is what to do when competitors are hurt *with economic justification*. In the area of price discrimination the apparent answer of the courts is that competitors are to be protected without extensive analysis of economic cause.

16

Tying and Exclusive Dealing Arrangements

Section 3 of the Clayton Act makes it illegal for any person to lease or sell commodities,

> . . . on the condition, agreement or understanding that the lessee or purchaser thereof shall not use or deal in the goods . . . of a competitor or competitors of the lessor or seller, where the effect . . . may be to substantially lessen competition or tend to create a monopoly in any line of commerce.

This provision has been directed, as have Sections 1 and 2 of the Sherman Act, against tying and exclusive dealing practices. Under such practices, the seller makes the sale of his product contingent on specified customer behavior toward another product or products.

The typical tying arrangement provides that the buyer can purchase one product—the *tying good*—from the seller only if he agrees to purchase something else—the *tied good*—as well. The seller states in effect: "I will sell you my tying good only if you also buy the tied good from me." Exclusive dealing arrangements are similar in certain respects, but are usually stated by the seller in the form of a negative prohibition: "I will sell you my product(s) only if you agree not to buy similar products from my competitors."

If we assume profit-maximizing behavior on the part of the firm, the question arises as to why any such arrangements would be desirable from its point of view. To maximize profits in any market, the firm need only produce that amount at which marginal cost and marginal revenue are equal, and charge the highest price that consumers are willing to pay. If the firm sells two different products, it presumably can maximize its total profit by maximizing in each market separately. Why, then, should the firm ever have an incentive to tie in the sale of one good to another?

The answer often given is that tying permits a firm to extend its power from one market to another—a practice known as *leverage*. Typically, the tying good is pictured as one with a strong market demand— for example, a patented machine—and the tied good as one with a relatively weak demand. Demand for the tied good is thus bolstered, but although demand for the tying good may suffer, it is presumably in a strong enough position so that the reduction is relatively small.

This view of why tie-ins pay, however, is a bit misleading, for it seems to imply that the tying process inevitably has a short-run effect that could not be accomplished by price changes. In fact, this is not always the case. If consumers are willing to purchase tied goods at some combined price, it is implicit that they would also be willing to purchase the goods separately at prices that add up to the combined price. Indeed, the tie-in might be analyzed as if it were a change in the price of both the tying and tied good; viewed in this way, it is difficult to see what the tie-in accomplishes that could not have been accomplished by direct price changes.

At this point an example may be helpful. Suppose that a firm produces a very popular brand of fountain pen and a very ordinary kind of ink, and decides to tie in the two goods. Instead of charging, say, $10 for the pen and $.50 for a bottle of ink, the firm now charges $10.50 for the pen-and-ink package. Its hope is that consumers will now buy more of the ordinary ink, yet will not reduce purchases of the popular pen by enough to offset the added profits on the ink. Consider, however, the implications of this hope. More ink will be purchased, but this result could also have been obtained by lowering the price of the ink. Fewer pens will be purchased, but this result could have been obtained by raising the price of the pen. Indeed, if it is more profitable to sell the combination at $10.50 than the individual units at $10 and $.50, then perhaps $10 and $.50 were not optimal prices to begin with; and the company could have expanded profits by raising the price of pens and lowering the price of ink.

The important point to remember is that there is no magical transformation when prices are quoted in combination. The combined price is just that—a combination of two separate prices. And consumers' willingness to pay the combined price implies a willingness to pay separate, though unspecified, prices. In the pen-and-ink example, any consumer who purchases the $10.50 package must rationally be willing to purchase the individual goods at some prices that add up to $10.50.[1]

We are still left with the initial questions: when and why do tie-ins pay? One possibility is that tying facilitates price discrimination, which might otherwise be impossible. Consider a simple case of two goods, A and B, and two consumers, 1 and 2. Suppose that consumer 1 is willing to buy a unit of A at any price up to $5 and a unit of B at any price up to $5; whereas consumer 2 will buy a unit of A at any price up to $6 and a unit of B at any price up to $4. If the seller offers A and B as a package at $10, each consumer will purchase the combination, and the seller will receive $20. But there is no *nondiscriminatory* set of prices at which separate sales of A and B will yield $20. (The maximum revenue obtainable with separate prices is $18: $10 for two units of A priced at $5 each plus $8 for two units of B priced at $4 each.) Tying, then, may permit a seller to take advantage of different demands by individual consumers. Because the price of any single product is never specified, consumers may in effect interpret a given package price in different ways.

Other possibilities also exist. It may be, for example, that the tie-in represents an acceptable form of competition for some markets in which direct price change is considered unacceptable. Tacit price agreements, for example, might not be considered to be violated if the product in question is tied to some other good; but a direct price reduction would be considered a violation and might precipitate price warfare. Perhaps more important, tie-ins may at times act as an effective long-run barrier to entry. When IBM, for example, tied service contracts to its computers, one result was to forestall entry of competing service organizations. Initially, IBM might have done just as well by lowering service prices and raising the prices on its machines; but it could not have been sure that someone—for example, its customers—would not have found out enough about the machines to enter the service market. It is possible that tie-in arrangements are often profitable for longer-run reasons of this type.

Analytically, exclusive dealing arrangements are distinct from tie-ins, although some similarities may be noted. Suppose, for example, that a shoe manufacturer decides to sell to retailers on an exclusive basis. It tells the retailers: "You can purchase our shoes only if you do not carry the shoes produced by our competitors." Such a condition has two contradictory affects on the demand for the manufacturer's shoes. To the extent that retailers accept the condition, demand will tend to rise, for these

---

[1] To be completely accurate, we should say that the consumer is willing to spend up to $10.50 on one or both goods priced separately. Conceivably, some consumers would not buy the ink even at a zero price; but if they pay $10.50 for the package, the implication is that they would have paid $10.50 for the pen alone.

stores must now fill their entire requirement from the one producer; but to the extent that retailers refuse to accept the condition, they will cease purchasing from this producer, and demand will tend to fall. The desirability of the arrangement from the producer's viewpoint depends partly on the calculation of the *net* effect of these tendencies.

The undesirable element in tying arrangements is commonly discussed in terms of leverage. In the case of exclusive dealing the undesirable effect is confined to one market and is somewhat analogous to vertical foreclosure (the shoe manufacturer in the above example is in effect foreclosing rival manufacturers from his retail outlets). In either case legal condemnation of these practices has been based on the idea that the practitioner may obtain a degree of market power that could not have been achieved purely on merit, according to the quality and price of goods offered. The Courts have dealt stringently with certain arrangements that imply exclusivity, taking the position that there is little to recommend such provisions and much to condemn them.

Of course many exclusive arrangements, particularly tie-ins, are trivial and even difficult to define. It could be argued, for example, that the sale of any product with separable components is really a tie-in sale of the components. A new car, for instance, could be viewed as a tie-in sale of innumerable parts—tires, transmission, body, engine, and so on. Similarly, a shirt involves a tie-in of buttons and cloth. In other cases, a trivial sort of tie-in arises because components can be used only in fixed proportions; a right shoe cannot be purchased without the left one. Such "tie-ins" have not been prosecuted under the antitrust laws; however, they show the need to define both products and the degree of significance that might make for a violation.

A. A Review of Relevant Cases

1. THE STANDARD FASHION-MAGRANE CASE (1922)

One of the earliest cases brought under Section 3 of the Clayton Act concerned an exclusive dealing arrangement imposed by a manufacturer of paper dress patterns.[2] Standard Fashion and Magrane-Houston entered into a contract that provided that Magrane would sell Standard's dress

---

[2] *Standard Fashion Co.* v. *Magrane-Houston Co.*, 258 U.S. 346 (1922).

patterns under the condition that the patterns of other companies would not be sold on its premises.

The question before the Supreme Court was whether the contract would tend to lessen competition or create a monopoly, and thus fall within the prohibition of Section 3. The Court agreed with the Circuit Court observation that:

The restriction of each merchant to one pattern manufacturer must in hundreds, perhaps in thousands, of small communities amount to giving each single pattern manufacturer a monopoly of the business in such community. Even in larger cities . . . [the practice] may tend to facilitate further combinations. . . .[3]

The exclusive dealing requirement was thus found by the Court to violate Section 3.

2. THE INTERNATIONAL SALT CASE (1947)

The International Salt Company,[4] the nation's largest producer of salt for industrial uses, held patents on two salt-dispensing machines. The company leased these machines under provisions that required the lessees "to purchase from it all unpatented salt and salt tablets consumed. . . ." That is, customers could lease the machines from International Salt only if they used the company's salt products in conjunction with the machines. The government charged violations of Section 1 of the Sherman Act as well as Section 3.

The Supreme Court held that although patents conferred a limited monopoly on the salt-processing machines, they "confer no right to restrain use of, or trade in, unpatented salt." The company argued that the trial court had precluded consideration of the reasonableness of the practices (under Section 1) and of the probability of lessened competition (under Section 3). The Supreme Court held, however, that it is "unreasonable per se" to foreclose competitors from any market; and found that the leasing provision had this effect by precluding rival salt producers from selling to users of International Salt Machines. The practice thus violated Section 1. Further, said the Court, Section 3 bars agreements that tend to create a monopoly, whether "the tendency is a creeping one rather than one that proceeds at full gallop; nor does the law await arrival at the goal before condemning the direction of the movement. . . ."

The company lodged one further argument that might have impressed the Court under different circumstances. It contended that because, under

[3] 259 Fed. 793, 170 C.C.A., 593.
[4] *International Salt Co.* v. *United States*, 332 U.S. 392 (1947).

the leasing arrangements, it was required to repair and maintain its machines, "it was reasonable to confine their use to its own salt because its high quality assured satisfactory functioning and low maintenance cost." The Court stated that "a lessor may impose . . . reasonable restrictions designed in good faith to minimize maintenance burdens," but noted also that no one had argued "that the machine is allergic to salt of equal quality" produced by other companies. Presumably the tie-in might have been permissible if it had been shown that salt produced by anyone other than International would have damaged the machines.

3. THE STANDARD STATIONS CASE (1949)

The Standard Oil Company of California and its subsidiary, Standard Stations,[5] had entered into exclusive supply contracts with 5937 independent service stations in the Western area of the United States. Under the contracts, service stations that were supplied by Standard were bound to fill their entire requirement for one or more products from the company. The provisions varied somewhat in product coverage, but the common effect of the agreement was that the stations served by Standard could not purchase some or all of the products they offered to consumers from any rival petroleum company.

The service stations involved in the exclusive contracts comprised 16 percent of total area outlets, and Standard was the largest seller of petroleum products in the area. There was thus little question of the substantiality of the commerce affected. Moreover, Standard's competitors practiced a similar kind of exclusive dealing; only 1.6 percent of the area service stations were "split-pump," that is, suppliers of more than one company's gasoline. The Supreme Court concluded that the exclusive requirements contracts created a "potential clog on competition," and were in violation of Section 3; but Justice Frankfurter's discussion of the issues was perhaps more significant than the actual decision.

The first substantive question considered by the Court was whether a showing that competition actually has been impaired is necessary under Section 3. The District Court had held that the substantiality of commerce affected implied a substantial lessening of competition, but Justice Frankfurter noted that there was no real precedent for such an implication. In some cases, he stated, an examination of the actual economic consequences of an agreement may be necessary; in others (such as *Inter-*

---

[5] *Standard Oil of California and Standard Stations, Inc.* v. *United States*, 337 U.S. 293 (1949).

national Salt), examination of actual consequences was not necessary once it was established that the volume of business affected was significant.

Justice Frankfurter distinguished between tying agreements, which, he stated, serve no purpose beyond the suppression of competition; and requirements contracts, which "may well be of some advantage to buyers as well as to sellers, and thus . . . to the consuming public." The advantage of such arrangements according to the Court, lies in the assurance of a steady source of supply to buyers and a steady demand for sellers. Long-term planning is facilitated and selling expenses may be lowered accordingly. The implication of this argument seems to be that tying ought to be illegal per se because it can have no positive justification; whereas exclusive dealing ought to be judged under some rule of reason, because positive benefits are possible. Interestingly, however, Justice Frankfurter refrained from applying a rule of reason in *Standard Stations*. It was true, he noted, that Standard's competitive position had not improved during the period covered by the exclusive requirements contracts, but it was impossible to say *what would have happened* to its position in the absence of the contracts. Said the Court:

> . . . to demand evidence as to what would have happened but for the adoption of the practice that was in fact adopted or to require firm prediction of an increase in competition as a probable result of ordering the abandonment of the practice, would be a standard of proof if not virtually impossible to meet, at least most ill-suited for ascertainment by courts. . . .[6]

The *Standard Stations* decision is thus something of an oddity. The Court said that exclusive requirements contracts—unlike tying arrangements—might be shown to be desirable. Yet because of the "serious difficulties" that would attend any effort to apply the necessary tests, a presumption was made against contracts involving a substantial volume of business. The Court seemed to argue for a rule of reason approach, while actually applying a per se test modified by the significance of commerce affected.

4. THE J. I. CASE COMPANY CASE (1951)

The J. I. Case Company,[7] a manufacturer of farm equipment, distributed its products through a dealership system. The company was charged with violations of Section 1 of the Sherman Act and Section 3 of the Clayton Act on the grounds that it entered into agreements with its dealers "which

---

[6] *Ibid.*, pp. 309–10.
[7] *United States* v. *J. I. Case Co.*, 101 F. Supp. 856 (1951).

require said dealers to confine their sale and purchase of farm machinery exclusively to the farm machinery manufactured and sold by Case." In addition the government charged that Case engaged in *full line forcing*, under which a dealer could carry Case products only if he agreed to handle the full line of goods offered by the company.

Case was the third largest farm machinery manufacturer, with 7 percent of the national market. Apparently its dealers were pressured in varying degree to act as exclusive agents by the threat that their Case contracts would not be renewed if they carried the products of other manufacturers. Such pressure was officially disowned by the company, which blamed it on overzealous salesmen, and the company had issued bulletins telling its managers not to use coercive tactics.

The District Court was influenced by the fact that exclusive-requirements provisions were not part of the actual written contracts between J. I. Case and its dealers. Coercion had been used to obtain exclusivity, but it was at least plausible to suppose that this was not the policy of the company itself. Beyond the absence of overt exclusive agreement, the District Court found that the instances of pressure that had been shown did not damage competition. Those dealers who lost their Case contracts through nonrenewal had little difficulty obtaining contracts from other manufacturers, and the Case dealers who continued were apparently happy to act as exclusive agents. The decision may have turned largely on the absence of exclusive provisions in Case contracts, but the Court's conclusion of innocence was based also on the fact that dealers were not adversely affected.

5. THE TIMES-PICAYUNE CASE (1953)

The Times-Picayune Publishing Company[8] owned and published two major New Orleans newspapers, the morning *Times-Picayune* and the evening *States*. Only one other major newspaper, the *Item*, was published in New Orleans. The company sold advertising space only in the two papers combined; a buyer of space could only purchase a joint advertisement that would appear in both the *Times-Picayune* and the *States*. Although this arrangement was akin to a tie-in, the government charged violations of Sections 1 and 2 of the Sherman Act rather than Section 3 of the Clayton Act. It argued that these unit or forced-combination contracts were unreasonable restraints of trade and represented an attempt to monopolize.

[8] *Times-Picayune Publishing Co.* v. *United States*, 345 U.S. 594 (1953).

The Supreme Court noted that tying agreements flout the purpose of the Sherman Act by reducing competition, and, for this reason, "fare harshly under the laws prohibiting restraints of trade." When a seller has a monopolistic position *or* when a substantial volume of commerce is affected, said the Court, such agreements violate Section 3; when *both* these conditions are met, Section 1 of the Sherman Act—which provides a more stringent standard of illegality—is breached as well. Under this interpretation, the government was required to show both that the Times-Picayune Company held a monopolistic position *and* that its advertising sales policy had restrained substantial commerce.

Justice Clark, for the Supreme Court majority, disagreed with the District Court's finding that the *Times-Picayune* paper held a dominant position in the New Orleans newspaper advertising market. Noting that there were only three significant publications in the area, the 40 percent share of advertising lineage that the paper received was not significantly different from the 33.3 percent it would have held were the market divided equally. On this rather curious basis Justice Clark concluded that the conditions of the case failed to meet the Sherman Act standard of illegality.

Further, the Court argued, the immediate circumstances did not amount to a tying arrangement. The essence of such arrangements, said Justice Clark, "is the wielding of monopolistic leverage; a seller exploits his dominant position in one market to expand his empire into the next." In the present case, however, Justice Clark found it impossible to identify distinct tying and tied goods, stating:

> Here . . . two newspapers under single ownership at the same place, time, and terms sell indistinguishable products to advertisers; no dominant "tying" product exists . . . ; no leverage in one market excludes sellers in the second, because for present purposes the products are identical and the market the same. . . . In short, neither the rationale nor the doctrines evolved by the "tying" cases can dispose of the Publishing Company's arrangements challenged here.[9]

The Company was acquitted of Sherman Act violations by a vote of five to four. Once again the Court had displayed strong hostility to tie-ins, yet its definition of such arrangements appeared narrow. The practice followed by the *Times-Picayune* Company was found not to be a tie-in because there were no identifiable strong and weak goods. The dissenting opinion argued for separate morning and evening markets. Under this construction the company almost certainly would have violated the Sherman Act, for its share of the morning market was 100 percent. Moreover, a tie-in could then be argued plausibly: advertisers wishing to reach either market alone were tied into the other market.

[9] *Ibid.*, p. 614.

6. THE NORTHERN PACIFIC RAILWAY CASE (1958)

The Northern Pacific Railway Company[10] had large land holdings that it leased and sold for various uses. In its leasing and selling agreements the company had preferential routing provisions that required lessees or buyers to ship on Northern Pacific lines all commodities produced on that land. The practice was challenged by the government as a violation of Section 1 of the Sherman Act.

The Supreme Court noted that the Sherman Act had not been read literally by the courts to prohibit *every* restraint on trade. However, said Justice Black,

. . . there are certain agreements or practices which because of their pernicious effect on competition and lack of any redeeming virtue are conclusively presumed to be unreasonable and therefore illegal without elaborate inquiry as to the precise harm they have caused or the business excuse for their use. This principle of per se unreasonableness not only makes the type of restraints which are proscribed by the Sherman Act more certain but it also avoids the necessity for an incredibly complicated and prolonged economic investigation. . . .[11]

Among the practices deemed per se illegal in past cases were: price fixing, division of markets, group boycotts, and tying arrangements. The present circumstances amounted to a tie-in according to Justice Black. He found no question "that the defendant possessed substantial economic power by virtue of its extensive landholdings," and that the volume of commerce affected was substantial. Accordingly, the Court held that the preferential routing clauses violated Section 1.

7. THE TAMPA ELECTRIC CASE (1961)

The Tampa Electric Company and the Nashville Coal Company had entered into a contract in which Tampa agreed to fill its entire coal requirements from Nashville for a period of 20 years. Nashville later advised Tampa that the agreement was illegal under Section 3 of the Clayton Act and refused to supply the coal. Tampa thereupon sued for a judgment declaring the agreement to be legal.

The Supreme Court disagreed with the District and Circuit Court decisions that the requirements contract violated Section 3.[12] The Court

[10] *Northern Pacific Railway Co.* v. *United States*, 356 U.S. 1 (1958).
[11] *Ibid.*, p. 5.
[12] *Tampa Electric Co.* v. *Nashville Coal Co.*, 365 U.S. 320 (1961).

assumed (without actually ruling) that the contract amounted to exclusive dealing. But whereas such prolonged contracts are suspect, said Justice Clark, they are not illegal per se. The amount of commerce involved in this contract—$128 million—was hardly trivial, but, said the Court, "the dollar volume by itself is not the test. . . ." The Court found that this sum amounted to less than 1 percent of the relevant market, and was not sufficient to imply a Section 3 violation. Once again the Court took the position that exclusive dealing arrangements may have positive benefits and are to be judged under a rule of reason approach.

8. THE LOEW'S CASE (1962)

At issue in the Loew's case[13] was the practice of block booking of copyrighted motion pictures. Six major distributors were charged with violating Section 1 of the Sherman Act by making the sale of one or more feature films to television stations conditional on the purchase of other films. The practice had forced buyers to purchase undesirable films in order to obtain features that they wanted. For example, to get *Treasure of the Sierra Madre, Casablanca, Sergeant York, Johnny Belinda,* and *The Man Who Came to Dinner,* WTOP (a Washington television station) also had to purchase such films as *Nancy Drew, Troubleshooter, Tugboat Annie Sails Again, Kid Nightingale, Gorilla Man,* and *Tear Gas Squad.*[14]

The Loew's case combined several lower court cases that raised identical issues and were considered together. The first issue considered by the Supreme Court was whether tying arrangements violate Section 1. Justice Goldberg reasserted the Court's earlier contention that tie-ins have no real justification and are viewed with concern because they may "force buyers into giving up the purchase of substitutes for the tied product . . . and they may destroy the free access of competing suppliers of the tied product to the consuming market." These effects, said the Court, may occur when the seller, "by virtue of his position in the market for the tying product, has economic leverage sufficient to induce his customers to take the tied product along with the tying item." The test of illegality thus rests on an assessment of the market power held by the seller. In the immediate case the Court held that a patent or copyright on the tying good creates the presumption of the requisite market power.

---

[13] *United States* v. *Loew's Inc.,* 371 U.S. 45 (1962).

[14] As George J. Stigler has noted, block booking may be inspired by the desire to price discriminate, as in the example cited earlier. See "A Note on Block Bookings," in Stigler, *The Organization of Industry,* Irwin, Homewood, Ill., 1968, pp. 165–70.

Loew's and the other distributors held copyrights on films desired by the stations, and this was taken to imply sufficient leverage. The defendants argued that the relevant line of commerce was television programming, of which motion pictures (at that time) comprised only 8 percent. The Supreme Court, however, agreed with the district judge that each copyrighted film block "was in itself a unique product." There was no question that block booking had adverse effects on competition, said Justice Goldberg. Stations that were forced to buy unwanted films were denied access to films marketed by other distributors; and the other distributors were in turn foreclosed from selling to the stations. The Court thus concluded that the practice violates Section 1. The motion picture distributors henceforth were required to quote prices for individual films on request, although they could continue to offer blocks for purchase.

B. The Legal Status of Tying and Exclusive Dealing Arrangements

The courts have been careful to distinguish between tie-ins and exclusive requirements, and to make distinctions within each category as well. Nevertheless, standards for judging the legality of this broad family of practices are not fully clear. The courts have held repeatedly that exclusive dealing may serve positive purposes, yet they have refrained from efforts to identify benefits in specific cases. The most prominent benefit cited is the assurance of a long-term source of supply that may permit sellers to plan more efficiently. At the same time, exclusivity can result in market foreclosure. This kind of effect may be trivial or important, and the courts have now taken the position that the legality of exclusive dealing provisions depends directly on the likely degree of foreclosure. In *Tampa Electric* the Supreme Court held that an exclusive requirements contract that was large in dollar terms would not foreclose "a substantial share of the line of commerce affected." A precise definition of substantial does not exist; however, 16 percent of the relevant market was sufficient in *Standard Stations*.

The legal status of tying arrangements differs from that of exclusive dealing, and also is subject to ambiguities. Because the courts have recognized no potential benefits, a harsher standard has been applied to tie-ins. The courts have claimed on several occasions that tying is per se illegal. Yet the actual treatment of such arrangements does not seem to conform to a per se standard as the term has been understood with respect to other kinds of violations. As Baldwin and McFarland state, "[per se] . . . means that . . . the Court need only be shown that the act itself was committed. If tying arrangements are illegal per se the plaintiff need only prove that the act itself was committed."[15] Despite judicial assertions of per se illegality, this is not the standard that has been employed. The courts have found tie-ins to be illegal only when monopolistic power in the market for the tying good or substantial market foreclosure in the tied good exist. In addition, tying arrangements have been permitted in at least one instance in which both market dominance in the tying good and substantial commerce in the tied good were present. In *United States* v. *Jerrold Electronics*[16] the District Court held that Jerrold could tie service contracts to community antenna television systems for a limited period of time. The equipment was "sensitive and unstable," and the business was new. There was reason to believe that, in the absence of a compulsory tie-in, customers might attempt to service their own antenna apparatus, a task for which few were qualified. Such efforts could lead to unsatisfactory performance of the equipment and damage to Jerrold's innovative business. In light of this situation the Court found that tie-ins were reasonable under Section 1 until the business was established.

Have tying arrangements, then, been subject to a per se standard? As Singer puts it,

A rose may be a rose, but it is quite clear that one per se violation is not equivalent to another. Four market practices are generally listed as per se violations of the antitrust laws; price fixing, division of markets, group boycotts, and tying arrangements. But the standard of proof associated with each of these market practices is quite distinct.[17]

In short, whether tying arrangements are per se illegal depends on what one may wish to call per se illegal; but the per se doctrine of tie-in sales is not the same thing as the per se doctrine of price fixing. As Singer goes on to point out, however, the argument over what should or should not be called per se is irrelevant to substantive antitrust questions. The pertinent issue is what kinds of proof the courts require in different types of cases.

[15] W. L. Baldwin and David McFarland, "Some Observations on 'Per Se' and Tying Arrangements," *Antitrust Bulletin*, VI, July–December 1963, pp. 433–39; quotation at p. 435.

[16] 187 F. Supp. 545 (E. C. Pa., 1960).

[17] Eugene M. Singer, "Market Power and Tying Arrangements," *Antitrust Bulletin*, VIII, July–August 1963, pp. 653–67; quotation on p. 653.

C. An Economic View of the Legal Criteria

The fundamental question before the courts in exclusive dealing and tying cases is: under what circumstances are such arrangements likely to do damage to competition? Here it is necessary to consider the two practices separately.

If an exclusive dealing agreement diminishes competition, it does so by foreclosing suppliers from distribution outlets (or vice versa). In other words, it makes it difficult for some suppliers to offer their commodities to the market, thereby hurting not only the suppliers themselves, but also the consuming public whose alternatives are reduced. The anticompetitive tendencies of exclusive dealing can be viewed in *reductio ad absurdum* fashion by noting that *any* sale by a supplier to a distributor forecloses other suppliers from that portion of the market. If a buying agent purchases something from me, he cannot buy it from you; you are thus foreclosed from making that sale. Shillinglaw, in a discussion of this point, notes that the restrictive effect is limited:

Among a group of sellers competing for a particular sale, one must be successful, the others unsuccessful. The essence of the competitive system lies in competition *before* each sale. The fact of the sale does not remove this competition but is its direct result.[18]

One effect of an exclusive dealing arrangement is to enlarge the *units* of sale, thereby reducing the number of sales that occur. If, for example, a shoe store is bound to a manufacturer by an exclusivity clause, competition has not necessarily disappeared. The manufacturer presumably won his contract—exclusivity provision and all—in competition with other manufacturers; and he will have to win it again on expiration. But the *interval* between sales has been lengthened; the unit of sale is enlarged. Rather than competing for every lot of shoes that the store requires, manufacturers now compete for every contract; contracts come up with relatively infrequency. The amount of competition might be said to diminish in the sense that fewer competitive confrontations occur, but it is not clear that such a reduction will imply inferior performance.

The courts have stated that competitive diminution should be weighed against the possibility that exclusive dealing will permit more efficient planning. This benefit is not readily measurable, but rather has caused the courts to insist that the negative effects of exclusivity be substantial

[18] Gordon Shillinglaw, "The Effects of Requirements Contracts on Competition," *Journal of Industrial Economics*, 2, April 1954, pp. 147–63; quotation on pp. 148–49.

for a finding of illegality. Again, however, the precise meaning of substantial is unknown.

The treatment of tying arrangements, although it is stricter, has not been as stringent as the language of the courts would sometimes suggest. The courts have argued that tie-ins serve no purpose beyond economic leverage, the extension of monopoly power from one market to another. This contention is a dubious one. Bowman has shown, for example, that a rational monopolist is unlikely to extend his monopoly to another market by means of tie-ins.[19] He points out that many of the tying cases that have come before the courts indicate a purpose other than leverage. I.B.M., for example, tied its computer cards to its computing machine leases until this practice was found to violate Section 3.[20] As Bowman notes, such a tie-in forces customers to pay in proportion to their use of the leased equipment—heavier users of the I.B.M. machines had to purchase more cards and thus pay more. The tie-in served the same function as a meter recording the use of the equipment.

In addition to this purpose, we have already noted that tying arrangements may actually serve as a means of price competition.[21] In some circumstances direct price cuts may be regarded as undesirable. Sellers may experiment instead with tying arrangements in which the tied good is akin to a bonus; for example: "If you buy my new razor, I will 'throw in' an extra supply of blades at especially favorable terms." Viewed in this context, it is clear that tie-ins need not serve the detrimental ends that the courts have envisioned.

What is more disquieting, however, is the courts' implicit view of the way tie-in contracts work. This view states that tie-in sales generally permit a seller with some market power over the tying good to extend this power to the market for the tied good. Although such a possibility cannot be precluded, the effects of tying arrangements are so complex and varied that no such generalization is easily defended. The pertinent question is whether a tie-in permits the seller to accomplish something that could not be accomplished by more usual means such as price change. Bowman has shown that a monopolist may be able to extend his position if the tied good is complementary and is used in variable proportions with the tying good.[22] Burstein has argued more generally that tie-ins of the requirements contract variety—those in which the buyer must fulfill his require-

---

[19] Ward S. Bowman, Jr., "Tying Arrangements and the Leverage Problem," *Yale Law Journal,* **67,** November 1957, pp. 19–36.

[20] *International Business Machine Corp.* v. *United States,* 298 U.S. 131 (1936).

[21] This point is made in Joel B. Dirlam and Alfred E. Kahn, *Fair Competition,* Cornell University Press, Ithaca, N.Y., 1954, pp. 189 ff.

[22] *Op. cit.*

ments through the seller, but no quantities are specified—may be profitable even if the goods are unrelated.[23] In these instances it appears that the tie-in may be a uniquely effective device for extracting monopoly gains from the tied market.

At the same time, it is very questionable whether extension of monopoly power results from most tie-ins that specify the quantities of goods to be purchased. As we have noted above, manipulation of individual prices may produce some of the results of tying in the short run. We have not considered the effects of market structure (in both the tying and tied markets) on the likelihood that a tie-in will be profitable, yet this is also a relevant consideration. In a competitive market, for example, any arrangement that effectively raises the price of a product must necessarily fail. The considerations bearing on the effects of tying arrangements are many and complex. Unfortunately, even a generous evaluation of the courts' treatment of such devices must conclude that it has been simplistic.

[23] M. L. Burstein, "The Economics of Tie-In Sales," *Review of Economics and Statistics,* **42,** February 1960, pp. 68–73.

17

Some Exceptions to Competition in Antitrust

As we have noted at several points, antitrust enforcement does not extend equally to all segments of the economy. It seems logical that policies designed to encourage competition would be restricted largely to those areas in which the market mechanism is thought to be workable. This would exclude most notably the "natural monopoly" or "public utility" industries. In fact, however, the application of the antitrust laws is not so consistent as a dichotomy between market-oriented and non-market-oriented sectors might suggest. Regulation of monopoly has not been fully substituted for encouragement of competition in many of the latter industries; and there are a number of significant exemptions and exceptions to the search for competition within the former sector.

In general, both these inconsistencies have been highly controversial. Some writers have argued that the government ought to fish or cut bait—decide when competition will work and when it will not, and pursue appropriate and consistent policies within each area. This is an appealing suggestion and it may imply policies that are superior to what we have. It is not, however, an easily implemented approach to public policy; for, as we shall see, the question of whether competition is in principle workable within specific areas often has no clear answer.

A. Exemptions and Exceptions for Particular Industries and Groups

1. THE PUBLIC UTILITIES INDUSTRIES

Public utilities industries may be described as those in which there is a substantial national concern with performance, and in which unrestricted competition would prove damaging to performance. The reasons why free competition would lead to poor results vary somewhat. Most typically the industry cannot support many firms. The distribution of electricity and natural gas, for example, require huge fixed investments by firms in order to operate at feasible cost levels. The role of economies of large scale is such that price competition would likely run amok. Competing firms would cut their rates (prices) in order to attract business and lower their unit costs of production. So long as a higher volume of business implied lower costs, firms would continue in this direction even though prices might be forced beneath the level sufficient to cover long-run average costs.[1] In these circumstances the expectation would be for one of two ultimate situations: a kind of chaos in which firms would go bankrupt, with the last survivor taking over monopoly control of the market; or some consolidations among firms to avoid disaster, with the end result again a market structure akin to pure monopoly. Since the inevitable result is monopoly, such industries are often subject to more direct regulation than is provided by antitrust. Rather than attempting to maintain competition when it is inherently destructive, the government may allow partial or complete monopolies and attempt to control their behavior.

The rationale of such control may be considered in reference to Figure 17.1. Monopoly equilibrium occurs at point E_M; whereas competitive equilibrium in the short run would be established at point E_C. The desired effect of public regulation is sometimes thought of as the establishment of position E_R. At this point excess profits are eliminated (since price equals average cost); however, the industry would not be forced to a competitive (price equals marginal cost) equilibrium.[2] This is, at least nominally, the objective of public utility regulation. Regulated firms are

[1] Firms would not leave the industry in the short run so long as prices (rates) exceeded average *variable* costs.

[2] Readers should note a similarity (but not an identity) between the regulated result and the market outcome under monopolistic competition.

generally allowed to price in such a way that they cover all costs including a "fair" rate of return.

Several industries are ordinarily considered to fall within the public utilities framework: electric power and gas; communications; and some forms of transportation, including pipelines. The rationale for public regulation is not always related exclusively to an economies of scale or

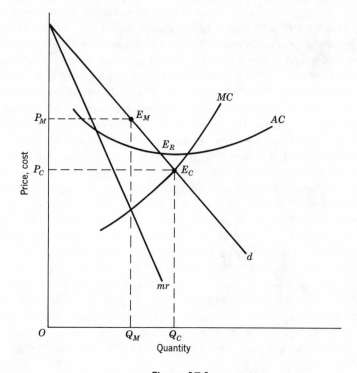

Figure 17.1

natural monopoly argument. In some cases competition may be possible, but only at the cost of poor performance.

One difficulty that arises in several areas is known as the peak-load problem. This refers to variation in demand for services over time. The demand for electricity, for example, may be higher at night than during the day; and it may reach unusually high levels during summer heat waves. Similarly, the demand for gas or for transportation services may vary substantially during each day or over the course of longer periods. Because the commodities in question tend to be nonstorable, and because they are considered to be important, the peak-load problem takes on significant dimensions. Industries, if left to their own devices, might choose not to build sufficient capacity to serve the peak demands; or the capacity, if built, might be priced in discriminatory or otherwise unsatisfactory ways. In either event there might be a need for public regulation.

Still other reasons for regulation exist. In at least one case—television —there exist purely technical restraints on the number of competitors (a problem, incidentally, that an appropriate public policy might have solved years ago)! The nature of demand itself may vary among the utilities industries, depending perhaps on how necessary different services are seen to be. The degree of mobility consumers have in switching among competitors may also differ considerably (it is relatively easy to switch modes of transportation, but somewhat difficult to switch a source of home heating). The reasons for public regulation are varied and, by similar token, so are the forms of public control.

In the case of electric power and gas, the Federal Power Commission has broad jurisdiction over interstate transmissions and sales. The functions of the Commission are varied, extending even to matters of conservation. From the standpoint of competition policy, however, its main activities have to do with the rates charged by the utilities companies. Rate making intrastate is directly regulated by state (and in some instances regional) public utilities commissions; the F.P.C. is broadly charged with responsibility for securing, on interstate commerce, just and reasonable rates that are also nondiscriminatory. Beyond this, the Commission has control over the level and type of services provided and over the entry and exit of firms from the market. In addition it has powers of approval over asset acquisitions (mergers).

The powers of the F.P.C. are in a general way typical of most public utility industries. In the telephone and radio and television industries, for example, the Federal Communications Commission is obliged to impose just and reasonable rates and to foreclose unjustified discrimination in interstate communications. The rates and services provided by the railroads and other carriers are subject to control by the Interstate Commerce Commission; and the airlines' rates and services are regulated by the Civil Aeronautics Board. In addition to controlling rates and services the various commissions generally are required to pass on merger proposals. A typical public utility company, then, finds itself in the following situation: the prices it charges must be approved by the appropriate state or federal commission; any change in the level or type of services provided must be similarly approved; and if it desires to acquire the facilities of another company, it must submit application to the appropriate commission.

The major issues of public utility regulation concern the effectiveness of the system, and are largely beyond the scope of this discussion.[3] What is pertinent here is rather the role of competition and the antitrust laws in the regulated industries. In the public utilities sector the regulatory apparatus is designed to control the pricing and output decisions of constituent firms. Such control is in a real sense the substitute for competition that is foregone when government sanctions the monopolistic position of utility companies. In these circumstances certain kinds of antitrust issues common to other industries tend not to arise. We would not expect, for example, that a power company holding a local or regional monopoly under the regulatory system would be challenged under the Sherman Act for monopolizing its market. Such a challenge would be contradictory to the very purposes of regulation, and would amount to a governmental attack on a government-granted market position. Similarly, it would not be expected that the rates charged by regulated companies would come under close antitrust scrutiny. The pricing decisions of the companies are controlled by the regulatory system in the form of the appropriate commission. If controls are ineffective, as they often may be, there exist a number of possible remedies. Once again, however, it might make little sense to attack regulated companies for pricing in ways that are sanctioned by the system of governmental regulation.

Relatively few antitrust questions are raised, then, in relation to either the monopoly power or the pricing policies of the utilities companies. Interestingly, the issue that seems to receive primary antitrust attention throughout the regulated sector is mergers. The regulatory commissions pass on merger applications. When an application is disapproved, that is generally the end of the matter; but frequently applications that have been approved by a commission are challenged in the courts.[4] Such challenges may arise on the rather technical point that a particular commission did not have jurisdiction over the merger in question; this is sometimes the case, for example, if the merger is effected through stock acquisition. A more basic question is raised, however, when the courts are asked to consider a merger on its merits. The question then is: what are the proper criteria—and particularly, *what weight is to be given to competition*—in passing on a merger that involves regulated companies?

---

[3] For more thorough discussions of public utilities, see Charles F. Phillips, Jr., *The Economics of Regulation*, Irwin, Homewood, Ill., 1965; and Roger C. Cramton, "The Effectiveness of Economic Regulation: A Legal View," *American Economic Review*, LIV, May 1964, pp. 182–91.

[4] Public utilities rates also have been challenged by private groups in the courts. Here the question ordinarily concerns a commission's judgment in defining a fair rate of return or an appropriate rate base.

We have already seen a major acquisition—Pacific Northwest by the El Paso Natural Gas Company—struck down by the Supreme Court. This merger had previously been approved by the Federal Power Commission, but the Court ruled in 1962 that the Commission had no authority to pass on acquisitions currently being challenged under the antitrust laws.[5] In considering the merger on its merits, however, the Supreme Court applied the standards of Section 7 of the Clayton Act,[6] and stated in effect that the consolidation of two regulated natural gas companies was to be judged by its probable impact on competition, that is, the test of the merger was to be no different from the test of any other corporate merger under the antitrust laws.

The Supreme Court has not always gone so far. In *McLean Trucking Co.* v. *United States*,[7] a case involving a merger of motor carriers, the Court held that the Interstate Commerce Commission has the power to approve a merger that might otherwise violate the antitrust laws. According to the Court, the Commission cannot ignore antitrust considerations in its decisions, but neither can it be required to apply antitrust standards to mergers of common carriers. The Commission's task is to further the goals of national transportation policy, such as an adequate and efficient system that imposes reasonable and nondiscriminatory charges. The attainment of these goals, the Court noted, is related to competitive factors. For this reason the I.C.C. must take such factors into account in judging the desirability of mergers. The special aspect of the transportation industries, however, is the public interest in something more than competition. It would be unsatisfactory to have an inefficient system of transportation, for example, even if the industry were highly competitive under accepted definitions. Therefore the Commission must consider other factors as well; and it may decide that a merger that reduces competition is, on balance, permissible.

The *McLean* doctrine has recently been reaffirmed by the Supreme Court in *Seaboard Air Line R. Co.* v. *United States*,[8] albeit in a somewhat different context. Here a merger of two railroad lines was approved by the I.C.C. despite apparent anticompetitive implications. The Court, in remanding the case, insisted that the Commission demonstrate rigorously the public benefit of a merger that reduces competition. However, the Court held, an adequate demonstration *could* insulate the merger despite the competitive problem.

The issues raised in such cases are typical of the problems that arise

---

[5] *California* v. *Federal Power Commission*, 369 U.S. 482 (1962).
[6] *United States* v. *El Paso Natural Gas Co.*, 376 U.S. 651 (1964).
[7] 321 U.S. 67 (1944).
[8] 382 U.S. 154 (1965).

in attempting to reconcile antitrust and regulatory interests. In general the Supreme Court has held that immunity from the antitrust laws is not to be lightly implied. The fact that certain aspects of a company's business are regulated, for example, does not imply antitrust immunity if the regulation is less than pervasive, and especially if it does not extend to the company's pricing policies.[9] In those instances in which regulation *is* pervasive, however, the proper weighting of competitive factors vis-a-vis other factors is seldom clear. The courts often have relied on the doctrine of *primary jurisdiction*, holding that the task of weighting competitive factors rests with the appropriate commission.

2. BANKING, INSURANCE, AND SECURITIES TRADING

Public regulation extends to areas in which the public utility type of argument for federal controls is absent. In commercial banking, insurance, and the securities markets there are two broad reasons for regulation.

1. The public is largely ignorant about the nature of the commodities it purchases in these markets, and is therefore vulnerable to fraudulent, or manipulative, or simply unsound practices. There is thus a special need for consumer protection.
2. The consequences of poor market performance could be severe for the national economy. In this respect the rationale for regulation is somewhat similar to that for traditional utilities areas.

Although the need for regulation in these markets may be fully as strong as it is in, say, the electric power industry, the type of regulation that has evolved is rather different. It is directed primarily toward the prevention of business practices that would mislead the consuming public or endanger the solvency of established firms, thereby threatening the stability of the markets.

(a) Banking

Nowhere have the consequences of widespread business failure been so dramatically demonstrated as in the commercial banking industry. During the late 1920's and early 1930's some 8000 banks failed, inflicting tremendous financial losses on depositors. The traumatic effects of these failures led directly to a system of rigorous and continuous scrutiny of banking operations. Three federal agencies—the Federal Reserve System,

[9] See, for example, *United States* v. *Radio Corp. of America*, 358 U.S. 334 (1959).

the Comptroller of the Currency, and the Federal Deposit Insurance Corporation—exert broad controls over many banks; those that do not fall within the purview of these agencies are subject to regulation by the states in which they are chartered.

There is no question as to the thoroughness of the regulatory system. Minimum bank reserves are specified; the quantity and quality of loans is prescribed; interest payments are prohibited on demand deposits and a maximum is imposed on time deposits; the banks are subject to independent audit and to unannounced examination. In addition, the structure of the industry is regulated by restrictions on branch banking and the necessity for approval of merger applications. Few persons would doubt that current conditions and safety differ vastly from those that prevailed in 1933.

As was the case with public utilities industries, antitrust issues in banking have arisen within narrow areas. Although control over the rates and services provided by banks is not quite so pervasive as that exercised by the utilities commissions, there has been virtually no antitrust challenge to the day-to-day operations of the industry. Rather, the major questions have arisen in connection with mergers. As we saw earlier, it was not until the Supreme Court decision in *Philadelphia National Bank*[10] that bank mergers were known to be vulnerable to Section 7 of the Clayton Act.

In this case the merging banks argued that bank acquisitions fell within the scope of the Bank Merger Act of 1960 rather than Section 7. Under this Act, the bank regulatory agencies were required to consider competitive factors in passing on merger applications. The defense position was that this requirement effectively immunized bank mergers from antitrust prosecution; and that the agencies could approve mergers that might otherwise violate Section 7, much as the I.C.C. had done in *McLean*.

The Supreme Court rejected this argument, citing its earlier statement that "immunity from the antitrust laws is not lightly implied." There was nothing in the language or history of Section 7, said the Court, that indicated Congressional desire to exempt the banking industry from its provisions. Further, the Bank Merger Act conferred no "express immunity. . . ." Said the Court, "Repeals of the antitrust laws by implication from a regulatory statute are strongly disfavored, and have only been found in cases of plain repugnancy between the antitrust and regulatory provisions. . . ."[11] If the Court was unwilling to find an implied exemption in existing law, it might yet have concluded that there was a

[10] *United States* v. *Philadelphia National Bank*, 374 U.S. 321 (1963).
[11] *Ibid.*, pp. 350–51.

repugnant relationship between antitrust and regulation in banking, and gone on to reconcile the conflict in favor of the regulatory agencies. Here, however, the Court stated:

> The fact that the banking agencies maintain a close surveillance of the industry with a view toward preventing unsound practices that might impair liquidity or lead to insolvency does not make federal banking regulation all-pervasive, although it does minimize the hazards of intense competition.[12]

At this point the Supreme Court was touching on the primary question in many similar cases: is the regulatory apparatus of an industry so complete that competition has literally no role to play? The Court's negative answer in this instance was unambiguous.

The legal status of bank mergers today appears to be in a state of conflict. Since the *Philadelphia National Bank* decision, Congress has passed the 1966 Bank Merger Act, providing explicitly that the regulatory agencies may approve a merger if it can be shown that adverse competitive effects are outweighed by the convenience and needs of the community affected.[13] The Supreme Court, however, has continued to hold that bank mergers fall within the antitrust laws, and has interpreted the 1966 Act to mean that the banking commissions are to make findings that may then become subject to independent judicial review. This position is plausible. The authority granted to the Justice Department to challenge approved mergers suggests that independent review was intended by Congress.

The fundamental dilemma in the banking industry, as in other areas, is that competition is at once desirable and feared. Competitive conditions may indeed encourage better performance, yet too much competition may lead to bank failure. In these circumstances the appropriate governmental attitude toward competition is difficult to define, and it seems safe to say that no obviously correct and consistent position has yet been determined.

(b) Securities

The stock market collapse of 1929 disclosed the remarkable extent of unsound and deceptive practices common in securities trading. It became clear that the investing public was in need of comprehensive protection, and the behavior of securities dealers and companies seeking to market their shares has been closely regulated in the period since the great crash.

---

[12] *Ibid.*, p. 352.

[13] Section 5(B) of the Act states that an agency shall not approve any merger "unless it finds that the anticompetitive effects are clearly outweighed in the public interest by the probable effect of the transaction in meeting the convenience and needs of the community to be served." The Act also provides that the Department of Justice may formally challenge any approved acquisition within 30 days of its approval.

Public concern over the operation of the market is related to the possibility of severe financial damage to those who lose their savings; however, this concern goes beyond sympathy for specific individuals. The securities markets serve a vital capital-raising function for private corporations, which could be impaired if public confidence in the markets were dissipated. Moreover, brokerage houses act in a fashion somewhat akin to commercial banks and savings institutions. They often hold the portfolios of investors, much as the banks hold the deposits of their customers. Accordingly, concern for the failure of investment houses is acute.

Unlike some other regulated industries, the antitrust issues raised in securities trading so far have not concerned mergers. This may be because of the relatively atomistic structure of the industry, which is such that few mergers could significantly alter the concentration of market shares. The issues that have been raised recently concern rather the rules and behavior of organizations such as the New York Stock Exchange.[14] The major exchanges are subject to control by the Securities and Exchange Commission. If the Commission finds that an exchange does not have rules that are "just and adequate to insure fair dealing and to protect investors," it may revoke the registration of that exchange; however, there are some significant gaps in regulation.

The issue of antitrust immunity for the N.Y.S.E., and for the securities markets generally, was raised in *Silver* v. *New York Stock Exchange*.[15] Silver, an over-the-counter dealer who was not an Exchange member, had his private telephone connections with 10 member firms discontinued by the Exchange without notice and without any statement of cause. The Supreme Court noted that this action, had it occurred "in a context free from other federal regulation," would have constituted a per se violation of Section 1 of the Sherman Act as a concerted refusal to deal.

The legal question was whether the Exchange was immune to antitrust prosecution by virtue of its regulated status. Here the Court noted that there were significant areas in which the jurisdiction of the S.E.C. was limited. It could insist on adequate rules for a stock exchange, but had no power to curb abuses by the exchanges in the enforcement of accepted rules. Under these circumstances, only a total exemption from the antitrust laws could have protected the actions of the Exchange, and the Court was unable to find a basis for such sweeping immunity. It left

[14] The Department of Justice did bring suit in 1947 against 17 investment banking firms, charging that the common practice of syndicating (joint underwriting) new issues violated the Sherman Act. These charges were dismissed in *United States* v. *Morgan*, 118 F Supp. 621 (S.D.N.Y., 1953), and no similar challenges have occurred since then.

[15] 373 U.S. 341 (1963).

open the possibility that specific immunity might be found in other circumstances, but where and when such immunity might exist has not since been determined.

Of special interest in the future is the legal status of exchange rules that have been specifically sanctioned by the S.E.C. but that also serve to limit competition. Here the courts will not have the relatively easy task of deciding on actions that occur within gaps in the system of regulation. This type of problem has not yet reached final determination in the courts, but some legal proceedings have been instituted and it is likely that decisions will be forthcoming in the near future.

The antitrust-regulation conflict in securities parallels a similar conflict in commercial banking. Intense competition raises the prospect of business failure, and business failure may imply unacceptable costs to the economy on a national level. The result is that some suppression of competition is accepted. At the same time, however, it may not be desirable to forego the benefits of all competition by completely ignoring competitive considerations. The conflict in securities is also tied to the extensive reliance on voluntary self-regulation that has been firmly established in the last 35 years. It would be virtually impossible for an agency such as the S.E.C. to regulate the behavior of all firms and their employees in a completely effective way. Accordingly, much of the responsibility for regulating behavior has been undertaken by private organizations such as the stock exchanges and associations of securities dealers. This type of control may be effective, but it implies, in the words of the S.E.C. itself, "private" formulation of restrictive standards of business conduct and their enforcement by, at the very least, exclusionary practices.[16] It is much as if an industry trade association were given unlimited power to determine and enforce comprehensive rules of behavior for members. This may be an effective way of securing adherence to the desired code; but it will, almost inevitably, imply the kind of concerted behavior that would normally violate the antitrust laws in a flagrant fashion. The key question—as yet unanswered and perhaps even unasked by responsible government bodies—is when and to what extent such behavior is truly necessary to assure safe and stable markets.

(c) Insurance

The insurance industry is regulated by the states to perhaps a greater degree than any other area within the government-controlled sector. Like banking, a primary purpose of regulation is to assure the financial

---

[16] *Report of Special Study of Securities Markets of the Securities Exchange Commission,* G.P.O., Washington, 1963, Part 4, p. 502.

soundness of companies; like securities, another significant purpose is to prevent fraudulent and misleading practices. The insurance industry had long been thought to be exempt from the antitrust laws because of an 1869 court decision that insurance is intrastate rather than interstate commerce.[17] This view was overturned in 1944,[18] and the industry responded in 1945 by securing passage of the McCarren-Ferguson Act, which exempted rate-making agreements in insurance from antitrust prosecution for a period of three years. The present status of antitrust in the insurance industry has been described by Brainard and Dirlam as follows:

If a state prohibits mergers that substantially lessen competition, enforcement in a specific case may stave off Federal action. But it is hard to see how . . . this . . . could be a bar to Federal Trade Commission or Department of Justice proceedings, if, despite the legislation, the consequence of mergers, market sharing or tying arrangements is substantially lessened competition.[19]

Despite the apparent applicability of antitrust to various agreements, however, the insurance industry has been relatively free from troublesome conflicts between regulation and competition. This is in large part because of the highly competitive nature of the insurance markets, in which the numbers of competing firms are large and barriers to entry are low.

3. LABOR UNIONS

One of the clearest departures from the procompetitive orientation of the antitrust laws occurs in the treatment of labor unions. Section 6 of the Clayton Act provides the following specific exemption:

. . . Nothing contained in the antitrust laws shall be construed to forbid the existence and operation of labor, agricultural, or horticultural organizations, instituted for the purposes of mutual help . . . or to forbid or restrain individual members of such organizations from carrying out the legitimate objects thereof; nor shall such organizations, or members thereof, be held or construed to be illegal combinations or conspiracies in restraint of trade under the antitrust laws.

[17] *Paul* v. *Virginia*, 8 Wall 168 (1869).

[18] *United States* v. *South-Eastern Underwriters Assn.*, 322 U.S. 533 (1944).

[19] Calvin H. Brainard and Joel B. Dirlam, "Antitrust, Regulation, and the Insurance Industry: A Study in Polarity," *Antitrust Bulletin*, XI, Jan.–Apr. 1966, pp. 235–316.

Yet as Mason has put it, "Whether labor unions are monopolies is a question hardly worth considering. Whatever else a union is, it is certainly an agreement among workers not to compete for jobs."[20]

Labor unions are, in Clayton Act terminology, mutual help organizations designed to secure desirable and improved working conditions for members. The monopoly aspect of the union lies in the agreement of members to bargain as a single group rather than as individuals. Members do not compete with each other for jobs, but band together to secure the best available terms for all. If a union seeks, for example, a $5 per hour wage for its members, workers who might be willing to take less are foreclosed from offering their services at the cheaper rate. Union members are thus enabled to engage in a form of price fixing without running afoul of antitrust prohibitions. Certainly such cooperative efforts alter the competitive situation of labor markets. Employers must negotiate with large groups of employees who often possess, in the aggregate, the power to shut down the employing company by means of a strike.

The rationale for the union exemption may never have had much to do with the Clayton Act assertion "that the labor of a human being is not a commodity or article of commerce." Indeed, the early motivation for allowing such organizations seems to have sprung from the belief that large employers could inevitably exploit their workers. The bargaining situation before unions was seen as a highly uneven one in which large business firms could offer terms to workers on a take-it-or-leave-it basis. Actually, the uneven bargaining problem does not arise unless firms are large relative to their market (i.e., they possess monopoly power). Presumably rival employers would compete for labor, and workers would gravitate toward firms offering the best conditions. The more general problem, however, is that labor mobility is limited; there are costs to switching jobs, and a switch that involves a geographic change may be especially difficult. Accordingly, workers might be exploited not because their employers were somehow bigger than they were, but rather because they could not take full advantage of the variety of offers that might be available.

Whatever the original merits of the exploitation argument, labor market conditions today are vastly different than they were 50 or 60 years ago. The labor force is now protected by a network of legislation encompassing health and safety conditions, restrictions on child labor, and minimum wage levels. Some observers have argued that unions are no longer needed to protect workers, but it should be noted that although the area

---

[20] E. S. Mason, "Labor Monopoly and All That," *Economic Concentration and the Monopoly Problem*, Harvard University Press, Cambridge, 1957, p. 196.

of possible exploitation has been reduced it may not have been eliminated completely.

Although the Clayton Act exemption for labor does not permit the unions to engage legally in any activity, the courts have interpreted it to imply considerable latitude for union behavior. In *Apex Hosiery Co. v. Leader*,[21] for example, the Supreme Court ruled that a striking union could seize a company's plant and stop outgoing hosiery shipments without violating the Sherman Act. The Court permitted this clear restraint of trade on the grounds that the restraint was only incidental to the union's legitimate purpose of advancing its own interests. In *United States v. Hutcheson*[22] the Supreme Court upheld the right of a carpenters' union to boycott the products of a brewing company that had contracted with machinists for certain dismantling jobs. Once again the reasoning was that the union was acting in pursuit of a legitimate interest, whatever the attendant restraints on commerce may have been.

An important limitation to union behavior under the antitrust laws was established by the Court in a 1945 case, *Allen Bradley* v. *Local 3, International Brotherhood of Electrical Workers*.[23] The union, which operated in New York City, had waged "aggressive campaigns" to obtain closed-shop agreements with employing manufacturers. The union then entered agreements with contracting firms that limited these firms to purchasing only from manufacturers with whom the union had closed-shop arrangements. The evident purpose of this agreement was to bolster the business of firms that employed members of Local 3 and had agreed to the closed-shop demands. The Supreme Court noted that the actions in question would violate Sections 1 and 2 of the Sherman Act unless immunized by the participation of the union. Such immunization, however, was not found. Said the Court, ". . . we think Congress never intended that unions could, consistently with the Sherman Act, aid non-labor groups to create business monopolies and to control the marketing of goods and services."[24] The principle that labor groups may not conspire with nonlabor groups to restrain trade was thus clearly established. This is, however, one of the few limits to labor union immunity to antitrust prosecution.

The exemption for labor unions is highly controversial, and there are many who advocate application of the antitrust laws in this area. Application of the laws could mean many things, however. Some proposals have suggested simply that the Sherman Act be invoked against certain restric-

[21] 310 U.S. 469 (1940).
[22] 312 U.S. 219 (1941).
[23] 325 U.S. 797 (1945).
[24] *Ibid.*, p. 408.

tive practices that now are protected by the exemption. Other, more severe suggestions would have the Act used as a basis for attacking the monopoly *power* of the unions rather than specific kinds of union behavior.

One's view of the appropriate way of dealing with unions depends on whether such organizations are seen to be good or bad. Many economists undoubtedly believe that some curbing of union practices is in order. At the same time, however, there are arguments about the merits of collective bargaining that suggest that the labor union *qua* union ought to be allowed to function. If the view is accepted (and it need not be) that union operations should be restricted, but not in ways that would cripple union effectiveness, a line between legitimate and illegitimate activity must be defined. Union effectiveness often implies restraint of trade, and the identification of those restraints that might be disallowed without doing damage to union interests is not obvious.

Our ability to formulate reasonable antitrust policies toward labor unions is handicapped by an absence of relevant empirical evidence. Despite the great interest economists have taken in these organizations, there is relatively little knowledge of their economic effects. It is known, for example, that wage-rate behavior in unionized and nonunionized areas does not differ as much as might be expected; yet we have little idea of what wage rates generally would look like had there never been a trade union movement. Similarly, we do not really know what the effects of restricting union activities or power might be. Any effort to apply the antitrust laws more fully implies a trade-off: there would be some gain in restricting restraints of trade and monopolistic pricing practices, but some loss in a weakening of the collective bargaining process. Conceivably the gain would be great and the loss negligible. But until we have some objective idea of relevant magnitudes, the debate over proper treatment of the unions will proceed on a frequently emotional level.

B. Exemptions for Particular Activities

Certain types of economic activity are also exempt from antitrust prosecution. Strictly speaking, the number of these activities is large, including such examples as price discrimination that is undertaken in good faith and tying arrangements that do not impair competition. Our interest, however, centers on actions that would clearly violate the antitrust laws were it not for the specific circumstances that have motivated exemptions.

1. PATENTS

A patent is in effect a temporary monopoly granted by the government to an inventor. The inventor of an original and significant process, product, or improvement may obtain exclusive rights to his invention for a period of 17 years under present law.[25] During this period the inventor is under no compulsion to utilize his invention in any way. He may put the invention to work or do nothing with it; or he may license others who wish to use the invention on his terms. The essence of the patent is its exclusivity, for no other person or company may make, use, or sell the patented invention during the period covered, except on terms agreed to by the patent holder.

The patent system may appear inconsistent with the antitrust objective of promoting competition, as one of its effects is to free the patent holder from competitive pressures. However, the two primary reasons for this procedure are actually procompetitive. The first harkens back to the familiar Schumpeterian idea that progress must be stimulated by the prospect of financial gain. Presumably the monopoly reward induces individuals[26] to greater inventive effort, and society is the ultimate beneficiary of improved products and processes. The second reason is to assure that the developers of original inventions will disclose their ideas. The patent holder need not do anything with his invention, and this may be a drawback of the system; but in order to obtain the patent he must provide all pertinent information. Society in effect strikes a bargain; in return for exclusive rights it receives information. Possibly this information may not be put to use during the term of the patent, but it becomes common property thereafter.

A host of legal problems are associated with the patent system. The Patent Office is understaffed, and standards of patentability suffer accordingly. Patents may be granted to different individuals for essentially the same product or process simply because the Office cannot adequately check the originality of every application. Patent infringement suits in such instances are common. Apart from this type of problem, patents are often involved in broader attempts to establish monopoly positions. Here conflicts with the antitrust laws arise.

[25] Standards of patentability, including an assessment of what is original and significant, are determined by the United States Patent Office.

[26] Patents are granted only to individuals, but are widely utilized by business firms. Commonly, employees work for companies under contracts that require them to transfer to the employing company the right to all inventions patented as a result of their work during the contract.

We have already discussed one case in which a company holding patent rights to salt dispensers attempted to tie in sales of nonpatented salt to its invention.[27] The Supreme Court refused to allow this practice, but in other instances the rights of the patent holder have been found to be extensive. In a landmark decision, *United States* v. *General Electric Co.,*[28] The Supreme Court ruled that a patent holder may specify the price at which a licensee sells his invention. In fact, the patent holder may restrict the terms of a license in virtually any way he desires, specifying not only price but the quantity to be produced.

Very commonly one company may hold a basic patent on a product or process and another company may patent some improvement on the original. In such instances the basic patent holder may not use the improvement and the improvement patent holder may not use the basic product or process. Such companies often will engage in *cross-licensing,* whereby each is granted the right to utilize the other's patented invention. Frequently a particular product or process will be covered by a large number of patents held by various companies. Here it is likely that the companies will *pool* their patents. Each company contributes its invention to the pool and receives the right to utilize the entire pool. Under these more complicated circumstances the doctrine of *General Electric* could permit a comprehensive system of price fixing to exist. The courts, however, have not extended the doctrine in such instances. In *United States* v. *Line Material Co.,*[29] two firms adopted restrictive cross-licensing agreements pertaining to patents on electrical equipment devices. The specific. sale prices to be charged by sublicensees were fixed in the agreement. The Supreme Court held that such agreements go beyond the rights conferred by patent. A clear conflict between competition and patent rights was thus resolved in favor of competition.

The use of patents and licenses to form a cartel also has been restricted by the Court. In a 1945 case, *Hartford Empire Co.* v. *United States,*[30] a group of glassware manufacturers had established a pool of several hundred patents pertaining to glassware manufacturing machinery. The group had formulated extensive cross-licensing agreements that had the effect of allocating particular portions of glassware manufacturing activities to particular companies. As the Supreme Court observed,

. . . control was exercised to allot production in Corning's field to Corning, and that in other restricted classes within the general container field to Owens, Hazel,

[27] *International Salt Co.* v. *United States,* 332 U.S. 392 (1947).
[28] 272 U.S. 476 (1926).
[29] 333 U.S. 287 (1947).
[30] 323 U.S. 386 (1945).

Thatcher, Ball, and such other smaller manufacturers as the group agreed should be licensed. The result was that 94% of the glass containers manufactured in this country on feeders and formers were made on machinery licensed under the pooled patents.[31]

The Court held that the formation of the patent pool and elaborate cross-licensing agreements had been employed to discourage invention of glass-making machinery and to suppress competition in the manufacture of unpatented glassware. The arrangement had effectively divided the market and set the prices of various glass containers. In so doing it had established powers that were beyond those conferred by the patents themselves.

A difficult and persistent problem arises when an individual company attempts to establish a monopoly market position by accumulating patents. In *Kobe, Inc.* v. *Dempsey Pump Co.*[32] a circuit court held that a company cannot buy up all the patents in an area as a means of monopolizing the industry. At the same time, however, mere possession of many patents has never been found to violate the law. The company that develops numerous inventions and as a result monopolizes an industry presents a thorny and unresolved problem. To limit the company's monopoly position seems to abridge patent rights; but to uphold the position is to pay a potentially large competitive price for new inventions.

Important problems in patent policy remain unresolved. In part these problems relate to the fact that there is an anticompetitive element in the patent grant. The accumulation of patents by an initially powerful firm or group may imply great market control; and whereas the courts have said that accumulation alone does not violate the law, there is a question as to whether society may not be giving up more than is necessary in such instances to induce invention and innovation.

Significant problems also are raised by the behavior of patent holders. Patentees may license their inventions, and there is little question that they have a right to impose restrictions that could have been accomplished by refusing to license in the first place. The difficulty is that licensing restrictions may go beyond this reasonable right. Cross-licensing arrangements present particular problems, for although they may serve a socially useful purpose—for example, to permit the use of complementary inventions in conjunction with one another—they may also be employed as a vehicle for cartelization. In extreme instances—for example, *Hartford Empire*—it may be apparent that patent holders have used their rights to monopolize a market. But, absent such an elaborate scheme, it is often

[31] *Ibid.*, p. 400.
[32] 198 F. 2d 416 (1952).

hard to determine when an arrangement goes beyond those rights that patents are intended to confer.

Perhaps the primary problem with the present patent system is its rigidity. All patents have the same legal status, whether they are trivial or significant. Accordingly, all may be used with equal force to impose restrictions through licensing provisions. The use of a trivial patent to impose important restrictions is not uncommon, and this aspect of the system demands reform.

Numerous reforms of the patent system have been suggested. Most observers would undoubtedly agree that upgrading the standards of patentability and eliminating duplication are desirable. Some have argued that the duration of the patent grant is excessive and ought to be shortened, either across the board or selectively (with less important inventions receiving shorter protection). It has also been proposed that, because the purpose of patents is to improve technology, patent protection be tied to actual use of the invention. Some proposed reforms would likely improve the system. As is often the case, however, evaluation of the present system and its alternatives is extremely difficult.

The current patent laws have coincided with a period of rapid technological advance. What we do not know is whether and to what extent the system has *caused* this progress. It is clear that we pay a price for patents in terms of competition foregone; what is less clear is the benefit we derive from such payment. Conceivably we could maintain our present rate of progress at a lower cost, for example, through shorter patent terms, but it is also possible that cutting the cost would sharply reduce the benefits. Whether the patent grant is a worthwhile device and, if so, whether we have today the optimal kind of grant, are questions that can only be answered reliably when better measures of costs and benefits are developed.

2. RESALE PRICE MAINTENANCE

Under resale price maintenance, or *fair trade*, the manufacturer of a branded or trademarked item sets a minimum price below which the item may not be resold. This in effect does away with price competition at the reselling (wholesale or retail) stage, because sellers are not free to cut price below the level stipulated. The history of fair trade has been turbulent. In 1931 California passed the first law exempting resale price-maintenance agreements from prosecution under state antitrust laws. The original statute proved ineffective, for retailers who declined to sign price maintenance agreements simply ignored manufacturers' price specifications. For this reason, California added a *nonsigners* provision in 1933. The nonsigners clause bound *all* resellers (usually retailers) to adhere to a manufacturer's resale price so long as *one* reseller within the state had signed a price-maintenance contract. The success of this amendment stimulated a rash of similar fair-trade legislation in other states.

The state laws were upheld by the Supreme Court in 1936. In *Old Dearborn Distilling Co. v. Seagram-Distillers Corp.*[33] the Court ruled that a manufacturer's right to protect his "good will" justified fair-trade legislation. Shortly thereafter Congress passed the Miller-Tydings Act, an amendment to the Sherman Act that exempted resale price-maintenance contracts in *interstate* commerce whenever such contracts are permitted in the reseller's state. This Act, which was passed as a rider to a District of Columbia appropriations bill, marked a high point in the coverage of fair-trade laws.

From 1937 to 1951 resale price maintenance was a pervasive fact of economic life. The beginnings of change occurred in 1951 with the Supreme Court decision in *Schwegmann Bros. v. Calvert Distillers Corp.*[34] Schwegmann, a supermarket operator in New Orleans, had sold Calvert whiskey at less than the minimum resale price established by Calvert in Louisiana, a fair-trade state. Schwegmann had not signed any price maintenance agreement, and Calvert sued to enforce its price. The Supreme Court held that Miller-Tydings applied only to signers of interstate contracts, and could not be used to enforce minimum prices against nonsigners such as Schwegmann. As a result of this decision, vigorous price competition broke out in some areas previously controlled by fair trading.

The fair-trade advocates regrouped, and in 1952 won Congressional passage of the McGuire-Keough Act as an amendment to Section 5 of the Federal Trade Commission Act. Under McGuire-Keough, resale price-maintenance contracts in interstate commerce are permissible when permitted by state law; *and* such contracts may be enforced against non-signing retailers whenever one retailer in a state signs and the rest are notified. The only limitation is that this antitrust exemption is confined to goods that are sold "in free and open competition."[35]

The immediate effect of the McGuire-Keough Act was to reverse the *Schwegmann* decision. The Supreme Court has since enforced resale price-

---

[33] 299 U.S. 183 (1936).
[34] 341 U.S. 384 (1951).
[35] As Ward S. Bowman points out, however, the restriction is an anomaly. Fair trade would make sense to a firm *only* if it held some degree of monopoly power. See "Resale Price Maintenance—A Monopoly Problem," *Journal of Business*, 25, July 1952, pp. 141–55.

maintenance against nonsigners. As recently as 1964, in *Hudson Distributors, Inc.* v. *Eli Lilli & Co.*,[36] the Court held that a nonsigner of an interstate contract was covered by the Act. Whether such a policy is wise, said the Court, "is a matter for Congress to decide."

Despite the broad reach of the fair-trade laws, very substantial erosion has occurred in recent years. A significant loophole to fair-trade legislation was established in a 1957 court decision, *General Electric Co.* v. *Masters Mail Order Co.*[37] Masters, a discount mail-order house, shipped G. E. appliances to New York buyers at less than the minimum price specified by G. E. The appellate court held that Masters was not subject to resale price maintenance because it was based in the District of Columbia, which had no fair-trade law. The Supreme Court refused to review this ruling, and it thus appears that retailers can legally undercut a manufacturer's specified price by shipping from a non-fair-trade state or district.

The major erosion of resale price maintenance has occurred within individual states. State courts have frequently refused to enforce resale price-maintenance contracts, and nonsigners provisions in particular. At the present time fair-trade laws have been rendered inoperative in at least half of the 46 states that originally adopted such legislation. This does not mean that resale price maintenance is dead or even insignificant. The impact of the laws that remain is far from negligible. Moreover, those retailers and manufacturers groups that have traditionally supported resale price maintenance continue to push for new federal enabling legislation, this time under the misleading title of quality stabilization.

The argument against fair trade is an obvious one. Price-maintenance agreements differ from other forms of price fixing only in that they are vertical—that is, they involve a price set between different stages of production, rather than among competitors at a single stage. There is no question that such agreements restrict competition. Empirical evidence is abundant that the prices of such items as drugs and alcoholic beverages are substantially higher in fair-trade then in non-fair-trade states. Why, then, does anyone advocate such legislation?

The answer from a small retailer's point of view is evident: price competition, especially when large discount houses are involved, is threatening. The local druggist or liquor store owner likely will do better under a price-maintenance system that has much the same result as effective collusion.

Why manufacturers should desire fair trade is somewhat less clear, and the factors that determine the desirability of resale price maintenance

[36] 377 U.S. 386 (1964).
[37] 244 F. 2d 681; 355 U.S. 824 (1957).

are not completely defined.[38] Indeed, it is noteworthy that in many areas manufacturers do not take advantage of existing fair-trade legislation; they do not set minimum resale prices even though they legally could. The determinants of fair-trade desirability may be considered in reference to a simple example. Suppose that a manufacturer of headache remedies knows that his retail drug outlets will charge customers less for his product if no minimum resale price is specified. The manufacturer would like his druggists to sell as much of his product as possible. From the manufacturer's point of view, then, competition at retail may be desirable. The price of his product will be lowered, and (if demand curves look the way economists think they do) more will be sold. The druggist, who receives a lower retail price, might be happier with fair trade; but the manufacturer need not be.

In this simplest case a manufacturer would not want to set a minimum resale price. There are, however, some further considerations. The headache remedies produced by the manufacturer may well be less attractive to druggists if they must be sold in active price competition. If prices and profit margins are driven down substantially, druggists may demand less of the product from the manufacturer than they otherwise would. For this reason the retail price competition could ultimately reduce the manufacturer's sales, especially if competing manufacturers offer druggists alternative headache remedies at fixed retail prices. A major consideration for the manufacturer, then, may be retailers' treatment of his products. Even if retailers continue to carry his headache remedies at all, they are likely to push the fixed-price products that offer the higher net return.

Another possible motivation for manufacturers to establish minimum resale prices is the fear that lower retail prices reduce the value of products in the eyes of consumers. Producers often believe that the consuming public judges the quality of a product by its price; if so, a lower price may damage the product's reputation and hurt its future marketability. This fear is especially strong if a product may be used by retailers as a *loss leader*. A loss leader may be defined as a product sold by a retailer at a price that does not cover his wholesale price plus distribution costs. Typically, stores may offer special sales on a single loss leader in order to attract customers who will also purchase other (profitable) products. From the retailer's point of view, the loss leader is simply a promotional device. For the manufacturer whose product is the loss leader it may be seen as a threat to the product's reputation or good will. A minimum resale price blocks this threat.

[38] For a thorough discussion, see Lester G. Telser, "Why Should Manufacturers Want Fair Trade?" *Journal of Law and Economics*, **3**, October 1960, pp. 86–105.

Whether and under what circumstances resale price maintenance is rational for manufacturers is not entirely clear. Apparently, however, manufacturers believe that it is rational often enough to make extensive use of such arrangements. In effect, fair-trade laws exempt vertical price fixing from antitrust prosecution. The only rationale for such laws is that active price competition is regarded as dangerous by those who would be forced to compete. A weaker defense for a significant exception to antitrust policy would be difficult to find.

C. Summary

This discussion has not attempted to survey all exceptions to a procompetitive policy in the United States.[39] Even within the relatively small group of significant exceptions that have been discussed, there is little homogeneity. The reasons for exempting particular groups or activities vary widely, as do the exemptions themselves. But if the situations differ, the questions that need to be asked about each do not. Any exemption from antitrust prosecution implies the possibility of a reduction in competitive vigor. A sensible policy must proceed to grant exceptions only when such a possibility can be justified.

If there is a generally applicable criticism that may be made of antitrust exemptions, it is that the justification for a competitive loss is often vague. In the case of fair trade, for example, this is because the purely intuitive arguments for exemption are unconvincing. In the case of patents the intuitive arguments are plausible, but the magnitudes of gain and loss that we reap from the system are unknown. The justifications for exempted industries and unions tend to be unclear on both counts; we do not necessarily know whether and to what extent the various systems of regulation should supersede competition, nor do we know whether the existing accommodations produce, on balance, good results.

In many exempt areas there is serious doubt as to the wisdom of our approach to competition, and it may well be asked whether even the nominal purposes of exemption are well served. There is, for example, a variety of conservation programs designed to slow the use of resources that are either exhaustible or can be restored only over a long period of time. Such programs may restrict the competitive exploitation of the

---

[39] For a fuller enumeration of exceptions, see Walter Adams, "Exemptions from Antitrust: Their Extent and Rationale," in Almarin Phillips (editor), *Perspectives on Antitrust Policy*, Princeton University Press, Princeton, 1965, pp. 273–311.

resource. But in some instances at least, it appears that conservation is used primarily to protect existing interests. The case of crude oil production may be relevant; for although there is something to be said for conservation here, the system by which states proration quotas serves also to maintain existing prices. It is not clear that the system achieves anything approximating an ideal rate of use of the scarce resource over time; nor is it clear how estimates of appropriate use rates ought to be made. The system does, however, preserve prices and profits for existing producers.

The regulation of some utilities-type industries seems, at best, badly out of date. Arguments for the regulation of airlines, trucking, and television simply are not the same today as they were when the regulatory systems were instituted. And while this does not necessarily mean that we have too much regulation, it may well indicate that the type of regulation we now have is anachronistic.

In order to grant safely any type of antitrust immunity, it is necessary to make two showings: first, that there exist *identifiable benefits* associated with such a move (i.e., we do not grant immunity without reasons); and second, that the benefits *are expected to outweigh* the anticipated costs of decreased competition. The latter showing, which is necessarily empirical, has not been attempted regularly, in large part because relevant magnitudes are difficult to measure.

The pertinent question at this point concerns the kinds of decisions that we ought to make, given existing uncertainty. Suppose that we grant antitrust exemptions and then discover that we have made a mistake. Is this preferable to not granting exemptions and finding out that we were wrong? At the very least, this is the kind of question that might usefully be asked. For if it is not, we may give up on competition in areas where its merits are in fact substantial.

18

Some Evaluations of
Antitrust Policies

Although simple characterizations of antitrust are impossible, it would be inappropriate to conclude without some assessments. Do the current rules of the game, developed largely by the courts, make economic sense? Is the effect of enforcement on the economy salutary or deleterious —or is it perhaps imperceptible? Such questions are important and demand attention even if satisfactory answers are difficult to find.

A. The Meanings of Competition in Antitrust

We have noted at many points that the ostensible purpose of the antitrust program is to encourage a system of competitive markets. Indeed, if we accept the statements of judges and other public officials, there has been little deviation in policy from this noble objective. The difficulty, as we have also noted, is that the term competition carries different meanings, and a wide variety of policies can be justified in its name.

We have now had more than three-quarters of a century of experience under the Sherman Act, and over half a century with the Clayton Act. It might be thought that in this time some definitions of competition and monopoly would have won broad acceptance. This is not the case. The points of disagreement over these terms are perhaps better clarified now than they were a few decades ago, but the disagreements themselves persist.

1. THE LEGAL-ECONOMIC DICHOTOMY

In a classic article written more than 30 years ago Mason pointed out that lawyers and economists use the word monopoly (and therefore the word competition) in very different ways.[1] The term monopoly as used in the law, Mason noted, is "a standard of evaluation." It is used simply to designate situations that are not in the public interest; competition, the antithesis of monopoly, designates situations that are in the public interest. In economics, on the other hand, monopoly and competition are used as tools of analysis rather than simply as labels for bad or good market situations.

It would be inaccurate to state that lawyers and economists are homogeneous groups, each holding identical views of competition and monopoly. Mason's dichotomy between legal and economic concepts, however, is as real today as it was in 1937. Under the legal approach, monopoly consists of *restriction*—some limitation on the freedom of business units to engage in legitimate economic activity. The economic definition of monopoly, on the other hand, is related to *control*—the power of business units to influence the terms at which they sell goods and services.

The difference between these views is evident, yet neither implies an obviously correct basis for public policy. If we ask what each view contributes to policy formulation, it appears that the legal outlook carries at least two important virtues: certainty and simplicity. Few persons would doubt that the elimination of restrictive practices is beneficial, both on economic and other grounds. Furthermore, restrictive practices frequently are easy to identify and thus to act against. The kind of policy that follows from the legal standard, then, is straightforward and, in an important sense, workable.

The economic view of monopoly carries neither virtue of the legal approach. Market control in the broadest sense may be easy to identify; there exists *some* control whenever the conditions of pure competition are absent, although the precise degree of control is much harder to define. But, within rather broad limits, the mere existence of control or power carries no certain policy implications. We often do not know whether policies that retard power are on balance desirable. It is for this reason,

[1] Edward S. Mason, "Monopoly in Law and Economics," *Yale Law Journal*, **47**, November 1937, pp. 34–49.

as Mason notes, that the economic contribution to antitrust policy has been largely negative. It has cast doubt on the adequacy of the legal approach, but has failed to provide a real alternative.

2. COMPETITION AS A GOOD CONDUCT PHENOMENON: THE SHERMAN ACT APPROACH

What Mason termed the legal view of monopoly has won substantial acceptance in the enforcement of Sections 1 and 2 of the Sherman Act. Under current judicial interpretation, restraints of trade and attempts to monopolize are defined to mean particular restrictive practices. Even the *fait accompli* of illegal monopolization, as we have seen, has been viewed by the courts as something necessarily attributable to past business conduct. In very extreme cases of market dominance a company may be found to violate the law even though it has been relatively well behaved; yet even here the courts have found it necessary to show the existence of some kind of restrictive action in the company's history.

Present Sherman Act standards thus parallel Mason's legal definition of monopoly. Some attention has of course been devoted to the economic aspect as well. If, for example, a company is charged with monopolization, a court will likely seek to determine whether its market position justifies the accusation. But market position, although sometimes necessary to sustain a monopolization charge, has in no case been sufficient grounds for establishment of a violation. There is apparently no way in which market power, taken alone, can breach the law.

The strongest challenge to this conduct-oriented approach is represented by the conscious parallelism reasoning of the late 1940's. Under a strict parallelism doctrine, a violation of law would continue to depend on observed conduct; but the point at which conduct would imply illegality would be very different from what it is today. Parallel behavior, of course, still has a place in the law, but its role has diminished. The courts may one day turn back in the direction of the stricter parallelism approach, but we have come a long way from the days when writers believed that parallel behavior among competitors was virtually illegal.

Economic criticisms of Sherman Act interpretation properly focus not so much on what the law does as on what it neglects to do. There is wide, although not universal,[2] agreement that a per se approach toward conspiratorial conduct, is justified. To the extent that conspiracies are effective, the chance for vigorous price competition is reduced. There is

[2] For a dissenting view see Almarin Phillips, *Market Structure, Organization and Performance*, Harvard University Press, Cambridge, 1962.

some evidence that suggests that price fixing is often ineffective, yet even if it were inevitably so the effort is so flagrantly anticompetitive that per se prohibitions might still be supported.

The difficulty, then, is not so much that per se prohibitions on certain kinds of behavior have undesirable economic effects, but rather that the Sherman Act is used to do little more than impose these prohibitions. Illegal monopoly exists only if firms behave in restrictive or anticompetitive ways; and, conversely, if firms are well behaved the state of competition is legally acceptable. The economic flaw in this position should be evident. We have seen as early as Chapter 1 that the economic problem posed by monopoly is independent of business conduct. Resource misallocation follows directly from the pricing power of a pure or partial monopolist, without reference to the specific business strategems employed.

Because the law focuses primarily on the strategems, it is not surprising to find that many economists are critical of Sherman Act enforcement.[3] There are, however, two qualifications that may serve somewhat to mitigate criticism. The first is that legal standards are not rigid or constant over time. As both Judge Hand and Judge Wyzanski have shown, the Sherman Act can be interpreted in ways consistent with economic notions of competition and monopoly, and nothing that the courts have said recently precludes future movement in this direction. If judges have failed to embrace economic concepts in monopolization proceedings, they have not yet made it impossible for this to occur.

The second and perhaps more compelling qualification arises from the observation that economic analysis does not provide a ready-made alternative to present policy. If we were to use the Sherman Act to curtail monopoly in the strict economic sense, the results would be difficult to imagine. Under a literal interpretation, the law would be invoked against any firm with a perceptible degree of market power, presumably not a course that most economists would recommend.

What, then, are the alternatives? One possibility is that action be taken only in cases of significant or highly concentrated market power. Kaysen and Turner have suggested, for example, that unreasonable market power be made a violation of a new antitrust statute, and have proposed guidelines for judging unreasonableness.[4] Companies charged

---

[3] Indeed, an economist could hardly find the Sherman Act approach fully satisfactory unless he believed that monopoly in the economic sense could arise *only* through illegal behavior. If this were the case, then economic monopoly could not exist unless a company engaged in practices that violated the Sherman Act, in which case it would be prosecuted. Unfortunately, it is difficult to place much credence in such a doctrine.

[4] Carl Kaysen and Donald F. Turner. *Antitrust Policy*, Harvard University Press, Cambridge, 1959.

with having excessive power could attempt to show justification—for example, efficiencies or patents—but the burden of justification would rest with the companies themselves. The Kaysen-Turner proposal represents something of a compromise between present-day Sherman Act policy and the alternative of a strict limitist position on market power. As such, it may be a step in the right direction, although the problems of measuring both power and its sources should not be underestimated.

3. COMPETITION AS A STRUCTURAL CONDITION: THE SECTION 7 (CLAYTON ACT) APPROACH

If competition has been defined in a legalistic fashion under the Sherman Act, its fate in merger cases has been substantially different. Horizontal mergers have been judged on almost a purely structural basis and have been found illegal whenever an increase in the centralization of market power is a probable result. The test for vertical mergers has been the degree to which customers or suppliers would be foreclosed from the part of the market represented by one of the merging firms. Our experience with conglomerates is limited, but decisions such as *Procter & Gamble*,[5] indicate that the courts may find anticompetitive implications in over-all firm size as well as in relative size within a given market.

Although the Court's emphasis on the structural effects of merger may place it in somewhat closer accord with economic notions of competition and monopoly, this approach also encounters difficulty. Two particular criticisms seem pertinent:

1. The specific structural tests adopted may be unduly harsh and, at times, overly rigid. Thus, although market structure may be the appropriate variable to examine for clues to competitive impact, it is subject to distortion.

2. The emphasis on market structure has been used to preclude other relevant information such as economies that may result from merger. Indeed, the Supreme Court has not merely held that possible efficiencies are irrelevant; it has implied that efficiencies may condemn a merger because the merged firm then gains "competitive advantages."[6]

The validity of these criticisms will be assessed differently by different individuals. The Supreme Court has very likely denied some mergers that would not have lessened competition perceptibly. Yet the Court must consider not only the immediate effects of its decisions but also their implications as future precedent. It is possible, for example, that one merger will not affect competition in an industry, but that 20 similar

[5] *Procter & Gamble Co.* v. *Federal Trade Commission*, 386 U.S. 568 (1967).
[6] See *Brown Shoe Co.* v. *United States*, 370 U.S. 294 (1962).

mergers would do so adversely. The dilemma of a court in this situation is a real one. To prohibit the merger is to act against an occurrence that is benign, and therefore by all logic legal; but to approve the merger may open the gates to future acquisitions that, *in toto*, damage competition substantially.

The Court's exclusive reliance on structural information presents a similar problem. Its hostility to suggestions that improved performance is a relevant factor in mergers, is not good economics. Yet the nature of a preferred alternative to the Court's position is not entirely clear. How ought assertions about performance effects to be treated? Such information tends to be speculative, and it is not obvious what weight ought to be accorded to it.

The issue of an appropriate public merger policy is ridden with uncertainty. For the moment the Supreme Court has taken the position that the sole objective of policy is to retard increases in market power concentrations, whether or not any cost in efficiency foregone is involved. An ideal policy could not proceed in this fashion, but rather would weigh the benefits on one side against the costs on the other. Such a manifestly sensible procedure, however, encounters many difficulties. Economic analysis does not provide a set of guideposts that would point the way toward correct decisions. The market power effects of a merger may outweigh its efficiency effects, or vice versa. There is nothing inevitable about the net result, and the question of whether a gain or loss on balance will occur is essentially empirical. Our measures, however, are often inadequate.

Estimates of the impact of mergers often cannot be specified with confidence, and even when reasonably accurate calculations are possible the issue of society's priorities remains. If we are to pursue a rational merger policy that in effect makes trades between market power and efficiency, we must know not only the actual terms of the trades (the empirical measures), but also our own judgment of the prospective bargain (the social priorities). At the moment, neither kind of information exists in ideal form.

4. PROTECTION OF COMPETITION VERSUS PROTECTION OF COMPETITORS

As we have noted earlier, some observers of antitrust have accused the courts of acting to protect the interests of competitors rather than competition. This issue arises largely in connection with the Clayton Act prohibitions that apply to certain actions only if their effect may be substantially to lessen competition. The courts are therefore required to consider not only the nature of the behavior in question but also its competitive impact.

It is clear that the courts have frequently considered competitive effects in terms of the fortunes of affected competitors. In price discrimination cases a primary question is whether the behavior at issue has made it more difficult for discriminated-against firms to operate successfully. Similarly, a major consideration in tying and exclusive dealing litigation has been the competitive disadvantage incurred by firms that are excluded from some portion of the market. Even in merger cases the courts have been concerned with the prospects of companies that would remain in competition with the merged firm. In general the imposition of competitive disadvantages on specific firms has been taken by the courts as a strong indication that competition may be lessened.

This sort of approach is not especially controversial so long as harm to firms flows from behavior of an anticompetitive nature. Actions that in fact restrict competition by doing damage to competitors are not uncommon. Controversy arises when firms are harmed by practices that are not obviously anticompetitive; and it is heightened when damage to firms is inflicted by behavior that itself *reflects* competition. A classic example of conflict occurs whenever a company achieves efficiencies that its rivals cannot match. Increased efficiency implies social benefits; but it must also hurt those firms that have not become more efficient.

Competition at times hurts competitors. *Anticompetitive* behavior also can hurt competitors. In Clayton Act cases the courts have at times failed to inquire carefully into the origins of harm to competitors. Rather, they have tended to assume implicitly that such damage, *whatever its cause*, is a uniformly unhealthy event.

Have the courts, then, been acting in an unwise and unsound way? Some will conclude that the answer is yes, but the issue is not a simple one. We must again return to the question of society's priorities. Perhaps the community wishes to protect competitors, even if they are inefficient. There is nothing in economics that condemns this objective, although the objective ought not to be confused with protection of *competition*. The problem with our legal treatment is not that a necessarily bad goal has been pursued; but rather that the pursuit of a goal proceeds without much explicit effort to assess its economic cost.

5. SUMMARY

That "competition" has no single, well-defined meaning in antitrust is perhaps more a symptom than a cause of policy confusion. Competition and monopoly are treated primarily as phenomena of conduct under the Sherman Act and structure under the Clayton Act. The mere fact that treatments of the terms differ is not surprising, for the purposes of the laws are not identical. The Sherman Act tends to deal with flagrantly anticompetitive practices often promulgated by firms holding substantial market power; the Clayton Act, on the other hand, deals more with borderline practices that may not be inevitably anticompetitive, and with mergers whose effect may be to create substantial market power when it did not previously exist.

In light of this simplified dichotomy it does not appear necessary that both laws view competition and monopoly in the same way. The existence of different definitions is less troublesome than the shortcomings of each definition taken alone. Under present construction of the Sherman Act, an effectively monopolized industry need not violate the law; whereas under the Clayton Act, events that reflect competition may be said to lessen competition if they damage the interests of some firms. This does not imply that the laws in general work poorly, but it does indicate that our legal system has not yet come to grips with some rather basic questions.

B. The Effectiveness of Antitrust

The effectiveness of the antitrust program is of course related to the definitions of competition and monopoly that have evolved under the laws, but it depends also on other factors. The vigor with which federal agencies, especially the Department of Justice and Federal Trade Commission, enforce the laws is highly significant, as is the receptiveness of the courts to the agencies' arguments and proposed remedies. Moreover, the magnitude of resources devoted to the program is important, for even the most stringent interpretations of law would mean little without broad enforcement.

1. CLUES TO EFFECTIVENESS

A common problem besets efforts to measure the effects of any economic policy. Because so many variables are changing at once it is difficult to isolate the portion of the behavior of relevant factors that is attributable to policy actions. In the case of antitrust the measurement problem is compounded, for the variables that reflect the impact of policy are themselves hard to define. Assessments of monetary or fiscal policies, for example, can proceed by examining the behavior of income and price levels, the elements that those policies seek to affect. But the element that antitrust seeks to affect—the competitiveness of the economy—is not subject to precise measurement. It is therefore necessary to look to some more proximate and definable variables.

One obvious candidate for examination is market concentration. Concentration and competitiveness of course are not the same thing; yet a policy that promotes competition is likely also to reduce concentration or keep it from rising in some sectors. If we look at the behavior of concentration in recent decades no trend is apparent. It has declined in some areas, risen in others, and showed no significant change in most. The absence of an obvious trend is not conclusive, however, for we do not know *what would have occurred* had there been no antitrust program. It is reasonable to suppose that there would have been more increases, for antitrust tends to retard upward movements in concentration; but there is no way to ascertain whether the increases would have been significant, or even perceptible.

If we look specifically at merger policy, it appears that antitrust has probably had a strong impact. Corporate mergers since the 1950 amendment of Section 7 show a sharp trend away from horizontal (and to a lesser extent vertical) acquisition, and toward conglomerates. Although part of this change may be from other factors, the trend coincides so closely with the development of a strong policy toward precisely those types of merger that have become less frequent that some cause-and-effect relationship seems likely. The trend toward conglomerate acquisition has produced more diversified companies and has undoubtedly kept concentration levels in specific industries below those that would have been attained otherwise.

The effect of other Clayton and Sherman Act prohibitions on conduct is even less clear. It is reasonable to suppose that the vast majority of American corporations attempt to comply with the law. This may alter their conduct somewhat, but precisely how and with what effect is hard to say. It is likely, for example, that there are fewer tying arrangements because of the Clayton Act restriction. But what does this mean for competition and performance? There is no accurate way to tell without knowing precisely the effects of firms' current behavior and the effects of their behavior as it would have been without the legal barrier. A similar situation exists with respect to price discrimination. Many firms have probably altered their pricing schedules to conform with the Robinson-Patman Act, but whether this has altered the competitive process depends again on the unknown impact of their current conduct, contrasted with the unknowable impact of the conduct that would have prevailed were there no price-discrimination law.

One of the more intriguing questions about the effectiveness of the antitrust laws arises with respect to policies toward conspiracy. The Department of Justice devotes a large proportion of its antitrust resources to rooting out and prosecuting such practices as price fixing, yet the consequences of this effort are not fully known. It is again reasonable to assume that firms attempt to comply with the law and, to this end, they may undertake fewer flagrantly illegal schemes than they would otherwise. As we have seen, however, prosecution under Section 1 of the Sherman Act is somewhat inconsistent. It has tended to penalize formal and overt conspiracy, but has been far more lenient with informal and tacit forms of parallel business behavior. It is therefore conceivable that although some firms have abandoned collusive patterns that they know to be illegal, they have simply substituted different patterns that, although more "legal," are no less collusive. The law may not have induced greater independence in decision making, but rather may have forced firms to adopt relatively difficult and inefficient methods of collusion.[7] If this has in fact been the case, then the economic implications of Sherman Act enforcement may be rather limited.

It may be noticed that little reference has been made to the court cases discussed in earlier chapters. This omission reflects the widely shared view that antitrust effects are, like an iceberg, only partially visible. The direct effects, which occur in actual litigation, can be seen; but the indirect implications, like the bottom of the iceberg, can only be guessed. Moreover, the indirect effects are potentially much more important than those that can be observed in judicial rulings. The finding of illegality in one merger is not itself so important as the possibility that 100 other mergers may be abandoned or never contemplated seriously because of that ruling. Similarly, a decision against a price-fixing conspiracy is less important than the probability that numerous other conspiratorial devices will never see the light of day because of that decision.

It is clear that the significance of the antitrust laws cannot be gauged simply by looking at the relatively few situations that reach final resolution in the courts. At the same time, however, there is no way to determine how much the behavior of firms may be affected by the small number of significant legal decisions. Among policy makers it is an article of faith that the unseen effects of antitrust are comparable in magnitude to the underside of the iceberg, but this simply is not a demonstrable proposition.

---

[7] This point is made by George J. Stigler in "The Economic Effects of the Antitrust Laws," *Journal of Law and Economics*, IX, October 1956, pp. 225–58.

2. THE PROBLEM OF REMEDIES

A separate aspect of antitrust effectiveness has to do with the sanctions that are imposed once a violation of law is found to exist, and with the terms on which out-of-court settlements are reached by mutual consent of the parties to a legal proceeding. Obviously a determination that the law has been breached means little if no effective action follows. It is necessary to find a remedy that, ideally, will assure that repetition of the violation does not occur.[8]

Several kinds of remedies have been widely employed in antitrust proceedings. One type is *punitive* (although there may be some doubt that such measures ought to be termed remedial). In criminal cases, often involving conspiracy, fines commonly are imposed on those found guilty of Sherman Act violations. The maximum fine under current law is $50,000 per defendant per violation, and it has been suggested that this maximum be sharply increased.[9] As noted earlier, such a sum may not mean much to a large company, especially since fines have been held to be tax deductible! The most important potential penalty in many proceedings is the treble-damage action, which may be invoked by parties who have suffered injury as a result of the illegal act. Although the determination of damages is an uncertain art, the sums that may be recovered from defendants are often vastly greater than the fines levied under the Act.

Potentially more meaningful remedies deal directly with the behavior of companies and with the circumstances surrounding initial violations. Of course illegal actions will ordinarily result in an injunction to discontinue the practice in question. At times, however, it is doubtful whether such a restriction—even if it is combined with other, positive conduct requirements—is sufficient. The nature of an appropriate remedy obviously depends on the violation that has occurred. In cases of patent abuse the courts may impose compulsory licensing requirements. The obvious remedy in cases of illegal merger is prohibition of the merger, or divestiture if it has already been consummated. And when illegal conduct such as price discrimination or tying arrangements is the issue, conduct prohibitions may be appropriate.

In the view of some economists remedies are the weakest link in the

[8] Determination that a violation exists may itself be significant if the action or situation in question was not previously known to be illegal. In general, however, the fact that a court defines something as illegal probably is not a sufficient remedy.

[9] Prison sentences of up to one year may also be imposed on individuals, but rarely are used.

chain of antitrust enforcement. The absence of attention paid to this important area is in fact remarkable. As Massel has put it:

Decrees are written following hunches, some of which are dressed in the intellectual cloth of theory. After a decree is written, some attention may be paid to its enforcement, but there is no mechanism for a systematic analysis of the effects of such decrees, either individually or collectively.[10]

Remedies appear to be least satisfactory in cases when violations of law are related to the market power of defendant companies. Even when the relationship is an obvious one, the courts have been reluctant to impose remedies that would reduce power directly. The result is that the government sometimes wins legal victories in antitrust proceedings but obtains inadequate economic relief.

Perhaps the primary case in point is the *American Tobacco* decision of 1946.[11] Although the Big Three cigarette manufacturers were found guilty of monopolizing trade, the only sanctions imposed were a series of fines that left the monopolistic group intact. Dissolution of the convicted companies might not have been an appropriate remedy, for physical facilities would have been easy to duplicate and the companies' power was not a function of their physical size. Rather, it appeared, power was tied to public loyalty to the existing brands of cigarettes. Conceivably, the power concentration could have been reduced by requiring divestiture of brand names, or perhaps by placing future limits on advertising, the primary source of the brand loyalty. Such potentially useful procedures were not adopted, however, and a landmark legal victory for the government produced virtually no meaningful change in the condition of the affected industry.

The *American Tobacco* case was unusual in that the ordinary kinds of remedy would have been ineffective. In many instances, however, the obvious remedy of dissolution is passed over in favor of pure conduct requirements. A notable example is the 1956 consent decree agreed to in *United States* v. *Western Electric Co. and American Telephone and Telegraph Co.*[12] The Department of Justice, acting under a recent Supreme Court ruling,[13] sought to require A.T. & T. to divest itself of Western Electric, the telephone company's equipment-producing subsidiary. The government's hope was that Western could be split into three companies that would then compete in selling to A.T. & T. At the time of the proceedings, Western was the only significant supplier of telephone equip-

[10] Mark S. Massel, *Competition and Monopoly*, Brookings, Washington, 1962, p. 99.
[11] *American Tobacco Co.* v. *United States*, 328 U.S. 781 (1946).
[12] Civil Action No. 17-49 (D.Ct.N.J., 1956).
[13] *United States* v. *Pullman Co.*, 330 U.S. 806 (1947).

ment. The actual decree effected none of these basic structural changes. Instead, strict constraints were placed on the companies' future behavior: Western was required to maintain a cost-accounting system that would enable state utilities commissions to determine whether equipment costs were excessive (excessive costs were not to be permitted to enter rate-making calculations); both companies were required to abandon noncommunications activities; and compulsory licensing of numerous patents was imposed. Possibly these restrictions have had some meaningful impact on market performance, but it is far from clear that they were an adequate substitute for a plan that would have introduced some degree of competition into the telephone communications industry.

The courts have occasionally compromised by imposing conduct-oriented remedies but providing for later review of structural conditions. This was done in the *United Shoe* case, and the effects of Judge Wyzanski's 1953 order were the subject of a hearing in 1964. At the hearing the government requested that United be broken into two companies, while the company asked for modification of certain conduct provisions in the earlier order. Judge Wyzanski denied both requests, finding that competitive conditions in the shoe machinery industry had improved substantially since 1953 (United's market share had fallen from an estimated 75–85 percent to 62 percent; and the gross revenues of its "most important domestic competitors" had doubled).

In two notable cases—*United States* v. *Eastman Kodak Co.*[14] and *United States* v. *International Business Machines Corp.*[15]—consent decrees were entered requiring specific conduct; but providing explicitly that divestiture would be required in the future if satisfactory structural conditions were not attained. The *Eastman* decision required that company to split the tie-in between its color film and color film processing activities. Eastman would be required to divest itself seven years hence of any processing facilities in excess of 50 percent of national capacity; but divestiture would not be required if in six years it were shown that purchasers of Eastman color film had easy access to processors other than Eastman.[16] Divestiture was not required; in 1961 both the government and the company agreed that independent processors had captured more than 50 percent of the market.

The *IBM* consent decree was in some ways similar to *Eastman*. IBM had been alleged to hold about 90 percent of the tabulating-card market

[14] Trade Cas. Par. 67,920 (W.D.N.Y., 1954).

[15] Trade Cas. Par. 68,245 (S.D.N.Y., 1956).

[16] In addition to splitting the tie-in, Eastman was required to license its processing patents at "reasonable" and "nondiscriminatory" royalty rates, thereby hopefully encouraging new entrants.

for computing machines in 1952. A consent decree required that the company follow specified conditions of conduct: machines were to be offered for sale or lease; IBM was not to purchase used machines; its lease periods were limited to one year for a period of 10 years; and its patents were to be licensed at reasonable terms to new competitors. The decree provided, however, that IBM would divest itself of any card-manufacturing capacity in excess of 50 percent of national capacity, unless it could show, seven years hence, that "substantial competitive conditions exist." In 1963 IBM was required to divest itself of 16 card-printing presses. According to at least one observer, however, the original decree had already resulted in "an impressive improvement in structure and in economic performance."[17]

The devising of appropriate remedies in cases involving substantial market power has proved to be difficult. If existing physical structures are easy to duplicate (e.g., *American Tobacco*), then market power rests on other things than size and there may be no point in splitting up a firm. If, on the other hand, structures are hard to duplicate, firms are likely to be hard to split up. In the latter instances the government often has been unable to produce clearly workable remedies that would yield the desired reduction in power without harming efficiency. When such difficulties are combined with the typical reluctance of the courts to tamper with existing concerns, the lack of meaningful structural remedies is understandable.[18]

What is less easily understood is the absence of general knowledge about remedy effects, both in monopolization and in other areas. Although some remedies are supervised by the courts, the large majority receive virtually no later scrutiny. The difficulty may be not so much that meaningless remedies are the rule, but rather that we simply *do not know* when remedies are effective and when they are not.

The identification of an antitrust violation and the formulation of a remedy for that violation are separate problems, but in reality they are not always considered independently. In some instances poor prospects for remedying a situation may influence the findings with respect to legality. This is a natural interaction since a finding of illegality may be insignificant—and courts may be reluctant to reach it—if the possibilities for a remedy are poor.

A more systematic and sensible approach to remedies will require,

[17] William Lee Baldwin, "The Feedback Effects of Business Conduct on Industry Structure," *Journal of Law & Economics*, 12, April 1969, pp. 123–54.
[18] Baldwin points out, however, that conduct remedies may have beneficial effects on structure. Possibly the strict "structuralists" have underestimated such effects, and may be prone to depict the remedy situation as somewhat worse than it is. *Ibid.*

first, knowledge of the effects of varied remedies in the past. Beyond this, it will also be necessary to develop new approaches, especially in the monopolization area. The remedy problem will always be difficult when excessive market power is the cause of an antitrust violation; and when divestiture of assets will not reduce this power, or when it might reduce power at a high cost in efficiency. Although the precise form that remedies might take in such circumstances is unclear, there are at least two avenues that bear exploration.

One concerns the possibility of acting to reduce market entry barriers rather than the size of offending firms. If dissolution is not a feasible solution, there may be some actions that would increase the likelihood of new entry and ultimately work toward a more competitive situation. One specific possibility would be to set limits on the advertising expenditures of established firms if product differentiation through advertising is an important entry barrier.

Another possibility that has received some attention would require divestiture of a firm's brand names, perhaps combined with limits on future advertising. Although the merits of such an approach are not well defined, it does appear that new kinds of remedies will be necessary. Until novel approaches are developed, and until we know more about the implications of the traditional approaches, the remedy problem must be expected to persist.

C. Some Plausible Interpretations of Antitrust

Why has antitrust policy evolved to its present state? Is modern antitrust something that has come about through design or through blunder? Does it reflect values that society holds to be important, or does it reflect an incompetent search for those values? Such questions cannot be answered categorically, but some alternative suggestions may be offered.

1. AS A COMMITMENT TO THE STATUS QUO

American antitrust policy can be interpreted partially as a commitment to the *status quo*. A survey of the various branches of antitrust indicates that, whatever its positive accomplishments may be, it has not often been a vehicle for sharp change. Indeed, it may be said to resist change effectively. That portion of the policy that is directed toward business conduct may have had the effect of reducing the frequency of conspiracy and other restrictive practices; however, it has stopped short of doing anything about the market conditions that make such practices possible. This may be a rational policy, for it is conceivable that the necessary alterations in market structures might do more harm than good. The thrust of policy, however, does not seem to have been based on this kind of calculation. Rather, it appears that the courts and the federal agencies have been reluctant to tamper with existing firms and markets almost as a matter of ethical principle.

Even merger policy, perhaps the most significant area of antitrust in recent years, may be viewed as a commitment to resist change. If we are unwilling to attack established monopolistic positions under the Sherman Act, we seem also unwilling to permit the establishment or extension of new positions through merger. There are obvious inconsistencies implied by this dual standard. The dominant firm that attained its monopoly power long ago will not have its position challenged; but even a modest increment in power that would accrue to a nondominant firm through merger may not be permitted.

The Sherman and Clayton Act approaches may be reconciled partially when viewed as part of a broader program to retard major changes in the structure of markets. Despite this, the *status quo* interpretation of antitrust cannot be carried too far. The policies have not been designed to freeze existing market structures, and they have proved to be amenable to changes that come about in certain ways. What can be said is that the posture of antitrust with respect to structural change has been strongly conservative, so much so that the *status quo* seems to be valued to some extent for its own sake.

2. AS THE PRODUCT OF AN INCONCLUSIVE ECONOMICS

A second interpretation of antitrust is that it has sought primarily economic objectives, but has been handicapped by a lack of economic guidelines. It is not unreasonable to suggest that the ultimate general goal of public competition policy has been good economic performance, subject to social and political constraints on the centralization of economic power.

If this be so, then the policy maker has received relatively little help from the economist. Traditional economic analysis suggests that optimal performance can be secured by establishing a regime of truly competitive markets, populated by relatively small and impotent firms. Once the impossibility of such a regime is conceded, however, the analysis does not provide clear choices among a large array of imperfect alternatives. The prime question is: to improve economic performance, should we rely on competition among as many as possible (and as small as possible) business units in each industry; or should we rely on the efficiency of fewer larger firms?

Such a question cannot be answered on the basis of a priori reasoning. Rather, the answer lies in empirical analyses of what actually happens in different markets. As we have seen, a great deal of relevant information has been gathered and some useful clues have emerged. Despite these clues, however, the evidence is still fragmentary and inconclusive; and it may be hypothesized that the absence of clear empirical distinctions has prevented policy makers from adopting a strong and consistent position on such basic matters as the treatment of industry concentration.

This interpretation of antitrust is not acceptable as a full explanation of policy evolution. It presupposes that our objectives are well defined and that policy is hindered only by an inability to predict which actions will best secure those objectives. Certainly this involves some overstatement of the clarity of policy priorities. It is true, nevertheless, that better notions of the economic implications of alternative policy actions would facilitate more rational choices.

3. AS THE PRODUCT OF CONFLICTING AND ILL-DEFINED GOALS

A third view of antitrust might stress the confusion in defining policy objectives rather than lack of economic information. Policy problems may not be a matter of knowing what we want to do but not having the information to do it, but, more simply, of *not* knowing what we want to do. This view has been touched on in earlier chapters. The objectives of antitrust are clear only so long as they are stated in a general way. Once it is recognized that various objectives are competitive, some specification of priorities is necessary, and it is at this point that the clarity in defining goals breaks down. It is easy to support economic progress, optimal allocation of resources, equitable distribution of income, and economic freedom; and difficult to stipulate precisely the order and degree of preference among them.

One common conflict is our desire for both economic efficiency and narrow limits to the extent of market power. Another policy complication is imposed by an apparently strong social emphasis on fairness throughout antitrust enforcement. To some degree the emphasis on fairness parallels that on restriction of power. For example, the large and powerful firm might be called unfair in the sense that it limits the opportunities of rivals.

The introduction of this consideration complicates further the definition of a consistent set of antitrust goals. Certainly we all want to be fair, and it would be surprising to find anyone challenging the legitimacy of such a public policy objective. The issue, however, is not whether to be fair, but rather how far to subordinate other legitimate objectives to this one. A competitive market system is not inherently fair, if by fair we mean assuring all participants of equal success. Quite the contrary, it is the essence of the market that those who do not perform well will be penalized by failure. Those who confuse competition with fairness misinterpret the meaning of one or both terms.

4. AS THE PRODUCT OF ULTIMATE WISDOM

Lest the preceding paragraphs appear too uniformly critical of antitrust policy, it must be noted that the policy can be—and perhaps ought to be—interpreted in a favorable way. If antimonopolization policies have been weak, this may simply reflect society's view that we ought to proceed cautiously in treating established firms; in light of our limited knowledge of the effects of dissolution, such caution may be justified. Similarly, if merger policy has been strong, this may only follow from the view that the growth of firm size and power ought to be subject to certain market tests that mergers may avoid. Finally, stringent antitrust treatment of restrictive practices can be rationalized on the grounds that the practices may reduce the vigor of competition without being likely to aid efficiency.

A full defense of antitrust suggests that the policies in fact represent the wishes of society; and that the wishes themselves reflect a desirable reconciliation of objectives. Such arguments cannot be easily treated within the framework of an economic approach to public policy. The proposition that antitrust does what we, collectively, want it to do, cannot be proved or disproved; and there is no objective basis for analyzing the suggestion that what the policy does is, on various grounds, good.

D. Conclusions

What, then, is the sum and substance of antitrust? Many answers have been proposed. Bork and Bowman see modern antitrust as an unwarranted attack on bigness, an effort to protect small and inefficient firms from the rigors of the competitive wars.[19] Galbraith also sees a protectionist quality, but in reverse: antitrust, he asserts, simply protects existing market power from the aggressive growth of smaller competitors.[20] Berle, on the other hand, regards the modern corporation as virtually a public institution that long ago succeeded in liberating itself from the constraints of the marketplace, and thus from policies designed to alter the market.[21]

The thrust of these diverse views is much the same: antitrust is a monumental irrelevancy. At best, it does nothing but squander a few million dollars of resources annually. At worst, it has the capacity for considerably more mischief.

It is easy, but not especially illuminating, to point out that these opinions are oversimplified. It is perhaps more pertinent to note that the world—our part of it, at least—has changed in ways that call into question the appropriateness of traditional policies. This is one factor the authors above have in mind. Firms are not only bigger than they once were, they are more diversified. Such changes are fundamental. From the economist's standpoint they not only make relevant information harder to obtain, but also greatly complicate the conceptualization and explanation of firms' behavior.

The economist's job is thus more difficult. In order to contribute usefully to policy it is necessary to delineate the consequences of alternative public actions. But our older theories, based implicitly on the idea of single-product, profit-maximizing business units, may not prove adequate. If this is the case a radical redirection of our thinking may be required before the contribution can be expanded much beyond its present bounds.

As we have noted at many points, ideal economic information is a necessary, but not sufficient, condition for rational public decision making. It will also be necessary to decide what kinds of economic results, and ultimately what kind of a society, we wish to have.

[19] Robert H. Bork and Ward S. Bowman, Jr., "The Crisis in Antitrust," *Fortune*, December 1963; reprinted in John A. Larson (editor), *The Regulated Businessman*, Holt, Rinehart & Winston, New York, 1966, pp. 78–94.

[20] John Kenneth Galbraith, *The New Industrial State*, Houghton Mifflin, Boston, 1967.

[21] A. A. Berle, Jr., *The 20th Century Capitalist Revolution*, Harcourt, Brace, New York, 1954.

Table of Cases

Index